EZRA

by
John M Riddle

JOHN RITCHIE LTD
CHRISTIAN PUBLICATIONS

40 Beansburn, Kilmarnock, Scotland

ISBN-13: 978 1 910513 09 5

Copyright © 2014 by John Ritchie Ltd.
40 Beansburn, Kilmarnock, Scotland

www.ritchiechristianmedia.co.uk

Typeset by John Ritchie Ltd., Kilmarnock
Printed by Bell & Bain Ltd., Glasgow

Contents

Preface

This book represents the substance of Bible Class discussions on Friday evenings at Mill Lane Chapel, Cheshunt, between January and November 1996 with regard to Ezra and Nehemiah, and before that in connection with Esther. The practice of dating the study notes was introduced at some point after the Esther studies, leaving long-standing members of the Bible Class fumbling around in their memories to no avail. It is a clear case of *tempus fugit*. The Esther studies were particularly memorable for the heat generated at the time over the precise meaning of "merry with wine" (1:10). Was Ahasuerus drunk or not? The argument continues to this day (jocularly), but it has to be said that if this were the only issue dividing believers, some assemblies would be infinitely stronger than they are today.

As in the case of Acts, 1 Samuel, 2 Samuel, and Luke, the original notes were written without any thought of their eventual appearance in the public domain, and like the previous publications, the current volume does not purport to be a commentary in the usual sense of the word.

The three books surveyed in this volume belong, obviously, to the 'historical section' of the Old Testament, and deal particularly with the affairs of God's people during the period of their return from exile in Babylonia. Having said this, Esther is rather different in that it records a crisis at the heart of the Persian Empire in connection with those who did not return to Judah, but what happened in the court at Shushan posed a threat to the lives of all Jews throughout the entire realm of Ahasuerus.

We must remember that "whatsoever things were written aforetime were written for our learning" (Rom 15:4) and we can therefore expect to encounter valuable lessons from the historical books of the Old Testament. Bible history should not be regarded in the same way as 'secular history'. How many of us struggled to remember the significance of such dates as 55BC, AD1066 and AD1666! Bible history is quite different. We are told that in political, economic and military terms, Jeroboam II, who reigned over Israel for forty-one years, was a power to be reckoned with, but the Bible devotes about five inches of typescript to him (2 Kings 14:23-29). The secular historian would not get particularly excited over Abraham, but the Bible devotes acres of space to him! God has not given us, by any means, a complete and detailed record of the entire history of His people in the Old Testament. He has been selective, giving us the record of those events best suited to convey important spiritual lessons. We must therefore read our Bible history with care and expectation.

The Bible Class at Cheshunt is indebted to John Ritchie Ltd for their continuing willingness to publish its notes, and to Mr Fraser Munro (not forgetting his colleagues) for his help in editing the material, thirty-eight studies in all, forwarded to him for that purpose. The Bible Class continues to be grateful to Miss Lesley Prentice for having checked and corrected the original manuscripts, something she continues to do, and to Mr Eric Browning for his invaluable help in continuing to distribute copies of current studies by Email to an increasing number of recipients.

Ezra's name means 'help', and the people at Jerusalem said to Nehemiah, "Let us rise up and build" (Neh 2:18), and if these are the results in the lives of those who kindly read this book, the effort on the part of all who have produced it will be very worthwhile.

John Riddle
Cheshunt, Hertfordshire
November 2014

EZRA

Introduction

Read 2 Chronicles 36.11-23, Ezra 1.1-3 & 7.1-6, Jeremiah 29.10-14
It might be helpful to commence our studies in the book of Ezra by considering *(1)* the background of the book, with reference to its period, place, purpose and priority; *(2)* the contents of the book.

1) THE BACKGROUND OF THE BOOK
The books of Ezra, Nehemiah, Esther, Haggai, Zechariah and Malachi all relate to the closing period of Israel's Old Testament history. As we will see, they describe a series of events which commenced with the edict of Cyrus in 536BC permitting the Jews to return to their homeland after seventy years' exile in Babylonia.

A) THE PERIOD
It is always important to see Bible books in their proper context, and a summary of events will be helpful.

a) The period before the Exile
After the death of Solomon (in 975BC, according to J.N.Darby), under whom Israel reached the zenith of its past history, the kingdom was tragically divided:

(i) In the north, ***Israel***, comprising ten tribes, with its capital Samaria (Tirzah at first), and its first king, Jeroboam the son of Nebat. His name is often followed by the chilling epithet, "who made Israel to sin" (see, for example, 1 Kings 22.52). Compare 1 Kings 12.28 with Exodus 32.4,8. Israel was ultimately taken into captivity by Assyria in 721BC. The reasons are clearly set out in 2 Kings 17.

(ii) In the south, ***Judah***, comprising the tribes of Judah and Benjamin, plus Levi, with its capital Jerusalem, and its first king, Rehoboam the son of Solomon. Judah became subject to Babylon (Nebuchadnezzar) in 606BC. Although the temple was not destroyed until 588BC (or 586BC), the nation became part of the Babylonian Empire from 606BC, and its remaining two rulers, Jehoiachin

and Zedekiah, were really only vassal kings. 2 Chronicles 36 sets out the reasons, and tells us that the Chaldeans "burnt the **house of God**, and brake down the **wall of Jerusalem**" (v.19). As we shall see, the book of Ezra describes the rebuilding of "the house of God", and the book of Nehemiah describes the rebuilding of "the wall of Jerusalem".

b) *The period of the Exile*
The Babylonian captivity lasted for seventy years, but this was far from a mere quirk of history. The period had been carefully calculated by God Himself (see 2 Chronicles 36.21 and Leviticus 26.34-43). The duration of the captivity was announced by Jeremiah. See 25.11-12 and 29.10-14. Seventy years after Babylon had annexed Judah in 606BC, and in fulfilment of Jeremiah's prophecy (2 Chronicles 36.22 and Ezra 1.1), Cyrus authorised the return of the exiles to Jerusalem to rebuild the temple. We must not forget that all this was also an answer to prayer. Read Daniel 9.1-19. We will say more about this in our next study. God gave His people "a little reviving in [their] bondage" (Ezra 9.8). The year was 536BC.

c) *The period after the Exile*
i) The first party of exiles returned under the leadership of Zerubbabel and Jeshua (also called Joshua: see Haggai 1.1 etc). These were civil and religious leaders respectively. Their names are often linked (see, again, for example, Haggai 1.1), and this emphasises a very important spiritual lesson. The expedition under these two leaders is covered by Ezra Chapters 1-6. The purpose of the expedition was to **rebuild** the temple. This work was completed in the sixth year of Darius (Ezra 6.15), i.e. 515BC (Darius commenced to reign in 521BC). The ministry of Haggai and Zechariah is relevant to this period. See Ezra 5.1-2 and 6.14.

ii) Fifty-seven years later, in 458BC, in the seventh year of Artaxerxes Longimanus (Ezra 7.7), who commenced to reign in 465BC, a second party of exiles returned under the leadership of Ezra himself. This is covered by Ezra Chapters 7-10. The purpose of this expedition was to **beautify** the temple. See Ezra 7.27.

iii) Between the two periods covered by the book of Ezra (1-6 and 7-10), we have events described in the book of Esther, although this is set in Persia, not in Israel. The reigning monarch at this time was Ahasuerus, known to history as Xerxes, the father of Artaxerxes above. He commenced to reign in 485BC, and as Esther became queen in the seventh year of his reign (2.16), the date was

478BC. Isaiah 45.15 is an apt commentary on the book of Esther: "Verily thou art a God that hidest thyself, O God of Israel, the Saviour".

iv) The book of Nehemiah continues the story of Ezra. It commences in 445BC, i.e. in the twentieth year of Artaxerxes. Nehemiah therefore came to Jerusalem thirteen years after Ezra, who was still in the city. See Nehemiah 8.4; 12.36. Nehemiah was twelve years in Jerusalem (see 5.14), after which he returned to Artaxerxes (see 13.6), so the major part of the book can be dated 445-433BC. Note: the decree of Artaxerxes for the rebuilding of the wall marks the commencement of the 'Seventy Weeks' prophecy of Daniel 9. Whilst the book of Ezra is concerned with the rebuilding of the **temple**, the book of Nehemiah is concerned with the rebuilding of the **wall.** In spite of Nehemiah's excellent leadership, the people were prone to backsliding, and the preaching of Malachi makes it very clear that conditions had continued to deteriorate.

A note of the Persian kings might be helpful: **Cyrus** (539-530); **Cambyses** (530-522); **Darius 1 Hystaspes** (521-486): not the Darius of Daniel 5.31; 6.1; **Xerxes** (486-465): the Ahasuerus of Esther: not the Ahasuerus of Daniel 9.1; **Artaxerxes 1 Longimanus** (465-423).

B) THE PLACE

The books of Ezra and Nehemiah, with the attendant ministry of Haggai, Zechariah and Malachi, deal with "last days". They describe the history of those Jews who were sufficiently concerned about the place where the Lord placed His Name, to turn their backs on Babylon and make the journey to their homeland. Jerusalem was the place "which the Lord shall choose to place his name there...the place which the Lord thy God shall choose to place his name in" (Deut. 16.2,6). See also Nehemiah 1.9. Deuteronomy 16 explains the significance of this expression: "Three times in a year shall all thy males appear **before the Lord thy God** in the place which he shall choose" (v.16). To "appear before the Lord" meant entering the temple precincts. In the New Testament, Paul describes the local assembly as "the temple of God". See 1 Corinthians 3.16-17. Another term for the temple in the Old Testament was "the house of God" (see, for example, Ezra 3.8), and Paul also describes the local assembly in the same way. See 1 Timothy 3.15. "The temple of God" and "the house of God" are terms which describe the dwelling-place of God, and it is there that He places His Name today. Quite clearly then, we can expect lessons from Ezra which will help us in **our** building work.

With this in mind, the remnant had turned their backs on Babylon, and set their faces to the 'place of the name'. That is precisely what is required of us today.

While the words, "Come out of her, my people" (Rev. 18.4) have particular reference to godly Jews in coming days, the principle is applicable today. The Ecumenical Movement will find its consummation in "Mystery, Babylon the Great, the mother of harlots and abominations of the earth" (Rev. 17.5). The godly Jew exclaimed "If I forget thee, O Jerusalem, let my right hand forget her cunning. If I do not remember thee, let my tongue cleave to the roof of my mouth; if I prefer not Jerusalem above my chief joy" (Psalm 137.5-6). We should display, from our hearts, similar devotion and enthusiasm for the 'place of the name' today. But why did the Jews actually return? This brings us to:

C) THE PURPOSE

It was more than just "Come out of her, my people". It was a case of building for God in the right place. These books describe people who **built** at 'the place of the name'. This immediately points us forward to the New Testament. In 1 Corinthians 3, Paul describes assembly building. He tells us *(i)* **where** we should be building (on the right foundation), *(ii)* **how** we should be building (with great care), and *(iii)* **what** should be used in building ("gold, silver, precious stones"), vv.10-12.

Perhaps this is a good opportunity to review the standard of our building, or even to ask ourselves if we are building at all! As we shall see, the good start in Ezra 3, was followed by inactivity in Ezra 4, and Haggai (Ezra 5.1) was obliged to open his preaching with a broadside against people who were simply content to be back from Babylon: "Thus speaketh the Lord of hosts, saying, This people say, The **time** is not come, the **time** that the Lord's house should be built. Then came the word of the Lord by Haggai the prophet, saying, Is it **time** for you, O ye, to dwell in your cieled houses, and this house lie waste?" (Hag. 1.2-4). They had time to 'do their own thing', but God's interests were firmly on the back burner. They were glad to be back in Jerusalem, but that was all. Some people are glad to be in the assembly, and **that is all!** But things did change for the better, as we shall see.

D) THE PRIORITY

The order of Ezra and Nehemiah is significant. The temple was rebuilt **first.** God's interests were given **priority.** The wall and gates followed. Worldly wisdom would have dictated otherwise. It was obviously far more sensible to get defences in position! But that is exactly what they did from the very start! "And they set the altar upon his bases; for fear was upon them because of the people of those countries: and they offered burnt offerings thereon unto the Lord, even burnt offerings morning and evening" (Ezra 3.3). That was their defence! We must never forget that our great bulwark against the enemy is to give God His rightful place in our lives. Failure to do this exposes us to disaster. See Revelation 2.4-5. It ought to be said of every assembly: "It was noised that **he** was in the house" (Mark 2.1).

This brings us to:

2) THE CONTENTS OF THE BOOK

The name "Ezra" means 'help', and we can therefore expect to discover how we too can help the people of God. It's all summed up in 7.10, "For Ezra had prepared his heart to **seek** the law of the Lord (so he **explored** the word of God), and to **do** it (so he **exemplified** the word of God), and to **teach** in Israel statutes and judgments (so he **expounded** the word of God)". He was a true priest: see Malachi 2.7, "For the priest's lips should keep knowledge, and they should seek the law at his mouth: for he is the messenger of the Lord of hosts". He is called "Ezra the **priest**, the scribe" (7.11-12). We have his priestly genealogy at the beginning of Chapter 7.

Although the book bears his name, we do not actually meet Ezra until Chapter 7. According to Jewish tradition, he was "one of the outstanding names in Jewish history. Associated with his name is the writing of the books of Chronicles, the compilation of the Old Testament canon, and even the inauguration of local centres called synagogues where the law could be read regularly in the hearing of the people" (Cyril Hocking, *The Work of Reconstruction, Precious Seed, 1957).*

Our final task in introducing Ezra is to attempt an analysis of the book. We have already noticed that it is in two parts. The first emphasises the problems encountered in connection with the **place**: the second emphasises the problems encountered in connection with the **people**. It can be summarised by 2 Corinthians 7.5, "**without** were fightings, **within** were fears". We shall discover that, as always, the work of God is never without difficulties. The two sections can be set out as follows:

Chapters 1 to 6	Interval	Chapters 7 to 10
The decree of Cyrus	57/58 years	The decree of Artaxerxes
BC 536	During this period	BC 458
The return under Zerubbabel	the events described	The return under Ezra
To build the Lord's house	in the book of	To beautify the Lord's house
About 50,000 people involved	Esther	About 2,000 people involved*
A period of 22 years	took place	A period of 1 year

* figures for males only

The two sections above could be analysed as follows, bearing in mind that chapter headings do not often fully reflect chapter contents!

The First Expedition, Chapters 1-6

A) The Repatriation: Chs. 1-2
Ch.1 The Permission Involved
Ch.2 The Personnel Involved

B) The Reconstruction: Chs. 3-6
Ch.3 The Work Commences
Ch.4 The Work Ceases
Ch.5 The Work Continues
Ch.6 The Work Completed

The Second Expedition, Chapters 7-12

A) The Repatriation: Chs. 7-8
Ch. 7 The Priest prepared
Ch. 8 The People prepared

B) The Reconsecration: Chs. 9-10
Ch. 9 The Intercession
(or Confession)
Ch.10 The Intervention
(or Correction)

In future studies, God willing, we will take one chapter of Ezra at each sitting, and follow this with studies in the companion book of Nehemiah. In your preparatory reading, remember that "God's word is no dry-as-dust textbook, but a **hungry man's meal**" (David Newell, *Believer's Magazine: April 1988*).

READ CHAPTER 1

"Let him go up to Jerusalem"

Ezra Chapters 1-6 describe the first repatriation of exiles from Babylon to Judah and Jerusalem. Seventy years had elapsed since Judah fell to Nebuchadnezzar. Psalm 137 expresses the feelings of the captives at the time: "By the rivers of Babylon, there we sat down, yea, we wept, when we remembered Zion...If I forget thee, O Jerusalem, let my right hand forget her cunning. If I do not remember thee, let my tongue cleave to the roof of my mouth; if I prefer not Jerusalem above my chief joy" (Psalm 137.1-6). But seventy years is a long time, and it is not unreasonable to suggest that Psalm 137 had died on many lips. No doubt many of the Jewish exiles 'made the best of a bad job', and settled down quite nicely in Babylon. Daniel and his three friends were certainly exceptions, but what about the rest of their contemporaries in Daniel Chapter 1? They evidently settled down reasonably well! It doesn't take a great deal for some Christians to forget their early Bible teaching either!

The book of Ezra commences with men and women who did **not** forget Jerusalem, and who evidently **did** prefer Jerusalem above their "chief joy". Chapter 1 can be easily divided into two sections: **(1)** the appeal to God's people (vv.1-4); **(2)** the response of God's people (vv.5-11).

1) THE APPEAL TO GOD'S PEOPLE, vv.1-4

"Now in the **first year** of Cyrus king of Persia, that the word of the Lord by the mouth of Jeremiah might be fulfilled, the Lord stirred up the spirit of Cyrus king of Persia, that he made a proclamation...Who is there among you of all his people? his God be with him, and let him go up to Jerusalem, which is in Judah, and build the house of the Lord God of Israel, (he is the God,) which is in Jerusalem". This must have thrilled Daniel, who "continued even unto the **first year** of king Cyrus" (Dan. 1.21) He lived to see the answer to his prayers! See Daniel 9.1-19. (Daniel lived at least till the "third year of Cyrus king of Persia" (Dan. 10.1).) Note: Cyrus had been king of Persia for some years: the "first year of Cyrus" refers to his conquest of Babylon, and therefore to the time he first entered Jewish history. We shall see shortly that God knew all about him years before he was born! However, we must notice first of all:

a) The promises of God

i) The promise. "That the word of the Lord by the mouth of Jeremiah might be **fulfilled**". Here is the mark of a true prophet. See Deuteronomy 18.20-22. Ezra 1.1 refers to Jeremiah 25.11-12, "And this whole land shall be a desolation, and an astonishment; and these nations shall serve the king of Babylon seventy years. And it shall come to pass, when seventy years are accomplished, that I will punish the king of Babylon, and that nation, saith the Lord, for their iniquity, and the land of the Chaldeans, and will make it perpetual desolations". Further details are given in Jeremiah 29.10-14, "For thus saith the Lord, That after seventy years be accomplished at Babylon I will visit you, and perform my good word toward you, in causing you to return to this place". The time had now come: Babylon had been overthrown and Cyrus reigned supreme. God had exactly fulfilled His promises. This is not surprising: after all, our God "cannot lie" (Titus 1.2); "God is not a man, that he should lie; neither the son of man, that he should repent: hath he said, and shall he not do it? or hath he spoken, and shall he not make it good?" (Num. 23.19). Paul tells us that "all the promises of God in him are yea, and in him Amen" (2 Cor. 1.20). Abraham was "fully persuaded that, what he (the Lord) had promised, he was able also to perform" (Rom. 4.21). We should be equally persuaded. "The Lord is not slack concerning his promise, as some men count slackness" (2 Pet. 3.9).

ii) The period. The duration of the captivity had been carefully calculated. See 2 Chronicles 36.20-21, "And them that had escaped from the sword carried he (Nebuchadnezzar) away to Babylon; where they were servants to him and his sons until the reign of the kingdom of Persia: to fulfil the word of the Lord by the mouth of Jeremiah, **until the land had enjoyed her sabbaths: for as long as she lay desolate she kept sabbath, to fulfil threescore and ten years**". This refers to Leviticus 25.3-4, "Six years thou shalt sow thy field, and six years thou shalt prune thy vineyard, and gather in the fruit thereof; but in the seventh year shall be a sabbath of rest unto the land, a Sabbath for the Lord: thou shalt neither sow thy field, nor prune thy vineyard". God ensured that His people would not be hungry during "the sabbath of the land" (Lev. 25.20-21). Every seventh year was to remind them that He was able to preserve and bless His people as tenants in His property. But although this was ignored (see Leviticus 26.33-43: note vv.34-35 particularly), God secured every one of those sabbaths! Each of those seventy years in captivity represented a "seventh year", which means that Israel had not "kept sabbath" for 490 years. Working back from 606BC, we reach 1096BC, the year in which Saul was anointed, and the monarchy commenced.

We must not fail to grasp the lesson. God is well aware if we disobey His word. It had become the norm to dispense with Leviticus 25.3-4, and if it ever crossed their minds at all, some Israelites might have concluded that since God had not intervened, it obviously no longer mattered. The seventy years' captivity proved that it did matter: God had not forgotten His word, and had not overlooked the disobedience of His people. We cannot play 'fast and loose' with the word of God, and escape unscathed.

iii) The prayer. Towards the end of this period, a man had been reading his Bible. His name was Daniel. "I Daniel understood by books the number of the years, whereof the word of the Lord came to Jeremiah the prophet, that he would accomplish seventy years in the desolations of Jerusalem" (Dan. 9.2). So he prayed about it: "And I set my face unto the Lord God, to seek by prayer and supplications, with fasting, and sackcloth, and ashes" Dan. 9.3-19). Daniel knew from Jeremiah 29, that God cared for His people in spite of their disobedience (Jer. 29.11). He also knew that God would answer prayer for restoration: "Then ye shall call upon me, and ye shall go and pray unto me, and I will hearken unto you. And ye shall seek me, and find me, when ye search for me with all your heart. And I will be found of you, saith the Lord: and I will turn away your captivity...and I will bring you again into the place whence I caused you to be carried away captive" (Jer. 29.12-14).

This is most important. Centuries later, John wrote: "And this is the confidence that we have in him, that, if we ask any thing according to his will, he heareth us" (1 John 5.14). Daniel knew the will of God from Jeremiah's prophecy, and prayed accordingly. Elijah did the same: compare 1 Kings 17.1 with Deuteronomy 11.16-17 and 28.23-24. When we pray, God expects us to claim His promises. After all, prayer is the language of faith. It follows that we cannot expect God to answer our prayers if they are at variance with His word. The prayer of Daniel was certainly heard as we will now see:

b) The providence of God
We now have a beautiful illustration of Isaiah 65.24, "And it shall come to pass, that before they call, I will answer; and while they are yet speaking, I will hear". Approximately **one hundred and eighty years** before Daniel prayed, God gave His answer. See Isaiah 44.24-28, "Thus saith the Lord...that confirmeth the

word of his servant, and performeth the counsel of his messengers; that saith to Jerusalem, Thou shalt be inhabited; and to the cities of Judah, Ye shall be built, and I will raise up the decayed places thereof...That saith of Cyrus, He is **my shepherd**, and shall perform all my pleasure: even saying to Jerusalem, Thou shalt be built; and to the temple, Thy foundation shall be laid". God continues to speak about Cyrus in Isaiah 45.1-14: "Thus saith the Lord to **his anointed**, to Cyrus, whose right hand *I* have holden, to subdue nations before him; and *I* will loose the loins of kings, to open before him the two leaved gates; and the gates shall not be shut...*I* will break in pieces the gates of brass, and cut in sunder the bars of iron (referring to the conquest of Babylon)...For Jacob my servant's sake, and Israel mine elect, *I* have even called thee by name: *I* have surnamed thee, though thou hast not known me. *I* am the Lord, and there is none else, there is no God beside me: *I* girded thee, though thou hast not known me...*I* have raised him up in righteousness, and *I* will direct all his ways: he shall build my city, and he shall let go my captives, not for price nor reward, saith the Lord of hosts".   But God always pays His servants!: see v.14 above.

This is an amazing passage. We are unable to say whether Cyrus was familiar with this prophecy, but we **do** know that he said, "The Lord God of heaven hath given me all the kingdoms of the earth; and he hath charged me to build him an house at Jerusalem, which is in Judah" (v.2). Compare the arrogant pride of Nebuchadnezzar: "Is not this great Babylon, that *I* have built for the house of the kingdom by the might of **my** power, and for the honour of **my** majesty?" (Dan. 4.30). Nebuchadnezzar soon discovered that "the most High ruleth in the kingdom of men, and giveth it to whomsoever **he** will, and setteth up over it the basest of men" (Dan. 4.17). The expression, "basest of men", probably refers to Nebuchadnezzar himself. Cyrus was quite different. God "raised him up in righteousness". But whether it is men like Nebuchadnezzar, or men like Cyrus, it remains that "the Lord hath prepared his throne in the heavens; and his kingdom ruleth over all" (Psalm 103.19). "The king's heart is in the hand of the Lord, as the rivers of water: he turneth it whithersoever he will" (Prov. 21.1). **He is in complete control of world affairs.** What an encouragement to pray!

The providence of God is also clear in what seems, at the time, to be quite a minor detail. Cyrus made the proclamation "throughout all his kingdom, and **put it also in writing**". Now read Ezra 6.1-5!

c) The presence of God
"Who is there among you of all his people? **his God be with him**, and let him go up to Jerusalem, which is in Judah, and build the house of the Lord God of

Israel, (he is the God,) which is in Jerusalem" (v.3). Cyrus acknowledged God as "the God of the heavens" (v.2, JND), and "the God of Israel" (v.3). In fact, he used the covenant name: "to build the house of the Lord (*Jehovah*) God (*Elohim*: plural) of Israel". It is sad to notice that Israel had "**polluted** the house of the Lord" (2 Chron. 36.14): now a Gentile proposes to "**build** the house of the Lord God of Israel!" We should notice the expressions, "the **house** of the Lord God of Israel" (v.3); "the **house** of God" (v.4); "the **house** of the Lord" (v.5). It is **His** house. The local assembly is similarly described: see 1 Timothy 3.15.

The historians tell us that Cyrus respected the gods of his subject peoples, restored their images, rebuilt the temples, and repatriated their worshippers. His decree therefore reflected "concern for correct religious protocol" (*Ezra and Nehemiah*, D.Kidner). We must make it clear, however, that this is **not** the perspective of Scripture. "The **Lord** stirred up the spirit of Cyrus king of Persia". God took the initiative.

Concern for the glory of God will be accompanied by the presence of God. The decree of Cyrus took the form of a personal appeal, rather than a general command. It was a question of willing devotion rather than onerous duty. Years later, "the people blessed all the men, that **willingly offered themselves** to dwell at Jerusalem" (Nehemiah 11.2). The Macedonian believers were "**willing of themselves**; praying us with much entreaty that we would receive the gift, and take upon us the fellowship of the ministering to the saints" (2 Cor. 8.3-5).

d) The provision of God

"And whosoever remaineth in any place where he sojourneth, let the men of his place help him with silver, and with gold, and with goods, and with beasts, beside the freewill offering for the house of God that is in Jerusalem" (v.4). This is very significant. *(i)* "Whosoever remaineth in any place where he sojourneth". The word "remaineth" means 'remnant' or 'survivor' (D.Kidner). The prophetic scriptures give an important place to the 'remnant'. See, for example, Isaiah 10.20-21. The word "sojourneth" stresses that the Jews were strangers in Babylon. They were away from home. They did not belong in Babylon, and no true child of God should be involved with the corrupt and confused religious world, which the Bible calls "MYSTERY, BABYLON THE GREAT, THE MOTHER OF HARLOTS AND ABOMINATIONS OF THE EARTH" (Rev. 17.5). *(ii)* The Jew *en route* for Jerusalem was to be helped by "the men of his place" in the same way that Israel was assisted by the Egyptians. See Exodus 12.35,36. The prophetic scriptures give an important place to a second Exodus: see, for example, again, Isaiah 10.20-22. We know from Ezra 6, that Cyrus also made provision from the royal treasury. While Ezra 1 does not fulfil Isaiah 10.20-22, it does foreshadow the future and final regathering of Israel. Isaiah 60.10 predicts Gentile participation.

Paul assured the Philippians that "my God shall supply all your need according to his riches in glory by Christ Jesus" (Phil. 4.19).

2) THE RESPONSE OF GOD'S PEOPLE, vv.5-11

"Then rose up the chief of the fathers of Judah and Benjamin, and the priests, and the Levites, with all them whose spirit **God** had raised ('stirred', JND: He had already "stirred up the spirit of Cyrus",v.1), to go up to build the house of the Lord which is in Jerusalem" (v.5). So it was not a case of natural inclination: these people responded to the call of God. We should notice the order: they "**rose up**" (v.5), having been '**stirred up**' (v.5), in order to "**go up**" (v.5), and finally they "**went up**" (2: 1). Some people 'rise up' without being 'stirred up': see Jeremiah 14.14. Some are 'stirred up', but never 'rise up': see Judges 5.15-16. We do well to heed the lesson!

a) They were stirred by God, v.5

i) **The leaders were stirred.** "Then rose up the chief of the fathers of Judah and Benjamin". The vessels were "numbered...unto Sheshbazzar, the prince of Judah" (v.8). Although there are alternative explanations, it does seem that Sheshbazzar and Zerubbabel (meaning 'born in Babylon': see also Matthew 1.12) are one and the same. Sheshbazzar could have been the court name for Zerubbabel, in the same way that Belteshazzar was the court name for Daniel. Elsewhere, he is called the "governor of Judah" (Haggai 1.1 etc), stressing "his subservient place in the Persian kingdom": but here he is called "the prince of Judah" which "stresses his relationship to his own people" (C.E.Hocking).

Little can be accomplished without good leadership. Deborah and Barak praised God for "the governors of Israel, that offered themselves willingly among the people" (Judges 5.9. In the New Testament, elders are to be "ensamples to the flock" (1 Pet. 5.3).

ii) **The priests were stirred.** In the Old Testament, there was a selective priesthood. Not all Israelites were priests. That privilege belonged only to the sons of Aaron. In the New Testament, all believers **are** priests. See 1 Peter 2: notice the expressions "an holy priesthood" (v.5) and a "royal priesthood" (v.9). They occur in a passage which speaks about "newborn babes" (v.2), those who have "tasted that the Lord is gracious" (v.3), and who "believe" (v.7). There is not even the slightest hint of a special group of people here! The word "priest" (Greek *hiereus)* means 'one who offers sacrifice' (W.E.Vine). How much are we stirred up to "offer up spiritual sacrifices, acceptable to God by Jesus Christ?" (1 Pet. 2.5). What about our daily prayer and worship? The local assembly, "the house of God", will suffer if this is lacking. We will have nothing to offer God in assembly meetings, if we have nothing to offer Him every day.

iii) The Levites were stirred. In the Old Testament, the Levites were responsible, originally, for the carriage and maintenance of the tabernacle, and latterly, for various duties in connection with the temple. They were involved in work for God. Paul stirs us *all* up in 1 Corinthians 15.58: "Be ye steadfast, unmoveable, always abounding in the work of the Lord, forasmuch as ye know that your labour is not in vain in the Lord".

b) They were supported by others, v.6
"And all they that were about them strengthened their hands with vessels of silver, with gold, with goods, and with beasts, and with precious things, beside all that was willingly offered". At first glance, this sounds rather noble, but if it includes Jews who were quite happy to contribute but who had no desire to return to Jerusalem, the picture is not quite so attractive. It does seem that the majority of the Jews were quite content to "stay in the place of temporal prosperity and religious confusion". In this case, all they did was to "pay a mere patronage to His work" (C.E.Hocking). Let us beware of adopting the same attitude. On the other hand, there must have been many who could not go back, but who gave support none-the-less. Daniel, for example, did not return, but he was an old man by this time. Either way, one thing is clear: God expects us to use our resources for His glory.

c) The were stewards of holy things, vv.7-11
The "vessels of the house of the Lord" (notice the two 'houses' in v.7), once used in service for God, and then for idol worship (see Daniel 5.3-4), were *(i)* "numbered...unto Sheshbazzar, the prince of Judah" and *(ii)* "*all* these did Sheshbazzar bring up with them of the captivity that were brought up from Babylon unto Jerusalem". Sheshbazzar was made a steward of the temple treasure. In a unique way, the apostles were "stewards of the mysteries of God" (1 Cor. 4.1) but, like Timothy, we are called upon to "keep the entrusted deposit" (1 Tim. 6.20 JND). At the end of his life, Paul could say, "I have kept the faith" (2 Tim. 4.7). Various types of vessels were committed to Sheshbazzar, and God commits various gifts to us. Can we say that we are "*good stewards* of the *manifold* grace of God?" (1 Pet. 4.10).

READ CHAPTER 2

"The children of the province that went up"

Ezra Chapter 1 records the appeal to God's people, and their response. Chapter 2 lists the names of those that responded to the appeal. "These are the children of the province that went up out of the captivity, of those which had been carried away, whom Nebuchadnezzar the king of Babylon had carried away unto Babylon, and came again unto Jerusalem and Judah, every one unto his city" (v.1). Years later, Nehemiah found this register: see Nehemiah 7.5.

The chapter may be divided as follows: *(1)* dividing the names (vv.1-58); *(2)* dealing with uncertainties (vv.59-63); *(3)* detailing the total (vv.64-67); *(4)* duties on arrival (vv.68-70).

1) DIVIDING THE NAMES, vv.1-58

Over these verses it could be written, "I know my sheep". It has to be said that first impressions are rather daunting, to put it mildly! We are confronted with some sixty verses of names. It wouldn't be so bad if we knew a little more about them, but names...names...names! Of course, not every one of the 50,000 are mentioned individually. That would have taken a lot of space! They are mentioned in groups: in some cases, family groups, and in others, city groups. We will analyse the list shortly, but first of all, why all the detail? Hebrews 6.10 supplies the answer: "For God is not unrighteous to forget your work and labour of love, which ye have shewed toward his name". Here were people who, at great personal sacrifice, had turned their backs on Babylon, and made the long journey back to Jerusalem, "the place which the Lord shall choose to place his name there" (Deut. 16.2). God took note of them all. Like Job, their record was "on high" (Job 16.19). Malachi tells us that "they that feared the Lord spake often one to another: and the Lord hearkened, and heard it, and a book of remembrance was written before him for them that feared the Lord, and that thought upon his name" (Mal. 3.16).

You see, heaven overlooks no one. You may think that your life and service for God is very ordinary, and that there is nothing much worth noting. But He knows all about your service and concern for His glory, even though it might not seem very spectacular. After all, this is the record of "all them whose spirit God had raised" (1.5): people who had responded to the voice of God. Numbers ch.7 proves that God doesn't bulk us all together, but takes note of the concern of each one of His people. Isn't that why the offerings of the twelve princes are individually recorded, even though they were completely identical? Isn't that why "Jesus, which is called Justus" is mentioned in Colossians ch.4, even though, unlike everybody else in the chapter, nothing at all is said about him? By the way, what about the many thousands that did not return from Babylon? Have you ever noticed that we only know the names of **two** of them? (Mordecai and Esther - excluding Daniel of course: he was probably too old to travel.) Significant, isn't it?!

God is no respecter of persons either: leaders (v.2) and servants (v.65) are all taken into account. As C.E.Hocking points out, "This fact should cause us to avoid noting secular and social distinctions amongst the saints. The poor rejoices in his elevation in Christ, whilst the rich rejoices in his being made low. We should be careful to observe 'the royal law', and love our neighbour as ourselves (see James ch.2)". Before we leave this, we must notice that in Ezra, God notices more than the concern of men and women for His house and His glory: He also notices men and women who have disobeyed His word. See 10.18-44. The list in vv.1-58 includes the following *(a)* the leaders (v.2); *(b)* the people (vv.3-35); *(c)* the priests (vv.36-39); *(d)* the Levites (v.40); *(e)* the singers (v.41); *(f)* the porters (v.42); *(g)* the Nethinims (vv.43-54); *(h)* the children of Solomon's servants (vv.55-57).

a) The Leaders, v.2

"Now these are the children of the province that went up out of the captivity... which came with Zerubbabel: Jeshua, Nehemiah (not the man who came 91 years later: Neh. 1.1), Seraiah, Reelaiah, Mordecai (not the man in Shushan 58 years later: Est. 2.5), Bilshan, Mispar, Bigvai, Rehum, Baanah". *Zerubbabel* (called Sheshbazzar in 1.8) was the **princely** man. He is called "the prince of Judah" (1.8), and was one of the ancestors of the Lord Jesus. See Matthew 1.12-13 where he is called "Zorobabel". Notice what is said about him in Haggai 2.20-23. He was the "Tirshatha" (see v.63) or Governor. The word means 'one to be feared or reverenced'. Years later, Nehemiah became "Tirshatha": see Nehemiah 8.9 & 10.1. *Jeshua* (or Joshua) was the **priestly** man. See, for example, Haggai 1.1.

Zerubbabel and Joshua are almost inseparable: see Ezra 3.2, 3.8, 4.3, 5.2,

Haggai 1.1, 1.12, 1.14, 2.2, 2.4. This is most significant. The people were led by a prince and a priest. That is, by a man who stood before the people, and a man who stood before God. Good leadership demands men who will do both! Assembly elders will be totally ineffective in standing before God's people (see Hebrews 13.7, 17, 24), if they do not stand before God. Assembly leaders must be priestly men. They must have a right relationship with God. "He that ruleth over men must be just, ruling in the fear of God" (2 Sam. 23.3). But let's make this applicable to us all. Our life of public service and testimony will crash if it is not supported by private prayer, worship and intercession.

b) The People, vv.3-35
What can we say about this section? There is nothing special said about these people. They were not leaders, priests or Levites. But they are all listed because they were people with a concern for God's house and God's glory. They loved the 'place of the name'. It appears that in vv.3-19, we have *family* names. "Pahath-Moab" (v6) looks like a place name, but it actually means 'Governor of Moab'. Then in vv.20-35, we have *place* names. "Gibbar" (v.20) is evidently 'Gibeon'. ("Senaah", v.35, does look like another family name!) Some of the people were associated with famous places, like "Bethlehem" (v.21); "Anathoth" (v.23: Jeremiah came from there); "Bethel and Ai" (v.28: an interesting combination: see Genesis 12.8); "Jericho" (v.34). But quite a number of the people were connected with lesser-known places, and really, no famous families are conspicuous at all. But *they are all listed!* That's the whole point! We may not be conspicuous people, and we may not come from conspicuous families, and we may not be associated with conspicuous places, but the devotion and service of every one of us is known to God.

c) The Priests, vv.36-39
There were 4,289 priests. Something like a tenth of the whole group: see v.64. The priests were vital to the whole enterprise. Once the exiles had arrived in Jerusalem, their first priority was to build the altar, and offer sacrifices to God. See 3.2-3, "Then stood up Jeshua the son of Jozadak, and his brethren the priests...and builded the altar of the God of Israel, to offer burnt offerings thereon, as it is written in the law of Moses the man of God". Nothing could ever be accomplished unless God was given pre-eminence. As we shall see in later studies, their entire security lay in giving God first place. We cannot expect God's blessing on our lives and service unless He receives His portion from us. This is emphasised in Acts 13.2, "As they *ministered to the Lord*, and fasted, the Holy Ghost said, Separate me Barnabas and Saul for the work whereunto I have called them". The word "ministered" here means to act as a priest. The same

word is used in Hebrews 8.2; 10.11. Now compare Acts 13.2 with Deuteronomy 21.5: "And the priests the sons of Levi shall come near; for them the Lord thy God hath chosen to *minister unto him*".

Let's say again (we said it in our last study): all believers, however young, are priests. We proved this from 1 Peter 2. Now we'll prove it again, but this time from Hebrews 10.22, "Let us draw near with a true heart in full assurance of faith, having our *hearts sprinkled from an evil conscience, and our bodies washed with pure water*". This refers to the consecration of the priests in Exodus 29: for the water, see v.4; for the sprinkled blood, see v.21. So Hebrews 10 describes priestly service. But who is involved? You will look in vain for any special class of Christians: Hebrews 10 refers to *all* Christians! Don't forget that *you* belong to "an holy priesthood, to offer up spiritual sacrifices, acceptable to God by Jesus Christ" (1 Pet. 2.5). Your priesthood is as vital to your Christian life, as the priesthood was to national life in Ezra ch.3!

d) The Levites, v.40
Not many Levites: only 74 in fact, although the singers (128 of them: v.41) and the porters (139 of them: v.42) were also Levites. The priests are associated with *worship*: the Levites are associated with *work.* 1 Chronicles 23.28 describes their work: "Their office was to wait on the sons of Aaron for the service of the house of the Lord, in the courts, and in the chambers, and in the purifying of all holy things, and the work of the service of the house of God". It seems that they were often in short supply. When the second repatriation took place, Ezra "viewed the people, and the priests, and found there none of the sons of Levi". They eventually managed to find 38! See Ezra 8.15-19. We can only speculate about the shortage of Levites. Perhaps they didn't volunteer in larger numbers through fear of poor support! This certainly happened in Nehemiah 13.10. Or perhaps they were just too comfortable in Babylon! Either way, one thing is certain: there is generally a lack of workers. Not too many of the Lord's people are "always abounding in the work of the Lord" (1 Cor. 15.58). But spiritual Levites are as vital now, as literal Levites were then.

e) The Singers, v.41
"The singers: the children of Asaph, an hundred twenty and eight". Amongst the servants, there were also "two hundred singing men and singing women" (v.65). *1 Chronicles 9.14-34* describes the work of the Levites, including the singers, *after the return from exile.* (The opening chapters of 1 Chronicles give genealogies from Adam to the Exile, and in some cases, beyond the Exile). "And these are the singers, chief of the fathers of the Levites, who remaining in the

chambers were free: for they were employed in that work *day and night*" (v.33). The following references show the importance of the singers: *1 Chronicles 15.16-22*, "And David spake to the chief of the Levites to appoint their brethren to be the singers with instruments of musick, psalteries, and harps and cymbals, sounding, by *lifting up the voice with joy*...So the singers, Heman, Asaph, and Ethan, were appointed to sound with cymbals of brass...And Chenaniah, chief of the Levites, was for song: he *instructed about the song, because he was skilful*". This was in connection with the transfer of the ark from the house of Obed-Edom to Jerusalem. *2 Chronicles 5.12-13*, "Also the Levites which were the singers, all of them of Asaph, of Heman, of Jeduthun, with their sons and their brethren, being arrayed in white linen, having cymbals and psalteries and harps, stood at the east end of the altar...It came even to pass, as the trumpeters and singers were as one, to *make one sound to be heard in praising and thanking the Lord*....that then the house was filled with a cloud, even the house of the Lord". This was in connection with the dedication of the temple. *2 Chronicles 20.19-22*, "And the Levites, of the children of the Kohathites, and of the children of the Korhites, stood up to praise the Lord God of Israel with a loud voice on high...And when he (King Jehoshaphat) had consulted with the people, he appointed singers unto the Lord, and that should praise the beauty of holiness, as *they went out before the army*, and to say, Praise the Lord; for his mercy endureth for ever". This was in connection with the defeat of the Moabites and Ammonites. Just imagine it: an army led by a choir! (Perhaps that's where the Russians got the idea of the Red Army Ensemble!).

The New Testament is silent when it comes to church choirs and musical instruments. It has been nicely said that in the New Testament "there is only one choir, we are all in it, and the Lord Jesus is the Leader of the praise" (A.Leckie, referring to Hebrews 2.12). However, we must not think that there was no singing in early New Testament churches! See 1 Corinthians 14.15, "What is it then? I will pray with the spirit, and I will pray with the understanding also: I will *sing* with the spirit, and I will *sing* with the understanding also". See also Colossians 3.16. "Let the word of Christ dwell in you richly in all wisdom; teaching and admonishing one another. In *psalms and hymns and spiritual songs, singing with grace in your hearts to the Lord*". Notice the altered punctuation. The RSV puts it as follows: "Let the word of Christ dwell in you richly, as you teach one another in all wisdom, and as you sing psalms and hymns and spiritual songs with thankfulnes in your hearts to God". (Note: Ephesians 5.19 refers to personal praise). Every local assembly should be vibrant with praise and thanksgiving. "By him therefore let us offer the sacrifice of praise to God continually, that is, the fruit of our lips giving thanks (confessing) to his name" (Heb. 13.15).

f) The Porters, v.42

"In all an hundred thirty and nine". Their job description is given in 1 Chronicles 9.17-29. We have already noticed that this chapter evidently refers to the resettling of Jerusalem, and to service in connection with the rebuilt temple. The passage makes most interesting reading. Notice the following: "They and their children had the oversight of the gates of the house of the Lord, namely, the house of the tabernacle, by wards (watches)" (v.23); "And they lodged round about the house of God, because the charge was upon them, and the opening thereof every morning pertained to them" (v.27). (Compare 1 Samuel 3.15). Amongst other things, the porters were therefore gate-keepers, and this required vigilance. The divisions of the porters are given in 1 Chronicles 26.1-19. These verses emphasise their valour and their strength. See vv.6-9. After the death of Athaliah, Jehoiada "set the porters at the gates of the house of the Lord, that none which was **unclean in any thing should enter in**" (2 Chron. 23.19). In the days of Josiah, "the porters waited at every gate; **they might not depart from their service**; for their brethren the Levites prepared for them" (2 Chron. 35.15). We get the overwhelming impression that the porters were principally concerned with the **purity** of the house of God. When the Lord Jesus came, there were either no porters in existence, or they just weren't doing their job. See Matthew 21.12-13 and John 2.13-17.

The need for spiritual "porters" remains. See Acts 20.29-31, "For I know this, that after my departing shall grievous wolves enter in among you, not sparing the flock...Therefore watch, and remember, that by the space of three years I ceased not to warn every one night and day with tears". Paul refers to "false brethren unawares brought in" (Gal. 2.4), Peter to "false teachers among you, who privily shall bring in damnable heresies" (2 Pet. 2.1), and Jude to "certain men crept in unawares" (Jude v.4). We must not therefore be surprised if elders interview unknown visitors, and if necessary, politely but firmly, refuse them fellowship. Laxity in the matter of reception has been the downfall of many assemblies. Whilst, sadly, the Lord Jesus was obliged to rebuke the assembly at Ephesus, He did commend them on this point. See Revelation 2.2.

g) The Nethinims, vv.43-54

The name 'Nethinim' means 'given' or 'dedicated', and this is explained in Ezra 8.20: "Whom David and the princes had appointed for the service of the Levites, two hundred and twenty Nethinims: all of them were expressed by name". They are sometimes thought to be the Gibeonites, who were made by Joshua "hewers of wood and drawers of water for the congregation, and for the altar of the Lord, even unto this day, in the place which he should choose". Compare

Joshua 9.27 with 2 Chronicles 2.17-18. D.Kidner observes that "the presence of some foreign-looking names in the list may indicate that some of these groups came into Israel from David's conquests, whether as immigrants or perhaps as prisoners of war". They certainly performed the more menial tasks. We learn from Ezra 2.58, that they were closely associated with:

h) The Children of Solomon's Servants, vv.55-57
They were evidently foreigners. See 2 Chronicles 8.9, "But of the children of Israel did Solomon make no servants for his work". D.Kidner suggests that "Solomon may have recruited them to supplement David's Nethinim". To sum up: both categories could be described as 'burden-bearers', which is something required of us all: "Bear ye **one another's burdens,** and so fulfil the law of Christ" (Gal. 6.2). It is worth noting that Paul uses two different words for 'burden' in Galatians ch.6: in v.2 it refers to a heavy load (Greek, *'baros'*), but in v.5 it refers to the burden of personal responsibility (Greek, *'phortion'*). This explains the apparent conflict between the two verses.

2) DEALING WITH UNCERTAINTIES, vv.59-63
This section of the chapter deals with two problems: *(a)* inability to prove national status (vv.59-60); *(b)* inability to prove priestly status (vv. 61-63).

a) Inability to prove national status, vv.59-60
There were 652 people who could not "shew their father's house, and their seed, whether they were of Israel". Presumably, they could not produce proper family records, and although not barred from repatriation, they could not enjoy the same status as others. We must be absolutely certain that *our* names are in "the book of life" (Phil. 4.3). The Lord Jesus told His disciples to "rejoice not, that the spirits are subject unto you; but rather rejoice, because your names are written in heaven" (Luke 10.20). The presence of this particular group in Ezra 2, reminds us that we should not ostracise people who lack knowledge and assurance. They may not be in full fellowship with us, but they should at least be warmly welcomed.

b) Inability to prove priestly status, vv.61-63
The fate of Korah and his associates was a standing warning to Israel of the peril in approaching God without proper qualification. Read Numbers 16.40. This is why applicants whose claim could not be substantiated were "as polluted, put from the priesthood". It does seem that years before, one of the priests had married into another family, and for reasons unknown to us, his family had lost its priestly identity. (For Barzillai, see 2 Samuel 19.31-32). *We* ought to be known as men and women who are in touch with God.

This group was told that "they should not eat of the most holy things, till there stood up a priest with Urim and with Thummim". For "Urim and Thummim" (meaning 'light' and 'perfection'), see Exodus 28.30. We are not told precisely what they were, but we do know that God spoke through them. See Numbers 27.21; 1 Samuel 28.6. 1 Samuel 14.19 & 41 might be helpful as well. D.Kidner has an interesting piece here: "Whether the Urim and Thummim (through which the answer might otherwise have come) had been lost in the exile, or whether the ability to use them had been withdrawn, is not entirely clear; but the latter seems to be implied by the wording of the sentence". Compare Psalm 74, which refers to the destruction of Jerusalem and the period of the exile: "We see not our signs: there is no more any prophet: neither is there among us any that knoweth how long" (v.9).

Two lessons emerge: *(i) Disobedience* will stop God speaking to us. The absence of a priest with Urim and Thummim was the direct result of Israel's disobedience years before. *(ii) Doubt* should make us wait for God's guidance: don't take risks.

3) DETAILING THE TOTAL, vv.64-67
The total number of returning exiles was 42,360, plus servants and maids totalling 7,337. As we have already seen, every one of them was known to God, from leaders to maids. The transport does seem rather inadequate. It works out at six people per animal! Most people evidently walked. Asses outnumbered the rest, which is usually the case.

4) DUTIES ON ARRIVAL, vv.68-70
We should notice the order of events: *(i)* offering for the house of God (vv.68-69); *(ii)* occupation of their own cities (v.70). This speaks for itself. We know from Nehemiah ch.7 that it wasn't only "the chief of the fathers" who "offered freely for the house of God to set it up in his place". Their good example was followed by "the rest of the people" (Neh. 7.72). The fact that "the chief of the fathers...gave after their ability", reminds us of our own responsibilities. See 1 Corinthians 16.2, "Upon the first day of the week let every one of you lay by him in store, as God hath prospered him".

This was followed by resettlement of the cities. The people recovered their lost inheritance. The chapter therefore concludes with encouragement. Perhaps we have good cause to sing:

> Where is the blessedness I knew
> When first I saw the Lord?
> Where is the soul-refreshing view
> Of Jesus and His word?

Ezra Chapter 2 proves that God can restore to us the joy of our inheritance in Christ. *But far better if we never lose it in the first place!*

READ CHAPTER 3

The work commences

Ezra Chapter 1 records the decree issued by Cyrus authorising the Jews to leave Babylon and rebuild the temple in Jerusalem: "Who is there among you of all his people? his God be with him, and let him go up to Jerusalem, which is in Judah, and build the house of the Lord God of Israel" (1.3). Chapter 2 records the names of those who responded to the invitation. Chapters 3 to 6 describe the work of reconstruction and can be summarised as follows:

> Chapter 3: The work commences.
> Chapter 4: The work ceases
> Chapter 5: The work continues
> Chapter 6: The work completed.

Ezra Chapter 3 may be divided as follows: *(1)* Preparation for the work (vv.1-6); *(2)* Participation in the work (vv.7-9) *(3)* Praise because of the work (vv.10-13).

1) PREPARATION FOR THE WORK, vv.1-6

"And when the **seventh month** was come, and the children of Israel were in the cities, the people gathered themselves together as one man to Jerusalem" (v.1). Three Jewish "feasts" or "holy convocations" (Leviticus 23.4) took place in the "seventh month". They were *(i)* the feast of trumpets (v.24), *(ii)* the day of atonement (v.27) and *(iii)* the feast of tabernacles (v.34). All three "feasts" prefigure Israel's ultimate regathering and blessing, and events in the book of Ezra are a faint picture of events in the future. We should now notice the following:

a) Unity amongst the people of God, v.1

"The people gathered themselves together **as one man** to Jerusalem". There are other references in the chapter to the unity of the people: "and **all** they that were come out of the captivity" (v.8); "and **all** the people shouted with a great shout" (v.11). David would have been delighted. See Psalm 133.1, "Behold, how good and how pleasant it is for brethren to *dwell together in unity*!"

This was a matter of great concern to Paul when he wrote to the Philippians. It is no accident that he frequently uses the word "all" in his introduction: see v.1 ("to *all* the saints in Christ Jesus"); v.4 ("Always in every prayer of mine for you *all*"); v.7 ("Even as it is meet for me to think this of you *all*, because...ye *all* are partakers of my grace"); v.8 ("For God is my record, how greatly I long after you *all* in the bowels of Jesus Christ"). The reason for this emphasis lies in Phil. 4.2 (two sisters in the assembly were evidently not talking to each together: they could not say with Paul, "I long after you *all* in the bowels of Jesus Christ", 1.8), and it also explains 1.27, "Stand fast in *one* spirit, with *one* mind striving together for the faith of the gospel". It also explains 2.2, "Fulfil ye my joy, that ye be *likeminded*, having the *same love*, being of *one accord*, of *one mind*". See also Acts 2.1: "they were all with *one accord* in one place." Notice too in Ezra ch.3 that they "gathered themselves *together*" (v.1), they "stood...*together*" (v.9), they "sang *together*" (v.11), and they built '*together*' (4.3). They were "labourers *together*" (1 Cor. 3.9).

It is sad to notice the progress of disunity at Corinth. *(i)* "Contentions *among you*" (1 Cor. 1.11). The word "contentions" means 'strife...quarrels...wrangling'. *(ii)* "Divisions *among you*" (1 Cor. 11.18). The word "divisions" is translated "rent" in Matthew 9.16. *(iii)* "Heresies *among you*" (1 Cor. 11.19). The word "heresies" means 'sects'. This just proves how necessary it is to deal with problems in their infancy. The old English proverb that "tall oaks from little acorns grow" applies here as much as anywhere! Notice what James says about this: "But if ye have bitter envying and strife in your hearts, glory not, and lie not against the truth. This wisdom descendeth not from above, but is earthly, sensual, devilish. For where envying and strife is, there is confusion and every evil work" (James 3.14-16).

b) Centre of gathering to God, v.1

"The people *gathered themselves together* as one man *to Jerusalem*". That is, to the place where the Lord had put His Name. We discussed this in our introduction. See Deuteronomy 16.2,6,16. This is the place of which they said in Psalm 137: "If I forget thee, O Jerusalem, let my right hand forget her cunning. If I do not remember thee, let my tongue cleave to the roof of my mouth; if I prefer not Jerusalem above my chief joy" (vv.5-6). Compare Psalm 26.8, "Lord, I have loved the habitation of thy house, and the place where thine honour dwelleth". Jerusalem was the centre of worship and gathering.

In the New Testament, believers *"came together* to break bread" (Acts 20.7). See also 1 Corinthians 11: "ye *come together*" (v.17); "when ye *come together* in (the) church" (v.18); "when ye *come together* therefore into one place" (v.20). The Jews valued their centre of gathering to God. How much do we value the local assembly?

c) *Basis of approach to God, vv.2-3*

"Then stood up Jeshua the son of Jozadak, and his brethren the priests, and Zerubbabel the son of Shealtiel, and his brethren, and builded the altar of the God of Israel, to offer burnt offerings thereon, as it is written in the law of Moses the man of God". Notice that Jeshua is placed before Zerubbabel in v.2, whereas the order is reversed in v.8. Jeshua (elsewhere spelt 'Joshua'), the high priest, is named first in connection with sacrificial matters: Zerubbabel is named first in connection with the building work. Each man ministered according to his God-given position. Altar-building was a priority for Abraham. It was the first thing he did on entering Canaan: "And the Lord appeared unto Abram, and said, Unto thy seed will I give this land: and there **builded he an altar** unto the Lord, who appeared unto him" (Gen. 12.7). (See also Gen. 12.8). There was no altar in Egypt, and no altar in Babylon!

Although the Jews were surrounded by enemies intent on their destruction, they made no attempt to defend themselves by rebuilding the ruined wall of Jerusalem, or even setting a guard. But this does not mean that they did not take any steps to ensure their safety. Their defence lay in giving God first place (see Exodus 23.22) by erecting the altar and offering sacrifice. "And they set the altar upon his bases; for fear was upon them because of the people of those countries: and they offered burnt offerings thereon unto the Lord, even **burnt offerings** morning and evening" (v.3). Just look at the references to "burnt offerings" in vv.2-6. The "burnt offering" (read Leviticus ch.1) was the first of three offerings described as "a sweet savour unto the Lord". It was an 'approach offering' (Newberry), or an 'offering for acceptance'. The offerer was accepted in the value of his offering. We are accepted in Christ: see Ephesians 2.6.

In the New Testament, Paul alludes to the 'sweet savour' offerings as follows: "Walk in love, as Christ also hath loved us, and hath given himself for us an offering and a sacrifice to God **for a sweetsmelling savour**" (Eph. 5.2). Those sacrifices were all pictures of the Lord Jesus Christ, and describe, in different ways, His devotion to God. In the Old Testament, the Jews brought pleasure to God by offering sacrifices which prefigured His Son. But we give God first place, and bring pleasure to Him, when we express to God our appreciation of Christ Himself. We do this together at the Lord's supper, but we ought personally to "offer up spiritual sacrifices" (1 Peter 2.5) "morning and evening". We cannot build successfully without true appreciation of Christ. This is our greatest defence against seen and unseen enemies.

d) Obedience to the word of God, vv.4-6
i) **On a daily basis, v.3.** As we have seen, the "burnt offerings" were offered "morning and evening". This wasn't their bright idea. They simply carried out divinely-given instructions: "**as it is written in the law of Moses** the man of God" (v.2). They went back to **original** instructions. (This is very important: see Galatians 1.8-9). This refers to Exodus 29.38-42 and Numbers 28.1-10. So it was the scriptural order. The word of God must be carried out on a daily basis.

ii) **On a monthly basis, v.5.** "And...the continual burnt-offering, both of **the new moons**, and of all the set feasts of the Lord that were consecrated". See Numbers 28.11.

ii) **On an annual basis, v.4.** "They kept also the feast of tabernacles, **as it is writte**n". (The words, "as the duty of every day required", are explained in Numbers 29). The "feast of tabernacles" (called "the feast of ingathering", Exodus 23.16 & 34.22) was the last "feast" of the year, and commemorated God's mercy to His people. In addition to 'harvest home' (Leviticus 23.39), it recalled the exodus from Egypt: "that your generations may know that I made the children of Israel to dwell in booths, when I brought them out of the land of Egypt" (Lev. 23.43). But the "feast of tabernacles" also looks forward. It anticipates the millennial reign of Christ: see Zechariah 14.16-19. But there was an "eighth day", and students of prophecy remind us that since God always works in sevens, the number eight points forward to the "new heaven" and the "new earth". We'll leave it there! We learn then, that the word of God must be carried out, not only on a daily basis, but on special occasions as well.

But although there was a great deal of progress thus far, "the foundation of the temple of the Lord was not yet laid" (v.6). There remained a great deal more to do. This brings us to

2) PARTICIPATION IN THE WORK, vv.7-9
The first section of the chapter describes the **spiritual** preparation for the work: now we are given details of the **material** preparation. The order is important. We cannot expect any progress unless things are right spiritually! We must notice

a) The variety of skills involved in the work, v.7

"They gave money also unto **the masons**, and to **the carpenters**; and meat and drink and oil, unto them of Zidon, and to them of Tyre, to bring cedar trees from Lebanon to the sea of Joppa ('at Joppa', JND), according to the grant that they had of Cyrus king of Persia". So there was a variety of workmen, and this reminds us of the teaching of 1 Corinthians 12: "The eye cannot say unto the hand, I have no need of thee: nor again the head to the feet, I have no need of you" (vv.14-21). Paul applies his analogy in v.27: "Now ye are (the) body of Christ, and members in particular". This speaks for itself. The local assembly needs a wide variety of spiritual ability if it is to function effectively. Let's ensure that we are fulfilling our God-given role in the assembly. "As every man (every one) hath received the gift, even so **minister the same** one to another, as good stewards of the **manifold grace** of God" (1 Pet. 4.10-11).

b) The cost involved in the work, v.7

"They **gave money** also unto the masons, and to the carpenters; and **meat, and drink, and oil**, unto them of Zidon, and to them of Tyre". Building for God required expenditure. In this case it was expenditure in 'cash' ("money") and 'kind' ("meat, and drink, and oil"). Work for God **still** requires expenditure in 'cash and kind'. We should be good stewards of our financial and material resources. The hymnwriter puts it like this:

> Naught that I have my own I call,
> I hold it for the Giver:
> My heart, my strength, my life, my all,
> Are His, and His for ever.

There is expenditure in other ways. Expenditure of time in reading and studying the word of God. Expenditure of time in prayer. Expenditure of energy in service. The work of God is costly. "Gold, silver, precious (costly) stones" are not easily found and gathered. Gold and silver have to be mined, and costly stones have to be quarried, unlike "wood, hay, stubble". This requires time and energy. But these materials will stand the test. Are we willing to obtain, and use, materials like that in our assembly-building? The work of God is also costly in other ways. It could involve the surrender of a relationship, and it could involve exposure to persecution.

c) The oversight involved in the work, vv.8-9

"They appointed the Levites, from twenty years old and upward, to **superintend** (AV 'set forward') the work of the house of Jehovah. And Jeshua stood up, his sons and his brethren, Kadmiel and his sons, the sons of Judah, as one man, to **superintend** (AV 'set forward') the workmen in the house of God" (JND). We gather from this that the priests supervised the Levites. Compare Numbers 4.16,28,33. So the building was guided and controlled by priestly men. Assembly work still requires oversight by priestly men.

Levites over age twenty were involved in this work. See also 1 Chronicles 23.24-32. Originally, the Levites commenced their ministry at age thirty (Num. 4.3), although they evidently entered probationary service at twenty-five (Num. 8.24). With the reduction in heavy work, they became eligible for service at twenty (1 Chron. 23.24-26). However, it was back to heavy work here - and they still started at twenty! But the priestly men and the working men reached the first mile-stone, and "the builders laid the foundation of the temple of the Lord" (v.10). This led to

3) PRAISE BECAUSE OF THE WORK, vv.10-13
"And when the builders laid the **foundation** of the temple of the Lord, they set the priests in their apparel with trumpets, and the Levites the sons of Asaph with cymbals, to praise the Lord, after the ordinance of David king of Israel". Previously, it was back to **Moses** (v.2): now it is back to **David**, who instituted the service of praise (see 1 Chronicles ch.25).

Foundations are important. See 1 Corinthians 3.10-11, "According to the grace of God which is given unto me, as a wise masterbuilder, I have laid the **foundation**...for other **foundation** can no man lay than that is laid, which is Jesus Christ". **When** did Paul lay this foundation? See Acts 18.1-18, "After these things Paul departed from Athens, and came to Corinth...and **he continued there a year and six months**, teaching the word of God among them" (vv.1,11). His stay was actually longer than eighteen months: see v.18. **How** did Paul lay this foundation? See again Acts 18.11, "And he continued there a year and six months, **teaching the word of God among them**". There can be no other foundation for a New Testament assembly.

Barnabas was "glad" ('rejoiced', JND) when he saw evidence of the "grace of God" at Antioch (Acts 11.23), and these people gladly recognised that their progress was entirely due to the goodness of God. There was no self-adulation: "And they sang together by course in **praising and giving thanks unto the Lord**; because he is good, for his mercy endureth for ever toward Israel" (v.11). We should notice at least three things here:

i) **The clothing of the priests.** "The priests in their apparel" (v.10). Exodus 28.39-42 gives details. They wore "coats" which were evidently made of the same material as Aaron's "coat", that is, of "fine linen". They wore "linen breeches". Their clothes were "for glory and for beauty". So there was purity (the white linen), glory, and beauty. What kind of clothes do we wear as "holy" and "royal" priests? (1 Pet. 2.5, 9).

ii) The conducting of the praise. It was not discordant or disorderly: "And they sang together by course ('alternately', see 1 Chronicles 25) in praising and giving thanks unto the Lord" (v.11). (Perhaps they sang Psalm 136 amongst others: "O give thanks unto the Lord; for he is good: for his mercy endureth for ever"). In the assembly, everything should be done "decently and in order" (1 Cor. 14.40).

iii) The contribution of the people. There were tears and cheers! "But many of the priests and Levites and chief of the fathers, who were **ancient men** (how old is 'ancient?!'), that had seen the first house, when the foundation of this house was laid before their eyes, **wept with a loud voice**; and many **shouted aloud for joy**" (v.12). Compare Haggai 2.1-9. It was evidently the **younger** people who "shouted aloud for joy". The young were not allowed to think that they were accomplishing something better. The old were not allowed to overlook the enthusiasm of the new generation. The enthusiasm of youth blended with the experience of old age. Younger people should not despise the experience, concern and sorrow of older believers. Older believers should not despise the zeal and initiative of younger believers. We need both today!

Whilst people in the locality could not distinguish between the differing notes, they did not fail to hear the loud shout: "The noise was heard afar off" (v.13). David said, "He hath put a new song in my mouth, even praise unto our God: many shall see it, and fear, and shall trust in the Lord" (Psalm 40.3). We should endeavour to emulate the Thessalonians, of whom it was said "from you **sounded out** the word of the Lord" (1 Thess. 1.8).

READ CHAPTER 4

The work ceases

We have noticed that Ezra Chapters 3-6 describe the work of reconstruction and can be summarised as follows:

Chapter 3: The work commences.
Chapter 4: The work ceases
Chapter 5: The work continues
Chapter 6: The work completed.

Chapter 3 describes the solid progress of the builders after careful preparation. *Spiritual* preparation (vv.1-6) preceded *material* preparation (v.7), and the foundation of the temple had been laid amidst praise and thanksgiving to God. But building for God always attracts opposition, and Ezra 4 describes the various ways in which the enemies attempted to halt the work. Sadly, they succeeded at the third attempt - on the ground of false accusation. It is most significant that once the work had ceased, the enemy lost interest. We know from Haggai ch.1, that the people shrugged their shoulders and said, "The time is not come, the time that the Lord's house should be built". So they built their own houses. That didn't bother the enemies one little bit. But immediately work for God recommenced (Ezra ch.5), the enemy reappeared. This highlights two important lessons:

i) Build for yourself, and the enemy is not particularly interested, but build for God, and he is galvanized into action. This is quite normal. See 1 Corinthians 16.8-9, "But I will tarry at Ephesus until Pentecost. For a great door and effectual is opened unto me, and there are many adversaries". Paul does not say '*but* there are many adversaries'. He was not at all surprised by their presence! It was quite usual.

ii) Progress is dangerous! We must be as spiritually alert when things are going well as we are when things are going badly. Hezekiah's reforms were wonderfully successful (2 Chronicles chs.29-31), but then we read the chilling words, "After these things, and the establishment thereof, Sennacherib king of Assyria came, and entered into Judah" (2 Chron. 32.1). We must never forget the New Testament injunction, "Wherefore let him that thinketh he standeth take heed lest he fall" (1 Cor. 10.12).

Ezra 4 describes three aspects of enemy strategy. He attempted *(1)* to *deceive* them as *"an angel of light"* (vv.1-3): *(2)* to *deter* them as an *"adversary"* (v.4); *(3)* to *defame* them as an *"accuser of our brethren"* (vv.5-24). As you can see, all three are descriptions of the devil. He is an angel of light" (2 Cor. 11.14); he is our great adversary ('Satan' means adversary): he is the "accuser of our brethren" (Rev. 12.10). Satan is persistent. Failure in one direction gives place to an attempt somewhere else. Remember, "he departed from him (the Lord Jesus) *for a season*" (Luke 4.13). Satan varies his tactics, and we should not be "ignorant of his devices" (2 Cor. 2.11). But although his tactics may vary, the objective is always the same. Read 1 Timothy 1.19; 4.1; 5.8; 5.12; 6.10; 6.21. Notice the word "some" here, and where they are all heading!

1) THE ATTEMPT TO DECEIVE THEM, vv.1-3
In these verses we must notice *(a)* the amalgamation proposed (vv.1-2); *(b)* the amalgamation rejected (v.3).

a) The amalgamation proposed, vv.1-2
Like Satan, the enemy transforms himself into *"an angel of light"*. "Now when the adversaries of Judah and Benjamin heard that the children of the captivity builded the temple unto the Lord God of Israel; then they came to Zerubbabel, and to the chief of the fathers, and said unto them, **Let us build with you: for we seek your God, as ye do**". It all looked very plausible. Now compare 2 Corinthians 11.13-15, "For such are false apostles, deceitful workers, transforming themselves into the apostles of Christ. And no marvel; for Satan himself is transformed into **an angel of light.** Therefore it is no great thing if his ministers also be transformed as the ministers of righteousness". Notice the words, "**transforming themselves**". Paul does not use the word 'metamorphoo', which emphasises change from within (Matt. 17.2; Rom. 12.2; 2 Cor. 3.18), but 'metaschematizo', which emphasises outward change, that is, change in fashion and appearance. They masqueraded *(i)* as "apostles of Christ", and *(ii)* as "ministers of righteousness", but they were actually *(i)* "false apostles" and *(ii)* "his (Satan's) ministers". They just followed their dark master: "and no marvel; for **Satan himself** is transformed into an angel of light". But this does not make identification impossible. Paul tells us what to look for earlier in the same chapter: "For if he that cometh preacheth **another Jesus**, whom we

have not preached, or if ye receive **another spirit**, which ye have not received, or **another gospel**, which ye have not accepted, ye might well bear with him" (v.4). (The last words are probably ironical, and can be rendered, 'ye bear well enough with him'.)

The enemy used fine words: "We seek your God, as ye do; and we do sacrifice unto him". It was an attempt by "good words and fair speeches" to "deceive the hearts of the simple" (Rom. 16.18). It was a case of wolves "in sheep's clothing" (Matt. 7.15). But Zerubbabel and his colleagues were not as simple as the enemy imagined! They knew only too well that these people **were not Jews at all.** They talked about their sacrifices, but without a properly constituted priesthood and a properly recognised place their sacrifices could not be acceptable to God. On their own admission, they were descendants of colonists from other parts of the Assyrian empire (v.2). For Esar-haddon, see 2 Kings 19.37. As D.Kidner points out, "Esarhaddon (681-669BC) began his reign forty years after the fall of Samaria, but the transplanting of populations was a longstanding policy". This is certainly true: See 2 Kings 17.24-41 which describe events following the fall of Samaria in 721BC. "So these nations feared the Lord, and served their graven images, both their children, and their children's children: as did their fathers, so do they unto this day" (v.41).

The enemy first attacked by attempting to deceive the Jews. Compromise could halt the work, and to achieve this they endeavoured to 'transform themselves' into something acceptable to God's people. "The kisses of an enemy are deceitful" (Prov. 27.6). But did it work?

b) The amalgamation rejected, v.3
It did not work! Listen to the answer from discerning men: "Ye have nothing to do with us to build an house unto our God; but we ourselves together will build unto the Lord God of Israel". Like the early preachers of the gospel, they took "nothing of the Gentiles" (3 John 7). Alliance with the world, in this case the religious world, was firmly rejected. It happened again in the days of Nehemiah: "Sanballat and Geshem sent unto me, saying, Come, let us meet together in some one of the villages in the plain of Ono. But they thought to do me mischief. And I sent messengers unto them, saying, I am doing a great work, so that I cannot come down: why should the work cease, whilst I leave it, and come down to you?" (Neh. 6.1-3).

We must beware of our associations. See 2 Corinthians 6.14-18: "Be ye not unequally yoked together with unbelievers: for what fellowship hath righteousness with unrighteousness? and what communion hath light with darkness? and what concord hath Christ with Belial? or what part hath he that believeth with an infidel? and what agreement hath the temple of God with idols? for ye are the temple of the living God". Let us be very clear about this: if our associations, religious or otherwise, require us to either deny or compromise any part of God's word, then we are far better off without them. This is particularly true with reference to church unity and the Ecumenical Movement. Don't be deceived by the plea that we must all sink our doctrinal differences in the greater interests of unity. We must be unswervingly loyal to the word of God. It is our only path of spiritual safety. Sometimes, we have to sink **personal** opinions and preferences in the interests of assembly unity, but that is something quite different. We **cannot** compromise on Bible teaching.

2) THE ATTEMPT TO DETER THEM, v.4

The enemies now show their true colours. They had tried to disguise the fact that they were really "the **adversaries** of Judah and Benjamin" (v.1). But that is all thrown to the winds now: "Then the people of the land weakened the hands of the people of Judah, and troubled them in building". Now we have a picture of Satan acting in true character. His name means '**adversary**', and he is the same in both Old Testament (Hebrew 'Satan') and New Testament (Greek 'Satanas'). He is named and described in this way in Zechariah 3.1, "And he shewed me Joshua the high priest standing before the angel of the Lord, and **Satan** standing at his right hand to **resist** him". See also 1 Thessalonians 2.18, "Wherefore we would have come unto you, even I Paul, once and again; but **Satan hindered us**". He opposes the **word of God:** "And these are they by the way side, where the word is sown; but when they have heard, **Satan** cometh immediately, and taketh away the word that was sown in their hearts" (Mark 4.15). He opposes the **people of God:** "And **Satan** stood up against Israel, and provoked David to number Israel" (1 Chron. 21.1). He opposed the **Son of God:** "Then saith Jesus unto him, Get thee hence, **Satan**" (Matt. 4.10).

Notice how the 'adversaries' worked. **(i)** They "**weakened the hands** of the people of Judah". The word "weakened" means to 'cast or throw down', and in this case means 'to destroy his courage'. (It is Strong's word 7503 in Gesenius' Hebrew-Chaldee Lexicon). Compare Ezra 6.22 where the Lord had "turned the heart of the king of Assyria (think about that one!) unto them, to **strengthen their hands** in the work of the house of God, the God of Israel". **(ii)** They "**troubled** them in building". The word "troubled" means 'to terrify, to frighten, to cause any one's mind to be cast down' (word 1089 in the above lexicon). It was a persistent campaign of harassment and went on for about sixteen years. (Work it out from various dates in the book!). The enemy didn't give up. Don't expect Satan to give up either. Part of the campaign was to 'get their victims discredited and on the wrong side of the authorities - and they were prepared to buy professional help (v.5) to achieve this' (D.Kidner). This brings us to the third attack:

3) THE ATTEMPT TO DEFAME THEM, vv.5-24
There is a technical problem in this section of the chapter. Its chronological limits are set in v.5: "All the days of Cyrus king of Persia, even until the reign of Darius king of Persia". The chapter begins in the reign of Cyrus (v.3), and ends in the reign of Darius (v.24). Ahaseurus (v.6) and Artaxerxes (vv.7-23) reigned **after** Darius, but in this chapter their reigns are placed **before** the reign of Darius.

Commentators take the view that references to them are inserted here to show that opposition to God's people continued **beyond** the immediate context, and that vv.6-23 could therefore be placed in brackets. But this does not satisfactorily explain v.24: "Then (i.e. after king Artaxerxes' letter had been received: see footnote) ceased the work of the house of God which is at Jerusalem. So it ceased **unto** the second year of the reign of Darius king of Persia". Neither does it explain the totally different kind of letter that king Artaxerxes gave to Ezra in Chapter 7, or the permission given by the same monarch to Nehemiah. In the view of your present commentator, the usual argument seems flawed. J.N.Darby's view that Ahaseurus (v.6) is "probably Cambyses, son of Cyrus"', and that Artaxerxes (vv.7-23) is Smerdis (see his footnotes), is more logical, but his reference to Smerdis can hardly be supported. He was the brother of Cambyses, and never actually reigned! Whatever the answer to the problem, the spiritual lessons of the section remain the same. We should notice that nobody wrote to king Cyrus. That would be more than their life was worth!

We must now notice **(a)** the letter to the king (vv.6-16); **(b)** the letter from the king (vv.17-24).

a) The letter to the king, vv.6-16
"And in the reign of Ahasuerus, in the beginning of his reign, wrote they unto him **an accusation** against the inhabitants of Judah and Jerusalem. And in the days of Artaxerxes wrote Bishlam, Mithredath, Tabeel, and the rest of their companions unto Artaxerxes king of Persia".

Now we have the enemy as a picture of the Devil, meaning 'an accuser, a slanderer (from *diaballo*, to accuse, to malign' (W.E.Vine)). He is now the "**accuser of our brethren**". As the Devil, he accuses **men before God**. See Revelation 12.10, "The accuser of our brethren is cast down, which accused them before our God day and night". See also Job chs.1-2. As the Devil, he accuses **God before men**, see Genesis 3.4-5: "Ye shall not surely die: for God doth know that in the day that ye eat thereof, then your eyes shall be opened, and ye shall be as gods, knowing good and evil". In other words, 'God doesn't want you to be like Him - that's why He placed this unnecessary prohibition on you'.

We should notice, however, that the New Testament word translated "devil" is also used in warning believers against false accusation. See 1 Timothy 3.11, "not slanderers", and Titus 2.3, "not false accusers". Let's make sure that we don't do the Devil's work for him. (We should also notice that in "the last days" men will be "false accusers", 2 Tim. 3.3). We ought to stay with this for a little while. Work for God is still marred, and sometimes terminated, not because God's people have been duped by the "angel of light" or have succumbed to 'the adversary', but because they have become 'accusers of the brethren'. One of the ways to study the book of Proverbs is to watch the various characters who appear and reappear on the stage. One of them is "the talebearer". He, or she, is a very dangerous character, and Proverbs 26.17-28 is most illuminating. We ought to think twice about saying nasty things behind people's backs after reading the following! The "talebearer" -

i) **Fails to mind his own business.** "He that passeth by, and meddleth with strife belonging not to him, is like one that taketh a dog by the ears" v.17). He meddles to his cost!

ii) **Fabricates foolish excuses.** "As a mad man who casteth firebrands, arrows, and death, so is the man that deceiveth his neighbour, and saith, **Am not I in sport**?" (vv.18-19). This is particularly relevant. When you nail the culprit, they say, 'I was only joking!'

iii) **Fuels trouble**. "Where no wood is, there the fire goeth out: so where there is no talebearer, the strife ceaseth. As coals are to burning coals, and wood to fire; so is a contentious man to kindle strife" (vv.20-21).

iv) **Feeds on titbits.** "The words of a talebearer are as dainty morsels" (v.22 JND). ("The words of a talebearer are as wounds", AV).

v) **Faces you with deception.** "Burning lips and a wicked heart are like a potsherd covered with silver dross" (vv.23-26).

vi) **Falls into his own trap.** "Whoso diggeth a pit shall fall therein: and he that rolleth a stone, it will return upon him" (v.27).

vii) *Fixes his heart on damage* "A lying tongue hateth those that are afflicted by it; and a flattering mouth worketh ruin" (v.28).

Now let's read the letter to Artaxerxes. It was sent by eminent men, backed by an impressive list of nine different groups of people from the surrounding nations (vv.7-10). In all, a powerful alliance in opposition to God's people and God's house. We must never forget that we too face a powerful alliance. "We wrestle not against flesh and blood, but against principalities, against powers, against the rulers of the darkness of this world, against spiritual wickedness in high places" (Eph. 6.12). The letter is quoted here to show just how skilfully truth can be blended with lies! For example:

i) *The case involved deliberate misrepresentation.* No reference is made to the temple. But there is a great deal about the city and its walls, See vv.12, 13, 15, 16. On the assumption that the letter was written before the reign of Darius, it was only the temple that was in course of reconstruction. Paul was deliberately misrepresented too. See Romans 3.8, "And not rather, (as we be **slanderously reported**, and as some affirm that we say) Let us do evil, that good may come". We can expect the same treatment. The Lord Jesus said to the Jews, "Ye are of your father the devil... When he speaketh a lie, he speaketh of his own: for he is a liar, and the father of it" (John 8.44). We may also encounter circumstantial misrepresentation. See, for example, Acts 21.28-29; "For they had seen before with him in the city Trophimus an Ephesian, whom they **supposed** that Paul had brought into the temple".

ii) *The case involved half truth.* Jerusalem is described as "the rebellious and the bad city" (v.12). This is amplified in v.15. All this was perfectly true: see 2 Chronicles 36.13, "He (Zedekiah) also rebelled against king Nebuchadnezzar, who had made him swear by God". But the decree of Cyrus, encouraging the Jews to return, was not mentioned. We must be careful that we don't do this kind of thing. Let's endeavour to give all the facts of a case - not just those that will put someone in a bad light, or a good light. It has been said that 'a half-truth is like a half-brick: it goes further and is more dangerous. The problem with a half-brick is that you are likely to get the wrong half!'

Let's remember too, that we should behave in a way that gives the enemy no reason to throw mud. Satan will make the most of our misdemeanours. "Give none occasion to the adversary to speak reproachfully" (1 Tim. 5.14).

iii) *The case involved crafty presentation.* It was weighted to appeal to the king. He was likely to lose revenue! See vv.13-14, 16. "It was not meet for us to see the king's dishonour, therefore have we sent and certified the king" (v.14). But they really had no concern at all for the king's honour! They just wanted to stop the work. They also omitted to say that they had originally asked to help too! (v.2). Jude sums them up nicely: "These are murmurers, complainers, walking after their own lusts; and their mouth speaketh **great swelling words, having men's persons in admiration because of advantage**" (v.16).

b) The letter from the king, vv.17-24

The petition to Artaxerxes was successful. "Then ceased the work of the house of God which is at Jerusalem. So it ceased unto the second year of the reign of Darius king of Persia" (v.24). God's work is often marred, and sometimes terminated, by tittle-tattle and character assassination. We must not become spiritual cannibals: (Gal 5.15).

The accusation succeeded. At least for the time being. The king evidently believed all he had been told. His reply does not mention the rebuilding of the temple. That's not surprising: he hadn't been told about it! On the other hand, it was "the work of the **house of God**" that ceased. No reference is made to the city! The work ceased by foul means.

But was that all? It could be argued that they could do nothing about it, and Jerusalem would echo with the tramp of Persian soldiers' feet if they continued to build. So all they could do was to forget about the whole project, and get on with life. But the work stopped, not so much through the "force and power" of opposition, but through the **apathy of the people.** Haggai makes this very clear indeed; see 1.1-11. Work ceased, we are told, for approximately fifteen years. But we will see from Chapter 5 that God did not allow the situation to continue.

Watch this space!

Footnote

"**Then** (i.e. after king Artaxerxes' letter had been received) ceased the work of the house of God which is at Jerusalem. So it ceased **unto** the second year of the reign of Darius king of Persia" (v.24). It has been pointed out that in each of the 10 other occurrences of the word "then" in Ezra, and in each of the 46 (Aramaic) occurrences in Daniel, the reference is apparently always to something following immediately.

READ CHAPTER 5

The work continues

We have noticed that Ezra 3-6 describe the work of temple reconstruction, and may be summarised as follows:

> Chapter 3: The work commences.
> Chapter 4: The work ceases
> Chapter 5: The work continues
> Chapter 6: The work completed.

The solid progress of the work in **Chapter 3** provoked opposition in **Chapter 4**, where the enemy attempted to terminate the work by acting *(i)* as an "angel of light"; *(ii)* as an adversary; *(iii)* as an accuser. He succeeded at the third attempt: "Then ceased the work of the house of God which is at Jerusalem. So it ceased unto the second year of the reign of Darius king of Persia" (4.24). For something like fifteen years, there was no further work for God, and the enemy remained inactive. This did not mean that the people had a fifteen year holiday on the Mediterranean beaches. They were evidently very busy indeed. But they were busy in their own interests, and God was obliged to say, through Haggai, "Is it time for you, O ye, to dwell in your ceiled houses, and **this house** lie waste?" (Hag. 1.4). As the result of preaching by Haggai and Zechariah, the work resumed in **Chapter 5**, and this brought fresh opposition. We must stress the lesson again: **build for yourself, and the enemy is not particularly interested, but build for God, and he is galvanized into action.**

We will explore this Chapter with reference to three phrases *(1)* "the prophets of God" (v.2); *(2)* "the eye of their God" (v.5); *(3)* "the servants of the God of heaven and earth" (v.11).

1) THE PROPHETS OF GOD, vv.1-2
"Then the **prophets,** Haggai the prophet, and Zechariah the son of Iddo, prophesied unto the Jews that were in Judah and Jerusalem in the name of the

God of Israel, even unto them. Then rose up Zerubbabel the son of Shealtiel, and Jeshua the son of Jozadak, and began to build the house of God which is at Jerusalem: and with them were the **prophets of God** helping them". We must notice: **(a)** the ministry of the prophets (v.1); **(b)** the response of the leaders (v.2).

a) The ministry of the prophets, v.1
i) The character of the ministry. "Then the prophets, Haggai the prophet, and Zechariah the son of Iddo, **prophesied** unto the Jews". Jeremiah 23.16-22 describe false prophets, but we also learn that the true prophet "stood in the counsel of the Lord, and hath perceived and heard his word" (v.18). The prophetic ministry involved **fellowship with God.** There is all the difference in the world between an address and a message. An address means time in the study, but a message means time in the study, and in the **sanctuary**. We tend to hear more addresses than messages. But don't reserve criticism for preachers: we **all** need to pray more over our service for God.

It is often said that a priest represented the people before God, and a prophet represented God before the people. But Malachi tells us that "the priest's lips should keep knowledge, and they should seek the law at his mouth: for he is the messenger of the Lord of hosts" (Mal. 2.7). The ministry of the prophet became necessary with the failure of the priests, and the poor condition of God's people.

ii) The emphasis on the ministry. We know very little about Haggai and Zechariah personally. But we do know a great deal about their ministry. This is important. We tend to place importance on a preacher's background, connections and personality, rather than on his service for God. Paul made the point quite forcibly in 1 Corinthians 3.5, "Who then is Apollos, and who Paul? Ministering **servants**, through whom ye have believed, and as the Lord has given to each" (JND). The RV is even more emphatic: "**What** then is Apollos? and **what** is Paul? Ministers through whom ye believed; and each as the Lord gave to him".

iii) The order in the ministry. Both men began to preach in the "second year of Darius the king", but they certainly didn't get under one another's feet! Notice when they preached:

Haggai:	**6th**.	month: see 1.1
Haggai:	**7th**.	month: see 2.1
Zechariah:	**8th**.	month: see 1.1
Haggai:	**9th**.	month: see 2.10
Zechariah:	**11th**.	month: see 1.7

We must notice these men only preached once they had received "the word of the Lord". We read this on each of these five occasions. So we can easily understand why the prophets didn't take any meetings in the 10th month. There was no word from the Lord. It would have been quite wrong for them to preach. God would have been obliged to say, "I have not sent these prophets, yet they ran: I have not spoken to them, yet they prophesied" (Jer. 23.21).

The harmony between Haggai and Zechariah in this way illustrates 1 Corinthians 14.40, "Let all things be done decently and in order". This verse summarises previous teaching in the chapter: for example, "Let the prophets speak two or three, and let the other judge. If any thing be revealed to another that sitteth by, let the first hold his peace. For ye may all prophesy one by one, that all may learn, and all may be comforted...*For God is not the author of confusion, but of peace, as in all churches of the saints*" (vv.29-33). There was no competition, collision, chaos or confusion amongst God's servants in Ezra 5, and there will be none today if we are all in fellowship with God.

Haggai and Zechariah evidently belonged to different age groups. Whilst it is sometimes inferred from Haggai 2.2-3 that the prophet was one of the "ancient men" (Ezra 3.12), it is quite certain that Zechariah was a young man. See Zechariah 2.4. It is therefore not unreasonable to think of these two men as older and younger respectively. We have only to think of Moses and Joshua in the Old Testament, and Paul and Timothy in the New Testament to see the importance of older and younger believers working together.

iv) The variety in the ministry. Whilst, as we have seen, the two men worked harmoniously together, their ministry was quite different. C.E.Hocking puts it nicely: "In this witness for God we find a grand illustration of the blending of ministries, the complementary character of their teaching effecting the desired result. Haggai's stirring words were aimed at the **conscience.** The Spirit convicted his hearers as he cuttingly asked, 'Is it time, O ye?' (Hag. 1.4). Zechariah's ministry however was directed to the **heart.** He indicated in his visions and prophecies the coming glories of 'that day'. He urged unbounded enthusiasm in the work of God's house in the light of the future prosperity and blessedness of Zion". Cyril Hocking continues, "How important for the spiritual welfare of God's people and the furtherance of His work is a ministry aimed at conscience and heart, combining challenge and comfort, leading to thought and action" (*The Work of Reconstruction: Precious Seed, January/February 1958).*

v) The authority of the ministry. Their preaching was "in the name of the God of Israel" (v.1). This was not an empty statement. As we have already noticed, "In the second year of Darius the king, in the sixth month, in the first day of the month, came **the word of the Lord,** by Haggai the prophet unto Zerubbabel the son of Shealtiel, governor of Judah, and to Joshua the son of Josedech, the high priest" (Hag. 1.1). See also Haggai 2.1; 2.10; Zechariah 1.1; 1.7. Our authority is no less: "And Jesus came and spake unto them, saying, All power (authority) is given unto me in heaven and in earth. Go ye therefore, and teach all nations (make disciples of all nations), baptizing them in the name of the Father, and of the Son, and of the Holy Ghost: teaching them to observe all things whatsoever I have commanded you" (Matt. 28.18-20). It is not a case of 'the teaching of the church', but the teaching of the Lord Jesus Christ.

vi) The example of the ministry. "And with them were the prophets of God *helping them*" (v.2). So Haggai and Zechariah were more than 'platform men'. Having delivered their messages, they rolled up their sleeves (pardon me, girded themselves!) and got stuck into the work with everybody else. Ministry has added effect when the servant becomes an example of what he is saying to other people. Hence 1 Timothy 4.11-12, "These things command and teach. Let no man despise thy youth; but **be thou an example** of the believers, in word, in conversation, in charity, in spirit, in faith, in purity". Hence Titus 2.6-7, "Young men likewise exhort to be sober minded. In all things shewing **thyself a pattern of good works**". See also 1 Peter 5.3. The Lord Jesus was the perfect example of His own ministry: see Acts 1.1.

We ought to say here that this was certainly not 'a flash in a pan'. Haggai and Zechariah kept on preaching. See Ezra 6.14, "And the elders of the Jews builded, and they prospered through the prophesying of Haggai the prophet and Zechariah the son of Iddo". C.E.Hocking has a very pertinent piece here: "In order that God's work might prosper, more than a week-end's ministry or the presenting of a fine address at a weeknight gathering will be needed. Consistently and consecutively, God's whole counsel will need to be unfolded to the saints".

b) The response of the leaders, v.2
The situation in Jerusalem was met by ministry of the word of God. The preaching, particularly of Haggai, was incisive, but it was undoubtedly effective. He was not concerned with outward opposition, but with inward apathy. The Jews were just content to be back from Babylon. Never mind about getting on with God's work. It was a far cry from the original enthusiasm of 3.10-13. They were in the right place, but that was all! They did not question the fact that it was right to build, **but not now!** "**The time is not come,** the time that

the Lord's house should be built" (Hag. 1.2). But it was "time...to dwell in your ceiled houses!" (v.4). Haggai preached against a background of indolence, indulgence and indifference.

We gladly notice that the word of God was not resisted. "Then rose up Zerubbabel the son of Shealtiel, and Jeshua the son of Jozadak, and began to build the house of God which is at Jerusalem". There are three important things here: *(i)* there was **leadership**: "Then rose up Zerubbabel the son of Shealtiel, and Jeshua the son of Jozadak"; *(ii)* there was **workmanship**: "and began to build the house of God which is at Jerusalem"; *(iii*) there was **fellowship**: "and with them were the prophets of God helping them". The ministry took effect within twenty-four days. See Haggai 1.12-15. Sadly, it generally takes far longer than twenty-four days for ministry to have much effect on us! As believers we are to "receive with **meekness** the engrafted word (the 'implanted' or 'rooted' word), which is able to save your souls. But be ye doers of the word, and not hearers only, deceiving your own selves" (James 1.21-22). In context, to "receive with meekness the engrafted word", refers to believers. How do we react to the word of God? We cannot afford to neglect or ignore it.

Notice that the divine command was more important than official permission. Compare Acts 4.19-20, "Whether it be right in the sight of God to hearken unto you more than unto God, judge ye. For we cannot but speak the things which we have seen and heard". This brings us to the second phrase:

2) THE EYE OF GOD, vv.3-5
The opposition now reappears: "At the same time came to them Tatnai, governor on this side the river (west of the Euphrates), and Shethar-boznai, and their companions, and said thus unto them, Who hath commanded you to build this house, and to make up this wall?" But it was no longer a case of making "them to cease by force and power" (4.23). We read, "But **the eye of their God** was upon the elders of the Jews, that they could not cause them to cease". This recalls Psalm 121.4, "He that keepeth Israel shall neither slumber nor sleep", and emphasises God's watchfulness over His people and His work. Peter quotes Psalm 34.15, "The **eyes of the Lord** are over the righteous, and his ears are open unto their prayers: but the face of the Lord is against them that do evil" (1 Pet. 3.12. The words, "the eye of their God was upon the elders of the Jews", obviously mean more than just watchfulness. The rest of the verse makes it quite clear that the builders enjoyed divine protection.

The phrase, "the eye of their God", also reminds us that He feels the hurt and damage done to His people: "he that toucheth you toucheth the **apple of his eye**" (Zech. 2.8); "Keep me as the **apple of the eye**" (Psalm 17.8). This refers, not to the best apple in the orchard, but to the pupil of the eye. The pupil is the most sensitive part of the human body. It is the "emblem of that which is tenderest and dearest, and therefore guarded with the most jealous care" (A.G.Clarke). This is why the Lord Jesus said to Saul of Tarsus, "Saul, Saul, why persecutest thou **me**?" (Acts 9.4). He is "touched with the feeling of our infirmities" (Heb. 4.15).

Failure to stop the work was followed by yet another letter. Compare 4.6-7. It worked before, so there was every possibility it would work again. "The copy of the letter that Tatnai, governor on this side the river, and Shethar-boznai, and his companions the Apharsachites, which were on this side the river, sent unto Darius the king". We have the text of the letter in vv.7-17. It quotes the Jewish leaders: "We are the servants of the God of heaven and earth, and build the house that was builded these many years ago, which a great king of Israel builded and set up" (v.11). This brings us to the third phrase:

3) THE SERVANTS OF GOD, vv.6-17
The letter tells us quite a lot about "the servants of the God of heaven and earth". All things considered, it's quite a complimentary letter, although this was probably quite unintentional. In fact, it wouldn't be altogether bad if it could be written about us! We should notice the following:

a) Their industry, v.8
"Be it known unto the king, that we went into the province of Judea, to the house of the great God, which is builded with great stones, and timber is laid in the walls, and this work goeth fast on, and prospereth in their hands". They were certainly "abounding in the work of the Lord!" Gaius is noteworthy for his prosperity of soul (3 John v.2). The letter here reports prosperity of work. The two are connected in Joshua 1.7-8.

b) Their authority, vv.9-11
When the elders were asked, "Who commanded you to build this house, and to make up these walls?", they answered, "We are the servants of **the God of heaven and earth**". While it was true that Cyrus had issued the original decree authorising their return, they did not serve an earthly potentate. Amos made this very clear to Amaziah, the priest of Bethel, "I was no prophet, neither was I a prophet's son; but I was an herdman, and a gatherer of sycomore fruit: and **the Lord took me** as I followed the flock, and **the Lord said unto me**, Go,

prophesy unto my people Israel" (Amos 7.14-15). Paul made this very clear to the ship's company in Acts 27.23, "For there stood by me this night the angel of God, **whose I am, and whom I serve**." The authority of the Lord is conveyed by His word, leading Paul to write, "If any man think himself to be a prophet, or spiritual, let him acknowledge that the things that I write unto you are **the commandments of the Lord**" (1 Cor. 14.37).

c) Their humility, v.11
"The **chief of them**" (v.10), described themselves as "**servants**" (v.11). We have already noticed 1 Corinthians 3.5 in this connection. While Paul describes himself as "the chief of sinners" (1 Tim. 1.15), it would not be amiss to say he was amongst "the chief of them" when it came to teaching and preaching. But he begins the Epistle to the Philippians with, "Paul and Timotheus, the **servants** of Jesus Christ" (1.1). See also 2 Corinthians 4.5. In his Second Epistle, Peter calls himself "a **servant**" and "an apostle" in that order!

d) Their testimony, vv.12-16
i) They admitted their wrongs in the past, v.12. "But after that our fathers had provoked the God of heaven unto wrath, he gave them into the hand of Nebuchadnezzar the king of Babylon, the Chaldean, who destroyed this house, and carried the people away into Babylon". They were ready to acknowledge their imperfection and failure. They did not reproach God for national defeat and captivity, and they did not reproach Nebuchadnezzar either. They were solely to blame. Daniel spoke for them all in praying, "O Lord, to us belongeth confusion of face, to our kings, to our princes, and to our fathers, because we have sinned against thee" (Dan. 9.1-8). It is to the credit of these leaders that there was nothing arrogant about them. We should never be reluctant to confess our sins and failures either. We must confess them to God, 1 John 1.9. In certain circumstances, we should confess them to each other, James 5.16. We should never make extravagant claims for ourselves before the world either.

It is encouraging to notice that although the Jews were very conscious of past failure, they also knew that God had not 'written them off'. We all have good cause to thank God for His patience, longsuffering and mercy.

ii) They asserted their rights in the present, vv.13-16. They carefully explained to their questioners that they had every right to be building the temple in Jerusalem. It had been officially sanctioned by Cyrus. Once again, there was nothing arrogant about these people. They claimed no credit for themselves.

Neither did they meekly apologise for 'all the inconvenience caused!' We too have no need to be ashamed in our service for God.

But were they telling the truth? Did Cyrus really issue a decree permitting the Jews to return and rebuild their temple? Zerubbabel and his colleagues knew it was true, and we know it was true. But could it be proved? Did a copy of the decree still exist? Could it be found? Everybody must have been holding their breath! Well, did "the eye of their God" continue to be upon them?

We shall find out in Chapter 6.

READ CHAPTER 6

The work completed

The work of reconstruction which **commenced** in Chapter 3, **ceased** in Chapter 4, and **continued** in Chapter 5, is **completed** in Chapter 6.

Chapter 3 describes the solid progress of the Jews, "and all the people shouted with a great shout, when they praised the Lord, because the foundation of the house of the Lord was laid" (3.11). Adversaries immediately appear in **Chapter 4.** Building for God always attracts enemy opposition. There were three attempts to stop the work. First of all, the enemy masqueraded as "**an angel of light**" (2 Cor. 11.14). That was unsuccessful, so he appeared in his true colours as the "**adversary**" (1 Pet. 5.8). That also proved unsuccessful, so he became "**the accuser of our brethren**" (Rev. 12.10). Here he succeeded, and the work ceased. In **Chapter 5**, following the preaching of Haggai and Zechariah, the work recommenced. Inactivity was countered by the word of God. The adversaries immediately reappeared, but "the eye of their God was upon the elders of the Jews, that they could not cause them to cease" (5.5). God's people obeyed His word through Haggai and Zechariah, and He honoured and protected them.

We left Chapter 5 with some apprehension. Tatnai and Shethar-boznai had written to Darius: "Now therefore, if it seem good to the king, let there be search made in the king's treasure house, which is there at Babylon, whether it be so, that a decree was made of Cyrus the king to build this house of God at Jerusalem, and let the king send his pleasure to us concerning this matter" (5.17). But **Chapter 6** dispels fear and anxiety! The "eye of God" was still "upon the elders of the Jews":

> Ye fearful saints, fresh courage take!
> The clouds ye so much dread
> Are big with mercy, and shall break
> In blessings on your head.

The chapter divides into two major sections: *(1)* confirmation from the king (vv.1-13); *(2)* completion of the work (vv.14-22).

1) CONFIRMATION FROM THE KING, vv.1-13

This section refers to the decree of Cyrus (v.3), and the decree of Darius (v.8). Both convey helpful lessons, all of which centre on the repeated expression "**house of God**" (vv.3,5,7,8,12), and the words, "And the God that hath caused his name to dwell there" (v.12). Darius refers to Him twice as "the God of heaven" (vv.9,10). We should notice *(a)* the original decrees of Cyrus (vv.1-5); *(b)* the confirmatory decree of Darius (vv.6-13).

a) The original decree of Cyrus, vv.1-5

The "house of the rolls" at Achmetha (Ecbatana, the capital of Great Media: JND margin) yielded the original documents authorising the Jews to return and rebuild the temple. The decree specified three things:

i) **The resumption of the sacrifices.** "Let the house be builded, the place where they offered sacrifices" (v.3) or, "Let the house be built for a place where they offer sacrifices" (JND).

ii) **The relaying of the foundations.** "Let the foundations thereof be strongly laid; the height thereof threescore cubits (90 feet), and the breadth thereof threescore cubits; with three rows of great stones, and a row of new timber: and let the expenses be given out of the king's house" (vv.3-5).

iii) **The restoration of the vessels.** "Let the golden and silver vessels of the house of God...be restored, and brought again unto the temple which is at Jerusalem, every one to his place ('in their place', JND), and place them in the house of God" (v.5).

So the **original documents** (in the providence of God, the decree had been "put in writing": see 1.1) confirmed that the Jews were acting correctly in rebuilding the temple. They were not acting on their own initiative: everything was properly authorised. This is very important. Unlike these Jews, we cannot claim earthly authority for our work and service, but we **can** claim the authority of the Scriptures. About one hundred and fifty years ago, through reading these **original documents**, there was a great recovery amongst God's people, particularly with regard to New Testament teaching concerning the coming of the Lord, and the local assembly. With the word of God as their sole guide, these Christians 'resumed sacrifices', 'relaid foundations', and 'restored vessels'. They followed the splendid example of the Jews in Nehemiah 8 who put something into practice that had lapsed for a thousand years (Neh. 8.17). They did it simply because "they found written" (Neh. 8.14). Many Christians today gladly do the same, not out of tradition, but out of love for God and His word. We must look at the three things above in New Testament terms:

i)   **The resumption of sacrifices**. The New Testament teaches us that **all** believers, "as lively stones, are built up a spiritual house, an holy priesthood, to offer up **spiritual sacrifices**, acceptable to God by Jesus Christ" (1 Pet. 2.5). The idea that the only people who can be called 'priests' are 'ordained clergymen', is totally foreign to the New Testament. The privilege of approaching God with worship and thanksgiving belongs to every believer in the Lord Jesus. We must remember too, that we are "a living sacrifice" (Rom. 12.1).

ii) **The relaying of the foundations**. A New Testament church does not rest on a man-made constitution, however well written, but on Christ Himself. Paul made this clear in 1 Corinthians 3.10-11: "According to the grace of God which is given unto me, as a wise masterbuilder, I have laid the **foundation**, and another buildeth thereon. But let every man take heed how he buildeth thereupon. For other **foundation** can no man lay than that is laid, which is **Jesus Christ**." Paul took at least eighteen months (Acts 18.11) to lay this foundation. He tells us about it in 1 Corinthians 15.1-4: "For I delivered unto you first of all that which I also received, how that Christ died for our sins according to the scriptures; and that he was buried, and that he rose again the third day according to the scriptures: and that he was seen..." The assembly at Corinth was founded on the doctrines of Christ. Each local assembly must rest on a proper doctrinal foundation. Christ **must** be pre-eminent.

iii) **The restoration of the vessels**. The temple vessels were used in the service of God. The New Testament makes no reference to "golden and silver vessels" in the "house of God" (1 Tim. 3.15), but it does refer to believers in this way: "If a man therefore purge himself from these, he shall be a **vessel** unto honour, sanctified, and meet for the master's use" (2 Tim. 2.21). To this end, "the manifestation of the Spirit is given to **every man** to profit withal" (1 Cor.12.7). See 1 Peter 4.10, "As **every man** hath received the gift, even so minister the same one to another, as good stewards of the **manifold** grace of God". Each brother and sister in the assembly should be encouraged to use their God-given gift, or gifts, for the glory of God, and for the good of His people. See Romans 12.6-8.

But there were enemies determined to impede and destroy the recovery in the book of Ezra, and there are enemies determined to do exactly the same in connection with the recovery of New Testament truth which took place in the Nineteenth Century. This brings us to the second decree:

b) The confirmatory decree of Darius, vv.6-13
The outstanding feature of the decree of Darius is that the original decree **must be recognised**. The proclamation of Cyrus **must be implemented**. There was no alteration or amendment **then**, and there is no alteration or amendment **now**. The decree was clear: "Let the work of this house of God alone" (v.7), but more than that, "That which they have need of...let it be given them day by day without fail" (v.9). We should notice:

i) Permission for the builders, vv.6-7.
"Let the governor of the Jews and the elders of the Jews build this house of God in his place". The adversaries are warned against interrupting and impeding the work of the "house of God".

ii) Provision for the builders, vv.8-10.
"I make a decree...that, of the king's goods, even of the tribute beyond the river, forthwith expenses be given unto these men, that they be not hindered". Notice that the function of the priests is emphasised in vv.9-10: "That they may offer sacrifices of sweet savours unto the God of heaven, and (significantly) pray for the life of the king, and of his sons". What are we supplying to enhance and enrich the priestly function of "the house of God?" It must be provided "day by day without fail".

iii) Protection for the builders, vv.11-13.
"Also I have made a decree that whosoever shall alter this word, let timber be pulled down from his house, and being set up, let him be hanged thereon". Compare Daniel 2.5; 3.29. A few years later, Haman was hung on his own gallows for attempting to destroy God's people. See Esther 7. The New Testament makes it equally clear that God does not stand idly by when His house, the local assembly, is damaged and polluted. See 1 Corinthians 3.17: "If any man defile the temple of God, him shall God destroy; for the temple of God is holy, which temple ye are".

2) COMPLETION OF THE WORK, vv.14-22
The work was completed "on the third day of the month Adar (March), which was in the **sixth year** of the reign of Darius the king". The work had been resumed in "the sixth month, in the **second year** of Darius the king" (Haggai 1.15), and during the four years, "the elders of the Jews builded, and they prospered through the prophesying of Haggai the prophet and Zechariah the son of Iddo" (v.14). They "prospered" by their **obedience to the word of God**. We have already

noticed the regularity with which God spoke to His people in the early days of reconstruction, and this evidently continued as work proceeded. See, for example, Zechariah 7.1, "And it came to pass in the *fourth* year of king Darius..."

It is also worth noticing that these prophets did not only give commands: they had a ministry of encouragement as well. See, for example, Haggai 2.4, "Yet now be strong, O Zerubbabel, saith the Lord; and be strong, O Joshua, the son of Josedech, the high priest; and be strong, all ye people of the land, saith the Lord, and work: for I am with you, saith the Lord of hosts"; Zechariah 4.9, "The hands of Zerubbabel have laid the foundation of this house; his hands shall also finish it".

Notice that "they builded, and finished it, according to the commandment *(i) of the God of Israel,* and according to the commandment *(ii) of Cyrus, and Darius, and Artaxerxes king of Persia"*. This was an acknowledgement that "the most High ruleth in the kingdom of men, and giveth it to whomsoever he will" (Dan. 4.32). Compare Romans 13.1, "The powers that be are ordained of God". Notice the closely-linked expressions, *"the children of Israel"* and *"the children of the captivity"* (v.16). See also vv.19-20. It's really a rather sad combination! But at least they "kept the dedication of this house of God *with joy"* (v.16). Ninety years before they said, "How shall we sing the Lord's song in a strange land?" (Psalm 137.4). This was the first of three things that were "*kept"*:

a) They "kept the dedication of this house of God with joy", vv.16-18
They re-established the house of God and its service. This emphasises the sacred character of the building. Compare 4.1, "Builded the temple *unto the Lord God of Israel"*. In the New Testament, the local assembly is called: *"the house of God,* which is *the church of the living God,* the pillar and ground of the truth" (1 Tim. 3.15). See 1 Corinthians 3.9, "Ye are *God's building"*. That's why Paul continues, "But let every man take heed *how* he buildeth" (v.10). This necessitates correct materials (v.12). There are at least three things to notice here:

i) Recognition of divine pleasure. See v.17. "And offered at the dedication of this house of God an hundred bullocks, two hundred rams, four hundred lambs". These were evidently burnt offerings, since sin offerings are specifically mentioned next. The burnt offering was the first of the 'sweet savour offerings', so God received the worship of His people. Compare the dedication of Solomon's temple: 22,000 oxen and 120,000 sheep (2 Chron. 7.5). A "day of small things" maybe (Zech. 4.10), **but there was something for God.**

ii) Recognition of divine unity. See v.17. "For a sin offering for all Israel, **twelve** he goats, according to the number of the tribes of Israel". This was an acknowledgement of national failure, from which this godly remnant did not disassociate themselves. They did not take a 'holier than thou' attitude. We must embrace **all** the people of God in heart and prayer. It may not be possible for us to walk where they walk, and do what they do, but we should at least recognise them as God's people.

iii) Recognition of divine order. See v.18. "As it is written in the book of Moses". They went back, beyond David who actually arranged the courses and divisions, to the ultimate authority, "the book of Moses". (Compare, again, Nehemiah 8.14). This involved "the **priests** in their divisions" (Num. 3.10), and "the **Levites** in their courses": see Numbers 3-4, which refer to the service of the sons of Kohath, Gershon, and Merari. The relevant New Testament passages are 1 Corinthians 14.40 and Romans 12.3-8. The word of God must regulate the corporate conduct of His people, and should not be replaced by human convenience and wisdom.

b) They "kept the passover", vv.19-21
They re-established the feast of remembrance. This took them back to their beginning as a nation, and reminded them that they were a redeemed people. "This month shall be unto you the beginning of months: it shall be the first month of the year to you" (Ex. 12.2). It all began with the blood of the lamb. The passover was kept by separated people and led by purified men.

i) Purification. "For the priests and the Levites were **purified** together, all of them were **pure**, and killed the passover for all the children of the captivity, and for their brethren the priests, and for themselves" (v.20) or "For the priests and the Levites had purified themselves as one man..." (JND). The New Testament reminds us that we must "draw near with a true heart in full assurance of faith, having our hearts sprinkled from an evil conscience, and our bodies washed with pure water" (Heb. 10.22). This alludes to the cleansing and consecration of the priests in Exodus ch.29. For the cleansing and consecration of the Levites, see Numbers ch.8.

ii) Separation. "And the children of Israel, which were come again out of captivity, and all such as had separated themselves unto them from the filthiness of the heathen of the land, to seek the Lord God of Israel, did eat" (v.21). This refers, either to the stranger (Numbers 9.14), or to Jews who had become immersed amongst the heathen. There was a moral fitness to eat the passover. There is a moral fitness required at the Lord's supper: "Let a man examine himself, and so let him eat" (1 Cor. 11.28). Compare Psalm 15. This leads to

c) They "kept the feast of unleavened bread seven days with joy", v.22 They re-established separation from evil. The feasts of passover and unleavened bread are never divided in Scripture. See Mark 14.12, "And the first day of unleavened bread, when they killed the passover, his disciples said unto him, Where wilt thou that we go and prepare that thou mayest eat the passover?"; Luke 22.1, "Now the feast of unleavened bread drew nigh, which is called the Passover". See also Luke 22.7. The lesson is very clearly stated in 1 Corinthians 5.7-8, "For even Christ our passover is sacrificed for us: **therefore** let us keep the feast (i.e. the feast of unleavened bread), not with old leaven, neither with the leaven of malice and wickedness; but with the unleavened bread of sincerity and truth".

Leaven is an appropriate symbol of sin. It is first mentioned by inference in Genesis 19 in connection with Sodom, where Lot "made them (the two angels) a feast, and did bake unleavened bread, and they did eat" (Gen. 19.3). The law of first mention is important in Scripture. Leaven has the property of converting sugar and allied substances, such as starch, into alcohol and carbon dioxide. In short, it changes the character of the substance involved. Its action in this way makes it an excellent picture of pervasive evil. (Matthew 13.33 is not an exception). Hence its presence is expressly forbidden in any sacrifice that speaks of **the Lord Jesus.** But notice its presence in the peace offering, and in the feast of weeks. This is because, in both cases, God's people are involved.

Amongst other things, we should note *(i)* That whilst the passover was kept in one place only, "the place which the Lord thy God shall choose", the feast of unleavened bread was kept in the tents of Israel for seven days (Deut. 16.7-8). The standard at the passover was to be maintained at home. *(ii)* That it was obligatory, "Ye **shall** observe the feast of unleavened bread....the feast of unleavened bread **shalt** thou keep" (Exodus 12.17,24; 34.18). Holiness is not an 'optional extra'. *(iii)* That it was comprehensive and embraced the individual and the home (Exodus 12.15,19), and the land as a whole (Deut. 16.4). *(iv)* That it reminded the children of Israel of their break with Egypt. See Deuteronomy 16.3, where it is called the "bread of affliction": the redeemed people had no time for leaven! In the New Testament, the disciples were warned by the Lord Jesus to beware of the leaven of the **Pharisees** (religious hypocrisy), of the **Sadducees** (wrong doctrine), and of **Herod** (moral evil).

So the section that began with **fear** (3.3), ends with **joy.** The returned exiles "kept the feast of **unleavened bread** seven days with **joy**: for the Lord had made them joyful" (v.22). Purity of life, and joy in life, are bosom friends. While "the people of the land **weakened the hands** of the people of Judah, and troubled them in building" 4.4), the Lord "turned the heart of the king of Assyria unto them, to **strengthen their hands** in the work of the house of God, the God of Israel" (v.22).

To quote Derek Kidner (*Ezra and Nehemiah*: Tyndale Old Testament Commentaries), "The word **Assyria** is a surprise here...Perhaps, however, it is meant to awaken memories of the traditional oppressor (cf. Nehemiah 9.32), whose empire first Babylon and then Persia had inherited, but whose policies were now dramatically reversed".

READ CHAPTER 7

Enter Ezra

According to the historians, there is a period of approximately fifty-seven years between Ezra 1-6 and Ezra 7-10. Chapter 6 ended in the reign of Darius (521-485 BC), and Chapter 7 commences in the reign of Artaxerxes (465-423 BC). The temple was completed in "the sixth year of the reign of Darius the king" (6.15), and Ezra started for Jerusalem in "the seventh year of Artaxerxes the king" (7.7). A little arithmetic will place these events in 515 BC and 458 BC respectively. Now you know where the fifty-seven intervening years come from! Ahasuerus (Xerxes) reigned for twenty of these fifty-seven years (485-465) so we can now date the book of Esther. It commences in "the third year of his reign" (Est. 1.3) and Esther became his new wife in "the seventh year of his reign" (2.16). So we are talking about 482 BC and 478 BC respectively. So Ezra left Babylon twenty years after Esther became queen of Persia. As Ezra 9 reveals, God's people in Jerusalem and Judea had declined during this period.

The first party of exiles returned under the leadership of Zerubbabel and Jeshua (Ezra 1-6), and their task was to **build** the temple. See 1.2. The second party of exiles returned under the leadership of Ezra (Ezra 7-10), and their task was to **beautify** the temple. See 7.27. C.E.Hocking (*Precious Seed March/April 1968*) entitles Chapters 1-6, 'Building the house', and Chapters 7-10, 'Building of character'.

This chapter can be divided into three sections: *(1)* Ezra's Task (vv.1-11); *(2)* Ezra's Testimonial (vv.12-26); *(3)* Ezra's Thanksgiving (vv.27-28).

1) EZRA'S TASK, vv.1-11

We now meet Ezra himself for the first time. His name means 'help', and that was his task: help for God's people. We learn that he was qualified to help them in two ways: *(a)* his **priestly descent** enabled him to help them (vv.1-5); *(b)* his **personal diligence** enabled him to help them (vv.6-11). We should all be keen to help God's people, and to help in God's work. There is something terribly wrong with a Christian who just doesn't want to help! Paul includes "*helps*" with the gifts detailed in 1 Corinthians 12.28. It really means 'to support', and involves "rendering assistance, perhaps especially of help ministered to the weak and needy" (W.E.Vine). It would be very nice indeed if we were all like Urbane, who is described as "our **helper** in Christ" (Rom.16.9). Some people hinder more than they help! But this does not apply to Ezra. We should notice that he is described as "Ezra the priest, the scribe" (vv.11,12,21). He was **firstly** a priest. The order is important. Devotion to God must precede all study and activity. So he was able to help God's people because of:

a) His priestly descent, vv.1-5

He traces his descent back to "Aaron the chief priest". This was most important in view of his responsibility. Not every candidate for the priesthood was able to do this. See 2.61-62: "These sought their register among those that were reckoned by genealogy, but they were not found: therefore were they, as polluted, put from the priesthood". They just couldn't produce their birth certificates! But whilst the Old Testament priesthood was selective, **every** believer in the Lord Jesus has been born into God's priestly family. We learn this from:

i) 1 Peter 2.

"Ye also, as lively stones, are built up a spiritual house, an holy **priesthood**" (v.5); "But ye are a chosen generation, a royal **priesthood**" (v.9). But to whom is Peter writing? Chapters 1 & 2 make it clear that he is not writing to a select few, but to **all believers.**

- **In Chapter 1**, Peter refers to: "The strangers scattered throughout Pontus, Galatia, Cappadocia, Asia, and Bithynia" (v.1); to those "elect according to the foreknowledge of God the Father" (v.2); to those "begotten...again unto a lively hope by the resurrection of Jesus Christ from the dead" (v.3).

- **In Chapter 2,** Peter refers to "newborn babes" (v.2); to those who have "tasted that the Lord is gracious" (v.3); to those "which believe" (v.7).

ii) Hebrews 10.

"Having therefore, brethren, boldness to enter into the holiest by the blood of Jesus, by a new and living way, which he hath consecrated for us, through the veil, that is to say, his flesh; and having an high priest over the house of God; let us draw near with a true heart in full assurance of faith, having our hearts sprinkled from an evil conscience, and our bodies washed with pure water" (vv.19-22). The words, "hearts sprinkled from an evil conscience, and our bodies washed with pure water", refer to the consecration of the priests in Exodus 29.4,21. The epistle is addressed to "holy brethren, partakers of the heavenly calling" (Heb. 3.1). It is therefore addressed to **all believers.**

The purpose of our priesthood is "to offer up **spiritual sacrifices**, acceptable to God by Jesus Christ" (1 Pet. 2.5); "By him therefore let us offer the **sacrifice of praise** to God continually, that is, the fruit of our lips giving thanks to his name" (Heb. 13.15).

But there is another way in which we exercise our priesthood. The best way in which we can help each other is to **pray for each other.** Let's watch a priest at work: "Epaphras, who is one of you, a servant of Christ, saluteth you, always labouring fervently for you in prayers, that ye may stand perfect and complete in all the will of God" (Col. 4.12). Epaphras was the man who first evangelised the district. He was now in prison (see Philemon 23), but he was still on very active service! Very energetic active service too. The words "labouring fervently" translate the Greek word *agonizomai,* and you don't have to be very clever to work out its meaning. Just think of our English word, 'agony'. It means 'to strive' or 'to wrestle'. There was nothing casual or 'laid back' about the prayers of Epaphras. He was in earnest. He was also most intelligent in his prayers for the assembly at Colosse. It wasn't just a case of 'Lord, bless the saints at Colosse'. He was quite specific: "that ye may stand perfect and complete in all the will of God". He knew all about the problems and pressures described by Paul in Colossians 2.8-23, and prayed for their spiritual preservation.

Ezra was able to help God's people because he was a priest. He was "Ezra the **priest".** But he was also "Ezra...the **scribe**".

b) His personal diligence, vv.6-11
Effective priesthood required a great deal more than a valid birth certificate. See Leviticus 10.9-11, "Do not drink wine nor strong drink, thou, nor thy sons with thee, when ye go into the tabernacle of the congregation, lest ye die: it shall be a statute for ever throughout your generations: and that ye may put difference between holy and unholy, and between unclean and clean; and that ye **may teach the children of Israel all the statutes which the Lord hath spoken unto them by the hand of Moses**". See Malachi 2.7, "For the priest's lips **should keep knowledge**, and they should seek the law at his mouth: for he is the messenger of the Lord of hosts". See 2 Chronicles 15.3, "Now for a long season Israel hath been without the true God, and without **a teaching priest**, and without law". So God's people were to be instructed by priestly men. We can only help God's people if we are in touch with **God himself**, and we can only help God's people if we are in touch with the **word of God.**

C.E.Hocking calls him "Ezra - Saint and Student", and continues: "As a student,

Ezra knew the word of God. He is called 'the scribe' (Neh. 8.1), not in the sense of being a state secretary, but a diligent student of the word of God". He was "a ready scribe in the law of Moses" (7.6); "a scribe of the words of the commandments of the Lord, and of his statutes to Israel" (7.11); "a scribe of the law of the God of heaven" (7.12, 21). The words "ready scribe" do not refer to "the dexterity of his pen, but to his wisdom and rich gift in handling God's word" (C.E.Hocking). Matthew makes it clear that scribes were more than writers: the Lord Jesus "**taught them** as one having authority, and not as **the scribes**" (Matt. 7.29). Scribes copied, studied, and communicated God's word.

We must now ascertain how Ezra became a competent Bible teacher. Three verses help us in this connection:

a) He was "a ready scribe", v.6
"This Ezra went up from Babylon; and he was a **ready** scribe in the law of Moses, which the Lord God of Israel had given". The word "ready" is rendered "diligent" in Proverbs 22.29: "Seest thou a man **diligent** in his business? he shall stand before kings; he shall not stand before mean men". According to Gesenius, it means "quick; hence *prompt, apt* in business". See also Psalm 45.1, "My tongue is the pen of a **ready** writer". Ezra therefore gave good workmanlike attention to his studies. He took it very seriously. He approached it eagerly. Compare 2 Timothy 2.15, "Study ('strive diligently', JND) to shew thyself approved unto God, a workman that needeth not to be ashamed, rightly dividing the word of truth". We shall see shortly that Ezra was quite painstaking in his studies.

It is stressed that he was "a ready scribe in the law of Moses, which **the Lord God of Israel had given**". Publishing was evidently in full swing even in Solomon's day: "Of making many books there is no end; and much study is a weariness of the flesh" (Eccl. 12.12). It was therefore most important that his son should remember that "the words of the wise are as goads, and as nails fastened by the masters of assemblies, which are given from one shepherd" (Eccl. 12.11). Education claims a very large part of our earlier years, but it is so important that we do not neglect the study of scripture. The habits of a lifetime are formed in youth.

b) He "prepared his heart", v.10
Ezra 7.6-9 are amplified in Ezra 8. The journey from Babylon to Jerusalem took four months (v.9). Ezra had specifically asked to make the journey (v.6), not out of idle curiosity, but because he had made it his aim to teach the word of God in Jerusalem: "For Ezra had prepared his heart to seek the law of the Lord, and to

do it, and to teach *in Israel* statutes and judgments". He was quite determined about it: "For Ezra had **directed his heart** to seek the law of Jehovah and to do it, and to teach in Israel the statutes and the ordinances" (JND). The force of this becomes clear when we understand the meaning of the word "heart". Its significance can be gauged from the first three references to it in the Bible. See Genesis 6.5 ("Every imagination of the **thoughts of his heart**"), Genesis 6.6 ("It **grieved him at his heart**"), and Genesis 8.21 ("And the Lord said in **his heart, I will not** again curse the ground any more for man's sake"). The heart therefore includes the intellectual (thinking is an intellectual process), emotional (grief is an emotion), and volitional (volition is a 'posh' word for the will) processes of our complex inner life. So when the Bible says that "Ezra prepared (directed) his heart", it means that his whole inner life was involved. How's that for commitment to study, apply, and teach the Bible?! It's rather more than 'prepared his head!'

Now let's notice where this commitment led him: "For Ezra had prepared his heart *(i)* to **seek** the law of the Lord, and *(ii)* to **do it**, and *(iii)* to **teach** in Israel statutes and judgments."

i) It led him to explore the word of God. "To **seek** the law of the Lord". Bible study is basically careful reading. We must

- Read the Scriptures **prayerfully**. See Psalm 119.18, "Open thou mine eyes, that I may behold wondrous things out of thy law". Notice what Ezra did when he opened "the book" in Nehemiah 8.5-6.

- Read the Scriptures **purposefully.** This involves planned reading, and for planned **reading** you need planned **time.** Read at length - but read in detail. Take time to think. "This book of the law shall not depart out of thy mouth; but thou shalt **meditate** therein day and night" (Joshua 1.8).

- Read the Scriptures **positively.** Determine to act on what you read. Remember that the scriptures should be allowed to inform our minds, warm our hearts, and direct our lives. See 2 Timothy 3.16-17.

- Read the Scriptures **primarily.** Don't let the commentaries take over! Make your own effort to understand the Bible!

ii) It led him to exemplify the word of God. "And to **do it**". Ezra did not "seek the law of the Lord" merely to increase knowledge and enhance his reputation as a preacher. He sought "the law of the Lord", firstly, to apply it to himself, then, and only then, to others. The Lord Jesus was a perfect example of his own teaching. See Acts 1.1, "The former treatise have I made, O Theophilus, of all that Jesus began both (firstly) to do and (secondly) teach". Every Bible teacher should be the same: "Whosoever therefore shall break one of these commandments, and shall teach men so, he shall be called the least in the kingdom of heaven: but whosoever shall (firstly) do and (secondly) teach them, the same shall be called great in the kingdom of heaven" (Matt. 5.19). Compare Matthew 23.2-3: "The scribes and the Pharisees...say, and **do not**". See also Acts 20.18-20, "Ye know, from the first day that I came into Asia, (firstly) after what manner I have been with you at all seasons...and (secondly) have taught you publickly, and from house to house". Compare 1 Thessalonians 2.10-11, "Ye are witnesses, and God also, how (firstly) holily and justly and unblameably we behaved ourselves among you that believe: as ye know how (secondly) we exhorted and comforted and charged every one of you, as a father doth his children". Read 1 Timothy 4.16, "Take heed (firstly) unto thyself, and (secondly) unto the doctrine; continue in them: for in doing this thou shalt both save thyself, and them that hear thee". James urges us to be "**doers** of the word, and not hearers only, deceiving your own selves" (James 1.22). Elders are to "feed the flock of God" and to be "**ensamples** to the flock" (1 Pet. 5.1-3). Our teaching may be right, but are **we** right? Talk must be exemplified in walk.

iii) It led him to expound the word of God. "And to teach in Israel (not Babylon!) statutes and judgments". Ezra was a man who desired to help God's people by teaching God's word. Let's remember that he acquired the moral right to teach other people by applying the Scriptures to himself. We see him at work in Nehemiah 8. This chapter is full of interest, but we shall have to confine ourselves, for the time being, to the statements in vv.7-8: "Also Jeshua, and Bani, and Sherebiah, Jamin, Akkub, Shabbethai, Hodijah, Maaseiah, Kelita, Azariah, Jozabad, Hanan, Pelaiah, and the Levites, caused the people to understand the law: and the people stood in their place. So they read in the book in the law of God **distinctly, and gave the sense, and caused them to understand the reading**".

While we acknowledge that the words "gave the sense" may mean, 'gave the interpretation' (that they were actually translating the Scriptures from Hebrew into Aramaic), these verses nevertheless set out the object of every Sunday School teacher, Bible Class leader, Gospel preacher, and Bible teacher. It is so important to teach the Scriptures clearly, so that people understand their meaning. We sometimes talk about 'deep ministry'. That can mean 'muddy ministry': it's so confused that no one can follow it! What's the use of that?! Aim for clarity and simplicity.

c) He studied in detail, v.11

The "ready scribe" (v.6) who had "prepared his heart" (v.10), studied in detail (v.11). "Now this is the copy of the letter that the king Artaxerxes gave unto Ezra the priest, the scribe, even a scribe of the **words** of the commandments of the Lord, and of his statutes to Israel". Not 'the word of the commandments of the Lord', but "the **words** of the commandments of the Lord". Ezra gave careful attention to the use and meaning of scriptural words. This is most important. We must remember that the inspiration of scripture extends to the very words in which it is expressed. If money is tight (it usually is!), and you haven't much left to spend on books, buy books that will help you understand the meaning of words. For example, *An Expository Dictionary of New Testament Word*', by W.E.Vine. Then there is *Strong's Exhaustive Concordance* coded to *Gesenius' Hebrew-Chaldee Lexicon to the Old Testament* and *Thayer's Greek-English Lexicon of the New Testament*. That will do for a start. The titles look rather daunting, but you'll soon get used to using them.

Paul gives us an example of the importance of words in Galatians 3.16, "Now to Abraham and his seed were the promises made. He saith not, And to **seeds**, as of many; but as of one, And to thy **seed**, which is Christ". The use of the singular, as opposed to the plural, is vital here. How about Ecclesiastes 12.1, "Remember now thy Creator in the days of thy youth". The word "Creator" is in the plural, so that we could read, 'Remember now thy **Creators** in the days of thy youth'.

2) EZRA'S TESTIMONIAL, vv.12-26

Yet another letter! But not quite like those in Chapters 4 & 5. "Now this is the copy of the letter that the king Artaxerxes gave unto Ezra the priest, the scribe" (v.11). Ezra certainly had "a good report of them which are without!" (1 Tim. 3.7). The letter mentions:

a) The uniqueness of God's people

Artaxerxes uses the expressions "God of heaven" (vv.12,21,23); "thy God" (vv.14,19,20,25-26); "the God of Israel" (v.15); "their God" (v.16); "your God" (vv.17-18); "the God of Jerusalem" (v.19). He never says 'my God' or 'our God'. The king evidently recognised that Ezra and the people had something that he did not have. We should be recognised in the same way.

b) The importance of God's word

It is striking to notice how Artaxerxes recognised the authority of God's word in the affairs of His people. Notice the following: "Ezra the priest, a scribe of **the law** of the God of heaven" (v.12); "According to **the law** of thy God which is in thine hand" (v.14); "Ezra the priest, the scribe of **the law** of the God of heaven" (v.21): "All such as know **the laws** of thy God" (v.25); "And whosoever will not do **the law of** thy God" (v.26). Are we known as people who are subject to God's word? Sadly, even the world knows that religious leaders conduct their debates and make their decisions without even a passing reference to the word of God. We should be known as people who say, "Thus saith the Lord".

b) The willingness of God's people

The letter emphasises the "freewill" of God's people. "I make a decree, that all they of the people of Israel, and of his priests and Levites, in my realm, which are minded of their own **freewill** to go up to Jerusalem, go with thee" (v.13);. "And all the silver and gold that thou canst find in all the province of Babylon, with the **freewill** offering of the people, and of the priests, offering **willingly** for the house of their God which is in Jerusalem" (v.16). Compare Ezra 1.4. We should be known as people who worship and serve God, not grudgingly, but gladly and readily.

d) The trustworthiness of God's servant

Artaxerxes was confident that Ezra was trustworthy enough to carry, not only the freewill offerings of the Jews, but the silver and gold donated by the king and his seven counsellors (vv.14-15). He was also authorised to carry "all the silver and gold that thou canst find in all the province of Babylon" (v.16), and given access to "the king's treasure house" if necessary (v.20).

Artaxerxes was confident that Ezra was trustworthy enough, and competent enough, to "set magistrates and judges, which may judge all the people that are beyond the river, all such as know the laws of thy God; and teach ye them that know them not" (vv.25-26). We should be recognised as people who are reliable and trustworthy.

3) EZRA'S THANKSGIVING, vv.27-28

Ezra took no credit for the favourable response to his application. He could have mentioned the fact that he had asked the king for permission to visit Jerusalem. But not a word about himself! "Blessed be the Lord God of our fathers, which hath put such a thing as this in the king's heart, to beautify the house of the Lord which is in Jerusalem: and hath extended mercy unto me before the king, and his counsellors, and before all the king's mighty princes. And I was strengthened as the hand of the Lord my God was upon me, and I gathered together out of all Israel chief men to go up with me".

Ezra recognised the hand of God in everything: see also vv.6,9. He might well have said with the Psalmist, "Not unto us, O Lord, not unto us, but unto thy name give glory, for thy mercy, and for thy truth's sake" (Psalm 115.1). Compare Acts 14.27, "they rehearsed all that **God** had done with them..."; Acts 15.12, where Barnabas and Paul declared "what miracles and wonders **God** had wrought among the Gentiles by them".

READ CHAPTER 8

The journey to Jerusalem

Ezra Chapter 8 expands the summary in the previous chapter: "This Ezra went up from Babylon...And there went up some of the children of Israel, and of the priests, and the Levites, and the singers, and the porters, and the Nethinims, unto Jerusalem, in the seventh year of Artaxerxes the king. And he came to Jerusalem in the fifth month, which was in the seventh year of the king. For upon the first day of the first month began he to go up from Babylon, and on the first day of the fifth month came he to Jerusalem, according to the good hand of his God upon him" (7.6-9). According to C.E.Hocking, "The most probable route involved a journey of approximately nine hundred miles". As we know, this was the second expedition to Jerusalem. Its purpose is stated at the end of the chapter: "They furthered the people, and the house of God" (v.36). You couldn't do that by remaining in Babylon, and you can't do that today by remaining in "MYSTERY, BABYLON THE GREAT" (the ultimate form of the Ecumenical Movement, with its 'Councils of Christian Churches'). See Revelation 17.5.

There are five paragraphs in the chapter: *(1)* the recorded names (vv.1-14); *(2)* the recognised need (vv.15-20); *(3)* the reliance upon God (vv.21-23); *(4)* the responsibility entrusted (vv.24-30); *(5)* the responsibility discharged (vv.31-36).

1) *THE RECORDED NAMES, vv.1-14*

So we have a second list of people who turned their backs on Babylon, and set their faces towards "the place which the Lord shall choose to place his name there" (Deut. 16.2). C.E.Hocking points out that "only the heads of the houses are mentioned by name, and the positions of honour at the head of the list are given to the priestly and royal houses". These people were "minded of their **own freewill** to go up to Jerusalem" (7.13). A quick burst on your pocket calculator will give you a total of 1,514 men. If we add the women and children, the total party must have been around 7000/8000. Compare this with the 50,000 in Chapter 2. It was a remnant, rather than a majority! When it was a case of **redemption**, the whole nation left Egypt. But when it was a case of **separation**, only a remnant left Babylon. How concerned are **we** about the "the place which the Lord shall choose to place his name there?" It is interesting to compare the names on this list with those in Chapter 2. In most cases, Ezra's colleagues were the descendants of the original pioneers. It therefore appears that the first expedition to Jerusalem under Zerubbabel left some families divided down the middle! For further reading on this point see Derek Kidner in *Ezra and Nehemiah* (Tyndale Old Testament Commentaries). Notice that this chapter is autobiographical: "this is the genealogy of them that went up with **me**".

The numbering of the people here is another reminder that God is completely aware of the convictions and movements of His people. We discussed this in connection with Chapter 2. Read the notes again! Numbers chs. 3-4 make it very clear that God knows whether or not we are taking responsibility commensurate with our age. The Levites were numbered twice. We are given the total of Levites over one month old in Numbers 3.14-39 (22,000, although you may have a surprise when you add up the figures), and over thirty years old in Numbers 4.34-49 (8,580: no surprises here). So God knew exactly how many Levites should be serving Him. It's also worth remembering that God knows every day of our faithful service for Him, and every day of our suffering too: that's why we are given a period of 1,260 days in Revelation 11.3 and 12.6. The same period is expressed in months in Rev. 11.2 ("forty and two months"), and by the formula "a time, and times, and half a time" in Rev. 12.14.

This list of names ought to encourage us. Once again, we have a register of people unknown to us, but all known to God. It recalls Malachi 3.16, "Then they that feared the Lord spake often one to another: and the Lord hearkened, and heard it, and a book of remembrance was written before him for them that feared the Lord, and that thought upon his name". But we mustn't forget that there is one more list of names in Ezra. It is sobering to remember that God also knows the names of people who are unfaithful to Him by disobeying His word. See 10.18-44.

2) THE RECOGNISED NEED, vv.15-20
"And I gathered them together to the river that runneth by Ahava; and there abode we in tents three days: and I viewed the people and the priests, and found there none of the sons of Levi" (v.15). We should notice the following:

a) The abode, v.15
It was by "the river that runneth to Ahava". The language "suggests a canal, since it is named after its destination (literally, 'the river that comes to Ahava'). There were many canals in Babylon. The location of Ahava is unknown" (D.Kidner).

Perhaps it was one of "the rivers of Babylon" by which the exiles sat and wept over a century before.

"There abode we in **tents**". They left cities to dwell in tents. In other words, they adopted the status of pilgrims. They were going home! They followed the footsteps of Abraham centuries before. He too left a city and dwelt in a tent. But he too was *en route* for a city. "By faith he sojourned in the land of promise, as in a strange country, dwelling in tabernacles (tents) with Isaac and Jacob, the heirs with him of the same promise: for he looked for a city ('the city', JND) which hath foundations, whose builder and maker is God" (Heb.11.9-10). Let's remember that we don't belong here. We certainly don't belong to religious Babylon. We are "strangers and pilgrims" in this world (1 Pet. 2.11).

b) The assessment, v.15

"And there abode we in tents **three days**: and I viewed the people, and the priests, and found there none of the sons of Levi". Those three days were valuable. Ezra was not prepared to commence the four month trek to Jerusalem without taking stock. The Hebrew word translated "viewed" *(bin)* means to understand or consider. It is translated "understanding" in v.16. (The word "understanding" in v.18 is different). In the New Testament, the work of 'viewing the people' is undertaken by assembly elders. They are called "overseers" (Acts 20.28: the word is usually rendered "bishops", but "overseers" is infinitely better!). It is their responsibility to observe and assess, out of concern for God's interests and glory.

Ezra's survey disclosed a deficiency. There were "none of the sons of Levi". Well, men who serve are generally in short supply. In fact, demand usually exceeds supply! We are not told why no Levites had volunteered to join the expedition. They were evidently not "minded of their own freewill to go up to Jerusalem" (7.13) We are not given reasons for their absence, but D.Kidner is probably right on target here: "It was only natural for these men to shrink from a prospect which was doubly daunting: not only the uprooting which all the pilgrims faced, but the drastic change from ordinary pursuits to the strict routines of the Temple". That sounds right! Service for God demands dedication in terms of time and energy, and Babylon was a very attractive place.

Barnabas evidently made a similar assessment in Acts 11. His ministry, following the meaning of his name, was exhortation. But the new assembly at Antioch needed teaching. Barnabas recognised the need and took appropriate steps: "Then departed Barnabas to Tarsus, for to seek Saul: and when he had found him, he brought him to Antioch. And it came to pass, that a whole year they assembled themselves with the church, and taught much people" (Acts 11.25-26).

c) The associates, v.16

"Then sent I for Eliezer, for Ariel, for Shemaiah, and for Elnathan, and for Jarib, and for Elnathan, and for Nathan, and for Zechariah, and for Meshullam, chief men; also for Joiarib, and for Elnathan, men of understanding". Ezra shared his burden with others, and enlisted their help. Notice the expression, "men of *understanding*". The Hebrew word is used in Psalm 119.130, "The entrance of thy words giveth light; it giveth *understanding* unto the simple". See also Proverbs 1.5, "A man of *understanding* shall attain unto wise counsels", and Proverbs 28.5, "They that seek the Lord *understand* all things". Compare 1 Kings 3.11, "Thou (Solomon)...hast asked for thyself *understanding* to discern judgment". Ezra shared his concern with men who understood the situation.

d) The action, v.17

"And I sent them with commandment unto Iddo the chief at the place Casiphia, and I told them what they should say unto Iddo, and to his brethren the Nethinims, at the place Casiphia, that they should bring unto us ministers for the house of our God". Notice the dignity of the Levitical service: "*ministers for the house of our God*". Ezra would not move from the "river that runneth to Ahava" until Levites were in attendance. He was not prepared to adopt unauthorised measures. The word of God must be obeyed.

e) The answer, vv.18-20

"And by the good hand of our God upon us they brought us a man of understanding, of the sons of Mahli, the son of Levi, the son of Israel; and Sherebiah, with his sons and his brethren, eighteen". Notice reference to the Nethinims. See our comments in connection with 2.43-54. The need was met, not so much by the diligent quest of Eliezer and his companions, but "by the *good hand of our God upon us*". See also 7.6,9,28, 8.22,31. God will respond to those who honour His word.

3) THE RELIANCE UPON GOD, vv.21-23

"Then I proclaimed a fast there, at the river of Ahava, that we might afflict ourselves before our God, to seek of him a right way for us, and for our little ones, and for all our substance". The journey was not undertaken lightly, just as no service for God should ever be undertaken casually. We often speak of 'our work for the Lord': perhaps we should think in terms of 'the Lord's work'. There is a great deal of difference between the two! We should notice the following:

a) Sacrificing our own interests

"I proclaimed a fast". Compare Acts 13.2. Fasting was saying 'no' to self. It was not a question of denying sinful practices. That was expected. But it did mean surrendering everything that might interrupt devotion to God. We must carefully control hobbies, sports, homes, gardens, and anything else that could get too big in our lives. So many of us are taken over by our own interests.

b) Self-judgment

"That we might **afflict** ourselves before our God". The Hebrew word means 'to lower', and is often rendered 'humble'. See, for example, "I **humbled** my soul with fasting" (Psalm 35.13); "And thou shalt remember all the way which the Lord thy God led thee these forty years in the wilderness, to **humble** thee, and to prove thee, to know what was in thine heart" (Deut. 8.2). Compare Isaiah 31.4, "He will not be afraid of their voice, nor **abase himself** for the noise of them". Peter writes on the subject as follows: "Likewise, ye younger, submit yourselves unto the elder. Yea, all of you be subject one to another, and be clothed with humility: for God resisteth the proud, and giveth grace to the humble. Humble yourselves therefore under the mighty hand of God, that he may exalt you in due time" (1 Pet. 5.5-6). God's way up, is down!

Self-judgment touches our motives. See 1 Corinthians 13.3: "And though I bestow all my goods to feed the poor, and though I give my body to be burned, and have not charity, it profiteth **me** nothing". If the motive is wrong, others may profit from my actions, but not **me.** The profit, or lack of it, will be revealed at the judgment seat of Christ.

c) Seeking a right way

The "right way" involved non-reliance on the world: "For I was ashamed to require of the king a band of soldiers and horsemen to help us against the enemy in the way: because we had spoken unto the king, saying, The hand of our God is upon all them for good that seek him; but his power and his wrath is against all them that forsake him". There was no discrepancy between profession and practice. It was one thing to say blithely to the king **before the journey,** when there was no immediate danger, that no escort was required because the "hand of our God is upon all them for good that seek him", but quite another to put it into practice when the journey was **actually beginning!** Ezra was consistent. He displayed the same faith when the test came. We mustn't think that he faced an imaginary enemy either. He refers to "the enemy in the way".

"So we fasted and besought our God for this: and he was **entreated of us**". We should always remember that we serve the only true God, and that He delights in faith, and answers prayer.

4) THE RESPONSIBILITY ENTRUSTED, vv.24-30

"Then I separated twelve of the chief of the priests, Sherebiah, Hashabiah, and ten of their brethren with them, and weighed unto them the silver, and the gold, and the vessels, even the offering of the house of our God, which the king, and his counsellors, and his lords, and all Israel there present, had offered". Like the preceding paragraphs, these verses are full of valuable lessons.

a) The sanctity of the charge

"And I said unto them, Ye are **holy** unto the Lord; the vessels are **holy** also; and the silver and the gold are a freewill offering unto the Lord God of your fathers" (v.28). So holy people handled holy things. See Isaiah 52.11, "Depart ye, depart ye, go ye out from thence, touch no unclean thing; go ye out of the midst of her; **be ye clean, that bear the vessels of the Lord**". While we do not carry vessels of silver and gold, we certainly carry holy vessels. Jude describes them as "the faith which was once delivered unto the saints" (Jude v.3). At Jericho, white-robed priests carried the ark of the covenant, but we carry spiritual realities. This emphasises:

b) The solemnity of the charge

"Watch ye, and keep them, until ye weigh them before the chief of the priests and the Levites, and chief of the fathers of Israel, at Jerusalem, in the chambers of the house of the Lord" (v.29). God has committed to us things for use in His house, and it is significant that teaching in connection with the house of God is committed to Timothy as a solemn charge. The charge lies between 1 Timothy 1.18, "This charge I commit unto thee, son Timothy", and 1 Timothy 6.20, "O Timothy, keep that which is committed to thy trust". The charge passes from one generation to another: see 2 Timothy 2.2, "The things that thou hast heard of *(i)* me among many witnesses, the **same** (so don't alter it) commit *(ii)* thou to *(iii)* faithful men, who shall be able to teach *(iv)* others also". See also 1 Corinthians 4.1, "Let a man so account of us, as of the ministers of Christ, and stewards of the mysteries of God"; 1 Thessalonians 2.4, "But as we were allowed of God to be put in trust with the gospel, even so we speak; not as pleasing men, but God, which trieth our hearts". In both cases, Paul refers particularly to the unique ministry of the apostles. Divine truth was **directly** revealed to them.

c) The integrity of the charge

Ezra "weighed unto them the silver, and the gold, and the vessels" (v.25). He "weighed unto their hand six hundred and fifty talents of silver, and silver vessels an hundred talents, and of gold an hundred talents; also twenty basins of gold, of a thousand drams; and two vessels of fine copper, precious as gold" (v.26-27). But everything was properly witnessed: "So took the priests and the Levites the weight of the silver, and the gold, and the vessels, to bring them to Jerusalem unto the house of our God" (v.30). This illustrates New Testament teaching: "Provide things honest in the sight of all men" (Rom. 12.17). We must be open and above board in spiritual matters: "The things that thou hast heard of me among **many witnesses**, the same commit thou to faithful men" (2 Tim. 2.2). We must be open and above board in financial matters. See 2 Corinthians 8.18-23. Note v.21, "Providing for honest things, not only in the sight of the Lord, but also in the sight of men". Proper supervision of assembly funds does not mean lack of confidence in the treasurer: it ensures that no charge of misappropriation **can** be brought, and therefore enhances the integrity of the treasurer. In this connection, it is worth noticing that whilst Ezra counted and weighed the vessels in Babylonia, **others** counted and weighed them in Jerusalem. See vv.33-34. Everything was verified by independent witnesses. We must, of course, be open and above board in every aspect of life, and this will reflect in assembly matters. It is a good policy for assembly offerings to be properly verified, and for assembly accounts to be properly audited. This brings us to:

5) THE RESPONSIBILITY DISCHARGED, vv.31-36
"Then we departed from the river of Ahava on the twelfth day of the first month, to go unto Jerusalem: and the hand of our God was upon us, and he delivered us from the hand of the enemy, and of such as lay in wait by the way. And we came to Jerusalem, and abode there three days". The gold, silver and vessels, were weighed in the temple on the fourth day, and nothing was missing: "All the weight was written at that time" (v.34). The enemy got nothing! But be assured that he continues to do all in his power to rob us of spiritual treasure! Paul lost nothing either: "I have fought a good fight, I have finished my course, I have **kept** (Greek *tereo*) **the faith**" (2 Tim. 4.7). He had the moral right to say, "That good thing which was committed unto thee **keep** (Greek *phulasso*) by the Holy Ghost which dwelleth in us" (2 Tim. 1.14).

It is sobering to remember that we too will have to give an account of our stewardship. Have we jettisoned any part of God's word? Will it be said that we committed the unabridged and unamended word of God to the following generation? The Lord Jesus taught His disciples the importance of faithful stewardship in the parable of the talents (Matthew 25.14-30) and the parable of the pounds (Luke 19.11-27). In Matthew, it is diversity of gift: in Luke 19, it is equality of opportunity.

But the chapter does not end here. The people involved in the expedition could have said with great personal satisfaction, 'We've arrived'. But they did three things:

a) They offered sacrifices, v.35
"Also the children of those that had been carried away, which were come out of the captivity, offered burnt offerings unto the God of Israel, twelve bullocks for *all Israel,* ninety and six rams, seventy and seven lambs, twelve he goats for a sin offering: all this was a burnt offering unto the Lord". They expressed their connection and concern for all the people of God. They understood that God was mindful of all His people. There was no sense of smug self-satisfaction. It is interesting to notice that here the sin offerings are called "a burnt offering unto the Lord".

b) They delivered the edicts, v.36
"And they delivered the king's commissions unto the king's lieutenants, and to the governors on this side the river". Ezra and his companions had evidently been entrusted with State business, and discharged this faithfully.

c) They helped God's people, v.36
"And they furthered the people, and the house of God". "Furthered" is the same word as "help" in 1.4. Remember, the name "Ezra" means 'help' too! We could say that "they furthered the people" - that is, individually, and they "furthered... the house of God" - that is, corporately.

READ CHAPTER 9

"We have forsaken thy commandments"

Ezra Chapters 1-8 record the faithfulness of God to His people: "the hand of the Lord" (7.28) had certainly been upon them, whether in connection with the first expedition to Jerusalem under Zerubbabel (Chapters 1-6), or the second expedition under Ezra himself (Chapters 7-8). Ezra puts it like this: "And now for a little space grace hath been shewed from the Lord our God, to leave us a remnant to escape...For we were bondmen; yet our God hath not forsaken us in our bondage, but hath extended mercy unto us in the sight of the kings of Persia, to give us a reviving, to set up the house of our God, and to repair the desolations thereof, and to give us a wall in Judah and in Jerusalem" (9.8-9). The temple had been built under Zerubbabel, and beautified under Ezra (7.27).

But all was not well. Having completed the business in hand, Ezra discovered that national life had been seriously undermined by intermarriage with the surrounding nations. Eight chapters of progress and achievement, though not without interruption, now give place to two chapters describing national decline. This is not the first time in the Old Testament that great national achievements had been followed by serious backsliding. It happened in the reign of Solomon, and it happened in the life of Gideon. It was not to be the last time either: it happened again after the rebuilding of the wall in the days of Nehemiah. These are solemn warnings: "Wherefore let him that thinketh he standeth take heed lest he fall" (1 Cor. 10.12). Chapters 9-10 describe the circumstances, and the steps taken by Ezra to recover the situation. Chapter 9 can be entitled *'Separation Lost'* and Chapter 10 can be entitled *'Separation Restored'.* Chapter 9 may divided into two main paragraphs: *(1) the compromise of the people* (vv.1-2); *(2) the confession of Ezra* (vv.3-15).

1) THE COMPROMISE OF THE PEOPLE, vv.1-2

"Now when these things were done, the princes came to me, saying, The people of Israel, and the priests, and the Levites, have not separated themselves from the people of the lands, doing according to their abominations...For they have taken of their daughters for themselves, and for their sons: so that the holy seed have mingled themselves with the people of those lands: yea, the hand of the princes and rulers hath been chief in this trespass". Notice the bad example of the leaders: "The hand of the princes and rulers hath been **chief** in this trespass" (v.2). They were particularly culpable, for "unto whomsoever much is given, of him shall be much required" (Luke 12.48).

Compare the report to Paul in 1 Corinthians 1.11, "For it hath been declared unto me of you, my brethren, by them which are of the house of Chloe, that there are contentions among you". This was not tittle-tattle. In both cases, the situation was brought to the attention of a man with the competence and authority to deal with the matter.

Derek Kidner points out that it was not the newcomers who brought the report to Ezra, but the established leaders. Ezra was evidently unaware of these mixed marriages. So within five months (compare 7.9, "the first day of the first month", with 10.9, "the ninth month, on the twentieth day of the month"), Ezra's ministry produced results. His preaching caused grave concern. We must remember that he had "prepared his heart to seek the law of the Lord, and to do it, and to **teach in Israel statutes and judgments**" (7.10). As D.Kidner observes, "Ezra's campaign to spread the knowledge of Scripture was bearing the characteristic fruit of reform". How deeply does the word of God affect **us**?

We should carefully notice the following: *(a)* that compromise destroys distinctiveness; *(b)* compromise means danger; *(c)* compromise is disobedience

a) Compromise destroys distinctiveness
It is summed up in the words: *(i)* "The people of Israel, and the priests, and the Levites, have not separated themselves from the people of the lands" (v.1), and *(ii)* "The holy seed have mingled themselves with the people of those lands" (v.2). The expression "holy seed" (see Isaiah 6.13), emphasises that God's people had been set apart for Him. See Deuteronomy 7.6, "For thou art an **holy people unto the Lord thy God:** the Lord thy God hath chosen thee to be a special people unto himself, above all people that are upon the face of the earth". We must remember that holiness is not cold and clinical. It is permeated with love for God. In fact, love is an essential part of holiness. See 1 Thessalonians 3.12-13: "The Lord make you to increase and abound in love one toward another, and toward all men, even as we do toward you: to the end he may stablish your hearts unblameable in holiness before God, even our Father, at the coming of our Lord Jesus Christ with all his saints". The Lord Jesus taught this: "Thou shalt love the Lord thy God with all thy heart, and with all thy soul, and with all

thy mind. This is the first and great commandment. And the second is like unto it, Thou shalt love thy neighbour as thyself" (Matt. 22.37-39).

We too are a "holy seed". See 1 Peter 2.9, "But ye are a chosen generation, a royal priesthood, **an holy nation,** a peculiar people; that ye should shew forth the praises of him who hath called you out of darkness into his marvellous light"; Hebrews 3.1, "Wherefore, **holy brethren,** partakers of the heavenly calling". Hence the exhortation of 1 Peter 1.15-16: "But as he which hath called you is holy, so be **ye holy** in all manner of conversation; because it is written, **Be ye holy; for I am holy**".

b) Compromise means danger
Whilst holiness is far more than abstention from evil, it does mean separation from everything that displeases Him, and this chapter highlights one of the greatest pitfalls we can encounter in this direction. Human emotions are very strong, and if we are not careful, they can override devotion to God. So many children of God have been spiritually ruined through marriage to unsaved, or unspiritual, partners. We must be good stewards of our affections. God warned His people against this in the Old Testament: "When the Lord thy God shall bring thee into the land whither thou goest to possess it, and hath cast out many nations before thee...and when the Lord thy God shall deliver them before thee; thou shalt smite them, and utterly destroy them; thou shalt make no covenant with them, nor shew mercy unto them: neither shalt thou make marriages with them; thy daughter thou shalt not give unto his son, nor his daughter shalt thou take unto thy son. **For they will turn away thy son from following me, that they may serve other gods**" (Deut. 7.1-4). This is exactly what had happened: the Jews had "not separated themselves from the people of the lands, doing according to their abominations...**for** they have taken of their daughters for themselves, and for their sons". Intermarriage was the first step to gross evil.

c) Compromise is disobedience
Ezra recalled this in vv.10-12: "And now, O our God, what shall we say after this? for we have forsaken thy commandments, which thou hast commanded by thy servants the prophets, saying, The land, unto which ye go to possess it, is an unclean land...Now therefore give not your daughters unto their sons, neither take their daughters unto your sons, nor seek their peace or their wealth for ever: that ye may be strong, and eat the good of the land, and leave it for an inheritance to your children for ever". Notice that separation ensured **(i) strength**: "that ye may be strong"; **(ii) satisfaction**: "and eat the good of the land" (compare Isaiah 1.19); **(iii) succession**: "and leave it for an inheritance

to your children for ever". Ezra also recalled that God's people were repeating past mistakes, which made the situation even more serious: "And after all that is come upon us for our evil deeds, and for our great trespass, seeing that thou our God hast punished us less than our iniquities deserve, and hast given us such deliverance as this; should we **again** break thy commandments, and join in affinity with the people of these abominations?" (vv.13-14).

The New Testament is equally forthright. "Ye adulterers and adulteresses, know ye not that the friendship of the world is enmity with God? whosoever therefore will be a friend of the world is the enemy of God" (James 4.4); "Love not the world, neither the things that are in the world. If any man love the world, the love of the Father is not in him" (1 John 2.15-17); "For what fellowship hath righteousness with unrighteousness? and what communion hath light with darkness? and what concord hath Christ with Belial? or what part hath he that believeth with an infidel? and what agreement hath the temple of God with idols?" (2 Cor. 6.14-18).

2) THE CONFESSION OF EZRA, vv.3-15
We should notice the following: *(a)* his sorrow for sin (vv.3-4); *(b)* his shame before God (vv.5-6); *(c)* his sharing of guilt (v.6); *(d)* his statement of facts (vv.7-15).

a) His sorrow for sin, vv.3-4
"When I heard this thing, I rent my garment and my mantle, and plucked off the hair of my head and of my beard, and sat down astonied" (v.3). The word "astonied" means 'desolated', and carries the idea of silence. See also v.5, "And at the evening sacrifice I arose up from my heaviness; and having rent my garment and my mantle, I fell upon my knees, and spread out my hands unto the Lord my God". Ezra's sorrow continues in Chapter 10: "Now when Ezra had prayed, and when he had confessed, weeping and casting himself down before the house of God" (10.1); "He did eat no bread, nor drink water: for he mourned because of the transgression of them that had been carried away" (10.6).

Instead of immediately convening a general assembly, and remonstrating with the people, Ezra was overwhelmed with deep sorrow. Like Ezra, we must never underestimate the solemnity of sin. Sin in our own lives, and sin in the lives of others, should cause us sorrow. Compare Joshua at Ai: "And Joshua rent his clothes, and fell to the earth upon his face before the ark of the Lord" (Joshua 7.6); Nehemiah at Shushan: "I sat down and wept, and mourned certain days, and fasted, and prayed before the God of heaven" (Neh. 1.4); Paul at Miletus: "Serving the Lord with all humility of mind, and with many tears" (Acts 20.19).

Ezra was not alone in his concern: "Then were assembled unto me every one that **trembled at the words of the God of Israel**, because of the transgression of those that had been carried away" (v.4). This describes the effect of Ezra's preaching. There were at least some who took his ministry seriously, and were deeply affected by the word of God. We cannot expect to enjoy God's blessing unless we do take His word seriously: see Isaiah 66.2, "To this man will I look, even to him that is poor and of a contrite spirit, and **trembleth at my word**".

b) His shame before God, vv.5-6

"I am ashamed and blush to lift up my face to thee, my God" (v.6). He exhibited a totally different reaction to an earlier generation of Israelites: see Jeremiah 6.15, "Were they ashamed when they had committed abomination? nay, they were not at all ashamed, neither could they **blush**". As D.Kidner observes, Ezra was "more deeply ashamed of the national guilt than any of them, and thus more fit to be their spokesman in confession". We must not miss the significance of "the evening sacrifice" (see Exodus 29.39). This was a lamb, and it was offered as a burnt-offering. The day began and ended in this way. Israel paid attention to the "continual burnt-offering", which expressed their devotion to God, but it had become a hollow ceremony. Their lives did not match their profession. We too must beware.

c) His sharing of guilt, v.6

Notice the expressions, "For **our** iniquities (v.6)...**our** trespass (v.6)...have **we** been in a great trespass (v.7)...**we** have forsaken thy commandments (v.10)... after all that is come upon **us** for **our** evil deeds, and for **our** great trespass (v.13)...**we** are before thee in **our** trespasses (v.15)". "His involvement with those for whom he spoke comes through at once, in the swift transition from 'I' in the first sentence (v.6), to 'our' and 'we' for the rest of the prayer" (D.Kidner). Ezra did not protest his personal innocence. Neither did Nehemiah (Neh. 1.6), or Daniel (Dan. 9.20), in similar circumstances. Ezra did not opt out of the situation, nor take a 'holier than thou' attitude. Although he had not personally subscribed to the trespass of the people, he identified himself with them in their guilt. It's very easy, when things go wrong in the assembly, to say 'nothing to do with me!'

d) His statement of facts, vv.7-15

Ezra's confession is a painful and detailed statement before God. He makes no attempt to gloss over the situation. We must carefully notice the language of 1 John 1.9. Not, 'If we confess our **sin**, he is faithful and just to forgive us our sins', but "If we confess our **sins**, he is faithful and just to forgive us our sins, and to cleanse us from all unrighteousness". Cleansing and forgiveness necessitate a **full** confession of our sins. It was painful for Ezra, and it is painful for us too. We must notice what this involved for Ezra:

i) **He acknowledged their rebellious history, v.7.** "Since the days of our fathers have we been in a great trespass unto this day; and for our iniquities have we, our kings, and our priests, been delivered into the hand of the kings of the lands, to the sword, to captivity, and to a spoil, and to confusion of face, as it is this day".

ii) He acknowledged their revival from God, vv.8-9. Though undeserved, there had been a measure of revival, when the nation could have been extinguished.

We should notice the way in which God had extended "grace" (v.8) and "mercy" (v.9) to His people. He had given them:

- **Honour for shame:** "to give us a nail ('tent pin') in his holy place" (v.8). Bearing in mind that a tent pin was a very small piece of equipment, the expression means that some small honour had been conferred upon them. Hence the expression a "little reviving" (v.8). Compare Zechariah 4.10, "Who hath despised the day of small things?"

- **Light for darkness:** "that our God may lighten our eyes" (v.8). Compare Psalm 137.1, "Yea, we wept, when we remembered Zion". See Psalm 13.3, "Consider and hear me, O Lord my God: lighten mine eyes, lest I sleep the sleep of death". To 'lighten the eye' means illumination after darkness and doubt.

- **Liberty for bondage:** "and give us a little reviving in our bondage. For we were bondmen; yet our God hath not forsaken us in our bondage, but hath extended mercy unto us in the sight of the kings of Persia, to give us a reviving" (vv.8-9).

- **Restoration for ruin:** "to set up the house of our God, and to repair the desolations thereof" (v.9). There had been recovery of worship and approach to God.

- **Security for danger:** "to give us a wall in Judah and in Jerusalem" (v.9). This should be compared with Zechariah 2.4-5, "For I, saith the Lord, will be unto her a **wall of fire round about**, and will be the glory in the midst of her".

iii) **He acknowledged their repeated failure,** vv.10-14. "And now, O our God, what shall we say **after this**? for we have forsaken thy commandments". Ezra then specified the commandments in question by referring to Deuteronomy 7.1-3, although he does not quote the passage verbatim. Quite obviously, the message of this passage had been proclaimed on numerous occasions by many people: "We have forsaken thy commandments, which thou hast commanded by thy servants the prophets". In view of the fact that God had punished His people for their disobedience, but had not punished them to the extent that they deserved (v.13), Ezra continues, "Should we **again** break thy commandments, and join in affinity with the people of these abominations? wouldest not thou be angry with us till thou hadst consumed us, so that there should be no remnant nor escaping?" They had failed to learn from their past mistakes.

iv)   He acknowledged the righteousness of God, v.15. "O Lord God of Israel, thou art righteous: for we remain yet escaped ('we are a remnant that is escaped', JND), as it is this day: behold, we are before thee in our trespasses: for we cannot stand before thee because of this". D.Kidner is probably right in saying, "the prayer ends with clear recognition that God has every reason to wash His hands of this community, as He once threatened to do with an earlier generation (Exodus 32.10)". These Jews had returned to Jerusalem through the grace and mercy of God (vv.8-9), and they had responded by transgressing His commandments. They could hardly expect further mercy from Him. Their conduct was an affront to His righteousness.

Sin destroys communion and fellowship with God. "We are before thee in our trespasses: for we cannot **stand before thee because of this**" (v.15). David sets out the qualifications for standing before God: "Who shall ascend into the hill of the Lord? or who shall **stand** in his holy place? He that hath clean hands, and a pure heart; who hath not lifted up his soul unto vanity, nor sworn deceitfully" (Psalm 24.3-4). Psalm 1 tells us that "the ungodly shall not **stand** in the judgment, nor sinners in the congregation of the righteous" (v.5). We must never forget that "If I regard iniquity in my heart, the Lord will not hear me" (Psalm 66.18).

We might have expected Ezra to enter a heartfelt plea for forgiveness. But there can be no forgiveness without repentance. Sin must be dealt with properly and thoroughly before we can enjoy God's presence again, and this is exactly what happens in Chapter 10.

READ CHAPTER 10

"There is hope in Israel concerning this thing"

The fifty-eight years between Ezra Chapter 6 and Ezra Chapter 7 had obviously witnessed a sad decline in the spiritual life of God's people. Unfortunately, it's the old, old story. As we have noticed, Chapters 1-6 describe progress and achievement, though not without interruption, and certainly not without difficulty. But they made it! The temple had been rebuilt, and "the children of Israel, the priests, and the Levites, and the rest of the children of the captivity, kept the dedication of this house of God with joy" (6.16). See also 6.22. The goal had been reached! End of story! But that was the sad part about it: they treated the completion of the temple as a goal, rather than a milestone. Flushed with success, it never occurred to them that there was a great deal more to accomplish. One look at the wall and gates of Jerusalem (see Nehemiah 1.3) should have made them flex their muscles and pick up their toolbags again! As it was, they lost their sense of vocation, and lapsed into backsliding and compromise. The sorry story is told in Chapter 9.1-2.

Let this be a lesson to us. There is **always** work to do for God. "Be ye stedfast, unmoveable, always abounding in the work of the Lord" (1 Cor. 15.58); "Preach the word; be instant in season, out of season" (2 Tim. 4.2). There is **always** need for progress in spiritual life. Even Paul acknowledged this: "Brethren, I count not myself to have apprehended: but this one thing I do, forgetting those things which are behind, and reaching forth unto those things which are before, I press toward the mark for the prize of the high calling of God in Christ Jesus" (Phil. 3.13-14). We cannot afford to relax and take it easy in spiritual life. It is a recipe for disaster. "Wherefore let him that thinketh he standeth take heed lest he fall" (1 Cor. 10.12). Ezra is now faced with the task of recovering the situation described in Chapter 9.

Chapter 10 may be divided into four main paragraphs: *(1)* the request for Ezra's help (vv.1-4); *(2)* the response to Ezra's command (vv.5-9); *(3)* the result of Ezra's preaching (vv.10-15); *(4)* the resolution under Ezra's guidance (vv.16-44). In the first paragraph, Ezra cast *"himself down"* (v.1); in the second, he *"rose up"* (vv.5-6); in the third, he *"stood up"* (v.10); in the fourth, he *"sat down"* (v.16).

1) THE REQUEST FOR EZRA'S HELP, vv.1-4

Ezra felt the situation very deeply indeed. The backsliding and compromise of God's people caused him great sorrow. See 9.3-6. Paul foresaw grave dangers for God's people, and "ceased not to warn every one night and day **with tears**" (Acts 20.31). How much are **we** affected when the welfare of God's people is threatened? In this case, Ezra's sorrow had a salutary effect on other people. We should notice the following: *(a)* sorrow for sin (v.1); *(b)* confession of sin (v.2); *(c)* dealing with sin (vv.3-4).

a) Sorrow for sin, v.1

"Now when Ezra had prayed, and when he had confessed, weeping and casting himself down before the house of God, there assembled unto him out of Israel a very great congregation of men and women and children: for **the people wept very sore**". His **preaching** had been effective: see 9.4, "Then were assembled unto me every one that trembled at the words of the God of Israel, because of the transgression of those that had been carried away". Now, his **sorrow** was effective. This reminds us that what we say will only be effective if people see its reality in our own lives.

b) Confession of sin, v.2

"And Shechaniah the son of Jehiel, one of the sons of Elam, answered and said unto Ezra, We have trespassed against our God, and have taken strange wives of the people of the land: yet now there is **hope in Israel** concerning this thing". "Instead of whipping a reluctant people into action, Ezra has pricked their conscience to the point at which they now urge **him** to act" (D.Kidner). Conviction and confession of sin marked the first stage of recovery. There would have been **no hope at all** if the people could not see, or did not wish to see, that they had sinned. It was when David said to Nathan, "I have sinned against the Lord", that Nathan replied, "The Lord also hath put away thy sin; thou shalt not die" (2 Sam. 12.13). We know that there can be no hope of salvation without conviction of sin: see Acts 2.37-40. But **we** need to pray with David, "Search me, O God, and know my heart: try me, and know my thoughts: and see if there be any wicked way in me, and lead me in the way everlasting" (Psalm 139.23-24).

Since Shechaniah's father, Jehiel, was guilty of marrying a 'strange wife' (v.26), it's quite conceivable that there were some heated words in the family that night!

c) Dealing with sin, vv.3-4

i) The covenant. "Now therefore let us make a **covenant** with our God to put away all the wives, and such as are born of them, according to the counsel of my lord, and of those that tremble at the commandment of our God; and let it be done according to the law". The use of the word "covenant" emphasises their strength of purpose. They were in earnest. Disobedience is a most serious matter. It should lead us to 'keep short accounts with God'. We should also notice that Shechaniah emphasised the need for the matter to be dealt with thoroughly: "Now therefore let us make a covenant with our God to put away *all* the wives, and such as are born of them". National disobedience must be dealt with by national obedience.

Obedience to the word of God can be a *painful* matter. It is not always easy to say, "Let it be done according to the law". In this case, wives and children were involved, and the fact that the marriages should have never been contracted in the first place, does not mean that there was no love and affection. Disobedience brings painful consequences. Whilst the New Testament does not demand separation from an unsaved husband or wife (see 1 Cor. 7.10-16; 1 Pet. 3.1-4), there are many ways in which obedience to the word of God cuts right across our natural inclinations and desires. Spiritual recovery is never easy.

ii) The counsel. The covenant was to be made "according to the counsel of my lord, and of those that tremble at the commandment of our God; and let it be done according to the law. Arise; for this matter belongeth unto thee: we also will be with thee: be of good courage, and do it". These verses mention five requirements in the man involved in the restoration of God's people:

- He must be **an authoritative man**: "according to the counsel of my lord" (v.3). The JND/RV margin has 'the Lord' *(Adonai)*. D.Kidner comments: "The consonants are the same, and while either alternative is possible, the latter ('my lord') seems preferable in view of the stronger terms used in the rest of the verse for what God Himself says". Either way, the authority of the man is emphasised: he speaks for God. See Hebrews 13.17.

- He must be **a God-fearing man**: "and of those that tremble at the commandment of our God" (v.3). See Ezra 9.4 and Isaiah 66.2. Note Galatians 6.1.

- He must be **a faithful man**: "and let it be done according to the law" (v.3). The word of God must be brought to bear upon the situation. Human expediency will not do. It is all too easy to be swayed by family ties and personal preferences, and to become guilty of operating double standards when dealing with problems amongst God's people.

-   He must be *a responsible man*: "Arise; for this matter belongeth unto thee" (v.4). Ezra was not to shirk his responsibilities as a leader of God's people. Elders should not shirk their responsibilities either.

-   He must be *a courageous man*: "be of good courage, and do it" (v.4). Sadly, things sometimes go wrong in assemblies, and good men haven't the courage of their convictions to intervene.

2) THE RESPONSE TO EZRA'S COMMAND, vv.5-9

Ezra displayed the sense of responsibility and courage required for the task: "Then arose Ezra". We should notice three things in this section: *(a)* the obedience he demanded (v.5); *(b)* the burden he felt (v.6); *(c)* the proclamation he made (vv.7-9).

a) The obedience he demanded, v.5

"Then arose Ezra, and made the chief priests, the Levites, and all Israel, to swear that they should do according to this word. And they sware". Nothing can be accomplished without obedience to the word of God. Progress and achievement in the Christian life is dependent on being "doers of the word, and not hearers only" (James 1.22).

b) The burden he felt, v.6

"Then Ezra rose up from before the house of God, and went into the chamber of Johanan the son of Eliashib: and when he came thither, he did eat no bread, nor drink water: for he mourned because of the transgression of them that had been carried away". It is significant that the words "then Ezra rose up" are followed, not by a public preaching, but solitary fasting and mourning. Ezra embarked upon his work, not with smug self-satisfaction, but with a deeply-burdened heart. We should notice that his sorrow was not engendered by pity *for* the people, but by the disobedience *of* the people. It was this that led to the painstaking and lengthy enquiry described in vv.16-44. Dealing with sin amongst God's people is a serious matter.

c) The proclamation he made, vv.7-9

"And they made proclamation throughout Judah and Jerusalem unto *all* the children of the captivity, that they should gather themselves together unto Jerusalem". Notice the word "gather" (v.7) and "gathered" (v.9). There was no 'hidden agenda'. Justice must be done, and justice must be **seen** to be done. The command to attend a "mass meeting at Jerusalem" (D.Kidner), was not over-reaction on Ezra's part. We must remember that God's word had been deliberately flouted, and public transgression must be dealt with publicly. This is why Paul confronted Peter at Antioch: "But when Peter was come to Antioch, I withstood him to **the face**, because he was to be blamed...But when I saw that they walked not uprightly according to the truth of the gospel, I said unto Peter **before them all**" (Gal. 2.11-14). At first glance, this seems to be rather uncharitable on Paul's part, but we must remember that Peter had been guilty of **publicly** misleading God's people, and therefore **public** correction was necessary. Private matters can be put right privately.

Attendance at Jerusalem was mandatory, and there were severe penalties for anyone who refused to come: "Whosoever would not come within three days, according to the counsel of the princes and the elders, all his substance should be forfeited, and himself separated from the congregation of those that had been carried away" (v.8). Ezra had authority to do this: see 7.25-26. It would be very unwise to suggest that there is an exact parallel in the New Testament. Elders are not to be dictatorial or autocratic, but they are responsible to God for the welfare of the assembly. So far as the flock is concerned, they are **shepherd**s (1 Pet. 5.1-4): so far as God is concerned, they are **stewards** (Titus 1.7). Whilst elders are responsible **for** the flock, they are not responsible **to** the flock. Their authority is to be recognised: "Obey them that have the rule over you ('obey your leaders', JND), and submit yourselves: for they watch for your souls, as they that must give account, that they may do it with joy, and not with grief: for that is unprofitable for you" (Heb. 13.17). See also 1 Thessalonians 5.12-13. These verses also remind us that we will certainly 'forfeit' spiritual blessing if we forsake "the assembling of ourselves together" (Heb.10.25), and that failure to meet with God's people will ultimately mean that we cease to be recognised as members of the assembly.

It was a most disconsolate group of people who duly assembled at Jerusalem. As D.Kidner observes, "It was late in the year, well into the equivalent of December, and verse 9 captures for us the shivering misery of the scene": "And all the people sat in the street of the house of God, trembling because of this matter, and for the great rain".

3) THE RESULT OF EZRA'S PREACHING, vv.10-15
Ezra did not wait until it stopped raining (see v.13). He got straight down to business. More correctly, he "stood up" and began to preach. This was an

urgent matter. We must notice *(a)* the subject of the preaching (vv.10-11); *(b)* the result of the preaching (vv.12-14); *(c)* the objection to the preaching (v.15).

a) The subject of the preaching, vv.10-11

"And Ezra the priest stood up, and said unto them, Ye have transgressed, and have taken strange wives, to increase the trespass of Israel. Now therefore make confession unto the Lord God of your fathers, and do his pleasure: and separate yourselves from the people of the land, and from the strange wives".

i) Ezra exposed their sin, v.10. Their disobedience had brought about captivity in the first place, and this had been followed by still more disobedience which only served to "increase the trespass of Israel".

ii) Ezra urged confession of sin, v.11. But confession of sin was not enough: something more was required.

iii) Ezra demanded separation from sin, v.11. There could be no such thing as confession of sin, and remaining in sin. Notice the words, "*and do his pleasure*". This should be the aim of us all: "Wherefore also we make it our aim, whether at home or absent, to be well-pleasing unto him" (2 Cor. 5.9, RV). Paul taught the Thessalonians how they "ought to walk and to please God" (1 Thess. 4.1).

b) The result of the preaching, vv.12-14

"Then all the congregation answered and said with a loud voice, As thou hast said, so must we do". Compare Hebrews 13.17. To their credit, the people, with a few exceptions (v.15), were willing to obey the word of God. We must remember that Ezra was not expressing his own opinion: he had chapter and verse for his preaching. See 9.11-12. We too must "receive with meekness the engrafted ('implanted', JND) word, which is able to save your souls" (James 1.21). We must not resist the word of God, but receive it "with meekness". Only then can it "save your souls" when temptation arises.

There was evidently some enthusiasm in their response: they "answered…with a *loud voice*". It was not a case of just giving it some thought: "As thou hast said, so *must* we do". Whilst it was impractical to deal with the matter there and then, they were quite prepared for a thorough examination. See vv.13-14.

c) The objection to the preaching, v.15

"Only Jonathan the son of Asahel and Jahzeiah the son of Tikvah stood up against this; and Meshullam and Shabbethai the Levite helped them" (JND).

There are usually some people who object when it comes to putting the word of God into practice!

4) THE RESOLUTION UNDER EZRA'S GUIDANCE, vv.16-44
The procedure took approximately three months. "And Ezra the priest, with certain chief of the fathers, after the house of their fathers, and all of them by their names, were separated, and sat down in the **first day of the tenth month** to examine the matter. And they made an end with all the men that had taken strange wives by the **first day of the first month**" (vv.16-17). This approximates to a period covered by our January, February and March.

A list of names terminates the book of Ezra. It contrasts vividly with earlier lists! We must remember that heaven notes the affairs of every child of God, whether it is their spiritual concern (as in Chapters 2 & 7), or their carnal compromise here. There was no partiality. **All** classes of society were involved.

i) The **priests** are named in vv.18-22. Eighteen priests are named, including four from the high priest's family (v.18). Not one of the priestly families that returned were guiltless. Sadly, the sons of Jeshua (see 2.36), Immer (2.37), Harim (2.39), and Pashur (2.38) are all included in the list. Ezra, himself a priest, did not extend them any special favours! Those who were most culpable are mentioned first. See Leviticus 21.7. Godly forebears and privileged positions do not guarantee preservation from spiritual decline. We should add that it is not usually very long before others follow the bad example of men with position and influence.

ii) The **Levites** are named in v.23: Jozabad, Shimei, Kelaiah, Pethahiah, Judah, and Eliezer.

iii) The **singers** and **porters** are named in v.24: Eliashib (a singer), Shallum, Telem and Uri (porters).

iv) The **people** are detailed in vv.25-43. The sons of Parosh (v.25), see 2.3; of Elam (v.26), see 2.7; of Zattu (v.27), see 2.9; of Bebai (v.28), see 2.11; of Bani (v.29), see 2.10); of Pahath-Moab (v.30), see 2.6; of Harim (vv.31-32), see 2.32,39; of Hashum (v.33), see 2.19; of Bani (vv.34-42); of Nebo (v.43), see 2.29.

"All these (priests, Levites, singers, porters and people) had taken strange wives: and some of them had wives by whom they had children". We learn from Malachi 2.10-16, that a scandalous number of Jewish wives had been abandoned in favour of heathen women. Malachi preached some years after Ezra, and it is not possible to say with certainty whether Ezra 10 and Malachi 2 are two sides of the same coin. Neither do we know what happened to these wives once they had been "put away". It seems most likely that they would have returned to their own families, but as D.Kidner rightly observes, "this is no more than an assumption". Disobedience to God's word brought the most awful consequences, and it still does. We must not forget that Ezra Chapters 9 & 10 teach a very clear lesson. Christians must carefully avoid alliances and relationships which will cause them spiritual harm. When discussing **marriage**, Paul uses the expression, "**only in the Lord**" (1 Cor. 7.39). Even marrying a Christian is not enough: it must be the **right** Christian. It must be "in **the Lord**".

On this solemn note we take our leave of Ezra. True to his name, he was a 'help' to God's people, and not least by the courageous way in which he taught and applied the word of God. But even Ezra was evidently not equipped or able do everything. Another mighty man - Nehemiah - was needed to initiate and supervise the reconstruction of the walls and gates of Jerusalem. Watch this space!

Having said this, it remains that we desperately need men like Ezra today. Who amongst us is willing to become one of his spiritual successors, and be a true 'Ezra' in our current day and generation? Remember the meaning of his name. Need we say more?

Ezra, Nehemiah, Esther

NEHEMIAH

by
John M Riddle

NEHEMIAH

Introduction

Read the whole book

Our introduction to the book of Nehemiah will cover the following: *(1)* the background of the book; *(2)* the structure of the book; *(3)* the character of the man.

1) THE BACKGROUND OF THE BOOK

The opening verse of the book forms a fitting introduction. "The words of Nehemiah the son of Hachaliah" (1.1). Nehemiah means **'consolation of the Lord'**, and Hachaliah means **'darkness of the Lord'.** The two names summarise the historical background. The key hangs at the door of the book! Israel had experienced the **'darkness of the Lord'**, and Nehemiah refers to this in his confession (1.5-7). God had fulfilled His promise, "If ye transgress, I will scatter you abroad among the nations". But now, after seventy years' captivity, judicial darkness had given place to the **'consolation of the Lord'.** The books of Ezra and Nehemiah describe this period, causing Ezra to say, "And now for a little space grace hath been shewed from the Lord our God...God hath not forsaken us in our bondage" (Ezra 9.8-9). This needs a little amplification:

a) 'Darkness of the Lord'

A summary of events might be helpful. After the death of Solomon (975BC, although more recent opinion gives a different date), the kingdom was divided, leaving Israel in the north, and Judah in the south. **Israel**, in the north, comprised ten tribes, with its capital Samaria (Tirzah at first), and its first king, Jeroboam the son of Nebat. Israel was ultimately taken into captivity by Assyria in 721BC. **Judah**, in the south comprised the tribes of Judah and Benjamin, plus Levi, with its capital Jerusalem, and its first king, Rehoboam the son of Solomon. Judah became subject to Babylon (Nebuchadnezzar) in 606BC. Although the temple was not destroyed until 588BC or thereabouts, (586BC is usually quoted today) the nation became part of the Babylonian Empire from 606BC, and its remaining two rulers were really only vassal kings.

The Babylonian captivity lasted for seventy years, but this was far from a mere quirk of history. The period had been carefully calculated (see 2 Chronicles 36.21 and Leviticus 26.34-43). The duration of the captivity was announced by Jeremiah. See, for example, Jeremiah 25.11-12. Seventy years after Babylon had annexed Judah in 606BC, in fulfilment of Jeremiah's prophecy (2 Chronicles 36.22 and Ezra 1.1) and in answer to Daniel's prayer (9.2-19), Cyrus authorised the return of the exiles to Jerusalem to rebuild the temple. The year was 536BC.

b) "Consolation of the Lord"
i) The first party of exiles returned under the leadership of Zerubbabel and Jeshua the priest. This is covered by Ezra Chapters 1-6. The purpose of the return was to **rebuild** the temple. This work was completed in the sixth year of Darius (Ezra 6.15), i.e. 515BC (Darius commenced to reign in 521BC). The preaching of Haggai and Zechariah is relevant to this period. See Ezra 5.1-2 and 6.14.

ii) Fifty-seven years later, in 458BC, in the seventh year of Artaxerxes Longimanus (Ezra 7.7), who commenced to reign in 465BC, a second party of exiles returned under the leadership of Ezra himself. This is covered by Ezra Chapters 7-10. The purpose of this return was to **beautify** the temple. See Ezra 7.27.

iii) Between the two periods covered by the book of Ezra (Chs.1-6 and Chs.7-10), we have the events described in the book of Esther, although this is set in Persia, not Israel. The reigning monarch at this time was Ahasuerus, known to history as Xerxes, the father of Artaxerxes. He commenced to reign in 485BC, and Esther became queen in the seventh year of his reign (Est. 2.16), i.e. in 478BC. Note: two other kings bear the name 'Ahasuerus' in Scripture (Ezra 4.6 & Daniel 9.1), but they are not identical with the monarch named in the book of Esther.

iv) The book of Nehemiah continues the story of Ezra. It commences in 445BC, i.e. in the twentieth year of Artaxerxes. Nehemiah therefore came to Jerusalem thirteen years after Ezra, who was still in the city. See Nehemiah 8.4 and 12.36. Nehemiah was twelve years in Jerusalem (see 5.14), after which he returned to Artaxerxes (see 13.6), so the major part of the book can be dated 445-433BC. We should carefully note that the decree of Artaxerxes authorising the rebuilding of the wall of Jerusalem marks the commencement of the 'Seventy Weeks' prophecy of Daniel 9.24-27. Whilst the book of Ezra is concerned with the rebuilding of the **temple**, the book of Nehemiah is concerned with the rebuilding of the **wall**. Malachi evidently preached some years after events described in the book of Nehemiah.

2) THE STRUCTURE OF THE BOOK

The book of Nehemiah can be divided into two main sections: Chapters 1-6 deal with the *place*, and Chapters 7-13 deal with the *people*. The overall picture produces some important lessons. They look something like this:

- *In Chapters 1-3 we learn that the work of God requires determination.* Once he had been informed of the situation at Jerusalem, Nehemiah determined to do something about it. This is clear from his *prayer* in Chapter 1: "Prosper, I pray thee, thy servant this day, and grant him mercy in the sight of this man" (v.11). This is clear from his *preparation* in Chapter 2: Not only did he have a plan of action ready, but he acquainted himself thoroughly with the actual task, before saying to his colleagues, "Come, and let us build up the wall of Jerusalem, that we be no more a reproach". This found a ready response: "And they said, Let us rise up and build" (vv.17-18). So, in Chapter 3, we have the *prosecution* of the work.

- *In Chapters 4-6 we learn that the work of God involves danger.* The dangers and difficulties experienced by Nehemiah were threefold. In the first place, the work was threatened by *opposition from without*. See Chapter 4. In the second place, it was threatened by *dissatisfaction from within*. See Chapter 5. In the third place it was threatened by *compromise and infiltration*. See Chapter 6. We could write Paul's words over these chapters: "we were troubled on every side; without were fightings, within were fears" (2 Cor. 7.5). There was certainly the threat of 'fightings without' in Chapter 4, and there were certainly 'fears within' in Chapters 5 & 6. It is noteworthy that Nehemiah was "very angry", not with Sanballat, Tobiah and Geshem, but with the Jews! See 5.6. Compare 13.8,11,17, and in particular, 13.25.

The work of God always attracts enemy attention. Notice the way in which this develops throughout the book. It began when the enemies were "grieved... exceedingly that there was come a man to seek the welfare of the children of Israel" (2.10). This was followed by scorn (2.19), anger (4.1,7), threat of attack (4.11), and finally by craft and stealth (6.1-14). The enemy hibernates where there is lethargy and indolence amongst God's people, but leaps into action when work for God commences. *See Chapter 4.* Disorders amongst God's people comprise a very real threat to the work. The dissatisfaction of disadvantaged Jews threatened disruption. *See Chapter 5.* The enemy still endeavours to get us on to his ground, where we will be vulnerable. The Lord's people today are not lacking fifth columnists amongst them. *See Chapter 6.* But the work never stopped!

- *In Chapters 7-12 we learn that the work of God requires devotion.* With the exception of Chapter 8, these are the less read and less expounded chapters of Nehemiah! They tell us that it is one thing to rebuild city walls and city gates, but it is another to give God His rightful place. There must be activity *for* God, but there must be obedience *to* God. Having recorded the names of those that returned under Zerubbabel and Joshua in **Chapter 7**, the scriptures are read publicly in **Chapter 8.** This had a twofold effect; *(i)* God's people recognised the authority of the Scriptures, and practised something that had not been done for a thousand years: see 8.13-18; *(ii)* they realised as never before their shortcomings, and determined to renew the covenant: see Chapters 9 & 10. Do the Scriptures have the same effect on *us*? This had a further effect: *(iii)* they ensured that Jerusalem, "the place which the Lord shall choose to place his name there" (Deut. 16.2) was properly inhabited and supported. See **Chapter 11.** We too are not to forsake "the assembling of ourselves together" (Heb. 10.25). Only then can there be *(iv)* true praise and thanksgiving. See **Chapter 12.**

- *In Chapter 13 we learn that the work of God can be followed by decline.* Spiritual achievement signals danger. We have only to remember the reign of Solomon, and the history of the church at Ephesus. In fact, Nehemiah refers to Solomon in this connection (13.26). In the absence of Nehemiah, the solemn vows of Chapter 10 had been jettisoned. Nehemiah was therefore obliged to reinstate provision for the Levites, recognition of the sabbath, and to deal with mixed marriages.

The tragedy was that Nehemiah's convictions were not shared by others. When he was absent, spiritual standards slipped, reminding us that it is not sufficient to have men of conviction at the helm of the assembly. We *all* need to be men and women of conviction.

C) THE CHARACTER OF THE MAN
His heart for God and God's work is seen in *(i)* his concern; *(ii)* his cries; *(iii)* his caution; *(iv)* his consistency; *(v)* his conviction; *(vi)* his confidence.

i) His concern
"And it came to pass, when I heard these words, that I sat down and wept, and mourned certain days, and fasted, and prayed before the God of heaven" (1.4). He was concerned for the *people,* and he was concerned for the *place*: "The remnant that are left of the captivity there in the province are in great affliction and reproach: the wall of Jerusalem also is broken down, and the gates thereof are burned with fire" (1.3). The apostle Paul displayed similar

sorrow: "Out of much affliction and anguish of heart I wrote unto you with **many tears**" (2 Cor. 2.4).

Nehemiah's comfortable situation, "In Shushan the palace…the king's cupbearer" (1.1,11), and his distance from Jerusalem, did not minimise his concern. He was not just sympathetic. He was stirred. But more than that, he was prepared to work. It meant a hard and lonely life at times, but he was willing to serve in the place of "the name". What about **our** concern for the people of God, and for the place of "the name?" Is it purely cosmetic, or are we stirred to action?

ii) His cries
Nehemiah cried to God on eight occasions. See 2.4; 4.4-5; 5.19; 6.14; 13.14; 13.22; 13.29; 13.31. These were 'ejaculatory prayers'. We have a further prayer in 4.9. Nehemiah could approach God in all circumstances. Even when conversing with the Persian emperor! But we would be quite wrong to suppose that he **only** prayed in this way. See 1.4-11. We cannot expect audience with God in emergencies if we are not prepared to spend time in His presence on a regular basis.

iii) His caution
Nehemiah carefully weighed up the situation. Notice that it was three days after arrival before he examined the ruined walls of Jerusalem: "And I arose in the night, I and some few men with me; neither told I any man what my God had put in my heart to do at Jerusalem" (2.11-12). When the internal problem arose in Chapter 5, Nehemiah says, "I consulted with myself" (v.7). He was "swift to hear, slow to speak, slow to wrath" (James 1.19). Another aspect of his caution surfaces in Chapter 6. He was not easily deceived: "they thought to do me mischief" (v.2). He was 'not ignorant of [their] devices' (2 Cor. 2.11).

iv) His consistency
The narrative liberally supplies us with examples. See, for example, chapters 4 & 5: "Likewise at the same time said I unto the people, Let every one with his servant lodge within Jerusalem, that in the night they may be a guard unto us, and labour on the day. **So neither I**, nor my brethren, nor my servants, nor the men of the guard that followed me, none of us put off our clothes, saving that every one put them off for washing" (4.22-23); "Moreover from the time that I was appointed to be their governor in the land of Judah, from the twentieth year even unto the two and thirtieth year of Artaxerxes the king, that is, twelve years, **I and my brethren** have not eaten the bread of the governor…"; (5.14-15); "Yet

for all this (his well stocked table) **required not I the bread of the governor,** because the bondage was heavy upon this people" (5.18). Nehemiah never asked anybody to do what he would not do himself.

This recalls 1 Timothy 4.16, "Take heed unto **thyself**, and unto the doctrine". There was to be no disparity between Timothy's teaching and Timothy's practice. Nehemiah did not belong to the class of people that "sit in Moses' seat...they say, and do not" (Matt. 23.2-3).

v) His conviction

Nehemiah was not afraid to tackle difficulties and problems. For example, when dealing with the lack of care amongst God's people in Chapter 5, he "rebuked the nobles, and the rulers, and said unto them, Ye exact usury, every one of his brother. And...set a great assembly against them" (v.7). In the case of the acquisition of the chamber in the temple by Eliashib for Tobiah, he "cast forth all the household stuff (belonging to Tobiah) out of the chamber" (13.8). Related or not to the high priest (see 13.4, JND), out it went! But he became even more militant: "And one of the sons of Joiada, the son of Eliashib the high priest, was son in law to Sanballat the Horonite: therefore I chased him from me" (13.28). Sadly, other people did not share Nehemiah's convictions. Standards slipped when he returned to Artaxerxes. Good leadership is important, but we must **all** be loyal to the word of God. **Our** convictions must be based on the Scriptures.

vi) His confidence

In fact, Nehemiah inspired confidence. Notice such expressions as, "Ye see the distress that we are in (so he was no ostrich), how Jerusalem lieth waste, and the gates thereof are burned with fire: come, and let us build up the wall of Jerusalem, that we be no more a reproach...And they said, Let us rise up and build. So they strengthened their hands for this good work" (2.17-18). When attack threatened, he rallied his colleagues: "Be not ye afraid of them: **remember the Lord**, which is great and terrible, and fight for your brethren, your sons, and your daughters, your wives, and your houses...In what place therefore ye hear the sound of the trumpet, resort ye thither unto us: **our God** shall fight for us" (4.14,20).

With all this, Nehemiah was none the less **a lonely man.** The first person singular punctuates the narrative. See for example, Chapter 2: "And **I** said unto the king...that **I** may build it...**I** set him a time...then **I** came to the governors...So **I** came to Jerusalem... And **I** went out by night...Then said **I** unto them..." Notice too the words, "Think upon **me**, my God, for good, according to all that **I** have done for this people" (5.19). Similar words occur three times in Chapter 13: "Remember *me*, O my God, concerning this, and wipe not out *my* good deeds that *I* have done for the house of *my* God, and for the offices thereof" (v.14); "Remember *me*, O my God, concerning this also, and spare *me* according to the greatness of thy mercy" (v.22); "Remember *me*, O my God, for good" (v.31).

This must not be construed as boasting. The fact is that Nehemiah acted alone, because there was no one else to whom he could turn. He had little fellowship. He was sustained by his personal relationship with God: hence the expressions "*my* God" and "O *my* God".

The book ends with Nehemiah's eighth 'ejaculatory prayer': "Remember me, O my God, for good". It is the prayer of a man who, in the face of great odds externally, and in the face of great discouragement internally, had been unswervingly faithful. Centuries later, another man wrote, "I have fought a good fight, I have finished my course, I have kept the faith: henceforth there is laid up for me a crown of righteousness (a rightly adjusted crown of reward), which the Lord, the righteous judge, shall give me at that day" (2 Tim. 4.7-8).

What will *we* be able to say at the end of life's journey?

Addendum

An analysis of Nehemiah

CHAPTERS 1-3

How to tackle a task for God

Chapter 1.   Our work must be born out of **Personal Concern**. "Moved with compassion" (Matt. 9.36).

Chapter 2.   Our work must be preceded by **Personal Preparation**. "Prepared unto every good work" (2 Tim. 2.21)

Chapter 3.   Our work must proceed with a sense of **Personal Responsibility**. "Workers together" (2 Cor. 6.1).

CHAPTERS 4-6

How to deal with the difficulties we meet

Chapter 4. The work threatened by **Opposition Without.** "Watch and pray" (Matt. 26.41).

Chapter 5. The work threatened by **Dissatisfaction Within.** "Consider one another" (Heb. 10.24).

Chapter 6. The work threatened by **Infiltration and Compromise**. "Try the spirits whether they are of God" (1 John 4.1).

CHAPTERS 7-12

How to plan for prosperous spiritual lives

Chapter 7. The Registration of their Names. "Written in the Lamb's book of life" (Rev. 21.27).

Chapter 8. The Reading of Scripture. "Give attendance to reading" (1 Tim. 4.13).

Chapter 9. The Review of their History. "All these things happened unto them for ensamples" (1 Cor. 10.11).

Chapter 10. Their Resolution to Obey. "We will serve the Lord" (Joshua 24.15).

Chapter 11. The Recognition of their Centre. "Set your affection on things above" (Col. 3.2).

Chapter 12. Their Rejoicing in God's Goodness. "In every thing give thanks" (1 Thess. 5.18.

CHAPTER 13

How to Become a Backslider

Chapter 13. How to become a backsliding Christian. "Ye did run well; who did hinder you...?" (Gal. 5.7).

READ CHAPTER 1

"I sat down and wept"

Nehemiah Ch. 1 may be divided into four sections as follows: *(1)* Nehemiah's anxiety for God's people (vv.1-3); *(2)* his anguish of soul (v.4); *(2)* his admission of sin (vv.5-7); *(4)* his appeal to God (vv.8-11). The book is clearly autobiographical: "The words of Nehemiah..." (v.1). The personal pronoun "I" is particularly prominent in chs.1-7.

1) HIS ANXIETY FOR GOD'S PEOPLE, vv.1-3

Nehemiah's concern for both the people and the place is expressed in v.2, "I asked them concerning the Jews that had escaped, which were left of the captivity, and concerning Jerusalem". When we look at the opening paragraph of the chapter, it is quite obvious that Nehemiah had at least two good reasons to forget all about the situation in Judah and Jerusalem. First of all, there was his **situation at Shushan**, and secondly, there was the **situation at Jerusalem.** To his credit, neither reason made him stay in Shushan. Nehemiah was probably born in captivity, but this did not lessen his deep concern for the city of which the Lord had said, "the place that I have chosen to set my name there" (1.9).

a) His situation at Shushan

Nehemiah enjoyed a very privileged position in life. In his own words, "I was in Shushan **the palace...**I was **the king's cupbearer**" (vv.1,11). This was no quirk of fate. In the wisdom and sovereignty of God, both Ezra and Nehemiah were in a position to act. Both were in close contact with the king. This is why Nehemiah, rather than Hanani (v.2), was used by God to mastermind the rebuilding of the wall of Jerusalem. Compare Philippians 1.12. It's worth noticing the details given by Nehemiah:

i) The person. "The words of **Nehemiah the son of Hachaliah**". As we noticed in introducing the book, Nehemiah means 'consolation of the Lord', and Hachaliah means 'darkness of the Lord', or 'disturbed of the Lord'. This certainly mirrors the background and contents of the book. The judicial darkness which had fallen on Jerusalem because of sin, now gives place to recovery and encouragement.

ii) The period. "And it came to pass in the **month Chisleu, in the twentieth year...**" Ellicott's Commentary is helpful here: "The names rather than the numbers of the months are generally employed after the captivity: Nisan, Iyar, Sivan, Tammuz, Av, Elul, Tishri, Marchesvan, **Chisleu** (answering nearly to our December), Tebeth, Shevat, Adar; with an intercalary month, the second Adar'. ('Intercalary' means a month inserted in the calendar to harmonise it with the solar year). The reference to "Chisleu" is significant in view of the mention of "***Nisan***" at the beginning of the next chapter (2.1). There was something like four months between the two dates. As we will see, Nehemiah spent the time in prayer.

The "twentieth year" refers to the reign of Artaxerxes Longimanus, which commenced in BC 465 and ended in BC 425. Ezra went to Jerusalem in the seventh year of Artaxerxes (see Ezra 7.8), so there were approximately thirteen years between the expedition of Ezra and the expedition of Nehemiah. See Nehemiah 5.14.

iii) The place. "I was in **Shushan (Susa)** the palace". Shushan was "the principal and favourite residence of the Persian court, alternating with Persepolis, the older capital, and Babylon" (Ellicott's Commentary). Compare, for example, Daniel 8.2; Esther 1.2.

iv) The position. "I was in Shushan the **palace**". He certainly wasn't the errand-boy there! "I was the king's cupbearer" (v.11). The word "cupbearer" is translated "butler" in Gen 40.1-2 etc. Nehemiah obviously enjoyed a secure and privileged position. Events proved that he was highly regarded by the king. As "the king's cupbearer", he was a man of absolute integrity in whom the greatest trust reposed. After all, there was always the likelihood of the king's cup being poisoned! It has been said that "the king's cupbearer" was far more than a kind of butler: he was a personal confidante of the king.

All this reminds us that we should be known for integrity and trustworthiness. While none of us are "servants" (slaves) in the New Testament sense, the principles of Ephesians 6.5-8, Colossians 3.22-25, and Titus 2.9-10 are relevant to all employees. Employers should see the reality of our Christian faith, even if it leaves them sometimes bewildered, or even antagonistic.

Nehemiah was not hypnotised by his privileges and responsibilities as "the king's cupbearer". As we shall see, he was willing to resign his exalted position for a period in the interests of his suffering brethren, and in the interests of the place of 'the name' (v.9). Compare Daniel 9.18-19. What about *our* priorities? If we are not careful, business or career interests will buy us body, mind and soul. We must remember that the Lord Jesus looked not on His "own things", but "on the things of others" (Phil. 2.4). He was willing to leave the glory of heaven, and identify Himself with needy mankind.

b) The situation at Jerusalem

Conditions in Judah and Jerusalem were enough to quench anybody's enthusiasm! Fancy leaving the security and opulence of the palace for a downtrodden people and a ruined city! But that's exactly what Nehemiah did! But he didn't undertake the daunting task of rebuilding the city wall with stars in his eyes. Nehemiah was not a romantic! He was well aware of the *problems*, but he was equally aware of the *power of God.* He got the information, and he prayed about it! The problem is very clearly stated in v.3: "The remnant that are left of the captivity there in the province are in great affliction and reproach: the wall of Jerusalem also is broken down, and the gates thereof are burned with fire". The information was given to Nehemiah by, amongst others, his brother Hanani. See also 7.2. It has been suggested that the words, "Hanani...came", could refer to diplomatic activity, and indicate movement between the provinces. His name means 'whom Jehovah graciously gave', and it is significant that Hanani and his colleagues did not harshly criticise Nehemiah for living in a palace, when his brethren were living in ruins. They simply described to Nehemiah the situation in Judah and Jerusalem. There's nothing like grace to win interest and stir gift in God's service! Notice Nehemiah's enquiry: "I asked them concerning the Jews that had escaped, which were left of the captivity, and concerning Jerusalem" (v.2). He was interested in the *people*: "I asked...concerning the Jews that had escaped". He was interested in the *place*: "I asked...concerning Jerusalem". We must of course have an interest in the *place* of 'the name', but we must remember that assemblies are made up of people. It is sadly possible to be interested only in the *place*, and appear to have little time for the *people.* We must, of course, ensure that the assembly gathers on scriptural principles, but we must also remember that God's people need care and help in their spiritual growth. That involves patience, courtesy, and grace. These commodities are not always in plentiful supply amongst leaders and teachers! The answer to Nehemiah's questions is given in v.3 which refers to the remnant, the reproach, and the ruin. We must notice:

i) **The people.** The words, "the remnant that are left" means 'the remnant that had escaped' (see Jeremiah 39.10). They were "in great *affliction* and *reproach*." See also 2.17, "Ye see the distress that we are in, how Jerusalem lieth waste, and the gates thereof are burned with fire: come, and let us build up the wall of Jerusalem, that we be no more a **reproach**". Compare Lamentations 2.15-16. Centuries before, David exclaimed, "And what one nation in the earth is like thy people, even like Israel, whom God went to redeem for a people to himself, and to make him a name, and to do for you great things and terrible" (2 Sam 7.23). But now, that same nation had become despised and afflicted, and the responsibility lay wholly at their own door. What about **our** testimony and spiritual health? Have **we** given the adversary opportunity to "speak reproachfully?" (1 Tim 5.14).

ii) The place. It has been said that the walls were to keep out those who should not be in, and the gates were to give access to those who should be in!

- "The **wall** of Jerusalem also is broken down". There was no protection, and no dividing line between the city and its surroundings. In Scripture, city walls stand for salvation and protection: "Salvation will God appoint for walls and bulwarks" (Isa. 26.1); "Thou shalt call thy walls Salvation" (Isa. 60.18). We must ensure that the doctrines of salvation are in place in our lives and in our assemblies. Sadly, speaking generally, there appears to be little or no distinction today between the professing church and the world. In many places, "the wall... is broken down", and the Lord's people need to heed the injunction, "Take heed unto thyself, and unto the doctrine; continue in them: for in doing this thou shalt both **save** thyself, and them that hear thee" (1 Tim. 4.16).

- "The **gates** thereof are burned with fire". See, again, Isaiah 60.18; "But thou shalt call...thy gates **Praise".** See also Proverbs 31.31, "Let her own works praise her in the gates". What about **our** praise and thankfulness to God? Is there any? Or are "the gates...burned with fire?"

The "gates" were places where administration and business were conducted. The city gate was recognised as an open court of justice where civil and criminal cases were investigated by the elders. See, for example, Deuteronomy 16.18-20, Ruth 4.1. We must ensure that nothing deprives us of the teaching of God's word. It is our only court of appeal in all matters of doctrine and conduct. In many places, "the gates...are burned with fire" when it comes to assembly practices. Notice too that the gates were connected with reception, but reception with authority.

2) HIS ANGUISH OF SOUL, v.4
"And it came to pass, when I heard these words, that I sat down and wept, and

mourned certain days, and fasted, and prayed before the God of heaven". (The phrase "God of heaven" is found particularly in Ezra, Nehemiah and Daniel: it signifies a change in His relationship with His people. Whilst He no longer dwelt amongst them in the same way as before, He had certainly not abdicated! It also emphasises His complete supremacy). Nehemiah's response to the sad news illustrates James 5.13 ("Is any among you afflicted? let him pray"), and exhibited deep sorrow in the spirit of 1 Cor. 12.26, "And whether one member suffer, all the members suffer with it". Paul was deeply moved when he foresaw the devastating effect of false teaching, saying to the Ephesian elders: "Therefore watch, and remember, that by the space of three years I ceased not to warn every one night and day **with tears**" (Acts 20.31). He was equally moved when he heard about conditions in the assembly at Corinth: "For out of much affliction and anguish of heart I wrote unto you **with many tears**; not that ye should be grieved, but that ye might know the love which I have more abundantly unto you" (2 Cor. 2.4). The Lord Jesus wept over Jerusalem in Luke 19.41. The word "wept" here means 'to sob'.

To what extent do conditions amongst God's people really concern us? We are all too ready to condemn and correct, and the word of God must certainly be brought to bear upon all spiritual departure and decline, but we are less ready to weep. The prophet Jeremiah sternly denounced the evils of his day, but he is known as 'the weeping prophet'. See Jeremiah 9.1; 13.17; 14.17; 22.10; 31.16; 48.32; Lamentations 1.16; 2.11; 2.18.

As we have seen, Nehemiah's deep sorrow brought him to God in prayer. There was nothing casual or 'laid back' about his prayer. Notice the threefold expression, "I beseech thee" (vv.5,8,11). His prayer is recorded in vv.5-11. We must notice: *(i) that he confessed sin to God* (vv.5-7); *(ii) that he claimed the promises of God* (vv.8-11). This brings us to:

3) HIS ADMISSION OF SIN, vv.5-7
Attention is drawn to *(a)* his care in approaching God (v.5); *(b)* his continuity of prayer to God (v.6); *(c)* his confession of sin to God (vv.6-7).

a) His care in approaching God, v.5
He prayed with great reverence. "I beseech thee, O Lord God of heaven, the great and terrible God, that keepeth covenant and mercy for them that love him and observe his commandments". We must notice:

i) That Nehemiah addressed the "**Lord** God of heaven", emphasising that He was still the covenant-keeping God. Cyrus acknowledged Him in this way (Ezra 1.1-2). He is the "Lord God of *heaven*" as opposed to idols on earth. Nehemiah evidently prayed with reference to the teaching of "the Preacher": "Be not rash with thy mouth, and let not thine heart be hasty to utter any thing before God: for God is in heaven, and thou upon earth: therefore let thy words be few" (Eccl. 5.2).

ii) That Nehemiah was deeply conscious of God's awesome might and majesty: He is "the great and terrible God". He was equally conscious of His faithfulness: "that keepeth covenant (compare 9.32) and mercy for them that *love him and observe his commandments*". Note the conditions here, and compare John 14.15,23; 15.10. The rainbow-circled throne in Revelation 4.3 proclaims that God is always faithful to His covenants. We must remember that "whatever promises of God there are, in him is the yea, and in him the amen"' (2 Cor. 1.20, JND).

b) His continuity in prayer to God, v.6
He persisted in prayer. "Let thine ear now be attentive (see also v.11), and thine eyes open, that thou mayest hear the prayer of thy servant, which I pray before thee now, *day and night*". Compare Psalm 34.15, "The eyes of the Lord are upon the righteous, and his ears are open unto their cry". This is cited in 1 Peter 3.10-12. Nehemiah prayed for four to five months. He prayed from Chisleu (December) to Nisan (April). Compare Acts 20.31, "By the space of *three years* I ceased not to warn every one night and day with tears". The Lord Jesus taught that "men ought always to pray, and not to faint" (Luke 18.1). See also Colossians 4.2, "Continue (persevere) in prayer, and watch in the same with thanksgiving". Do remember that Moses' "hands were *steady* until the going down of the sun" (Ex. 17.12).

c) His confession of sin to God, vv.6-7
Nehemiah was certainly most unlike the proud Pharisee at prayer: "God, I thank thee, that I am not as other men are..." (Luke 18.11). We should notice the three stages in his confession: "Hear the prayer of thy servant, which I pray before thee now, day and night, for the children of Israel thy servants, and confess the sins of *(i)* the **children of Israel** (not just Judah, but all God's people), which *(ii)* **we** have sinned against thee (there is no self-righteousness here): *(iii)* both *I* and my father's house have sinned". This extends beyond admission of corporate failure: Nehemiah was conscious of personal failure. He identified himself with the situation: compare Daniel 9.20. It was a detailed confession. See 1 John 1.9, "If we confess our sins..." (not 'if we confess our sin...'). It involved humility: Nehemiah describes himself as "thy servant" and Israel as "thy servants". Confession is linked with joy in Psalm 51.8. But the process is painful: "The

sacrifices of God are a broken spirit: a broken and a contrite heart, O God, thou wilt not despise" (Psalm 51.17). See also Isaiah 66.2. His confession to God is followed by:

4) HIS APPEAL TO GOD, v.v8-11
It is based on the word of God. Nehemiah asked God to honour His own promises. He quoted God's word to God! Let's remember that God loves His own word! In his appeal to God, Nehemiah:

a) Cited the promises of God, vv.8-9
His appeal was based on the promises of God. Nehemiah prayed intelligently. He knew the word of God, and cited Leviticus 26.33; Deuteronomy 4.25-27; 28.63-67; 30.1-5. God had certainly honoured the first of these three passages, and now, since there had been repentance and confession, Nehemiah calls upon Him to honour the fourth. As the "great and terrible God", He had judged His people. Now Nehemiah asks Him to act as the covenant-keeping and merciful God. The early church also quoted the word of God in prayer, and called upon Him to give them strength and boldness. See Acts 4.24-31. Then Nehemiah:

b) Claimed relationship with God, v.10
His appeal was based on relationship with God. "Now these are thy servants and thy people, whom thou hast redeemed by thy great power, and by thy strong hand". Nehemiah does not criticise God's people, but emphasises that as a redeemed people, they are God's "servants" and God's "people". They belong to Him. Then there was:

c) Companionship in prayer to God, v.11
"O Lord, I beseech thee, let now thine ear be attentive to the prayer of thy **servant**, and to the prayer of thy **servants**, who desire (*chaphets*, meaning 'delight') to fear thy name". There was fellowship in prayer, together with reverential awe: "Thy servants, who desire to fear thy name." Finally, Nehemiah was:

d) Clear in request to God, v.11
"Prosper, I pray thee, thy servant this day, and grant him mercy in the sight of **this man.** For I was the king's cupbearer". Nehemiah did not waffle: He came to God with a definite request. His prayer was focused. Although Artaxerxes was the Persian emperor, he was simply "this man" to Nehemiah. After all, Nehemiah was in touch with the "great and terrible God", and that put things into proper perspective. For the same reason, Micaiah was not in the least overawed when confronted by two kings (Ahab of Israel and Jehoshaphat of Judah) in royal

attire. He had seen "the Lord sitting on his throne, and all the host of heaven standing by him on his right hand and on his left" (1 Kings 22.19). A proper appreciation of the power and majesty of God will help us cope with the "fear of man" (Prov. 29.25).

We should notice that Nehemiah asked the Lord to hear and answer immediately: "let **now** thine ear be attentive...and prosper, I pray thee, thy servant **this day**, and grant him mercy in the sight of this man". There was a delay of between four and five months before Nehemiah's prayer was answered. But that did not mean that his prayer was unheard. Because **our** prayers are unanswered, that does not mean that they are unheard either! There were at least three reasons for the delay:

i) **Practical considerations.** The delay gave Nehemiah opportunity to prepare for the time when his prayer **would** be answered. We shall see from Chapter 2, that Nehemiah had not been idle in the intervening months. He obviously **expected** an answer!

ii) **Prophetic considerations.** God's timing was perfect! See Daniel 9.25, "Know therefore and understand, that from **the going forth of the commandment to restore and to build Jerusalem** unto the Messiah the Prince shall be seven weeks, and threescore and two weeks: the street shall be built again, **and the wall**, even in troublous times". God knew exactly when He would answer Nehemiah's prayer!

iii) **Personal considerations.** God wanted Nehemiah to be involved in the answer to his own prayer, and waited until circumstances were ideal. When the opportunity came, it could hardly be mistaken! It was a case of "assuredly gathering" (Acts 16.10) that this was a divinely-given opportunity.

READ CHAPTER 2

"So I prayed to the God of heaven"

Chapter 1 ends with Nehemiah in the presence of God: "Prosper, I pray thee, thy servant this day, and grant him mercy in the sight of this man". Chapter 2 commences with Nehemiah in the presence of the king, and his prayer is about to be answered. We cannot expect to stand successfully in the presence of men unless we have stood in the presence of God. Elijah was told to hide himself (1 Kings 17.3) before he was told to shew himself (1 Kings 18.1).

Nehemiah Chapter 2 may be divided as follows: *(1)* the opportunity he took (vv.1-8); *(2)* the obstacles he saw (vv.9-16); *(3)* the optimism he shewed (vv.17-18); *(4)* the opposition he met (vv.19-20).

1) THE OPPORTUNITY HE TOOK, vv.1-8
We must notice *(a)* his sorrow of heart (vv.1-3); *(b)* his prayer to God (v.4); *(c)* his request to the king (vv.5-8).

a) His sorrow of heart, vv.1-3
The Artaxerxes of Nehemiah, and of Ezra (see Ezra 7), is the Longimanus of secular history. There can be little doubt that he is also mentioned in Ezra 4, although it has been suggested that the king here, whilst bearing the name Artaxerxes, was actually the Cambyses of secular history. We should notice:

i) The **reality** of his sadness, v.1. Notice three occurrences of the word "sad" (vv.1,2,3). There was nothing cosmetic about his sadness! Nehemiah had been burdened about the situation in Jerusalem for four months (from Chisleu to Nisan), although he had not allowed this to show in the king's presence. He was consistent and single-minded in his concern. James tells us that "a double minded man is unstable in all his ways" (Jas. 1.8). We have already explored the reasons for the four-month delay in answering Nehemiah's prayer (see our previous study), but it is worth making the point here that prayer must be accompanied by patience. The well-known hymn makes the point perfectly:

Take time to be holy, let Him be thy Guide;
And **run not before Him**, whatever betide.

This may mean praying for a long time in some cases. We are urged to "continue (persevere) in prayer" (Col. 4.2). We read that "Isaac intreated the Lord for his wife, because she was barren: and the Lord was intreated of him, and Rebekah his wife conceived" (Gen. 25.21). It is only when we reach the words, "And Isaac was threescore years old when she bare them" (Gen. 25.26) that we realise that he must have prayed for twenty years! Compare vv.20,26. It was probably even longer before God said to Zacharias, "Thy prayer is heard; and thy wife Elisabeth shall bear thee a son" (Luke 1.13).

ii) The **reflection** of his sadness, v.2. Now, for the first time, Nehemiah's sadness showed whilst on duty: "I had not been beforetime sad in his presence" (v.1). While we know that God provided the opportunity for Nehemiah to speak to Artaxerxes, we are not told what triggered his sadness in the king's presence. Perhaps it was the time of year. After all, it was the month Nisan, otherwise known as Abib, and therefore Passover time, when Israel celebrated deliverance from Egypt. But now things were so different. God's people, once redeemed from Egypt, were again in captivity, and their beautiful city lay in ruins. It was enough to make any good Hebrew sad.

To his credit, Artaxerxes noticed Nehemiah's sadness, which is more than **we** do sometimes. We can be so insensitive. Perhaps Nehemiah's fear derived from the fact that he knew rebuilding work had once been halted by the decree of Artaxerxes himself, Ezra 4.7-23. However, it is clear that Nehemiah was no superman: like Elijah, he was "a man subject to like passions as we are" (Jas. 5.17). He was "sore afraid".

iii) The **reason** for his sadness, v.3. Nehemiah was courteous: "Let the king live for ever". But he went straight to the point! He stressed his personal concern, rather than any political reason, by referring to Jerusalem as "the place of my fathers' sepulchres", illustrating 1 Corinthians 12.26, "And whether one member suffer, all the members suffer with it".

b) His prayer to God, v.4
He spoke to God before he spoke to the king: "So I prayed to the God of heaven". We must remember that the man who could pray like this was the man who prayed at length in Chapter 1. He was prepared in heart and mind, and knew what it was to "pray without ceasing" (1 Thess. 5.17). He was therefore able to

pray with confidence at the critical moment. There was no time for bowed knees and closed eyes, and it certainly wasn't a 'set prayer!' But he gained immediate audience with the God of heaven. No doubt Nehemiah prayed in the spirit of Ephesians 6.19: "And for me, that utterance may be given unto me, that I may open my mouth boldly, to make known the mystery of the gospel".

c) His request to the king, vv.5-8

i)   He asked to be **sent,** vv.5-6.   Notice his courtesy and diplomacy. We sometimes lack these commodities. Peter urges us to be courteous (1 Pet. 3.8). Daniel refused to "defile himself with the portion of the king's meat", but he was courteous about it! See Daniel 1.11-13.

The man in touch with God made a large request, and moved the hand of the potentate! He requested *(i)* to be sent to Jerusalem, and *(ii)* to be allowed to build there. He was ready with his plans. Good planning is important in the Lord's work, provided that we ask for His guidance **first.** He that aims at nothing usually hits it! There can be no doubt that Nehemiah's excellent character gave weight to his request. Artaxerxes obviously held him in high esteem. After all, his visit to Jerusalem was a lot longer than two weeks' annual leave! We know that the wall took fifty-two days to rebuild (6.15). It was completed 25th Elul, i.e. in September, the sixth month. But don't forget travelling time. See Ezra 7.9. There were no airlines in those days! Whilst the total period covered by the book was evidently twelve years (5.14; 13.6), it does seem unlikely that this was the "time" (v.6) set for his return. As D.Kidner observes, "he is more likely to have reported back after the dedication of the walls, within the year, and then to have his appointment as governor renewed". This says a great deal for Nehemiah's reputation. "The whole interview gives the impression that it was Nehemiah's personal qualities that won him the right to speak and that gained his point, overriding all the political obstacles" (D.Kidner). We should also notice the fascinating words: "The **queen** (Newberry has 'wife' here: her name was *Damaspia,* according to Cyril J. Barber) also sitting by him". This could suggest that "the king's decision owed something to her influence" (D.Kidner), but perhaps it is another example of Nehemiah's courtesy. He acknowledged the presence of the queen. Good manners will enhance our testimony.

ii)   He asked for **security**, v.7. He knew about previous problems with the governors "beyond the river" (Ezra 4.17), and took care to ensure that those problems did not reoccur. It is one thing to deal with problems when they arise, but it's quite another to ensure that they don't arise in the first place! The king gave him far more than letters to the governors. He ended up with an escort:

"Now the king had sent captains of the army and horsemen with me" (v.9). Compare Ezra 8.22, but it would be quite unfair to say that Ezra was obviously more spiritual than Nehemiah! After all, Nehemiah did not ask for an escort, and in any case he had **not** said that the Lord would protect him: so he was not inconsistent in accepting an escort!

iii) He asked for **supplies**, v.8. Nehemiah was quite meticulous in planning: he even had a note of Asaph's name! We have an appropriate commentary on this in 1 Corinthians 14.40! Nehemiah requested suitable building materials, and we must use the same. See 1 Corinthians 3.10-13. We must notice that Nehemiah was **unassuming.** He recognised that the Lord had answered his prayer in v.4. It wasn't his own brilliant planning or superb diplomacy that secured the king's favour, rather "according to the good hand of **my God upon** me". God was glorified. Nehemiah was also **unselfish.** He put God's house **first,** and his own house last! Compare Haggai 1.4, where the Jews were putting their own houses first, and God's house **last!** We could add here that Nehemiah was **unsuspecting.** The command to rebuild Jerusalem marked the beginning of the 'seventy weeks prophecy' (Dan. 9.25-27). Nehemiah's prayer was answered beyond his wildest dreams!

2) THE OBSTACLES HE SAW, vv.9-16
God's work is almost inevitably accompanied by difficulties, as Paul knew: "a great door and effectual is opened unto me, and there are many adversaries" (1 Cor. 16.9). Nehemiah refers to *(a)* the resolute enemies (v.10); *(b)* the ruined city (vv.11-16).

a) The resolute enemies, v.10
"It grieved them exceedingly that there was come a man to seek the welfare of the children of Israel". This was the first evidence of opposition. It was going to get worse. The work of God always attracts enemy attention. Notice the way in which this develops throughout the book. Their annoyance here was followed by scorn (2.19), anger (4.1,7), threat of attack (4.11), and finally by craft and stealth (6.1-14). The enemy hibernates where there is lethargy and indolence amongst God's people, but leaps into action where there is work for God.

We now meet **Sanballat** the Horonite. The Elephantine papyri, dated 407BC, some years after the date of this chapter, refers to Sanballat as 'governor of Samaria'. He evidently came from Horonaim in Moab, although this has been questioned. See JND margin here. Then we have **Tobiah** the Ammonite. The arrival of Nehemiah was a serious threat to these two men. A man had come to "seek the welfare of the children of Israel", and that could only mean the lessening of their own power and influence. Perhaps they remembered what happened years before when Zerubbabel flatly refused to liaise with the "adversaries of Judah and Benjamin" (Ezra 4.1-3). It is worth remembering that Nehemiah had come to "seek the welfare of the children of Israel" by building! We can always expect opposition when we build for God. Faithfulness to God always gives concern to the enemy. "Marvel not, my brethren, if the world hate you" (1 John 3.13). Have **we** made it clear that the interests of God and His people are our business in life?

It is worth thinking again about the ancestry of Sanballat and Tobiah. Had Abram completely obeyed the word of God, and left his "country...kindred, and... father's house" (Gen. 12.1), Moab and Ammon would not have been born (Gen. 19.30-38). But "Lot went with him" (Gen. 12.4). Incomplete obedience has dire results for us, and for other people. But there was a third enemy. We are introduced to **Geshem** the Arabian in v.19. He was descended from Ishmael whose mother was Hagar, an Egyptian (Gen. 16.1). Did Sarai obtain Hagar in Egypt? If so, we have another sad lesson from Abram's life. That stay in Egypt had disastrous results, and they are still with us today. Witness the current Middle East situation. Let us be warned!

b) The ruined city, vv.11-16
Nehemiah faced the facts! He was completely different to the man described by the Lord Jesus: "This man began to build, and was not able to finish" (Luke 14.28-30). We should notice the following:

i) **The interval** before surveying the ruins, v.11. "So I came to Jerusalem, and was there three days". Nehemiah took his time: he didn't act like 'a bull in a china shop!'

ii) **The intention** of Nehemiah, v.12. While he acted quietly in order to avoid raising people's hopes and expectations, he was quite settled and confident in his heart: "Neither told I any man what **my God** had put in my heart". Nehemiah acted in fellowship with God.

iii) **The inspection** of the walls and gates, vv.13-16. Nehemiah did not accept a second hand or garbled report. He verified his facts. That is always a very wise thing to do! Be sure of your ground. It gave Nehemiah the authority to speak when the time came. His case would have been severely eroded if he had expressed "half-formed ideas piecemeal to every acquaintance" (D.Kidner).

Nehemiah did not even publicise his mission as soon as he had verified the facts. He waited for the right moment to show his hand (v.16). Notice too that he made his survey "by night". He was willing to forego his sleep. There is a silent aspect to service for God. We know that Nehemiah looked at the ruined wall and gates objectively. Some people enjoy seeing what is wrong, but they have no enthusiasm when it comes to putting things right!

It is now necessary to consult the accompanying map! (see page 121). As you can see, Nehemiah commenced his inspection on the west side of the city. He emerged from the Valley Gate, turned left towards the south where the Dung Gate was located (the Valley Gate and the Dung Gate were about 500 yards apart), and so round to the Fountain Gate on the eastern side. He was then forced to dismount and proceed on foot a little way up the eastern side of the city before returning to the Valley Gate.

3) THE OPTIMISM HE SHOWED, vv.17-18
Amongst other things, we should notice here *(a)* Nehemiah's exhortation (v.17), together with *(b)* his experience (v.18) and *(c)* his effect (v.18).

a) His exhortation, v.17
Nehemiah was realistic, but his realism did not mean inactivity. "Then said I unto them, Ye see the distress that we are in, how Jerusalem lieth waste, and the gates thereof are burned with fire: come, and let us build up the wall of Jerusalem, that we be no more a reproach". He was thoroughly aware of the problems, and identified himself with them: "Ye see the distress that *we* (not 'you') are in". It is very important to face facts in the service of God. There is no mileage in trying to ignore them. But Nehemiah was also thoroughly aware of the power of God (vv.18,20). He pleaded for action: "Let *us* (not 'let you') build up the wall of Jerusalem". He followed the excellent example of Haggai and Zechariah (Ezra 5.2). The future governor of Jerusalem was willing to 'roll up his sleeves' with everybody else. He would have entirely agreed that elders should be "ensamples to the flock" (1 Pet. 5.3) His zeal was fuelled by the fact that Jerusalem was "a reproach". It should have been known as "the joy of the whole earth" and "the city of the great King" (Psalm 48.2).

c) His experience, v.18
"Then I told them of the hand of my God which was good upon me; as also the king's words that he had spoken unto me". Notice the order: God first: then the king. It was a case of 'cause and effect!' He had already experienced God's help and guidance.

c) His effect, v.18

Enthusiasm is infectious. The people responded: "Let us rise up and build". The test of leadership qualities is whether or not people follow. But words can be cheap, and the old proverb says: "After all is said and done, there's more that's said than done!" But not here: "So they strengthened their hands for this good work". Building for God is always "good work". Notice the expressions "so I" and "so we" in Nehemiah (see, for example, 2.4; 2.11; 4.6, 4.21).

4) THE OPPOSITION HE MET, vv.19-20

Attention is drawn to *(a)* the contempt of the enemy (v.19); *(b)* the confidence of Nehemiah (v.20); *(c)* the claim rejected (v.20).

a) The contempt of the enemy, v.19

Enemy concern (v.10) now becomes mockery: "They laughed us to scorn, and despised us, and said, What is this thing that ye do? will ye rebel against the king?" As D.Kidner observes, with Geshem now involved, "Judah was virtually encircled, and the war of nerves had begun!" They despised the **people**: "they laughed **us** to scorn". But they did not see the invisible God. They despised the **work**: "What is this **thing** that ye do?" The enemy uses the same tactics today. He will endeavour to stop our service for God by telling us that we're not really accomplishing anything, and it's all a waste of time! The enemy also threw in the threat of misrepresentation: "Will ye rebel against the king?" This implied the possibility of some kind of trumped-up charge, and was all part of the war of nerves. Paul knew something about this kind of thing: "as we be slanderously reported, and as some affirm that we say" (Rom. 3.8).

b) The confidence of Nehemiah, v.20

"Then answered I them, and said unto them, The God of heaven, he will prosper us". Jehoshaphat was equally confident: "O our God, wilt thou not judge them? for we have no might against this great company that cometh against us; neither know we what to do: but our eyes are upon thee" (2 Chron. 20.12). So was Hezekiah: "Be strong and courageous, be not afraid nor dismayed for the king of Assyria, nor for all the multitude that is with him: for there be more with us than with him: with him is an arm of flesh; but with us is the Lord our God to help us, and to fight our battles" (2 Chron. 32.7-8). In New Testament language, "If God be for us, who can be against us?" (Rom. 8.31). Compare the words, "**He will** prosper us", and, "**we...will** arise and build". In the first place, we have **God's** resources: in the second, we have **our** responsibilities. We are without excuse!

c) The claim rejected, v.20

All claims on Jerusalem by the enemy were thrown out of court. There would be no compromise. "Ye have no portion (present), nor right (future), nor memorial (past), in Jerusalem". See Deuteronomy 23.3. Nehemiah was a worthy successor of Zerubbabel and his colleagues who said, "Ye have nothing to do with us to build an house unto our God; but we ourselves together will build unto the Lord God of Israel" (Ezra 4.3). After all, "What fellowship hath righteousness with unrighteousness? and what communion hath light with darkness? and what concord hath Christ with Belial? or what part hath he that believeth with an infidel? And what agreement hath the temple of God with idols?" (2 Cor. 6.14-18).

Jerusalem's Wall in Nehemiah's Day

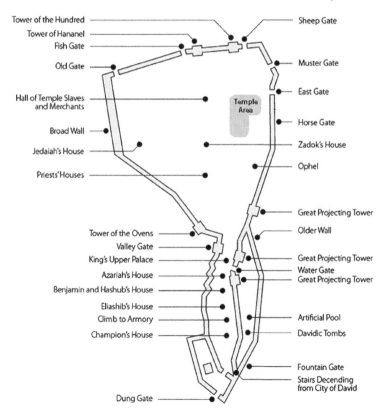

READ CHAPTER 3

"And they builded"

Nehemiah faced a daunting task. We can get some idea of the situation from Sanballat's question, "Will they revive the stones out of the heaps of the rubbish which are burned?" (4.2) But Nehemiah was a man of great conviction. It was more than dogged determination. He knew that he was carrying out the will of God: "Neither told I any man what **my God had put in my heart to do at Jerusalem**" (2.12). It was that conviction that prompted him to say to the people, "Let us build up the wall of Jerusalem". The response was admirable, "And they said, Let us rise up and build. So they strengthened their hands for this good work". Opposition in the form of laughter and scorn left Nehemiah undaunted: "The God of heaven, he will prosper us; therefore we his servants will arise and build" (2.17-20), and it was not a case of 'after all that's said and done, there's more that's said than done!' In Chapter 3, the work of rebuilding commences.

Cyril J. Barber (*Nehemiah and the Dynamics of Effective Leadership*) calls this chapter, "The Formula for Success", and says "The problem we face as we look at this chapter - at the long list of names - is that we are tempted to turn the page and continue the story at Nehemiah 4. Yet this chapter is one of the most important in the entire book! By noting repetitious statements, certain vitally important principles emerge. From these principles we will learn the secret of Nehemiah's success". We must therefore notice *(1)* the co-ordination of the work; *(2)* the co-operation in the work; *(3)* the commendation of the work; *(4)* the completion of the work.

1) THE CO-ORDINATION OF THE WORK
Recurring phrases in the chapter make it very clear that there was nothing haphazard about the work. It was not a case of everybody 'doing their own thing'. There was an overall plan. Nehemiah did not 'hope it would happen': he 'made it happen!'

a) "Next unto him", or "next unto them": "after him", or "after them"
Everybody was working! The work involved fellowship, but it also involved

integration. All had to work in view of each other. Otherwise there could have been some dangerous gaps in the wall! Quite obviously, Nehemiah "must have planned his strategy well. He knew where each person or group would work, and he assigned the men from Tekoa, Gibeon, Jericho and Mizpah etc., to sections of the wall where no residents were close at hand" (C.J. Barber). Everybody knew where they belonged, and everybody knew their particular responsibilities. Some people were required to rebuild sections of the wall from scratch, and some people were required to undertake repairs. For some, it was a case of labouring on their own doorstep. Others had a wider brief. See, for example, Hanun and the inhabitants of Zanoah, who rebuilt the valley gate and "a thousand cubits (something over a quarter mile) on the wall unto the dung gate" (v.13). Whether it was a small project, or a large project, **everything was vital.** But everybody knew what his work entailed. This superbly illustrates Romans 12.6-8 and 1 Corinthians 14.40! Nehemiah coordinated his workmen in the same way that the Holy Spirit coordinates activities in the local assembly. See 1 Corinthians 12.4-11.

b) "Over against his house" or "over against their house"
"Nehemiah took advantage of convenience (see vv.10,23,29,30). He did not have people 'commuting' from one end of Jerusalem to the other. This would have wasted time, and reduced efficiency" (C.J. Barber.) He continues, "By arranging for each man to work close to his own home, Nehemiah made it easy for them to get to work, to be sustained while on the job, and to safeguard those who were nearest and dearest to them. This relieved each worker of unnecessary anxiety. It also ensured that each person would put his best effort into what he was doing". As J.Sidlow Baxter observes: "Nehemiah set each of the forty-two different work-groups to work on that part of the wall which was nearest to where its members themselves lived. This gave them a special interest in the work. *Our first obligation for Christ is always to our own neighbourhood*". This statement may not be completely accurate, bearing in mind help received from elsewhere, but the principle is absolutely right!

2) THE CO-OPERATION IN THE WORK
Men from different places and different walks of life worked together on the wall. There were groups: for example, "the men of Jericho" (v.2); the Tekoites (v.5). There were individuals: men and women (v.12). There were priests and Levites (vv.1,17,22,28). There were rulers (vv.9,12,14,15,16,17,18). There were professional men: the goldsmiths (vv.8, 31), the apothecaries (v.8), the merchants (v.32). There were ordinary people: lesser known people. But all were known to God. It was a case of "*labourers together*" (1 Cor. 3.9), and "*with one mind striving together*" (Phil. 1.27). We must remember that while we should

recognise job titles, professional qualifications, and other distinctions *in the world,* all these disappear in the assembly. We are simply "brethren in Christ" (Col. 1.2). Let's take a closer look at them. There were:

a) The priestly men

The priests might have absolved themselves from responsibility for working on the wall by pleading their involvement with sacred things. But they actually took the lead in the rebuilding programme! "Then Eliashib (meaning 'God will restore' or 'Whom God restored') the high priest rose up with his brethren the priests, and they builded the sheep gate (without locks and bars); they sanctified it, and set up the doors of it; even unto the tower of Meah they sanctified it, unto the tower of Hananeel" (v.1). The priests did not consider such manual work 'beneath their dignity!' There is something wrong with the Bible teacher who has little or no interest in Gospel and Sunday School work, and the public preacher who would never think of distributing tracts. There's also something wrong with the preacher who considers that it isn't his business to lend a hand with some of the less glamorous jobs in assembly life. Let's remember that the Lord Jesus washed His disciples' feet.

Having commended Eliashib and his brethren for taking the initiative in the work of reconstruction, it is sobering to notice that in Nehemiah's absence, he provided accommodation in the temple for Tobiah the Ammonite: "And before this, Eliashib the priest, having the oversight of the chamber of the house of our God, was allied unto Tobiah: and he had prepared for him a great chamber, where aforetime they laid the meat offerings, the frankincense, and the vessels, and the tithes of the corn, the new wine, and the oil" (13.4-5). Nehemiah describes this as "evil": "And I came to Jerusalem, and understood of the evil that Eliashib did for Tobiah, in preparing him a chamber in the courts of the house of God" (13.7). It is hardly surprising that one of his grandsons married the daughter of Sanballat! (13.28).

So the man who led the people in building the wall to keep Tobiah out, provided a haven for him in the temple! It could be said of him, as it could be said, sadly, of so many: "Ye did run well" (Gal. 5.7).

b) The ruling men

Various rulers worked on the wall. There was "Rephaiah the son of Hur, the ruler of the half part of Jerusalem" (v.9), and "Shallum the son of Halohesh, the ruler of the half part of Jerusalem" (v.12). The word translated "ruler" here, is usually translated "prince" in the Old Testament, although it has no royal implication. Rephaiah and Shallum were certainly "ensamples to the flock" (1 Pet. 5.3). But rulers from Beth-haccerem (v.14), Mizpah (v.15), Beth-zur (v.16), and Keilah (v.17) laboured as well. Even rulers didn't consider it *infra dig* to get stuck into the work!

But Nehemiah did not succeed in motivating **all** the leaders: "And next unto them the Tekoites repaired; but **their nobles** put not their necks to the work of their Lord" (v.5). It seems that there will always be **some** of the Lord's people who just don't want to get involved, or at best, will only do the job half-heartedly. But it's particularly sad when those people like to be known as leaders. Some people like to be 'on the oversight', but do very little in the assembly. Paul urged the Thessalonians to "know them which **labour** among you, and are over you in the Lord, and admonish you; and to esteem them very highly in love for their **work's** sake" (1 Thess. 5.12-13).

Nehemiah uses two very significant expressions in describing the Tekoite nobles. The name means 'the sound of a trumpet', perhaps indicating that they were watchmen (Jer. 6.1), in which case it was a rather poor outlook with watchmen like them on the walls! We must notice that **(i)** "Their nobles put not their **necks** to the work of their Lord". D.Kidner (*The Tyndale Old Testament Commentaries: Ezra and Nehemiah*) calls this "a glimpse of petty pride rather than half-heartedness. The unbending neck is a standard picture of this unbiddable attitude". See Psalm 75.5, "Lift not up your horn on high: speak not with a stiff neck". Compare Romans 16.3-4, "Greet Priscilla and Aquila my helpers in Christ Jesus: who have for my sake laid down ('staked', with a margin note, 'risked, hazarded', JND) their own necks ('neck', singular, JND)". Priscilla and Aquila were willing to expose themselves to risk for Paul's sake, but the Tekoite nobles were not prepared to risk anything. We must also notice that **(ii)** "Their nobles put not their necks to the **work** of their Lord". They were rather like Peter when he said "Not so, Lord!" (Acts 10.14), which was a contradiction in terms if there was ever one! It is all too easy to pay lip-service to the Lord Jesus, and leave it there. He said, "Why call ye me, Lord, Lord, and do not the things which I say?" (Luke 6.46).

In view of the bad example of their nobles, it is most gratifying to notice that the Tekoites didn't stop work. They laboured between Zadok (v.4) and Jehoiada who, with Meshullam repaired the old gate (v.6). But they also "repaired **another piece**, over against the great tower that lieth out, even unto the wall of Ophel" (v.27)! The Tekoites put their nobles to shame. It might be opportune to say here that in some assemblies, the leadership leaves a lot to be desired, but that does not mean to say that everybody else is therefore entitled to 'throw in the towel', and do nothing. The Tekoites followed the example of one of their noblest sons who described himself as "among the herdmen of Tekoa" (Amos 1.1). Amos was quite prepared to put himself at risk (Amos 7.10-17). He wasn't amongst the nobility of Tekoa, but he was certainly amongst God's nobility!

The Gibeonites (v.7) certainly weren't 'ruling men'. They were "hewers of wood and drawers of water for the congregation" (Joshua 9.27), but they had a heart for the work. Their menial status did not become an excuse.

c) The professional men
"Next unto him repaired Uzziel the son of Harhaiah, of the **goldsmiths** (see also v.31). Next unto him also repaired Hananiah the son of one of the **apothecaries**, and they fortified Jerusalem unto the broad wall" (v.8). Like the priests, "the goldsmiths might have excused themselves. After all, they were used to intricate and delicate work: not the clumsy, cumbersome task of laying bricks" (C.J. Barber). (Don't quote C.J. Barber to a bricklayer!). The same could be said of the apothecaries. We call them 'pharmacists' today! For an example of their fine work, see Exodus 30.22-25, "And thou shalt make it an oil of holy ointment, an ointment compound after the art of the apothecary". There is a further example of "the art of the apothecary" in Exodus 30.34-38.

So men laboured who were used to priestly work, precious work, and perfumed work, but they were not afraid to get their hands dirty!

d) The merchant men
"And between the going up of the corner unto the sheep gate repaired the goldsmiths and the **merchants**" (v.32). Like the goldsmiths and the apothecaries, the merchants were willing to leave their business interests in order to help on the wall. It would be quite wrong to infer from this that we should all leave our employment in the interests of the Lord's work. He does call some believers to do this: some on a permanent basis, and some on a short-term basis. On the other hand, He does require us to put His interests first in our lives. Business and career can buy us body, mind, and soul, if we let them. This does not mean that we should be anything less than reliable, diligent, and dedicated as employees. But we must remember the words, "No man that warreth (on active service) **entangleth** himself with the affairs of this life; that he may please him who hath chosen him to be a soldier" (2 Tim. 2.4). There's all the difference in the world between being **involved** "with the affairs of this life", and being "**entangled**" in them! Sadly, the well-known hymn sometimes applies to Christians too:

Room for pleasure, room for business;
But for Christ the crucified -
Not a place where He can enter
In the heart for which He died?

e) The labouring women

"And next unto him repaired Shallum the son of Halohesh, the ruler of the half part of Jerusalem, he and **his daughters**" (v.12). Compare Philippians 4.3, "And I entreat thee also, true yokefellow, help those women which **laboured with me** in the gospel". See also Romans 16.12, "Salute Tryphena and Tryphosa, who **labour in the Lord.** Salute the beloved Persis, which **laboured much in the Lord**". Phebe is described as "a servant of the church which is at Cenchrea" (Rom. 16.1). While the Scriptures totally reject 'unisex', they do make it clear that the service of sisters is of immense value. We should never place restrictions on sisters (or brothers) other than those imposed by the word of God.

In the New Testament Paul employs the analogy of the human body to describe assembly diversity and harmony. Every member is necessary, however different in form and function: "And the eye cannot say unto the hand, I have no need of thee: nor again the head to the feet, I have no need of you" (1 Cor. 12.21). In Nehemiah 3 we have diversity yet unity. We must do all we can to ensure that this example of co-operation between so many different types of people is followed in the local assembly.

3) THE COMMENDATION OF THE WORK

Nehemiah took a keen interest in his labourers. He knew their names, where they worked, and what they did. They were not just people with National Insurance numbers, or numbers on a computerised pay-roll! Notice his eye for detail, and his tacit commendation: "Malchijah the son of Harim, and Hashub the son of Pahathmoab, repaired the **other piece** ('a second piece', JND), and the tower of the furnaces" (v.11). "And next to him repaired Ezer the son of Jeshua, the ruler of Mizpah, **another piece** over against the going up to the armoury at the turning of the wall. After him Baruch the son of Zabbai earnestly repaired the **other piece** ('another piece', JND), from the turning of the wall unto the door of the house of Eliashib the high priest" (vv.19-20). See also vv.24,27,30. We might have expected Nehemiah to praise Hanun and the inhabitants of Zanoah. After all, they repaired fifteen hundred feet of broken-down wall (v.13). But right next to them was Malchiah who apparently worked alone in repairing the dung gate (v.14). As C.J. Barber observes, "Nehemiah commended Malchiah's honest effort as well. He did not allow the size of one person's accomplishments to prevent him from recognising the efforts of another".

But Nehemiah also noticed, and commended, **how** the work was done. "After him Baruch the son of Zabbai **earnestly** repaired the other piece ('a second piece', JND margin), from the turning of the wall unto the door of the house of Eliashib the high priest" (v.20). That would be a very nice testimony to have! There was nothing nominal about Paul's service either: "God is my witness, whom I serve **with my spirit** in the gospel of his Son" (Rom. 1.9). We must not forget that "all things are naked and opened unto the eyes of him with whom we have to do" (Heb. 4.13), and that when the Lord Jesus comes, He will "bring to light the hidden things of darkness, and will make manifest the counsels of the hearts: and then shall every man have **praise of God**", (1 Cor. 4.5).

4) THE COMPLETION OF THE WORK
It has been pointed out that the words "built" and "repaired" are in the perfect tense, which means that each person completed the task assigned to him. As C.J.Barber observes, "Each one knew what was expected of him. Each one worked in his place. And each one finished the work he had undertaken". As we will see in the following chapters, the work was far from easy: "Without were fightings (Chapter 4), within were fears (Chapter 5)" (2 Cor. 7.5). But the "wall was finished in the twenty and fifth day of the month Elul, in fifty and two days" (6.15).

Centuries later, Paul addressed Archippus with the words, "Take heed to the ministry which thou hast received in the Lord, that thou fulfil it" (Col. 4.17). Nehemiah's workmen completed the task. We must have the same resolution and determination.

In our next study, we will discuss the significance of the gates.

READ CHAPTER 3 AGAIN

The gates

"The Lord loveth **the gates of Zion** more than all the dwellings of Jacob" (Psalm 87.2). Like "the holy Jerusalem, descending out of heaven from God" (Rev. 21.10), earthly Jerusalem had twelve gates. Ten of them are mentioned in this chapter: the **sheep** gate (vv.1,32), the **fish** gate (v.3), the **old** gate (v.6), the **valley** gate (v.13), the **dung** gate (v.14), the **fountain** gate (v.15), the **water** gate (v.26), the **horse** gate (v.28), the **east** gate (v.29), and the **Miphkad** gate (v.31). Two further gates are mentioned later: the "gate of **Ephraim**" (8.16), and the "**prison** gate" (12.39). While we must be careful not to let our imagination run riot, the names of the gates, and the order in which they occur, remind us of important Bible teaching. If "the Lord loveth the gates of Zion", we ought to reflect on their significance. Boaz was sitting in the gate of Bethlehem when he said, "Ho, such a one! turn aside, sit down here" (Ruth 4.1). **We** must now "turn aside" and "sit down" in the gates of Jerusalem.

But we are certainly not going to "sit down" and look at the scenery. The gates were places of praise. David prayed: "Have mercy upon me, O Lord; consider my trouble which I suffer of them that hate me, thou that liftest me up from the gates of death: that I may shew forth **all thy praise in the gates of the daughter of Zion**: I will rejoice in thy salvation" (Psalm 9.13-14). When "the Redeemer shall come to Zion" (Isa. 59.20), the city will be transformed. Isaiah 60 describes its millennial glory: "Arise, shine; for thy light is come, and the glory of the Lord is risen upon thee...thou shalt call thy walls Salvation, and **thy gates Praise**" (vv.1,18). (Do read the **whole** chapter). **We** shall find good cause for praise as we visit the:

1) THE SHEEP GATE, v.1
The chapter, and the work, begins and ends with the **sheep gate** (vv.1, 32). The whole project was undertaken with reference to this gate. It is mentioned in the New Testament: "Now there is in Jerusalem, at **the sheepgate** ('sheep market', AV), a pool, which is called in Hebrew, Bethesda, having five porches"

(John 5.2, JND). It was through this gate that the sheep destined for sacrifice were brought. We are immediately reminded that the Lord Jesus was "brought as *a lamb* to the slaughter, and as a sheep before her shearers is dumb, so he openeth not his mouth" (Isa. 53.7). This verse is cited in the New Testament, but the order is reversed: "He was led as *a sheep* to the slaughter; and like a lamb dumb before his shearer, so opened he not his mouth" (Acts 8.32). It has been pointed out that it would be nothing short of barbaric to shear a lamb, and the words have been reversed to make this very point. The Lord Jesus was treated with the utmost cruelty.

Israel's calendar began with the Passover: "And the Lord spake unto Moses and Aaron in the land of Egypt, saying, This month shall be unto you the beginning of months: it shall be the first month of the year to you" (Exod. 12.1-2). The passover lamb was to be "without blemish, a male of the first year: ye shall take it out from the sheep, or from the goats" (Exod. 12.5). We are reminded that "Christ our passover is sacrificed for us" (1 Cor. 5.7). For Israel, and for us, everything begins with the blood of the Lamb. We cannot proceed with our tour of the gates, unless we have visited the sheep gate: "And almost all things are by the law purged with blood; and **without shedding of blood is no remission**" (Heb. 9.22). We have good cause to sit in the sheep gate and say with David, "I will rejoice in Thy salvation" (Psalm 9.14):

> The blood of Christ, Thy spotless Lamb,
> O God, is all my plea;
> Nought else could for my sin atone;
> I have no merit of my own
> Which I can bring to Thee.

It is most significant that while "locks" and "bars" are mentioned in connection with the next five gates (see vv.3,6,13,14,15), they are not mentioned in connection with the sheep gate. This reminds us that salvation is free to all: the Gospel message proclaims that "whosoever will may come". It also reminds us that the Lord Jesus is the "door of the sheep" (John 10.7).

We meet the high priest and the priests at the sheep gate: "Then Eliashib the high priest rose up with his brethren the priests, and they builded the sheep gate; they sanctified it, and set up the doors of it; even unto the tower of Meah they sanctified it, unto the tower of Hananeel (see Jer. 31.38)" (v.1). The word "sanctified" is only used in connection with the sheep gate. The death of Christ is sacred. But like the gate itself, every effort has been made to destroy the significance and value of His death. In Christendom, the "sheep gate" has been "burned with fire" (1.3), but His work cannot be overthrown. As our great high priest, the Lord Jesus has "not entered into the holy places made with hands, which are the figures of the true; but into heaven itself, now to appear in the presence of God for us" (Heb. 9.24). Our great high priest serves in virtue of His perfect sacrifice. A greater than Elishib is here! But that is not all. The priests are called Eliashib's "brethren", and the Lord Jesus is 'not ashamed to call **us** brethren' (Heb. 2.11). As priests, we can stand in the sheep gate and "offer the sacrifice of **praise** to God continually, that is, the fruit of our lips giving thanks to his name" (Heb. 13.15).

2) THE FISH GATE, v.3

If the sheep gate reminds us that the Lord Jesus gave His life for us, then the fish gate reminds us that we should give our lives for Him. He said, "Follow me, and I will make you fishers of men" (Matt. 4.19). It has been observed that the believers at Thessalonica kept their fish gate in good repair: "For from you sounded out the word of the Lord not only in Macedonia and Achaia, but also in every place your faith to God-ward is spread abroad" (1 Thess. 1.8). One day, the Saviour will say, "Bring of the fish which **ye** have now caught" (John 21.10). He still says to us, "Launch out into the deep, and let down your nets for a draught" (Luke 5.4). Perhaps we feel exactly like Simon: "Master, we have toiled all the night, and have taken nothing", but that did not prevent him from continuing: "Nevertheless at thy word **I will** let down the net" (Luke 5.5). Like Peter, we must be 'willing in the day of His power' (Psalm 110.3).

It is significant that between this gate and the next, we encounter the Tekoites whose nobles "put not their necks to the work of their Lord" (v.5). See our comments in the previous study.

3) THE OLD GATE, v.6

"The Preacher" said that there was "no new thing under the sun" (Eccl. 1.9), and we must not forget this in our service for God as "fishers of men". Paul insisted that the Galatians stood in "the old gate": "But though we, or an angel from heaven, preach any other gospel unto you than that which we have preached unto you, let him be accursed" (Gal. 1.8). It is important to remember that the original teaching is the right teaching. It is a mark of a false teacher that he goes beyond what is written: "Whosoever goes forward and abides not in the doctrine of the Christ has not God" (2 John v.9, JND). The false teacher always knows better than Scripture, and always has something new to say. He ignores the solemn teaching of Deuteronomy 4.2, "Ye shall **not add** unto the word which I command you, neither shall ye **diminish** ought from it, that ye may keep the commandments of the Lord your God which I command you". See also Proverbs 30.5-6, "Every word of God is pure: he is a shield unto them that put their trust in him. **Add thou not unto his words**, lest he reprove thee, and thou be found a liar". Compare Revelation 22.18-19. Peter insisted that his readers stood in "the old gate": "Wherefore I will not be negligent to put you always in remembrance of these things, though ye know them, and be established in the present truth" (2 Pet. 1.12).

We must stand in "the old gate", and we must walk in "the old paths": see Jeremiah 6.16, "Thus saith the Lord, Stand ye in the ways, and see, and ask for the old paths, where is the good way, and walk therein, and ye shall find rest for your souls". Jeremiah also refers to them as "the ancient paths" (18.15). But there are some "old paths" which we must not take! We must never forget that "if any man be in Christ, he is a new creature: **old things** are passed away; behold, all things are become new" (2 Cor. 5.17).

4) THE VALLEY GATE, v.13

Some people are very proud of their orthodoxy! Their adherence to "the old paths" gives them a sense of superiority. The "valley gate" is therefore a very important place. We all need to "walk humbly" with God (Micah 6.8). Paul puts it like this: "For I say, through the grace given unto me, to every man that is among you, not to think of himself more highly than he ought to think; but to think soberly, according as God hath dealt to every man the measure of faith" (Rom. 12.3). Peter puts it like this: "Yea, all of you be subject one to another, and be clothed with humility: for God resisteth the proud, and giveth grace to the humble. Humble yourselves therefore under the mighty hand of God, that he may exalt you in due time" (1 Pet. 5.5-6). The Lord Jesus exemplified this *par excellence*: see Philippians 2.5-11. It is in the "valley gate" that fellowship is promoted; "Let nothing be done through strife or vainglory; but **in lowliness of mind** let each esteem other better than themselves" (Phil. 2.3).

The valley gate also reminds us of Psalm 23: "Yea, though I walk through the **valley** of the shadow of death, I will fear no evil: for thou art with me" (v.4). The valley gate was near the "tower of the furnaces", and service for God often brings us into the valley of opposition and persecution. He is with us too when death casts its shadow over our pathway. But opposition and difficulty do have a cleansing and purifying affect in our lives. See 1 Peter 1.7. We are told that a refiner would remove the dross from the crucible, until he could see a clear reflection of his face in the molten metal. The removal of the dross in our lives brings us to the dung gate. The city refuse went out through this gate.

5) THE DUNG GATE, v.14

This gate also reminds us that if we are going to serve God as "fishers of men", we need a similar gate in our lives: "Having therefore these promises, dearly beloved, let us **cleanse ourselves** from all filthiness of the flesh and spirit, perfecting holiness in the fear of God" (2 Cor. 7.1); "Let us **lay aside** every weight, and the sin which doth so easily beset us" (Heb. 12.1). This necessitates the practice of 1 John 1.9, "If we confess our sin**s** (notice it is "sins" here: each one of them), he is faithful and just to forgive us our sins, and to **cleanse us** from all unrighteousness".

Paul referred to the "dung gate" when describing his conversion: "Yea doubtless, and I count all things but loss for the excellency of the knowledge of Christ Jesus my Lord: for whom I have suffered the loss of all things, and do count them but dung ('filth', JND), that I may win Christ ('have Christ to my gain', JND margin)" (Phil. 3.8). We have the "dung gate" again in 2 Timothy 2.21: "If a man therefore purge himself from these (see vv.16-17), he shall be a vessel unto honour, sanctified, and meet for the master's use, and prepared unto every good work".

6) THE FOUNTAIN GATE, v.15

The "fountain gate" follows "the dung gate" in the same way that the enjoyment of the Holy Spirit's ministry in our lives is dependent upon daily cleansing from sin. Springing water in Scripture is a picture of the Holy Spirit. See John 7.38-39, "He that believeth on me, as the scripture hath said, out of his belly ('inner man') shall flow rivers of living water. (But this spake he of the Spirit, which they that believe on him should receive: for the Holy Ghost was not yet given; because that Jesus was not yet glorified)". There will be no "fountain gate" in our lives if we grieve the Holy Spirit. See Ephesians 4.30. The surrounding verses explain that we can grieve Him with "corrupt communication...bitterness...wrath...anger...clamour....evil speaking...malice". To the "dung gate" with it!

7) THE WATER GATE, v.26

If springing water in Scripture describes the Holy Spirit, then still water describes the word of God: "Christ also loved the church, and gave himself for it; that he might sanctify and cleanse it with the washing of water by the word" (Eph. 5.25-26). It was therefore most appropriate that the reading of the law in Chapter 8 took place in "the street that was before the **water gate**!" Still water symbolises the cleansing power of the word of God: "Wherewithal shall a young man cleanse his way? by taking heed thereto according to **thy word**" (Psalm 119.9). But the word of God is also preventative: "**Thy word** have I hid in mine heart, that I might not sin against thee" (Psalm 119.11). The word of God cleanses us when we **apply its teaching**.

In John 13, the Lord Jesus washed His disciples' feet, and overruled Peter's objection by saying, "If I wash thee not, thou hast no part **with** me" (v.8). It is vital to notice that the Lord Jesus did say, 'Thou hast no part **in** me'. He was not talking about salvation here, but about fellowship with Him. Sin interrupts fellowship with Him, and must be cleansed before that fellowship can be restored. We must let the Lord Jesus wash **our feet** by allowing Him to apply the word of God to our lives, and that means reading the Scriptures every day. Our lives have dark corners that need spiritual spring-cleaning, and once we have dealt with them by confession, we are assured of cleansing and renewed communion with Him. The priests had to use the laver constantly (see Exodus 30.17-21), and **we** need the cleansing of God's word constantly.

8) THE HORSE GATE, v.28
The "horse gate" reminds us that life is not a play-ground, but a battle-ground. We are required to "fight the good fight of faith" (1 Tim. 6.12). The horse is the symbol of warfare. God was obliged to reprove backsliding Israel with the words, "What have I done? every one turned to his course, as the **horse rusheth into the battle**" (Jer. 8.6). See also Revelation 19.11: "And I saw heaven opened, and behold a white horse; and he that sat upon him was called Faithful and True, and in righteousness he doth judge and **make war**". The horse gate therefore reminds us of conflict, and that we are engaged in spiritual warfare. We will only be fit for battle if we heed the teaching of the previous gates! God is looking for humble (the "valley gate"), clean (the "dung gate"), and Spirit-filled (the "fountain gate") warriors. (Don't forget the other gates either).

9) THE EAST GATE, v.29
Paul was acutely conscious of the spiritual battle when writing 2 Corinthians 4. Notice what he says: "We are troubled on every side, yet not distressed; we are perplexed, but not in despair; persecuted, but not forsaken; cast down, but not destroyed" (vv.8-9). But he continues: "For our light affliction, which is but for a moment, worketh for us a far more exceeding and eternal weight of **glory**" (v.17). Paul was standing in the "east gate!" The east has strong associations with the coming of the Lord. See, for example, Ezekiel 43.1-2, where the prophet was brought by God "to the gate, even the gate that looketh toward the **east**: and, behold, the glory of the God of Israel came from the way of the east: and his voice was like a noise of many waters: and the earth shined with his glory". Israel's hope is connected with the east: "But unto you that fear my name shall the **Sun of righteousness** arise with healing in his wings" (Mal. 4.2). While our hope is connected with Christ as "the bright and morning Star" (Rev. 22.16), rather than Christ as the "Sun of righteousness", we do "rejoice in hope of the

glory of God" (Rom. 5.2), and look "for that blessed hope, and the glorious appearing of the great God and our Saviour Jesus Christ" (Titus 2.13).

10) THE MIPHKAD GATE, v.31

"Miphkad" means 'review' or 'appointment': a 'place of meeting'. The Companion Bible gives the meaning as 'the registry gate'. See Psalm 87.6, "The Lord shall count, when he writeth up the people, that this man was born there". We must never forget that the "east gate" is followed by "the gate Miphkad". We "must all appear before the judgment seat of Christ; that every one may receive the things done in his body, according to that he hath done, whether it be good or bad" (2 Cor. 5.10); "So then every one of us shall give account of himself to God" (Rom. 14.12).

After leaving "the gate Miphkad", we return to the "**sheep gate**" (v.32). But we have approached it from a different direction. Everything **began** with the "sheep gate": now everything **ends** with the "sheep gate". The Lord Jesus is the "Alpha and Omega, the beginning and the end, the first and the last" (Rev. 22.13). The "sheep gate" reminds us that we will never forget Calvary. The cross will be the theme of our praise for ever and ever. The Lord's coming will enable us to praise and worship Him without distraction.

We will never leave the "sheep gate!"

READ CHAPTER 4

"What do these feeble Jews?"

Chapters 4-6 deal primarily with the difficulties surrounding the reconstruction of the wall of Jerusalem. In the first place, the work was threatened by **opposition from without**. See Chapter 4. In the second place, it was threatened by **dissatisfaction from within**. See Chapter 5. In the third place it was threatened by **compromise and infiltration**. See Chapter 6. The words of 2 Corinthians 7.5 are applicable to Chapters 4 & 5-6: "Without were fightings" (Chapter 4); "within were fears" (Chapters 5-6).

Although the builders faced dangerous opposition, the work proceeded with only one temporary halt (see v.15). "We builded the wall" (v.1); "So we built the wall" (v.6); "the walls of Jerusalem were made up" (v.7); "we returned all of us to the wall, every one unto his work" (v.15); "They which builded on the wall" (v.17); "So we laboured in the work" (v.21). They continued to work with the assurance that God was greater than their enemies, and that He was on their side! They addressed Him as "**our** God" (vv.4,9,20). They said, in effect, "God, even **our own God,** shall bless us" (Psalm 67.6). Paul went further and called Him "**my** God" (Phil. 4.19). But so did Nehemiah: "Remember me (or 'them'), O **my** God" (13.14,22,29,31).

The overall purpose of the enemy was to hinder (v.8), and to "cause the work to cease" (v.11). With this in mind, we can divide the chapter as follows: *(1)* the scorn of the enemies (vv.1-6); *(2)* the strength of the enemies (vv.7-9); *(3)* the strategy of the enemies (vv.10-23).

1) THE SCORN OF THE ENEMIES, vv.1-6

"But it came to pass, that when Sanballat heard that we builded the wall, he was wroth, and took great indignation, and mocked the Jews". (This is an enemy tactic: see Acts 2.13; 17.32. The Lord Jesus was mocked: Matt. 27.41; Luke 22.63; 23.11,36). We have already met Sanballat and his cronies, Tobiah and Geshem. See 2.10,19. We must not forget that their ancestry teaches us some sobering lessons. This calls for revision! See our comments on 2.10.

We have also noticed that their initial annoyance (2.10), was followed by scorn (2.19); anger (4.1,7); threat of attack (4.11); and finally by craft and stealth (6.1-14). Their tactics varied, and their opposition intensified, as the work proceeded. This is a timely reminder that we should not be "ignorant of his (Satan's) devices" (2 Cor. 2.11).

It has been pointed out that throughout this chapter, the enemies use the weapon of **fear** in different ways. Here, they endeavoured to engender fear by **ridicule**: "What do these feeble Jews? will they fortify themselves? will they sacrifice? will they make an end in a day? will they revive the stones out of the heaps of the rubbish which are burned? Now Tobiah the Ammonite was by him, and he said, Even that which they build, if a fox go up, he shall even break down their stone wall". They ridiculed the **people** themselves ("What do these feeble Jews?"); they ridiculed their **plans** ("will they fortify themselves?"); they ridiculed their **faith** ("will they sacrifice?"); they ridiculed their **energy** ("will they make an end in a day?"); they ridiculed their **materials** ("will they revive the stones out of the heaps of rubbish, seeing they are burned?", RV); they ridiculed their **achievements** ("if a fox go up, he shall even break down their stone wall"). The standard of their work was dismissed with contempt, and in any case, their very materials were an eloquent reminder of past defeat. See, for example: "the wall of Jerusalem...is broken down, and the gates thereof are burned with fire" (1.3). Their sarcasm was a cloak for their anger (v.1).

Ridicule is both cowardly and contagious. It is **cowardly:** Sanballat spoke obliquely, not directly. He "spake before his brethren and the army of Samaria". It is very easy to speak boldly when you have a sympathetic audience! It is **contagious:** Tobiah chimes in with his little piece as soon as Sanballat stops! Nothing like a few derisory jokes to get the audience cheering! Scorn and ridicule have often been enemy weapons. Hezekiah's messengers were "laughed...to scorn" as they announced the passover at Jerusalem (2 Chron. 30.10). The Lord Jesus was "laughed...to scorn" in the house of Jairus (Matt. 9.24. We must not therefore be surprised if we are ridiculed too. We can expect open ridicule from some quarters, but niggling doubts and nagging fears are even more potent. Haven't we all heard that little voice within: 'are you really achieving anything?... is it really worthwhile?' We must always remember **why** the enemy mocked: "it grieved them exceedingly that there was come a man to seek the welfare of the children of Israel" (2.10). **No work - no mockery!** We must expect ridicule if we are busy for God. If the enemy succeeds in making you feel "feeble", just remember that "God hath chosen the weak things of the world to confound the things which are mighty" (1 Cor.1.27).

The scorn of the enemy was met by **prayer and work.** Sanballat left God out: Nehemiah did not! Nehemiah did not underestimate the enemy, but he **prayed.** Like Hezekiah (2 Kgs. 18.36), he did not "answer a fool according to his folly", but looked up to God by prayer (Matthew Henry): "Hear, O our God; for we are despised" (vv.4-5). We know that it was confident prayer by the way in which the work continued: "So built we the wall; and all the wall was joined together unto the half thereof: for **the people (not just Nehemiah!) had a mind to work**" (v.6). They were "stedfast, unmoveable, always abounding in the work of the Lord" (1 Cor. 15.58). Paul could say of his service, "For God is my witness, whom I serve **with my spirit** in the gospel of his Son" (Rom. 1.9). He too "had a mind to work!" The taunts of the enemy left the people **undaunted in their enthusiasm.** They set us a good example, for we are to "stand fast in one spirit, with one mind striving together for the faith of the gospel" (Phil. 1.27). Note: the "reproach" in 1.3 was to their shame, but in 4.4 it was to their honour.

2) THE STRENGTH OF THE ENEMIES, vv.7-9

"But it came to pass, that when Sanballat, and Tobiah, and the Arabians, and the Ammonites, and the Ashdodites, heard that the walls of Jerusalem were made up ('being repaired', JND), and that the breaches began to be stopped, then they were very wroth, and conspired all of them together to come and to fight against Jerusalem" (vv.7-8). (The expression "the breaches began to be stopped" is very picturesque in Hebrew. It reads quite literally that 'a bandage was applied' to the walls of the city!). The united labour of God's people was met by united enemy opposition. The enemies now endeavoured to engender fear by **intimidation.** There is a very thin line between mockery and intimidation. It was a strong conspiracy: Arabians, Ammonites, Ashdodites. Jerusalem was ringed with enemies: to the **north**, Samaria (v.2): to the **south**, the Arabians: to the **east**, the Ammonites: to the **west**, the Ashdodites (Philistines). It was an intelligent and concerted attempt to overthrow the work. They "conspired **all of them together** to come and fight against Jerusalem, and to hinder it" (v.8). Behind the conspiracy was "wroth" (v.7). Like Nehemiah, we are faced by an intelligent enemy alliance: "We wrestle not against flesh and blood, but against principalities, against powers, against the rulers of the darkness of this world" (Eph. 6.12). The Lord Jesus was confronted by a most unlikely alliance of enemies. See Matthew 22.15-22. The Pharisees and Herodians were normally sworn enemies. But they united against Christ. Pilate and Herod were "made friends" in rejecting the Lord Jesus (Luke 23.12).

The strength of the enemy was met by **prayer and watchfulness**. "Nevertheless we made our prayer unto **our** God, and set a watch against them **day and** *night*, because of them" (v.9). In the words of Derek Kidner, "the celebrated remark *we prayed...and set a guard*, exactly reflects the faith of Nehemiah. The partnership of heaven and earth, of trust and good management, is taken for granted as something normal and harmonious; and the order of precedence between them is no formality". We too must "watch and pray". In New Testament language, "Be sober, be vigilant; because your adversary the devil, as a roaring lion, walketh about, seeking whom he may devour" (1 Pet. 5.8). The strength of the enemy was met by **unshaken faith**: "Remember the Lord, which is great and terrible" (v.14); "**Our** God shall fight for us" (v.20). So it was "Sanballat, and Tobiah, and the Arabians, and the Ammonites, and the Ashdodites", versus God! Jehoshaphat thought similarly: "We have no might against this great company that cometh against us; neither know we what to do: but **our eyes are upon thee**" (2 Chron. 20.12). John puts it like this: "Greater is he that is in you, than he that is in the world" (1 John 4.4).

It has been nicely said that they had a mind to work, a heart to pray, and an eye to watch. It was a case of "praying always" and "watching thereunto" (Eph. 6.18).

3) THE STRATEGY OF THE ENEMIES, vv.10-23
It was the strategy of surprise attack. It has been described as a concerted attack (vv.7-8), a cruel attack (v.11, "slay") and a confident attack (v.11): "And our adversaries said, They shall not know, neither see, till we come in the midst among them, and slay them, and cause the work to cease". The strategy was facilitated by **rubbish** and **declining strength** (v.10). After facing fear by ridicule (vv.1-3), the people now faced fear resulting from **weariness and discouragement.** We should notice what various people "said":

i) "And Judah **said**, The strength of the bearers of burdens is decayed, and there is much rubbish; so that we are not able (shall not be able) to build the wall" (v.10). But what about Isaiah 40.31, "they that wait upon the Lord shall renew their strength"? Those responsible for clearing the rubbish had become weary in their immense task - and it **is** an immense task. It is amazing how much rubbish from the past gets in the way of God's work. There is nothing quite so discouraging! Everything seemed to be against the builders: when they looked **in,** "the strength of the bearers of burdens is decayed": when they looked **down**, "there is much rubbish; so that we are not able to build the wall": when they looked **around,** "our adversaries said, They shall not know, neither see, till we come in the midst among them". We are told that the Hebrew text reads, literally, 'we shall not be able to build the wall'. God's people were doubting their ability to **complete the task.**

ii)) "And our adversaries *said*, They shall not know, neither see, till we come in the midst among them, and slay them, and cause the work to cease" (v.11). Compare the furtive, surreptitious activities of false teachers in Galatia: "false brethren *unawares* brought in" (Gal. 2.4). Peter knew all about this tactic: "there shall be false teachers among you, who *privily* shall bring in damnable heresies" (2 Pet. 2.1), and so did Jude: "there are certain men crept in *unawares*" (Jude v.4).

iii) "And it came to pass, that when the Jews which dwelt by them came, they *said* unto us ten times, From all places whence ye shall return unto us they will be upon you" (v.12). There was the likelihood of attack from any point: "Then the Jews who lived near them came and told us ten times over, "Wherever you turn, they will attack us"." (NIV) or "Whatever place you turn to, they are against us" (Matthew Henry). This time it is fear engendered by *rumour.* Fear from looking at the danger. People kept on making the point ("they said unto us ten times"), and therefore it must be right! Sadly, they didn't even mention the power of God!

The strategy of the enemy was met by *watching and working.* Nehemiah set an *uninterrupted guard.* But he did something even more important. He reminded them of God's great power: They were not to look *down*, and be discouraged: they were not to look *within,* and be depressed: they were not to look *around,* and be dismayed: they were to look *up!* Nehemiah looked beyond the immediate circumstances, and encouraged them. "Be not ye afraid of them: *remember the Lord*, which is great and terrible, and fight for your brethren, your sons, and your daughters, your wives, and your houses" (v.14).

We must notice *(a)* how he dealt with the immediate danger (vv.13-15), and *(b)* with the ongoing danger (vv.16-23). Battling must not impede building!

a) The immediate danger, vv.13-15
Bearing in mind the likelihood of imminent attack, Nehemiah took immediate steps to secure the city. This evidently involved a temporary halt in the work. Notice the following:

i) Consciousness of weakness, v.13. "Therefore set I in the lower places behind the wall, and on the higher places, I even set the people after their families with their swords, their spears, and their bows" or "I set in the lower places behind the wall in *exposed places*…" (JND). Nehemiah did not assume that all was well in the defences of Jerusalem. Weak places were guarded. Notice that reference is made to "swords" (hand to hand fighting), "spears" (taking the battle to the enemy) and "bows" (long distance fighting). They had the weapons to engage the enemy man to man, and at a distance.

ii) **Confidence in God, v.14a.** "And I looked, and rose up, and said unto the nobles, and to the rulers, and to the rest of the people, Be ye not afraid of them: remember the Lord, which is great and terrible". Notice the sequence:

- **"I looked".** Nehemiah was a man who carefully assessed the situation. Compare 2.12-16 and 5.7 ("I consulted with myself"). See James 1.19, "Wherefore, my beloved brethren, let every man be swift to hear, slow to speak, slow to wrath".

- **"I...rose up".** Nehemiah was equally a man of action. Some people only look!

- **"I...said".** This comes last, and only after careful thought, reminding us of the saying that 'He that thinketh by the inch, and speaketh by the yard, deserves to be kicked by the foot!'

iii) **Commitment to their brethren, v.14b.** "Fight for your brethren, your sons, and your daughters, your wives, and your houses". It wasn't a case of approaching the problem dispassionately. It was in their own interests and the interests of their families and homes. There was so much at stake. It was a 'life or death' situation. Pressure and persecution gets rid of the dross in our lives, and makes us focus on the most important issues!

The strategy of the enemy was unsuccessful: "And it came to pass, when our enemies heard that it was known unto us (see, again, 2 Cor. 2.11), and God had brought their counsel to nought, that we returned **all of us** to the wall, **every one unto his work**" (v.15). **No one dropped out**! They resumed work with gratitude to **God:** He had "brought their counsel to nought". But the passing of the immediate crisis **did not mean relaxation.** Nehemiah knew that the enemy was not likely to give up easily. He therefore takes steps to ensure future security:

b) The ongoing danger, vv.16-23
Unremitting vigilance was the order of the day. No one must allow his guard to drop. There were to be no off-days, and no days off! See v.23. We must notice the following:

i) Labouring with a guard, vv.16-18. The vigilance of vv.9,13 continued. Half of Nehemiah's servants "wrought in the work" and half "held both the spears, the shields, and the bows, and the habergeons". (A habergeon was a sleeveless coat of mail - and perhaps answers to "the breastplate of righteousness" in Ephesians 6.14). Those who laboured were armed: "They which builded on the wall, and they that bare burdens, with those that laded ('loaded', JND), every one with one of his hands wrought in the work, and with the other hand held a weapon. For the builders, every one had his sword girded by his side, and so builded". Do notice that "the rulers were behind all the house of Judah" (v.16), or "And the leaders stood behind all the house of Judah, who were building on the wall. Those who carried burdens were laden in such a way that each with one hand laboured on the work and with the other held his weapon. And each of the builders had his sword girded at his side while he built" (RSV). See also RV margin. The lesson is expressed in New Testament language: "Put on the whole armour of God, that ye may be able to stand against the *wiles* of the devil" (Eph. 6.11). The passage continues by referring to "the sword of the Spirit, which is the word of God", and to "the shield of faith". Constant readiness is the order of the day. We are to "watch, and remember" (Acts 20.31).

ii)   Listening for the trumpet, vv.19-20. The strategy of the enemy might well have been successful had Nehemiah not provided for his scattered resources, "one far from another" (v.19). An attack on one section of the wall would be repulsed, not only by those in the immediate vicinity, but by the whole community. The New Testament refers to this as follows: "And whether one member suffer, all the members suffer with it" (1 Cor. 12.26).

This required a good sense of hearing! It also required a clear alarm: "If the trumpet give an uncertain sound, who shall prepare himself to the battle?" (1 Cor. 14.8). Whilst this did not apparently involve the 'silver trumpets' (Numbers 10), the *principle* was the same: "Our *God* shall fight for us". See Numbers 10.9. Whilst Nehemiah's workmanlike precautions were good, they had limited value. His confidence went deeper: "Our God shall fight for us". He knew that "Except the Lord build the house, they labour in vain that build it: except the Lord keep the city, the watchman waketh but in vain" (Psalm 127.1).

With this measure in place, the work continued: "So we laboured in the work: and half of them held the spears from the rising of the morning till the stars appeared". They were on guard for extensive periods, and under extremes of temperature. We too can experience considerable variations in spiritual temperature! There are cool winds, and warm periods!

iii)   Lodging in the city, vv.22-23. "Likewise at the same time said I unto the people, Let every one with his servant lodge within Jerusalem, that in the night they may be a guard to us, and labour on the day". Their own interests were to be subordinated to the interests of the place where the Lord placed His Name! Compare 1 Cor. 7.29-31, "Brethren, the time is short: it remaineth, that both they that have wives be as though they had none; and they that weep, as though they wept not; and they that rejoice, as though they rejoiced not; and they that buy, as though they possessed not".

But Nehemiah was far more than an able governor. He was an 'ensample to the flock': "So neither I, nor my brethren, nor my servants, nor the men of the guard which followed me, none of us put off our clothes, saving that every one put them off for washing", or "None of us put off our garments: *every one had his weapon on his right side*" (JND), or "None of us put off our clothes, every one went with his weapon to the water" (RV).

READ CHAPTER 5

"Will ye even sell your brethren?"

We have already noticed that Chapters 4-6 deal primarily with the difficulties surrounding the reconstruction of the wall of Jerusalem. In Chapter 4, the work was threatened by **opposition from without**: in Chapter 5, it was threatened by **dissatisfaction from within**: in Chapter 6, it was threatened by **compromise and infiltration**. We can write over Chapter 4, "without were fightings", and over Chapter 5, "within were fears" (2 Cor. 7.5).

Nehemiah 5 requires some preliminary reading, and this must include Leviticus 25.35-36: "And if thy brother be waxen poor, and fallen in decay with thee; then thou shalt relieve him: yea, though he be a stranger, or a sojourner; that he may live with thee. Take thou no usury of him, or increase: but fear thy God; that thy brother may live with thee". See also Exodus 22.25 and Deuteronomy 15.1-11. Sadly, these instructions had been disregarded, with consequent hardship for many of God's people.

The chapter may be divided in the following way *(1)* unbrotherly conduct (vv.1-5); *(2)* uncompromising protest (vv.6-11); *(3)* unreserved obedience, (vv.12-13); *(4)* unselfish example (vv.14-19).

1) UNBROTHERLY CONDUCT, vv.1-5
"And there was a great cry of the people and of their wives against **their brethren the Jews**". Chapter 5 describes an internal problem. For Sanballat, Tobiah, Arabians, Ammonites and Ashdodites in Chapter 4, read "**brethren**" and "**brother**" in Chapter 5. See vv.1,5,7,8. Compare 1 Corinthians 6.6, "**Brother** goeth to law with **brother,** and that before the unbelievers". There was an absence of "brotherly kindness" (2 Pet. 1.7). The wealthy were evidently determined to build up their estates at the expense of their poorer brethren. This had happened before: see Isaiah 5.8-10. "Woe unto them that join house to house, that lay field to field, till there be no place, that they may be placed alone in the midst of the earth!" Oppression in this way from foreigners could be expected, but not from fellow Jews.

There was no help forthcoming to alleviate the problems of poorer brethren. The oppressed were not relieved. Previous instruction was ignored: "Learn to do well; seek judgment, relieve the oppressed, judge the fatherless, plead for the widow" (Isa 1.17). They faced two main problems:

a) Feeding their families, vv.3-4

"For there were that said, We, our sons, and our daughters, are many: therefore we take up corn for them, that we may eat, and live", or "and we must procure corn that we may eat and live" (JND). The passage continues: "Some also there were that said, We have mortgaged our lands, vineyards, and houses, that we may buy corn, because of **the dearth**". The famine would have sent food prices rocketing, and no one was interested in the welfare of God's people. Speaking literally, feeding 'the flock of God' was not a priority. Whilst there are some very practical lessons to learn here, we must never forget that God's people need to be "nourished up in the words of faith and of good doctrine" (1 Tim. 4.6).

b) Finding the tribute, v.5

"There were also that said, We have borrowed money for the king's tribute, and that upon our lands and vineyards". See also v.18: "the bondage was heavy upon this people". We must remember that although the books of Ezra and Nehemiah chronicle great progress, the Jews were still part of the Persian empire. The Persian kings, like any other conqueror, wanted their 'pound of flesh', and the poorer Jews were hard-pressed to find the money. As Christians, we are to "render...to all their dues: tribute to whom tribute is due; custom to whom custom" (Rom. 13.6-7). The Welfare State provides help where necessary, but this does not exempt us from helping in cases of need amongst God's people. But there was no help available here. We must remember that the world can make it hard for God's people in other ways, and we must be ready to assist and encourage in every way.

In order to meet both demands, the people were obliged to mortgage their lands and homes, and worse, to sell their children into servitude: "Lo, we bring into bondage our sons and our daughters to be servants, and some of our daughters are brought unto bondage already: neither is it in our power to redeem them; for other men have our lands and vineyards". This might be expected from foreigners, but not from fellow-Jews: "Yet now our flesh is as the flesh of our brethren, our children as their children". There was no mutual care, **and this threatened the work as much as Sanballat and his henchmen.**

Both Old and New Testaments stress God's concern for the poor and needy amongst His people. See, for example, Deuteronomy 24.10-15; Acts 2.44-45; 4.34-37; 6.1-6; 11.27-30. We need to remember that the local assembly should be a caring community. The early church "had all things common" (Acts 2.44), and whilst this is not enjoined in the New Testament epistles, the principle remains: "be ye kind one to another, tenderhearted..." (Eph. 4.32); "let us consider one another to provoke unto love and to good works" (Heb. 10.24); "Put on therefore, as the elect of God, holy and beloved, bowels of mercies, kindness..." (Col. 3.12); "But whoso hath this world's good, and seeth his brother have need, and shutteth up his bowels of compassion from him, how dwelleth the love of God in him?" (1 John 3.17); "If a brother or sister be naked, and destitute of daily food, and one of you say unto them, Depart in peace, be ye warmed and filled; notwithstanding ye give them not those things which are needful to the body; what doth it profit?" (Jas. 2.15-16).

2) UNCOMPROMISING PROTEST, vv.6-11

These verses tell us about *(a)* Nehemiah's anger (v.6); *(b)* action (v.7); *(c)* argument (vv.8-9); *(d)* abstention (v.10); *(e)* admonition (v.11).

a) Nehemiah's anger, v.6

"And I was very angry when I heard their cry and these words". It is rather striking to notice that there is no mention of anger in Chapter 4. There was little point in getting angry with Sanballat and Tobiah: after all, what else could you expect from people like that? But God's people should know better. Nehemiah expected a far higher standard of conduct from them. No wonder Nehemiah was "very angry". We should remember that there is such a thing as righteous anger: "who is offended, and I burn not?" (2 Cor. 11.29); "Be ye angry, and sin not: let not the sun go down upon your wrath" (Eph. 4.26). Anger becomes sinful when it turns into a smouldering overnight fire!

b) Nehemiah's action, v.7

i) **"Then I consulted with myself".** Presumably, there was no one else he could consult! Hence his prayer, "Think upon **me,** my God, for good" (v.19). See also 13.14,22,31. Nehemiah evidently reflected on the problem. He was never a hasty planner! Compare 2.11-16. He followed David's advice, "Commune with your own heart upon your bed, and be still" (Psalm 4.4). James would certainly approve: "Let every man be swift to hear, slow to speak, slow to wrath" (Jas. 1.19).

(ii) **"And I rebuked the nobles, and the rulers, and said unto them, Ye exact usury, every one of his brother".** Nehemiah did not avoid the issue, but addressed it directly: "Ye exact usury, every one of his brother". He was quite uncompromising in approach. The matter must be properly resolved. It must not be glossed over. Division amongst God's people is a very serious matter. Read, for example, Philippians 4.2-5. Discord between two believers at Philippi was serious enough to merit apostolic intervention.

(iii) *"And I set a great assembly against them"*. Public evils must be rectified publicly. There was no 'hidden agenda'. Justice must be done, and justice must be **seen** to be done. We must remember that God's word had been deliberately flouted, and public transgression must be dealt with publicly. This is why Paul confronted Peter at Antioch. "But when Peter was come to Antioch, I withstood him to **the face**, because he was to be blamed...But when I saw that they walked not uprightly according to the truth of the gospel, I said unto Peter **before them all**" (Gal. 2.11-14). At first glance, this seems to be rather uncharitable on Paul's part, but we must remember that Peter had been guilty of **publicly** misleading God's people, and therefore **public** correction was necessary. Private matters can be put right privately.

c) Nehemiah's argument, vv.8-9
"And I said unto them, We after our ability have redeemed our brethren the Jews, which were sold unto the heathen; and will ye even sell your brethren? or shall they be sold unto us? Then held they their peace, and found nothing to answer. Also I said, It is not good that ye do: ought ye not to walk in the fear of our God because of the reproach of the heathen our enemies?" Nehemiah used a dual argument:

i) Deliverance from bondage to aliens should not be followed by bondage to fellow Jews. That simply repeated the first situation. What happened in the surrounding nations should not happen amongst God's people. They should have different standards.

ii) Testimony before others must not be endangered. "Ought ye not to walk in the fear of our God because of the reproach of the heathen our enemies?" or "so as not to be the reproach of the nations our enemies" (JND). Preachers often refer to Genesis 13.7-8 in this connection. We must not overlook the reference here to "the fear of our God" (v.9). See also v.15. The New Testament equivalent is 'godliness' or 'piety'. The successors of these people caused "the name of God" to be "blasphemed among the Gentiles" (Rom. 2.24). We must studiously avoid doing the same. See 1Timothy 5.14; Titus 2.5.

d) Nehemiah's abstention, v.10
"I likewise, and my brethren, and my servants, might exact of them money and

corn: I pray you, let us leave off this usury". In the New Testament, Paul refers to three things to which he had legitimate right, but which he refused. See 1 Corinthians 7-9, especially 9.13-15. Nehemiah surrendered his legitimate claim to support. This is expanded in vv.14-19. Paul did the same: "For ye remember, brethren, our labour and travail: for labouring night and day, because we would not be chargeable unto any of you, we preached unto you the gospel of God" (1 Thess. 2.9). Nehemiah had the moral right to rebuke the malpractices of others. He was an example of his own teaching. What we **say** may be right, but are **we** right? The Ephesian elders were told: "Take heed therefore unto **yourselves**, and to all the flock..." (Acts 20.28) and Timothy was told: "Take heed unto **thyself**, and unto the doctrine" (1 Tim. 4.16).

We should also notice that Nehemiah was able to cite his own example in the matter. Generally speaking, it would be quite inappropriate to publicise our good deeds: after all, God knows all about them, and that is quite sufficient. On the other hand, it is sometimes very important that both God **and men** should know about them. See, for example, 2 Corinthians 8.21, "Providing for honest things, not only in the sight of the Lord, but also in the sight of men".

e) Nehemiah's admonition, v.11

"Restore, I pray you, to them, **even this day,** their lands, their vineyards, their oliveyards, and their houses, also the hundredth part of the money, and of the corn, the wine, and the oil, that ye exact of them". The words, "the hundredth part of the money" could mean 1% per month, i.e. 12% per annum, although there are alternative suggestions. D.Kidner discusses these in his 'Tyndale' commentary (*Ezra and Nehemiah*). This brings us to:

3) UNRESERVED OBEDIENCE, vv.12-13

We must notice **(a)** the promise made (v.12); **(b)** the promise witnessed (vv.12-13); **(c)** the promise fulfilled (v.13).

a) The promise made, v.12

"Then said they, We will restore them, and will require nothing of them; so will we do as thou sayest". Progress was being made. To begin with, when the gravity of the situation had been put to them, they had "held...their peace, and found nothing to answer" (v.8). Now they were prepared to address their malpractices. They did not 'fly off the handle'. On the contrary, they evidently received "with **meekness** the engrafted (implanted) word" (Jas. 1.21). They recognised that Nehemiah had highlighted a very serious problem, reminding us that "Faithful are the wounds of a friend" (Prov. 2.6). It might be going a little too far to include them in this category, but spiritually-minded people will recognise a just rebuke or reproof. It certainly seems that they adhered to their promise. The practices condemned here are not mentioned in Chapter 13.

b) The promise witnessed, vv.12-13
"Then I called the priests, and took an oath of them, that they should do according to this promise". This should be read in conjunction with guidance given by Solomon: "When thou vowest a vow unto God, defer not to pay it… neither say thou before the angel (the messenger, i.e. the priest, see Malachi 2.7), that it was an error" (Eccl. 5.4-6). The promise to repay was made to God, rather than Nehemiah: hence the solemn warning if restoration was not made: "Also I shook my lap, and said, So God shake out every man from his house, and from his labour, that performeth not this promise, even thus be he shaken out, and emptied". Obedience always brings joy: "And all the congregation said, Amen, and *praised the Lord*" (v.13). They recognised the hand of God in Nehemiah's intervention.

c) The promise fulfilled, v.13
"And the people did according to this promise" in the same way that the believers at Antioch responded to the prophetic ministry of Agabus: "Then the disciples, every man according to his ability, *determined* to send relief unto the brethren which dwelt in Judea: which also they *did*, and sent it to the elders by the hand(s) (it is singular: 'hand') of Barnabas and Saul" (Acts 11.29-30). They performed "the *doing* of it" (2 Cor. 8.11). It was *not* a case of 'after all that's said and done, there's more that's said than done!'

4) UNSELFISH EXAMPLE, vv.14-19
We should notice here that *(a)* the fear of God was all-important (vv.14-15); *(b)* the work of God was all-important (v.16); *(c)* the people of God were all-important (vv.17-18).

a) The fear of God was all-important, vv.14-15
"Moreover from the time that I was appointed to be their governor in the land of Judah, from the twentieth year even unto the two and thirtieth year of Artaxerxes the king, that is, twelve years (the entire period covered by the book, see 13.6, rather than the period of rebuilding, see 6.15), I and my brethren have not eaten the bread of the governor. But the former governors that had been before me were chargeable unto the people, and had taken of them bread and wine, beside forty shekels of silver; yea, even their servants bare rule over the people: but so did not I, *because of the fear of God*".

To have added to the existing burdens of his brethren, would have grieved the Lord. Nehemiah's desire was to please Him. The "fear of the Lord" is an attitude of mind that avoids all that displeases Him. A Greater than Nehemiah, a Greater than all, deliberately refused available help in order to secure the highest blessing for men and women. See Matthew 26.52-54.

b) The work of God was all-important, v.16

"Yea, also I *continued* in the work of this wall, *neither bought we any land*: and all my servants were gathered thither unto the work". Nehemiah exemplified the injunction to be "always abounding in the work of the Lord" (1 Cor. 15.58), and demonstrated very clearly where his priorities were located. The Lord Jesus said, "where your treasure is, there will your heart be also" (Matt. 6.21). Nehemiah's heart was set on the work, not on feathering his own nest: "Yea, also I continued in the work of this wall". He was not governed by materialism. We must, of course, provide for our families and pay our bills, but there is all the difference between this, and selling our souls in the pursuit of wealth and acquisition. Nehemiah's servants were so different to the servants of previous governors: "Even *their servants* bare rule over the people" (v.15), but Nehemiah was able to say, "All *my servants* were gathered thither unto the work" (v.16).

c) The people of God were all-important, vv.17-18

"Yet for all this required not I the bread of the governor, because **the bondage was heavy upon this people**". Nehemiah evidently paid for official entertaining himself, and this obviously involved considerable sacrifice on his part. We should notice that visitors were welcome. He refers particularly to "those that came unto us from among the heathen that are about us", that is, to Jews living amongst the surrounding people. We should also notice Nehemiah's well-stocked table, reminding us of Paul's words, "My God shall supply all your need according to his riches in glory by Christ Jesus" (Phil. 4.19). Nehemiah refused his legal rights as governor, in order to ease the burden on poorer brethren, but his table was very well furnished! God is no man's debtor.

Nehemiah reflects on his work in v.19, and looks to God alone for recompense: "Think upon me, my God, for good, according to all that I have done for this people".

Could **we** say this?

READ CHAPTER 6

"They thought to do me mischief"

As we have seen, Nehemiah Chapters 4-6 deal particularly with the difficulties encountered in rebuilding the wall of Jerusalem. Each chapter presents a different problem. In Chapter 4, the work was threatened by **opposition from without.** In Chapter 5, the work was threatened by **dissatisfaction from within.** In Chapter 6, the work was threatened by **compromise and infiltration.** The dangers remain, and these chapters therefore give us valuable guidance in similar circumstances, proving again that "whatsoever things were written aforetime were written for our learning" (Rom.15.4).

The former part of Chapter 6 records the **progress** of the work. "Sanballat, and Tobiah, and Geshem...heard that I **had builded the wall,** and that there was no breach left therein; (though at that time I had not set up the doors upon the gates;)" (v.1). The little piece in brackets emphasises that Nehemiah was not given to exaggeration: there was still work to be done. The latter part records the **completion** of the work. "So the **wall was finished** in the twenty and fifth day of the month Elul, in fifty and two days" (v.15). Frontal assault was no longer possible, but this did not mean for one moment that the enemies of God's people had lapsed into lethargy and indifference. The scorn, strength and strategy in Chapter 4, defeated by the undaunted enthusiasm, unshaken faith and unbroken vigilance of Nehemiah and his companions, gave place to new tactics. Compromise and infiltration were now tried by the enemy. They used the weapon of fear: see vv.9,13,14,19. We need to be aware that the strategy of the enemy can quickly change, "lest Satan should get an advantage of us: for we are not ignorant of his devices" (2 Cor. 2.11). Periods of success and progress can be spiritually dangerous. The enemy is not yet finally defeated.

In Nehemiah Chapter 4, the enemies act as "a **roaring lion**, walketh about, seeking whom he may devour" (1 Pet. 5.8). In Nehemiah Chapter 6, they change their approach and act as "an angel of light". See 2 Corinthians 11.13-14, "For such are false apostles, deceitful workers, transforming themselves into the apostles of Christ. And no marvel; for Satan himself is transformed into an *angel of light*". With Nehemiah Chapter 6 before us, we must notice some of his activities under this guise: *(1)* they attempted to disguise their tactics (vv.1-4); *(2)* they attempted to discredit his intentions (vv.5-9); *(3)* they attempted to destroy his faith (vv.10-14); *(4)* they exploited the disloyalty of his brethren (vv.15-19).

1) THEY ATTEMPTED TO DISGUISE THEIR TACTICS, vv.1-4

We should notice the following: *(a)* Nehemiah's discernment (vv.1-2); *(b)* Nehemiah's dedication (v.3); *(c)* Nehemiah's determination (v.4).

a) Nehemiah's discernment, vv.1-2

"Sanballat and Geshem sent unto me, saying, Come, let us meet together in some one of the villages in the plain of Ono. But they thought to do me mischief". The proposition looked quite innocent, but Nehemiah was not fooled. He knew very well that they were still "enemies" (vv.1,16), and he was well aware of their intentions: "they thought to do me mischief" (v.2). Notice the enemy's *information*: they "*heard* that I had builded the wall, and that there was no breach left therein"; the enemy's *invitation*: "*Come*, let us meet together in some one of the villages in the plain of Ono"; the enemy's *intention*: "But they *thought* to do me mischief". Had Nehemiah gone to Ono, it would have been a case of "A righteous man falling down before the wicked" (Prov. 25.26).

Sanballat and Geshem are not the only people who say, "Come, let us meet together". The Ecumenical Movement issues its invitation to all and sundry, and while its adherents would disown any desire to do us "mischief", there can be no doubt that this is the intention of their unseen master, "the angel of light". The meeting proposed by Sanballat and Geshem was to take place on *their* ground, not at Jerusalem. In fact, Nehemiah recognised that it was dangerous for him to leave 'the place of the name' (1.9), and it is equally dangerous for us to leave the safety, certainty and enjoyment of New Testament church teaching for the uncertainty and heresy of Christendom.

Notice where the proposed meeting was to take place: "some one of the villages…of Ono". It is elsewhere called, "Ono, the valley of craftsmen" (11.35). We should notice two things. Firstly, Ono was located in a *valley.* It lay some twenty-five miles north-west of Jerusalem in the territory of Benjamin. People went *up* to Jerusalem: but *down* to Ono! (v.3). Secondly, it is called "the valley of *craftsmen*". The proposed meeting was to take place in a commercial environment, and it is deeply significant that apostate religion and commerce are closely linked in Revelation chs.17-18.

b) Nehemiah's dedication, v.3

"And I sent messengers unto them, saying, I am doing a great work, so that I cannot come down: why should the work cease, whilst I leave it, and come down to you?" Building for God is "*a great work*!" Paul described the local assembly as "*God's husbandry*" and "*God's building*" (1 Cor. 3.9). He continues, "According to the grace of God which is given unto me, as a wise *masterbuilder*, I have laid the foundation, and another *buildeth* thereon. But let every man take heed how he *buildeth* thereupon. For other foundation can no man lay than that is laid, which is Jesus Christ" (1 Cor. 3.10-11). A "great work" demands quality materials, and Paul describes them as "gold, silver, precious (costly) stones" (1 Cor. 3.12). Nehemiah gave a positive answer: his involvement in "the place which the Lord shall choose to place his name there" (Deut. 16.2), precluded him from involvement anywhere else. There was, therefore, no question of leaving such "a great work". On a wider front, the believer who says "necessity is laid upon me; yea, woe is unto me, if I preach not the gospel!" (1 Cor. 9.16), will not be easily diverted from such "a great work". He will recognise that "no man that warreth entangleth himself with the affairs of this life: that he may please him who hath chosen him to be a soldier" (2 Tim. 2.4).

Nehemiah recognised his personal responsibility: "*I* am doing a great work, so that *I* cannot come down: why should the work cease, whilst *I* leave it". Nehemiah's presence in Jerusalem was essential to the work. Contrary to "much hard modern criticism" (Ellicott's Commentary), Nehemiah was not given to self-confidence and self-assertion. Quite evidently, there was scarcely anybody to whom he could turn for support and fellowship. Sadly, this is not an unusual situation. Nehemiah's personal commitment to the work at Jerusalem should remind us that we are all 'key personnel' in God's work. There is nothing mysterious about the condition of a local assembly: it simply reflects the spiritual vigour or spiritual weakness of those in fellowship. Individual responsibility rests upon every believer, and Paul's reference to the human body in 1 Corinthians ch.12 in describing an assembly stresses the necessity for each believer to ensure peak spiritual health. Finally in connection with this opening section of the chapter, we must notice:

c) Nehemiah's determination, v.4

"Yet they sent unto me four times after this sort; and I answered them after the same manner". Nehemiah was consistent in the face of pressure. He "*continued* in the work of this wall" (5.16). He was "stedfast, unmoveable, always abounding in the work of the Lord" (1 Cor. 15.58). All too often, when pressure grows, believers take the first opportunity to transfer their presence and energies elsewhere. The Lord Jesus warned, "No man, having put his hand to the plough, and looking back, is fit for the kingdom of God" (Luke 9.62).

2) THEY ATTEMPTED TO DISCREDIT HIS INTENTIONS, vv.5-9

Four successive defeats (v.4) did not mean the end of the war. "Then sent Sanballat his servant unto me in like manner the **fifth time** with an open letter in his hand". The enemy unleashes a new weapon: "For they all made us **afraid,** saying, Their hands shall be weakened from the work, that it be not done" (v.9). Solomon described it as follows: "The **fear of man** bringeth a snare" (Prov. 29.25). This was the weapon used by Jezebel against Elijah: "So let the gods do to me, and more also, if I make not thy life as the life of one of them by tomorrow about this time. And when he saw that, he arose, and went for his life" (1 Kgs. 19.1-3). Sanballat's communication is described as "an **open letter**" and, according to Ellicott's Commentary, "It was hoped that Nehemiah would be alarmed by the thought that its contents had been read by the people". Perhaps Sanballat intended that his "open letter" would induce the people to bring pressure on Nehemiah. Attention is drawn to the following:

a) Sanballat's accusation, vv.6-7

The weapon of fear depended on deliberate misrepresentation: "It is reported among the heathen, and Gashmu (Geshem) saith it, that thou and the Jews think to rebel: for which cause thou buildest the wall, that thou mayest be their king, according to these words. And thou hast appointed prophets to preach of thee at Jerusalem, saying, There is a king in Judah: and now it shall be reported to the king according to these words". This serves to remind us that whether deliberately or otherwise, we can expect to be misunderstood and misreported. Paul suffered deliberate misrepresentation: see Romans 3.8 where he refers to a **slanderous report.** See also 2 Corinthians 6.4,8: "in all things approving ourselves as the ministers of God...by honour and dishonour, by **evil report and good report: as deceivers, and yet true**". The Lord Jesus suffered deliberate misrepresentation: "for many bare false witness against him, but their witness agreed not together" (Mark 14.56).

We should notice that Sanballat made sure that he was well covered in the event of an enquiry. After all, he was only quoting a report! "It is reported among the heathen, and **Gashmu saith it**". Sanballat's reference to Geshem could have been a veiled threat. Historians tell us that in the days of the Persian Empire, Geshem and his son ruled a league of Arabian tribes which took control of Moab and Ammon together with part of Arabia and the approaches to Egypt. Far from being a comparative nonentity, Geshem, it seems was "an even more powerful figure than his companions, though probably less earnestly committed to their cause" (D.Kidner).

b) Sanballat's aim, v.7

"Come now therefore, and let us take counsel together". It was not necessary for Nehemiah to add this time, "But they thought to do me mischief!" Ellicott's Commentary is probably right in saying, "the letter suggests the desirableness of friendly counsel to avert the danger".

c) Nehemiah's answer, v.8

"Then I sent unto him, saying, There are no such things done as thou sayest, but thou feignest them out of thine own heart". The report was firmly denied, and that was all. Nehemiah had no need to argue his cause in detail. He was able to speak with confidence. It is very important to ensure that "he that is of the contrary part may be ashamed, **having no evil thing to say of you**" (Titus 2.8). Paul was able to say, "Men and brethren, I have lived in all good conscience before God until this day" (Acts 23.1); "And herein do I exercise myself, to have always a conscience void of offence toward God, and toward men" (Acts 24.16). Hence he could say, "And they neither found me in the temple disputing with any man, neither raising up the people, neither in the synagogues, nor in the city: neither can they prove the things whereof they now accuse me" (Acts 24.12-13). But Nehemiah's confident reply did not mean he was totally immune from fear. Like Elijah, he was "a man subject to like passions as we are" (Jas. 5.17).

d) Nehemiah's assurance, v.9

"For they all made us afraid (or 'For they all **would** have made us afraid', RV/JND), saying, Their hands shall be weakened from the work, that it be not done (that was the enemy's avowed intention). **Now therefore, O God,** strengthen my hands". He followed the example of Hezekiah when threatened by Sennacherib: "And Hezekiah received the letter of the hand of the messengers, and read it: and Hezekiah went up into the house of the Lord, and spread it before the Lord. And Hezekiah prayed before the Lord" (2 Kgs. 19.14-15). Both Hezekiah and Nehemiah acted on the advice of Proverbs 29.25; "The fear of man bringeth a snare: **but whoso putteth his trust in the Lord shall be safe**". See also Psalm 27.1, "The Lord is my light and my salvation; whom shall I fear? the Lord is the strength of my life; of whom shall I be afraid". Even Paul needed divine reassurance: "Then spake the Lord to Paul in the night by a vision, Be not afraid, but speak, and hold not thy peace: for I am with thee, and no man shall set on thee to hurt thee: for I have much people in this city" (Acts 18.9-10). The apostle had encouraging words for the believers at Philippi: "And in nothing terrified by your adversaries: which is to them an evident token of perdition, but to you of salvation, and that of God" (Phil. 1.28).

It is worth noting that Nehemiah was evidently more concerned with the progress of the work than for his personal safety. He prayed for strength to continue *the work*: "Now therefore, O God, strengthen my hands" (v.9).

3) THEY ATTEMPTED TO DESTROY HIS FAITH, vv.10-14
Nehemiah would not come down to them, so they endeavoured to go up to him! Here we have infiltration: the enemy now concentrates on undermining the single-mindedness of Nehemiah from a different direction, in fact, from amongst his own people. These verses have great significance for us today. Once again, the enemy uses the weapon of fear. Attention is drawn to *(a)* Shemaiah's prophecy (vv.10-11); *(b)* Nehemiah's perception (vv.12-13); *(c)* Nehemiah's prayer (v.14).

a) Shemaiah's prophecy, vv.10-11
Nehemiah calls Shemaiah's gloomy advice a "prophecy": "And, lo, I perceived that God had not sent him; but that he pronounced this **prophecy** against me" (v.12). It was a case of "perils among **false brethren**" (2 Cor. 11.26). Nothing could be more pessimistic: "Let us meet together (another meeting) in the house of God, within the temple, and let us shut the doors of the temple: for they will come to slay thee; yea, in the night will they come to slay thee". Just what Nehemiah needed! He was surrounded by problems and difficulties, "without were fightings, within were fears" (2 Cor. 7.5), and could have well done without such pessimism. In the New Testament, Tychicus is described as "a beloved brother, and a faithful minister and fellowservant in the Lord: whom I have sent unto you for the same purpose, that he might know your estate, and comfort (encourage) your hearts" (Col. 4.7-8). We can be like Shemaiah, leaving aside for the moment that he was hired to scare Nehemiah, or we can be like Tychicus. The writer to the Hebrews urged his readers: "Let us hold fast the profession of our faith without wavering; (for he is faithful that promised;) and let us consider one another **to provoke unto love and to good works**: not forsaking the assembling of ourselves together, as the manner of some is; but exhorting one another: and so much the more, as ye see the day approaching" (Heb. 10.23-25). Moses found things rather different: "Our brethren have discouraged our heart, saying, The people is greater and taller than we" (Deut. 1.28). 'Wet blankets' are not unknown amongst us today!

Nehemiah dealt with the false prophecy by outright refusal to listen. He did not parley with Shemaiah: "And I said, Should such a man as I flee? and who is there, that, being as I am, would go into the temple to save his life? I will not go in".

b) Nehemiah's perception, vv.12-13
"And, lo, I perceived that God had not sent him; but that he pronounced this prophecy against me: for Tobiah and Sanballat had hired him". Nehemiah reached the conclusion that "God had not sent him" for the following reasons:

- **Shemaiah engendered fear**: "Therefore was he hired, that I should be **afraid**" (v.13). Nehemiah had declared, "our God shall fight for us" (4.20). To act on the advice of Shemaiah was to substitute fear for faith. This was just the intention of the enemy.

- **Shemaiah encouraged sin**: "Therefore was he hired, that I should be afraid, and do so, and **sin**". This evidently means that he had suggested refuge in the temple building itself, not merely the court, in which case intrusion into the sphere of the priests was involved. The advice was therefore unscriptural: it ran contrary to the word of God.

- **Shemaiah endangered testimony**: "Therefore was he hired, that I should be afraid, and do so, and **sin**, and that they might have matter for an evil report, that they might reproach me".

Nehemiah applied the test, "By their fruits ye shall know them" (Matt. 7.20). The need for that test remains: "Beloved, believe not every spirit, but try the spirits whether they are of God: because many false prophets are gone out into the world. Hereby know ye the Spirit of God: Every spirit that confesseth that Jesus Christ is come in the flesh is of God: and every spirit that confesseth not that Jesus Christ is come in the flesh is not of God" (1 John 4.1-3). In the Old Testament, it was "to the law and to the testimony: if they speak not according to this word, it is because there is no light in them" (Isa. 8.20). This involves care in assembly reception, and the Lord Jesus commended the assembly at Ephesus for this: "Thou hast tried them that say they are apostles, and are not, and hast found them liars" (Rev. 2.2).

c) Nehemiah's prayer, v.14
"My God, think thou upon Tobiah and Sanballat according to these their works, and on the prophetess Noadiah, and the rest of the prophets, that would have put me in fear". Nehemiah dealt with the false prophecy, but asks God to deal with the false prophets. God does not do for us what we can do for ourselves.

4) THEY EXPLOITED THE DISLOYALTY OF HIS BRETHREN, vv.15-19
The final paragraph in this chapter covers: *(a)* the completion of the work (v.15); (b) the consternation of the enemies (v.16); *(c)* the compromise of the nobles (vv.17-19).

a) The completion of the work, v.15
"So the wall was finished in the twenty and fifth day of the month Elul (September), in fifty and two days". No need to say more! Except to 'cast an eye' over our own spiritual progress.

b) The consternation of the enemies, v.16
"And it came to pass, that when all our enemies heard thereof, and all the heathen that were about us saw these things, they were much cast down in their own eyes: for they perceived (Nehemiah was equally perceptive: see v.12) that this work was **wrought of our God**". The **enemies** acknowledged that this was a work of God, yet many of the **Jews** were allied to those same enemies!

c) The compromise of the nobles, vv.17-19
"Moreover in those days the nobles of Judah sent many letters unto Tobiah, and the letters of Tobiah came unto them. For there were many in Judah **sworn unto him**, because he was the son in law of Shechaniah the son of Arah; and his son Johanan had taken the daughter of Meshullam the son of Berechiah". It was a case of "the friendship of the world is enmity with God" (Jas. 4.4). These intermarriages between Israelite and Ammonite illustrate the New Testament warning, "Be ye not unequally yoked together with unbelievers: for what fellowship hath righteousness with unrighteousness? and what communion hath light with darkness? and what concord hath Christ with Belial? or what part hath he that believeth with an infidel? and what agreement hath the temple of God with idols? for ye are the temple of the living God" (2 Cor. 6.14-16). The work of God did not benefit from these marriages. They served to promote the interests of Tobiah and his colleagues. The 'unequal yoke' can only prove detrimental to the believer personally, and detrimental to the Lord's work. See 13.24. Compare Deuteronomy 7.3-4.

There was a total lack of loyalty on the part of these nobles. In fact, there was nothing 'noble' about them: "Also they reported **his** good deeds **before me**, and uttered **my** words **to him**". Tobiah evidently believed that 'the pen is mightier than the sword'. He "sent letters to put me in fear" (v.19). In the first place, "They reported his good deeds before me": the nobles endeavoured to paint Tobiah, an enemy, in the best possible light. In the second place, "They...uttered my words ('matters', JND margin) to him": was a case of 'every word taken down in evidence against him!' This highlights the danger of relating assembly matters to outsiders. It also reminds us that it can be highly dangerous to speak critically or disparagingly about assembly members in front of children at home. Young minds are very impressionable. "Let your speech be alway with grace, seasoned with salt" (Col. 4.6).

We have now completed the first section of the book (Chapters 1-6), which deals with the **place.** The second section of the book (Chapters 7-13) deals with the **people.** Nehemiah had rebuilt the place, now he turns to the equally important task of rebuilding the spiritual strength of the place. Jerusalem had been destroyed because it had lost its spiritual character. The city had no purpose at all if there was nothing for God. The local assembly and our individual lives have no purpose either if there is nothing for Him.

READ CHAPTER 7

"The genealogy of them which came up at the first"

This chapter commences with reference to the completed reconstruction of the walls of Jerusalem. At the beginning of Chapter 6, the doors had not been hung, but the work was finished by the end of the chapter: "So the wall was finished in the twenty and fifth day of the month Elul, in fifty and two days" (v.15). Nehemiah refers to this in Chapter 7: "Now it came to pass, when the wall was built, and I had set up the doors..." (v.1). As we said in our previous study, Chapters 1-6 deal with the **place**, whereas Chapters 7-13 deal with the **people.** The place would be meaningless if there was nothing for God in the lives of His people. Having rebuilt the place, Nehemiah now begins to rebuild the **significance** of the place.

Nehemiah 7 may be divided as follows *(1)* the responsibility for administration (vv.1-4); *(2)* the registration of the names (vv.5-69); *(3)* the record of the offerings (vv.70-72); *(4)* the resettlement of the cities (v.73).

1) THE RESPONSIBILITY FOR ADMINISTRATION, vv.1-4

These verses suggest that Nehemiah was on the verge of leaving Jerusalem, and taking steps to ensure that responsibility for the city was left in capable hands. Perhaps the agreed period of absence from Shushan (see 2.6) had almost expired. The transfer of responsibility to Hanani, "a *faithful man*" (v.2), reminds us of Paul's instructions to Timothy: "The things that thou hast heard of me among many witnesses, the same (so don't alter it) commit thou to *faithful men*, who shall be able to teach others also" (2 Tim. 2.2). We should notice the following:

a) The service of the Levites, v.1

"Now it came to pass, when the wall was built, and I had set up the doors, and the porters and the singers and the Levites were appointed..." We will meet the porters, singers and Levites again in vv.43-45, and all we will do at this juncture is to note that Nehemiah did not introduce new ideas. He simply took steps to ensure that life in 'the place of the name' was regulated by the word of God, and therefore **orderly**. See 1 Corinthians 14.40. God's word is never out of date. We should remember that the singers did not entertain the general public. You would have been hard put to find a 'box office' in Jerusalem! They sang to the Lord.

b) The selection of leaders, v.2

"I gave my brother Hanani, and Hananiah the ruler of the palace, charge over Jerusalem: for he was a **faithful** man, and **feared** God above many". It was Hanani who first brought news of conditions in the city (1.2). Hananiah was already "ruler of the palace". He is now promoted to higher authority. Whilst his position as "ruler of the palace" could hardly be described as "least", we are nevertheless reminded of the Lord's teaching: "He that is faithful in that which is least is faithful also in much." (Luke 16.10). He was a man who had proved himself. Hanani certainly fulfilled the qualifications for rule set out by David: "He that ruleth over men must be just, ruling in the **fear of God**" (2 Sam. 23.3). We must not forget our obligations to godly leaders: "Obey them that have the rule over you ('obey your leaders', JND), and submit yourselves: for they watch for your souls, as they that must give account, that they may do it (the work) with joy, and not with grief: for that is unprofitable for you" (Heb. 13.17).

iii) The security of the city, vv.3-4

"Let not the gates of Jerusalem be opened until the sun be hot; and while they (the rulers) stand by, let them (the porters) shut the doors, and bar them: and appoint watches of the inhabitants of Jerusalem, **every one in his watch**, and every one to be **over against his house**". The need for care and vigilance remained. Hanani and Hananiah were instructed to "stand by" to ensure that the gates were securely shut. The city was thinly populated. The words, "and the houses were not builded", suggest that all the effort had been put into the wall. Notice that the assignment of responsibilities to the leaders **did not absolve everybody else** from responsibility.

There is a sense in which assembly gates need to be securely shut. Four apostles (if you believe Jude was an apostle) warn against slack spiritual security. **Paul** does so in referring to "false brethren unawares brought in ('brought in surreptitiously', JND), who came in privily (the same word: 'surreptitiously') to spy out our liberty which we have in Christ Jesus" (Gal. 2.4). **Peter** does so in warning that "there shall be false teachers among you, who privily shall bring in (introduce secretly) damnable (destructive) heresies" (2 Pet. 2.1). **John** does so in saying "Beloved, believe not every spirit, but try the spirits whether they are of God: because many false prophets are gone out into the world" (1 John 4.1-3). **Jude** does so in saying that "There are certain men crept in unawares" (Jude v.4). The Lord Jesus commended the assembly at Ephesus for its care in this way: "thou hast tried them which say they are apostles, and are not, and hast found them liars" (Rev. 2.2). It is part of an assembly overseer's responsibility to ensure the spiritual safety of the flock.

2) THE REGISTRATION OF THE NAMES, vv.5-69

With administrative arrangements in place, Nehemiah now turns in earnest to the people themselves. Unlike David, who numbered Israel for his own satisfaction (2 Samuel 24), Nehemiah was directed by God. "And *my God put into mine heart* to gather together the nobles, and the rulers, and the people, that they might be *reckoned by genealogy*" (v.5). This is not the first time that Nehemiah acknowledges divine guidance in this way. He said the same thing in connection with the rebuilding project: "neither told I any man what *my God had put in my heart* to do at Jerusalem" (2.12). Do notice that Nehemiah uses the expression "my God". This emphasises his personal devotion to God, his personal appreciation of God, and his personal responsibility to God. Paul also said "my God" (Phil. 4.19).

We look in vain at this point for any further information about the census conducted by Nehemiah. Instead, we are given "an extract from the archives" (D.Kidner) in the form of "a register of the genealogy of them which came up at the first" (v.5). The "register" was first made ninety years before, and forms the larger part of Ezra 2. This raises two questions:

- *Why did God want Nehemiah to "gather together the nobles, and the rulers, and the people, that they might be reckoned by genealogy", and what happened when the results were known?* The census was taken in preparation for repopulating Jerusalem. This actually took place in Chapter 11. We have already noticed that "the city was large and great: but the people were *few therein*" (v.4). The intervening chapters tell us how the people were spiritually prepared to "dwell at Jerusalem".

No doubt the census also served to assure the valiant inhabitants of Jerusalem, who had helped rebuild "the wall, even in troublous times" (Dan. 9.25), that their names were not forgotten, even though they were "few therein". It is encouraging to remember that although "the harvest truly is plenteous, but the labourers are *few*" (Matt. 9.37), every labourer is known to the Lord of the harvest.

- *Why did Nehemiah place on record the contents of the "register of the genealogy of them which came up at the first"?* It was to remind the people both of their inheritance and their calling. They were the successors of men and women whose devotion to God made them resign the pleasures and security of Babylon to rebuild 'the place of the name'. By citing the old "register", Nehemiah said in effect, "whose faith follow" (Heb.13.7).

We should notice that Nehemiah was concerned, not only with names, but with genealogies. This is particularly important when we come to vv.61,64. The list that now follows differs in some details from the record given by Ezra, and we should notice that it is said to be, not '**the** register of the genealogy of them which came up at the first', but "**a** register of the genealogy of them which came up at the first". Cyril J. Barber cites John J. Davis in *Biblical Numerology (1968)* here: "The list in Nehemiah 7, whilst made many years before Nehemiah's appointment as governor, gives evidence of having been compiled **after** the people arrived in 'the land beyond the river'. It reflects changes which Zerubbabel's list (Ezra 2) could not". In other words, the list in Ezra 2 was made **before** the expedition left Babylon for Jerusalem, and the list in Nehemiah 7 was made **after** they arrived. Bearing in mind the length of the journey (it took Ezra's expedition four months) there are bound to have been some amendments!

We must now examine, as best we can, the vast array of names and information before us, noting *(a)* the categories (vv.5-60); *(b)* the exclusions (vv.61-65); *(c)* the total (v.66-69).

a) The categories, vv.5-60
These verses (plus vv.61-63) record the names of those who responded to the original appeal: "Who is there among you of all his people? his God be with him, and let him go up to Jerusalem, which is in Judah, and build the house of the Lord God of Israel, (he is the God,) which is in Jerusalem" (Ezra 1.3). But why the detail? All are mentioned: family by family. The New Testament supplies the answer: "God is not unrighteous to forget your work and labour of love, which ye have shewed towards his name" (Heb. 6.10). It is worth remembering at this juncture that the offerings of the princes, on the day that the tabernacle was finally assembled and sanctified, are given in detail, man by man, even though each offering was identical! See Numbers 7.1-88. Heaven overlooks no one. Nobody is 'lost in the crowd! The people named in the "register" are described in Ezra 1.5 as "**them whose spirit God had raised**". He is well aware of our response, or otherwise, to His guidance. The classification of the names is significant. For a more detailed study of the names as given by Ezra, see our study in Ezra ch.2. Here now are the categories as given by Nehemiah:

i) The leaders, v.7. "These are the children of the province, that went up out of the captivity...who came with Zerubbabel, Jeshua, Nehemiah (not Nehemiah the son of Hachaliah!), Azariah, Raamiah, Nahamani, Mordecai (not the Mordecai of Esther!), Bilshan, Mispereth, Bigvai, Nehum, Baanah". Leadership was recognised. Notice the oft-repeated combination of Zerubbabel and Jeshua: governor and priest led the people. See, for example, Ezra 3.2,8; 4.3; 5.2; Haggai 1.1,12. Zerubbabel was the man who served before the people: Jeshua was the man who served in the presence of God. It is a most important combination: we will never be anything for God before men, unless we spend time in the presence of God. Zerubbabel was in the royal line: see Matthew 1.12-13; Haggai 2.21-23. He was "the Tirshatha" (v.65), meaning one to be feared or reverenced. He was evidently succeeded by Nehemiah (8.9; 10.1).

ii) The people, vv.8-38. Nothing special is said about them. They were not leaders, priests or Levites. But they are all listed. They were people with concern for God's glory and God's house. Paul mentions ten brethren in Colossians 4.7-17, and tells us something about them all, with the exception of "Jesus, which is called Justus" (v.11). The absence of detail is instructive. Like the people in Nehemiah 7, nothing is said about him, but the very mention of his name assures us that his "record is on high" (Job 16.19). We must say again that heaven overlooks no one.

Do notice that this section of the "register" refers to a great number of places, some well known as Bethlehem (v.26), Anathoth (v.27), Bethel and Ai (v.32), Jericho, (v.36), but most of them quite obscure to us. The end of the chapter explains the significance of these details: "So the priests, and the Levites, and the porters, and the singers, and (some) of the people, and the Nethinims, and all Israel, *dwelt in their cities*" (v.73). They went back to their original possessions.

iii) The priests, vv.39-42. There were 4,289 priests. We must remember that there can be no true worship without priestly exercise: "By him therefore let us offer the sacrifice of praise to God continually, that is, the fruit of our lips giving thanks to his name" (Heb. 13.15). God receives His portion from us in our worship. How about *our* ministry "to the Lord" (Acts 13.2). In the Old Testament, it was the function of "the priests the sons of Levi" to "come near; for them the Lord thy God hath chosen *to minister unto him*" (Deut. 21.5). We should carefully note that it was as the "prophets and teachers" named (or, more likely, the whole church) "ministered *to the Lord*", that He revealed His will through the Holy Spirit. He communicates His mind and will to those who are devoted to Him.

iv) The Levites, v.43. There were only seventy-four Levites, although the singers (148) and porters (138) were also Levites. There is always a lack of serving men. Ezra discovered this when he "viewed the people, and the priests" by "the river that runneth to Ahava". He "found there none of the sons of Levi" (Ezra 8.15). Service for God demands dedication and sacrifice, and life is full of easier options, even for Christians! The duties of the Levites are set out as follows: "their office was to wait on the sons of Aaron for the service of the house of the Lord, in the courts, and in the chambers, and in the purifying of all holy things, and the work of the service of the house of God" (1 Chron. 23.28). See also Numbers chs.3-4 for their service in connection with the tabernacle. The priests were concerned with **worship**: the Levites were concerned with **work**. **We** are both priests and Levites!

v) The singers, v.44. The singers (148) outnumbered Levites (74) by two to one! This does seem rather unbalanced, and it is a sad fact that some Christians would rather sing in a choir than go out tracting! The following verses describe the work of the Levitical singers: "They were employed in that work day and night" (1 Chron. 9.33); "And David spake to the chief of the Levites to appoint their brethren to be the singers with instruments of musick...by lifting up the voice with joy" (1 Chron. 15.16.); "the Levites which were the singers...being arrayed in white linen...the trumpeters and singers were as one, to make one sound to be heard in praising and thanking the Lord" (2 Chron. 5.12-13); "he (Jehoshaphat) appointed singers unto the Lord, and that should praise the beauty of holiness, as they went out before the army, and to say, Praise the Lord; for his mercy endureth for ever" (2 Chron. 20.21-22); "such as taught to sing praise" (2 Chron.23.13). (There were evidently other singers besides the Levites: see v.67).

Turning to the New Testament, we must note the following: "I will sing with the spirit, and I will sing with the understanding also" (1 Cor. 14.15); "speaking to yourselves in psalms and hymns and spiritual songs, singing and making melody in your heart to the Lord" (Eph. 5.19); "Let the word of Christ dwell in you richly in all wisdom; teaching and admonishing one another in psalms and hymns and spiritual songs, singing with grace in your hearts to the Lord" (Col. 3.16) or, altering the punctuation, 'Let the word of Christ dwell in you richly in all wisdom; teaching and admonishing one another. In psalms and hymns and spiritual songs, singing with grace in your hearts to the Lord'.

We have already noticed that one aspect of our priesthood is to "offer the **sacrifice of praise** to God continually" (Heb. 13.15). All too often, prayer becomes a series of requests. The word "sacrifice" implies that worship and praise involve time and preparation. Our daily devotions should be unhurried and thoughtful. Our petitions will then be made in the spirit of praise and thankfulness.

vi) The porters, v.45. They functioned as gate-keepers. Their work is described in 1 Chronicles 9.17-27. Here are some extracts from their 'job description'. "They and their children had the oversight of the gates of the house of the Lord, namely, the house of the tabernacle, by wards" (v.23). The expression "by wards" means 'by watches', involving security and vigilance. "In four quarters were the porters, toward the east, west, north and south" (v.24); "They lodged round about the house of God, because the charge was upon them, and the opening thereof every morning pertained to them" (v.27). This is what Samuel did when he was a young Levite (1 Sam. 3.15). Notice that the tabernacle is described here (1 Sam. 3.15) as "the house of the Lord"; earlier it is called "the temple of the Lord" (1 Sam. 1.9). The porters were responsible for the purity of the house of God: "And he (Jehoiada the priest) set the porters at the gates of the house of the Lord, that none which was unclean in any thing should enter in" (2 Chron. 23.19). Paul pointed out the ongoing need for spiritual "porters": "For I know this, that after my departing shall grievous wolves enter in among you, not sparing the flock…Therefore watch and remember, that by the space of three years I ceased not to warn every one of you night and day with tears" (Acts 20.29-31).

vii) The Nethinims, vv.46-56. The word Nethinim is already plural: the English plural ending isn't really necessary! The name means 'given' or 'dedicated'. Ezra refers to them as those "whom David and the princes had appointed for the service of the Levites, two hundred and twenty Nethinims" (Ezra 8.20). They are thought to be the Gibeonites, who were made by Joshua "hewers of wood and drawers of water for the congregation, and for the altar of the Lord, even unto this day, in the place which he should choose" (Joshua 9.27). We could call them 'burden-bearers'. We all ought to be spiritual Nethinims: see Galatians 6.2. We must not be like the lawyers: see Luke 11.46.

viii) The children of Solomon's servants, vv.57-59. These were associated with the Nethinims (v.60). We could conclude that since "of the children of Israel did Solomon make no servants for his work" (2 Chron. 8.9), that the "children of Solomon's servants" were foreigners.

b) The exclusions, vv.61-65
There were two categories here: *(i)* those who could not prove their national status (vv.61-62); *(ii)* those who could not prove their priestly status (vv.63-65).

i) Those who could not prove their national status, vv.61-62. There were 642 people who "could not shew their father's house, nor their seed, **whether they were of Israel**". We must be absolutely certain that our names are in "the book of life" (Phil. 4.3). The Lord Jesus told His disciples to "rejoice not, that the spirits are subject unto you; but rather rejoice, because your names are written in heaven" (Luke 10.20).

ii) Those who could not prove their priestly status, vv.63-65. "And of the priests...these sought their register among those that were reckoned by genealogy, but it was not found: therefore were they, as polluted, put from the priesthood". The lesson is clear: **in cases of doubt, don't take risks: wait on God.** The purity of the priesthood must be preserved. For "Urim and Thummin" (v.65), meaning 'lights' and 'perfections', see Exodus 28.30. We are not told precisely what they were, but we do know that they were used in connection with discerning the will of God. See Numbers 27.21; 1 Samuel 28.6. (Further help could well be found in 1 Samuel 14.19,41). They are a picture of the Lord Jesus in whom God has finally spoken and revealed Himself (Heb. 1.1-3). Like the "Urim and Thummin", He is beyond human understanding. He is 'light' and 'perfection'.

c) The total, vv.66-69
The total number of returning exiles was 42,360, plus servants and maids numbering 7,337. Every one was known to God, from leaders to maids. The transport available seems rather inadequate. It works out at six people per animal. Most people evidently walked.

3) THE RECORD OF THE OFFERINGS, vv.70-72
"And *some* of the **chief of the fathers** gave unto the work", including the Tirshatha himself, Zerubbabel at that time (vv.70-71). Ezra puts it like this: the "chief of the fathers...offered freely for the house of God to set it up in his place: they gave after their ability" (Ezra 2.68-69). The New Testament gives us guidance on the subject as follows: "Upon the first day of the week let every one of you lay by him in store, as God hath prospered him" (1 Cor. 16.2). The "chief of the fathers" were followed by "the **rest of the people**" (v.72). The leadership set a good example for others to follow.

4) THE RESETTLEMENT OF THE CITIES, v.73
"So the priests, and the Levites, and the porters, and the singers, and *some* of the people, and the Nethinims, and all Israel, dwelt in **their** cities; and **when the seventh month came**, the children of Israel were in their cities". The people

recovered their lost inheritance, but it would have been far better if it had not been lost in the first place. We must remember that God makes provision for **our** spiritual recovery too, but like the Nazarite who became defiled, "the days that were before shall be lost, because his separation was defiled" (Num. 6.12).

The Chapter ends with reference to "the seventh month". This was no coincidence. Something very important took place in this month every seven years, as we shall see in Chapter 8.

READ CHAPTER 8

"Bring the book"

We have already noticed that Nehemiah Chapters 1-6 deal with the **place,** and Chapters 7-13 deal with the **people.** Nehemiah's prayer makes it very clear that whilst he was deeply concerned about the ruin of Jerusalem (1.3), he was equally concerned about the underlying reason for its destruction (1.7-9). He had successfully addressed the first problem: the broken walls had been rebuilt, and the burnt gates had been restored. Even the enemies recognised "that this work was wrought of our God" (6.16). But even more important work lay ahead, and Nehemiah now turns his attention to **spiritual rebuilding**. Listen again to his prayer: "Remember, I beseech thee, the word that thou commandest thy servant Moses, saying, If ye transgress, I will scatter you abroad among the nations: but if ye turn unto me, and **keep my commandments, and do them**; though there were of you cast out unto the uttermost part of the heaven, yet will I gather them from thence, and will bring them unto the place that I have chosen to set my name there" (1.8-9).

This section of Nehemiah (Chapters 7-12) therefore deals with the preparation of the people to dwell in "the place which the Lord thy God hath chosen to place his name there" (Deut. 16.11). We must not miss the lesson. It is very important that "all the counsel of God" (Acts 20.27) should be in place in the assembly, but this will accomplish very little unless the word of God is allowed to influence our life and conduct. The assembly must be right in doctrine and practice, but the people must be right as well.

This section of the book may be summarised as follows: **Chapter 7** - Registering the names (this reminded the people both of their inheritance and their calling: they were **God's** people); **Chapter 8** - Reading the scriptures (as God's people they had an appetite for His word, and so should we); **Chapter 9** - Reviewing their history; **Chapter 10** - Resolving to obey; **Chapter 11** - Recognising their centre; **Chapter 12** - Rejoicing in God's goodness.

Nehemiah Chapter 8 is punctuated by references to "the book" (vv.1,3,5,8,18).

Quite clearly, Nehemiah lost no time in preparing for the reading of God's word. The wall had been completed just days before: compare 6.15 (Elul was the sixth month) with 8.2, "the first day of the seventh month". It was on this day that the 'feast of trumpets' was to be kept. See Leviticus 23.24. Over the chapter we could write Paul's exhortation to Timothy, "Give attendance to *reading*" (1 Tim. 4.13). While "reading" here (*anagnosis*) can refer to private or public reading, the context shows that Paul is referring here to public reading, and it is significant that in the Septuagint (the Greek translation of the Old Testament), exactly the same word is used in Nehemiah 8.8 ("caused them to understand the *reading*"). The public reading of the word of God is most important. The Scriptures should be read at every assembly meeting. They should be read carefully and clearly.

The chapter may be divided as follows: *(1)* their desire for the book (v.1); *(2)* their attention to the book (vv.2-3); *(3)* their reverence for the book (vv.4-6); *(4)* their understanding of the book (vv.7-8); *(5)* their response to the book (vv.9-12): *(6)* their obedience to the book (vv.13-18). Ezra now makes his first appearance in the book of Nehemiah.

1) THEIR DESIRE FOR THE BOOK, v.1
"And they spake unto Ezra the scribe to *bring the book*". There is a little more to this than meets the eye! The people were evidently familiar with Deuteronomy 31: "And Moses commanded them, saying, At the end of every seven years, in the solemnity of the year of release, in the feast of tabernacles, when all Israel is come to appear before the Lord thy God in the place which he shall choose, thou shalt read this law before all Israel in their hearing. Gather the people together, men, and women, and children, and thy stranger that is within thy gates, that they may hear, and that they may learn, and fear the Lord your God, and observe to do all the words of this law: and that their children, which have not known any thing, may hear, and learn to fear the Lord your God, as long as ye live in the land whither ye go over Jordan to possess it" (vv.10-13). This striking passage would make the basis of a good sermon! Do notice **when** the law was to be read, **where** the law was to be read, to **whom** the law was to be read, and **why** the law was to be read. Nehemiah 8 is a classic illustration of Deuteronomy 31!

We should particularly notice the first of these points: the law was to be read, "at the end of every seven years". Nehemiah travelled to Jerusalem in BC445, ninety-one years after Zerubbabel led the first group of exiles back from Babylon in BC536, at which time the children of Israel "kept also the feast of tabernacles" (Ezra 3.4). The intervening period is exactly thirteen periods of seven years, so we can conclude that they had got it exactly right in Nehemiah 8! We must notice the following:

a) The unity with which they gathered
"**All** the people gathered themselves together as **one man** (compare Ezra 3.1) into the street (square, or open place) that was before the water gate". Very clearly, they were **all there** ("all the people gathered"), and they were all there **with the same enthusiasm** ("as one man"). Both are very important. They were all there to hear the word of God read publicly, which recalls the New Testament injunction: "not forsaking the assembling of ourselves together" (Heb. 10.25). The people who say that 'fellowship is more than coming to meetings', are usually people who are conspicuous by their absence from meetings! The people who faithfully attend assembly gatherings are usually first to promote fellowship in other ways. We should value every opportunity to hear the word of God read and expounded. There is a vast difference between a **reason** for not attending, and an **excuse** for not attending. These people valued the word of God. Unlike them, we have a **personal** copy of the Scriptures, but do we value them in the same way?

But it was even more than that: they "gathered themselves together as **one man**". There was a **common** desire to hear the word of God. It wasn't a case of reluctantly trudging down to the water gate because everybody else was going, and absentees would be noted! Everybody was there because they wanted to be there! It is a very happy assembly indeed when that is the case. Is it really too much to ask?

b) The place in which they gathered
"And all the people gathered themselves together as one man into the street that was before the **water gate**". We noticed the significance of the water gate when studying Chapter 3. Generally speaking, springing water in Scripture is a picture of the Holy Spirit, and still water is a picture of the **word of God.** See, for example, John 7.37-39 in the first case, and Ephesians 5.25-26 with Psalm 119.9 in the second. The law was therefore read at a most appropriate place! We should also notice that the Scriptures were read, not in the temple court, but in one of the centres of city life. Read Proverbs 1.20-21. Now that's worth thinking about!

c) The purpose for which they gathered
"They spake unto Ezra the scribe to **bring the book** of the law of Moses, which the Lord had commanded to Israel". Although preparation had already been

made (v.4), this was "clearly a general desire...and not a formality imposed by the leadership" (D.Kidner). The strength of their desire to hear the word of God is reflected in the translation, "they **told** Ezra to bring the book of the law of Moses" (RSV). They had not come to be entertained, or to indulge in dance or drama, but to hear the word of God. It is a sad fact that many believers today prefer anything but the word of God, so unlike the Psalmist who exclaimed, "O how I love thy law! it is my meditation all the day" (Psalm 119.97), and Job who said, "I have esteemed the words of his mouth more than my necessary food" (Job 23.12). There can be no spiritual growth in our personal lives or in our assembly life, without Bible teaching. We must be "nourished up in the words of faith and of good doctrine" (1 Tim. 4.6). Notice too that these people recognised the authority of God's word. They came prepared to listen to "the book of the **law** of Moses, which the Lord had **commanded** to Israel". In the first place, they wanted to hear the **original** word of God: "The book of the law of Moses". We must not be satisfied with anything less than the unvarnished Scriptures. So many people like a Bible suitably adapted to accommodate their own ideas. In the second place, they recognised the **divine authority** of the Scriptures: "which **the Lord** had commanded to Israel". God's word is binding upon us, simply because it **is** God's word.

2) THEIR ATTENTION TO THE BOOK, vv.2-3

"And the ears of all the people were **attentive unto the book** of the law" (v.3). They evidently lost sight of the reader, Ezra, and gave undivided attention to the word of God itself. So often we get absorbed by the personality and mannerisms of the preacher, rather than his message. We must remember that authority does not lie with the man, but with the word of God. We should now notice:

a) The people who listened

"And Ezra the priest (he is described as "the scribe" in v.4, and "the priest the scribe" in v.9) brought the law before the congregation both of **men and women, and all that could hear with understanding**". Men, women and children all listened to the reading of God's word. We are therefore reminded that all age groups need instruction from the word of God, and that part of the spiritual education of younger people is to listen and observe in the company of older people. Whilst there are legitimate exceptions from time to time, it is a mistake not to bring children to the Lord's supper, either by keeping them at home or by arranging a crèche, and it is a mistake not to encourage young people to attend all assembly meetings. We must also remember that assembly meetings are as incomplete without sisters as they are without brothers.

b) The time for which they listened
Ezra "read therein before the street that was before the water gate *from the morning until midday*". While, for obvious reasons, we should certainly endeavour to ensure that Gospel meetings end at the appointed time, it is decidedly sad when believers shut their Bibles, start to sigh, clear their throats, and shuffle their feet, just because the meeting, perhaps even the Lord's supper, has gone a little 'over the time'. While some preachers are wearisome, we should at least remember that the word of God is open.

c) The way in which they listened
"The ears of all the people were *attentive* unto the book of the law". They gave careful attention to its reading. It is quite amazing how quickly some people seem to forget what has been said at a meeting. Perhaps they weren't really listening at all. The Lord Jesus said, "Take heed therefore *how* ye hear" (Luke 8.18). In fairness, it has to be said that some things said by preachers are best forgotten!

3) THEIR REVERENCE FOR THE BOOK, vv.4-6
"And Ezra *opened the book* in the sight of all the people; (for he was above all the people;) and when he opened it, all the people stood up". They did this quite spontaneously. We must carefully note the following;

a) "Ezra the scribe stood upon a pulpit of wood"
He "*stood* upon a pulpit of wood". Proper arrangements were made for the reading of Scripture. It has been said that 'this is the only place in the Bible where we find a man on a platform!' (Jeffrey Harrison). The word of God was read with dignity. Whether publicly or otherwise, we must never forget whose book we are reading, and whose voice we are hearing when it is read. The public reading of Scripture must be undertaken with care. If you are a preacher, or aspire to be a preacher, remember to read God's word with great reverence. No hands in pockets!

b) "Ezra opened the book in the sight of all the people"
He "*opened* the book". Everybody could see what he was reading. It is good practice to clearly display an open Bible. We then proclaim our authority for all to see. We must let people see that we really do mean "thus saith *the Lord*", and that we really do ask, "What saith *the scripture*?" Preachers should remember that it is helpful to ask people to look at their Bibles with them when making or emphasising a point. Do notice what followed when Ezra "opened the book": "And when he opened it, all the people *stood up*". That was the measure of their reverence and respect for the word of God. "To this

man will I look, even to him that is poor and of a contrite spirit, and trembleth at my word" (Isa **66**.2).

c) *"Ezra blessed the Lord, the great God"*
Nehemiah "**blessed** the Lord, the great God". Notice Nehemiah's appreciation of God's greatness. We do need to remember that he is "the **great God**". The people responded beautifully: "And all the people answered, Amen, Amen, with lifting up their hands: and they bowed their heads, and worshipped the Lord with their faces to the ground". The law was read in the spirit of thankfulness, worship, and humility. There was a spirit of expectation on the part of the people. Can you think of a better way to read the Scriptures?!

4) *THEIR UNDERSTANDING OF THE BOOK, vv.7-8*
"So they **read in the book** in the law of God distinctly, and gave the sense, and caused them to understand the reading". There were evidently thirteen men on the platform with Ezra (v.4) and, presumably, these were the men who actually **read** the Scriptures. There were also thirteen men who **explained** the Scriptures (v.7). Perhaps the first part of v.8 refers to the readers, and the second part to the teachers. It is quite possible that the teachers circulated amongst the people, hence the words, "and the people stood in their place" (v.7). Very clearly, the word of God was given a good hearing. We have already noticed that "the ears of all the people were attentive unto the book of the law" (v.3). Now we read that "the people stood in their place". Remember, they did this "from the morning until midday"! They didn't move!

We are told **how** the Levites "caused the people to understand the law": "So they read in the book in the law of God distinctly, and gave the sense, and caused them to understand the reading" (v.8). Some understand the expression, "gave the sense", to mean, 'gave the translation', that is, from Hebrew into Aramaic, but this is far from certain, and it seems best to give the expression its normal meaning. The verse speaks for itself: good clear reading, plus good clear explanation. After all, this is the purpose of all Bible teaching. There is little good in 'ministry' that is so 'deep' that no one can understand it! We often come to a rather strange conclusion that preachers like this must be quite wonderful! The best compliment you can ever pay to a preacher is to go home scratching your head and wondering why you never saw it for yourself, because, after all, the meaning is really so simple! That man has done his job! Whether Gospel preacher, Bible teacher in whatever capacity, or Sunday School teacher, strive to be accurate, but **study to be simple.** The aim is to help people understand the Scriptures. So far as the first is concerned, we must remember Paul's advice to Timothy: "Study (be diligent) to shew thyself approved unto God, a workman that needeth not to be ashamed, rightly dividing the word of truth" (2 Tim. 2.15). This involves reference to the context of any verse or passage. Remember that a *text* taken out of its *context* becomes a *pretext* for just about anything!

5) THEIR RESPONSE TO THE BOOK, vv.9-12
We should notice here that they wept before rejoicing (v.9), and that they shared their blessings with others (vv.10-12).

a) They wept before rejoicing, v.9
"And Nehemiah, which is the Tirshatha, and Ezra the priest the scribe, and the Levites that taught the people (notice the unity of the leadership here: they spoke with one voice: this is very important), said unto all the people, This day is holy unto the Lord your God; mourn not, nor weep. For all the people wept, when they heard the words of the law". There was conviction of sin before enjoyment of the word of God, which is the order in which David places them: "I acknowledge my transgressions: and my sin is ever before me...Make me to hear joy and gladness; that the bones which thou hast broken may rejoice" (Psalm 51.3,8). Paul does the same: "godly sorrow worketh repentance to salvation not to be repented of" (2 Cor. 7.10). Derek Kidner makes the point that three times in this short paragraph we are reminded that holiness and gloom go ill together.

b) They shared their blessings with others, vv.10-12
"Then he said unto them, Go your way, eat the fat, and drink the sweet, and send portions unto them for whom nothing is prepared". Perhaps this refers to the poor widows and the fatherless. Their joy from understanding "the words that were declared unto them" (v.12) was to benefit others. If you have received blessing and help through an assembly meeting, or in your personal study, why not share it with a brother or sister who can't get out much, if at all, to the meetings? And what about sharing the Gospel with unsaved friends and neighbours?

6) THEIR OBEDIENCE TO THE BOOK, vv.13-18
"And on the second day were gathered together the chief of the fathers of all the people, the priests, and the Levites, unto Ezra the scribe, even to understand the words of the law" (v.13), or "to give attention to the words of the law" (RV), or "to study the words of the law" (RSV). It was a meeting of leaders, and involved a week of Bible Readings! While it is important for all God's people to have a working knowledge of God's word, it is particularly important for leaders. An overseer must hold "fast the faithful word as he hath been taught, that he may be able by **sound doctrine** both to exhort and to convince the gainsayers"

(Titus 1.9). The "gainsayers" will not be convicted ('convinced', AV) by charm on one hand, or brow-beating on the other: Only "sound doctrine" will achieve the desired result.

Their study of God's word produced something of a shock. They discovered that part of God's word had not been practised for a thousand years! "And they found written in the law which the Lord had commanded by Moses, that the children of Israel should dwell in booths in the feast of the seventh month" (v.14). The last time this had been done was in "the days of Jeshua the son of Nun" (v.17). Since such a long time had elapsed, and there had been no evidence of divine displeasure over the omission, we might have expected them to 'let sleeping dogs lie', but they did nothing of the kind. The commandments of God must be obeyed, even though it meant restoring something that had lapsed for a thousand years.

Over one hundred and fifty years ago, godly men and women in various places became convinced that the religious practices of the day were far removed from the teaching of the New Testament. Their convictions, formed solely by the word of God, led them to abandon denominational affiliations and meet simply on the grounds of Holy Scripture. Some did this at great personal cost. They followed the injunction "Buy the truth, and sell it not" (Prov. 23.23). These believers were guided by the Scriptures, not written a thousand years before, but **eighteen hundred years** or so before! It is a sad fact that so many of their spiritual successors have gone back to those very denominational circles from which those men and women of the Nineteenth Century, and many since, separated themselves because "they found written". Let us be warned: God has not changed His word: we have a duty to obey it in exactly the same way as Nehemiah and his colleagues. Do notice, in passing, that their obedience to the word of God was displayed on their houses, in the house of God, and in the streets (v.16). There must be a sermon here!

Obedience to God's word always brings joy, and it is not surprising to read, "and there was very great gladness" (v.17). Compare v.10. The Lord Jesus said, "If ye keep my commandments, ye shall abide in my love; even as I have kept my Father's commandments, and abide in his love. These things have I spoken unto you, that my joy might remain in you, and that your joy might be full" (John 15.10-11).

This is not the time for a detailed investigation of "the feast of the seventh month" (v.14). It was, of course, the feast of tabernacles. This was kept from the fifteenth day of the seventh month. Amongst other things, it was a feast of remembrance: "that your generations may know that I made the children of Israel to dwell in booths, when I brought them out of the land of Egypt" (Lev. 23.43). Being the last feast in the Jewish calendar, "when ye have gathered in the fruit of the land", it spoke of the time in which Israel could dwell upon God's goodness, and enjoy it. It was therefore a prophetic picture of millennial joy. See Zechariah 14.16. The eighth day of the feast (eight in Scripture signifies a new beginning) anticipates the eternal state. The millennium will lead to the "new heavens and the new earth".

READ CHAPTER 9.1-15

"They confessed, and worshipped the Lord their God"

In our previous study, we noticed that "the people wept, when they heard the words of the law" (8.9), and that they made "great mirth, because they had understood the words that were declared unto them" (8.12). Their obedience to a long-forgotten commandment brought "very great gladness" (8.17). But if these were the only results, we could be forgiven for questioning the reality of their response. We all know that initial enthusiasm can disappear very quickly, especially if it is rooted in the emotion of a big meeting! Hosea put it like this, "Your goodness is as a morning cloud, and as the early dew it goeth away" (Hos. 6.4). Nehemiah Chapters 9-10 demonstrate that the reading of God's word produced a deep desire to please God on an on-going basis. The short term results were good: the long term results were better. They are summed up in Chapter 10.29, "They clave unto their brethren, their nobles, and entered into a curse, and into an oath, to walk in God's law, which was given by Moses the servant of God, and to observe and *do* all the commandments of the Lord our Lord, and his judgments and his statutes". James urges us to be "*doers* of the word, and not hearers only, deceiving your own selves. For if any be a hearer of the word, and not a doer, he is like unto a man beholding his natural face in a glass: for he beholdeth himself, and goeth his way, and straightway forgetteth what manner of man he was" (Jas. 1.22-24). How much effect does God's word have on *our* lives?

Nehemiah Chapter 9 prepares the way for the covenant described in Chapter 10. Chapter 9 is far more than a resume of Israel's history. It is a record of God's **covenant faithfulness** to His people. Hence the words, "Now therefore, our God, the great, the mighty, and the terrible God, who keepest **covenant and mercy**..." (v.32). But, at the same time, it is a record of Israel's lamentable **failure**: "thou art just in all that is brought upon us; for thou hast done right, but we have done wickedly" (v.33). The faithfulness of God to the covenant with His people, and the unfaithfulness of the people to their obligations under the covenant, brought a resolve to renew the covenant: "And because of all this we make a **sure covenant**, and write it; and our princes, Levites, and priests, seal unto it" (v.38). As noted above, the covenant is described in Chapter 10.

The chapter may be divided as follows: *(1)* their approach to God (vv.1-3); *(2)* their appreciation of God (vv.4-31); *(3)* their appeal to God (vv.32-38). If Chapter 8 majors on the word of God, then Chapter 9 majors on prayer to God.

1) THEIR APPROACH TO GOD, vv.1-3
The feast of tabernacles (8.18) ended on the twenty-third day of the seventh month, but nobody went home. They remained in the presence of God after the feast was over. They had serious business to transact. This involved:

a) Self-denial, v.1
"Now in the twenty and fourth day of this month the children of Israel were assembled with fasting, and with sackclothes, and earth upon them". Fasting is self-denial. It was evidently practised in the New Testament (see Acts 13.2-3; 14.23), but not commanded. Even legitimate things can sometimes prove distracting in our service and devotion to God, so much so that the Lord Jesus said, "If any man will come after me, let him **deny himself**, and take up his cross daily, and follow me" (Luke 9.23). Our current chapter emphasises that nothing was allowed to divert the attention of the people from confession and prayer. They approached Him with deep sorrow. But fasting is not an end in itself. In the words of Matthew Henry, "Fasting without prayer is a body without a soul". Fasting promotes undistracted prayer, which promotes spiritual power. When the disciples asked the question, "Why could not we cast him out? (the 'dumb spirit')", the Lord replied, "This kind can come forth by nothing, but by prayer and fasting" (Mark 9.28-29).

b) Separation, v.2
"And the seed of Israel separated themselves from all strangers ('foreigners', JND), and stood and confessed their sins, and the iniquities of their fathers". We must remember that this was the result of reading the word of God. Deuteronomy 7.2-3 explains why it was necessary. Compromise would be disastrous. Paul deals with the question of separation in 2 Corinthians 6: "Be ye not unequally yoked together with unbelievers (the passage refers particularly to idolatry, but it also *applies* to marriage and to every other relationship): for what fellowship hath righteousness with unrighteousness? and what communion hath light with darkness? and what concord hath Christ with Belial? or what part hath he that believeth with an infidel? and what agreement hath the temple of God with idols? for ye are the temple of the living God; as God hath said, I will dwell

in them, and walk in them; and I will be their God, and they shall be my people. Wherefore come out from among them, and be ye **separate**, saith the Lord" (vv.14-17). We should carefully notice that Paul does not say that there was to be no **contact** with evil (in this case, idolatry), but no **contract** with evil. This applies as much to ecclesiastical evil as it does to moral evil.

Having done this, and "confessed their sins, and the iniquities of their fathers", evidence of their reality before God, they gave themselves to the Scriptures. After all, we cannot expect to hear God's voice if sin remains unconfessed.

c) Study, v.3
"And they stood up in their place, and read in the book of the law of the Lord their God". Compare 8.7-8. See 1 Timothy 4.13, "Give attendance to (public) reading". The results follow: "they confessed, and worshipped the Lord their God". The reading of scripture should promote a right attitude to sin, and a right attitude to God. "Three hours they spent in reading, expounding, and applying the scriptures, and three hours in confessing sin and praying; so that they stayed together six hours, and spent all the time in the solemn acts of religion, without saying, 'Behold what a weariness is it.'" (Matthew Henry). Notice their reverential posture: they "stood...they stood up...Then stood up...Then the Levites... said, Stand up" (vv.2-5). There should be no slouching in the presence of God.

2) THEIR APPRECIATION OF GOD, vv.4-31
This part of the proceedings is introduced by: *a sense of need*: they "cried with a loud voice unto the Lord their God" (v.4), and *a sense of wonder*: they said, "Stand up and bless the Lord your God for ever and ever: and blessed be thy glorious name, which is exalted above all blessing and praise" (v.5). They appreciated *(a)* His creatorial majesty (v.6); *(b)* His covenant mercy (vv.7-31).

a) His creatorial majesty, v.6
Try looking for the word 'creatorial' in the dictionary. You will be surprised at what you won't find! However, since this 'new' word will probably enter our official vocabulary one day, we will proceed!

"Thou, even thou, art Lord alone; thou hast made heaven, the heaven of heavens, with all their host, the earth, and all things that are therein, the seas, and all that is therein, and thou preservest them all; and the host of heaven worshippeth thee". It is not without significance that this great prayer should begin in this way. It was Israel's failure to remember the greatness and glory of God that led to her downfall through idolatry and all its associations.

Amongst other things, we should notice the following in vv.5-6: God's **eternity**: "bless the Lord your God *for ever and ever*"; God's **transcendence**: "*exalted above all blessing and praise*": God's **solitariness**: "Thou, even thou, art Lord **alone**"; God's **creatorial power**: "Thou *hast made* heaven...the earth...the seas"; God's **maintaining power**: "and thou *preservest them all*". Verse 6 concludes: "and the host of heaven worshippeth thee", which must refer, not so much to the starry heavens, but to the created heavenly intelligences. Why not take time to amplify the statements in these verses from other parts of Scripture? Make a start with the following: "For by him were all things created, that are in heaven, and that are in earth, visible and invisible, whether they be thrones, or dominions, or principalities, or powers: all things were created by him, and for him: and he is before all things, and by him all things consist" (Col. 1.16-17).

b) His covenant mercy, vv.7-31
The passage therefore follows the order of Psalm 19, where David links the revelation of God in the skies ("The heavens declare the glory of God: and the firmament sheweth his handiwork...", vv.1-6) with the revelation of God in scripture ("The law of the Lord is perfect, converting the soul: the testimony of the Lord is sure, making wise the simple...", vv.7-14). Stephen connected the **creatorial majesty** of God, with the **covenant mercy** of God: "The God of glory appeared unto our father Abraham, when he was in Mesopotamia, before he dwelt in Charran" (Acts 7.2). When we think of **our** calling, we can only be filled with wonder that such a God as this could choose such people as us!

We have already said that this section is far more than a review of their history: it is a record of God's covenant mercy and faithfulness. Hence v.32: "Our God... who keepest **covenant and mercy**". The Levites prayed over Israel's history. They cited the faithfulness of God to the covenant in five ways: *(i)* the covenant established with Abraham (vv.7-8); *(ii)* The covenant implemented in the exodus (vv.9-15); *(iii)* The covenant maintained in the wilderness (vv.16-21); *(iv)* the covenant fulfilled in the conquest (vv.22-25) *(v)* the covenant maintained to the restoration (vv.26-31).

i) The covenant established with Abraham, vv.7-8
In these verses, the Levites referred, firstly, to God's call (v.7), and, secondly, to God's covenant (v.8).

- **God's call.** "Thou art the Lord the God, who didst choose Abram, and broughtest him forth out of Ur of the Chaldees, and gavest him the name of Abraham" (v.7). The Levites refer here to Genesis 17.5. "Abram" means 'high father' and "Abraham" means 'father of a multitude'. The change is explained by the verse itself: "for a father of many nations have I made thee".

This emphasises divine choice, and therefore the doctrine of election. God's choice can only be explained by His love. See Deuteronomy 7.7-8 and 10.14-15. The New Testament has plenty to say on the subject: for example, "According as he hath chosen us in him (Christ) before the foundation of the world, that we should be holy and without blame before him. In love having predestinated us unto the adoption of children by Jesus Christ to himself, according to the good pleasure of his will" (Eph. 1.4-5, with altered punctuation). But we must never forget the practical issues connected with the call of God. See, for example, Deuteronomy 10.16, and Ephesians 2.10. The reference to Ur of the Chaldees reminds us of the historical and earthly setting of Abraham's call. Ur was evidently a highly-civilised place. Abraham exchanged the city for a tent, but God is no man's debtor: Abraham anticipated another city: "He looked for a city which hath foundations, whose builder and maker is God" (Heb. 11.10).

- *God's covenant.* "And foundest his heart faithful before thee, and madest *a covenant* with him to give the land of the Canaanites, the Hittites, the Amorites, and the Perizzites, and the Jebusites, and the Girgashites, to give it, I say, to his seed, and hast performed thy words; for *thou art righteous*" (v.8). This refers to God's *unconditional* promise to Abraham in Genesis 15.7-21, "In the same day, the Lord made a covenant with Abram, saying, Unto thy seed have I given this land, from the river of Egypt unto the great river, the river Euphrates" (v.18). While the final fulfilment of the covenant is still future, God has *already* fulfilled His word. Hence the statement by the Levites here: "And hast performed thy words; for thou art righteous" (v.8). Israel *did* possess the land, even though, through disobedience, they had been expelled. They will possess it again, and never be expelled! In passing, notice the "fowls" in Genesis 15.11. They are a picture of Satan's attempt to rob men of the value of God's work. The covenant was based on blood (Gen. 15.9-10), and made good to faith (Gen. 15.6).

ii) The covenant implemented in the exodus, vv.9-15
In these verses, the Levites refer to redemption (vv.9-11); direction (v.12); instruction (vv.13-14); provision (v.15).

- *Redemption, vv.9-11.* "And didst see the affliction of our fathers in Egypt, and heardest their cry by the Red sea" (v.9). It was in these circumstances that "God heard their groaning, and God remembered his *covenant* with Abraham, with Isaac, and with Jacob" (Exodus 2.24). See also Exodus 6.5. The people delivered from Egypt were not freeborn: they were born in bondage, and therefore accurately depict bondage to sin. But it would have been their fault had they remained in bondage! God planned their redemption. Moses underwent eighty years of preparation until, to apply New Testament language, "the fulness of the time was come". Israel was simply required to obey God at the given time. God did the rest! The nation was delivered from Egypt on the basis of shed blood, reminding us our own redemption was by the blood of Christ: "In whom we have redemption through his blood" (Eph. 1.7). See also 1 Peter 1.18-19. Redemption was practical: it severed Israel from Egypt: "there shall not an hoof be left behind" (Ex. 10.26). We must read Titus 2: 14 and 1 Peter 1.17-19 in this connection. Redemption should affect our relationships, and mould our behaviour. Redemption will ultimately be consummated in the "redemption of the purchased possession" (Eph. 1.14), and in the "redemption of our body" (Rom. 8.23).

We should notice the words, "So didst thou get thee a name, as it is this day" (v.10). Redemption from Egypt was, for Israel, the supreme never-to-be-forgotten demonstration of God's power. Our redemption is exactly the same, and it will be celebrated in heaven: "Thou wast slain, and hast redeemed us to God by thy blood" (Rev. 5.9).

This section also reminds us that redeemed people are completely dependent on their Redeemer. The pursuit by the Egyptians proved this beyond question. Redemption is by divine power as well as by blood. As the redeemed people, Israel enjoyed divine **direction,** divine **instruction,** and divine **provision**, reminding us of the words of the Lord Jesus, "I am the way (direction: Christ our Leader), the truth (instruction: Christ our Teacher), and the life (provision: Christ our Sustainer)" (John 14.6).

- **Direction, v.12.** "Moreover thou leddest them in the day by a cloudy pillar; and in the night by a pillar of fire, to give them light in the way wherein they should go". The cloud and fiery pillar were indicative of God's presence: see Exodus 19.9,18. Their movement gave guidance to Israel. They spelt doom for Egypt: see Exodus 14.24. How necessary to wait and watch for divine guidance at all times! God's guidance lay as much in the **stationary** periods as it did in the **active** periods. In the words of David, "The meek will he guide in judgment: and the meek will he teach his way" (Psalm 25.9). See also Proverbs 3.5-6. In grace, God did not withdraw His guidance after the rebellion at Kadesh-barnea (v.19).

- **Instruction, vv.13-14.** "Thou camest down also upon mount Sinai, and spakest with them from heaven, and gavest them right judgments, and true laws, good statutes and commandments". Moses emphasised this: "And what nation is there so great, that hath statutes and judgments so righteous as all this law, which I set before you this day?" (Deut. 4.8); "Did ever people hear the voice of God speaking out of the midst of the fire, as thou hast heard, and live?" (Deut. 4.33). The Levites stressed the utter purity of the law: "right judgments...true laws...good statutes and commandments" (v.13). Paul did the same: "the law is holy, and the commandment holy, and just, and good" (Rom. 7.12). Israel was instructed by the law, but we are privileged to have the completed Scriptures, and the Holy Spirit to instruct us from them. God has "given unto us all things that pertain unto life and godliness" (2 Pet. 1.3). We should add that "right judgments...true laws...good statutes and commandments" are "the basic foundation without which a nation cannot expect to prosper (Prov. 14.34)" (Cyril J. Barber).

- **Provision, v.15.** They had "***bread from heaven for their hunger***". The manna, God's provision for His pilgrim people, is a lovely picture of the Lord Jesus who said, "I am the bread of life: he that cometh to me shall never hunger" (John 6.35). He is "the bread which came down from heaven" (John 6.41). He imparts life and sustains life. We must notice *some* (that's all!) simple lessons from Exodus 16. It was found, "***upon the face of the wilderness***" (v.14), suggesting His incarnation. He certainly came to a "wilderness". Like the manna, He came quietly and without ostentation. The manna came on the dew (Ex. 16.13-14; Num. 11.9). Dew is a picture of divine blessing: see, for example Job 29.19. The coming of the Lord Jesus was the greatest blessing God bestowed on mankind. The manna is described as, "***a small round thing***" (v.14). It was "small", suggesting His humility: see Isaiah 53.2. It was "round", suggesting His eternity: without beginning and without end. "Round" also suggests the perfect harmony of every divine attribute in Him: no one attribute outweighed another. The manna resembled "***the hoar frost***" (v.14), suggesting the absolute purity of the Lord Jesus. The manna had to be gathered, "***every man according to his eating***" (v.16). There was sufficient for all age-groups and all appetites. Christ meets the need of all His people, young and old. Its taste was "***as the taste of fresh oil***" (Num. 11.8). The Lord Jesus always lived and taught in the power of the Holy Spirit. There is much more!

Then they had "***water for them out of the rock for their thirst***". See Exodus 17.6. Paul enlarges on this in 1 Corinthians 10.4, "And did all drink the same spiritual drink: for they drank of that spiritual Rock that followed them: and that Rock was Christ". The Lord Jesus satisfies both hunger and thirst: see, again, John 6.35, "and he that believeth on me shall never thirst". Read John 4.14. If the *manna* is a picture of the Lord Jesus, then the *water* is a picture of the Holy Spirit. We must remember that we can only enjoy His ministry because the Lord Jesus was smitten at Calvary.

READ CHAPTER 9.16-38

"Thou hast done right, but we have done wickedly"

We have already noticed that this chapter may be divided as follows: *(1)* their approach to God (vv.1-3); *(2)* their appreciation of God (vv.4-31) *(3)* their appeal to God (vv.32-38). We have also noticed that the central section (vv.4-31) is far more than a review of Israel's history. It is a record of God's *covenant faithfulness* to His people: "Now therefore, our God, the great, the mighty, and the terrible God, who keepest *covenant and mercy*..." (v.32). It is, at the same time, a record of Israel's lamentable *failure*: "Thou art just in all that is brought upon us; for thou hast done right, but we have done wickedly" (v.33).

1) THEIR APPROACH TO GOD, vv.1-3
In our previous study we noted their self-denial (v.1), their separation (v.2), and their study (v.3).

2) THEIR APPRECIATION OF GOD, vv.4-31
In their prayer, the Levites (vv.4-5), praised God for His 'creatorial' majesty (v.6) and his covenant mercy (vv.7-31).

a) His creatorial majesty, v.6
"Thou, even thou, art Lord alone; thou hast made heaven, the heaven of heavens, with all their host, the earth, and all things that are therein, the seas, and all that is therein, and thou preservest them all; and the host of heaven worshippeth thee".

b) His covenant mercy, vv.7-31
The faithfulness of God to the covenant is spelt out with reference to five chapters in Israel's history: *(i)* the covenant established with Abraham (vv.7-8); *(ii)* the covenant implemented in the exodus (vv.9-15); *(iii)* the covenant maintained in the wilderness (vv.16-21); *(iv)* the covenant fulfilled in the conquest (vv.22-25) *(v)* the covenant maintained to the restoration (vv.26-31).

i) The covenant established with Abraham, vv.7-8

"Thou art the Lord the God, who didst choose Abram, and broughtest him forth out of Ur of the Chaldees, and gavest him the name of Abraham; and foundest his heart faithful before thee, and madest *a covenant* with him to give the land..."

ii) The covenant implemented in the exodus, vv.9-15

"Thou...didst see the affliction of our fathers in Egypt, and heardest their cry by the Red sea..." This brings us to:

iii) The covenant maintained in the wilderness, vv.16-21

After redemption (vv.9-11), direction (v.12), instruction (vv.13-14) and provision (v.15), we have *rebellion*: "But they and our fathers dealt proudly, and hardened their necks, and hearkened not to thy commandments, and refused to obey, neither were mindful of thy wonders that thou didst among them; but hardened their necks, and in their *rebellion* appointed a captain to return to their bondage". There was no question of making a mistake: it was flagrant disobedience. We must notice the following:

- It all began with *pride*. "But they and our fathers dealt proudly, and hardened their necks" (v.16). In essence, pride is love for self as opposed to love for God. It manifests itself in self-sufficiency, self-centredness and self-assertiveness, leading to the warning, "Let not the wise man *glory in his wisdom*, neither let the mighty man *glory in his might*, let not the rich man *glory in his riches*..." (Jer. 9.23). Pride heads the list of the seven things that God hates in Proverbs 6.16-19. It was Satan's original sin. See 1 Timothy 3.6, where an overseer must not be "a novice (a recent convert: literally, someone 'newly planted'), lest being lifted up with *pride* he fall into the condemnation ('fault', JND) of the devil", perhaps referring to Isaiah 14.12-15. Pride constitutes a danger to us all: "Yea, *all of you* be subject one to another, and be clothed with humility: for God resisteth the proud, and giveth grace to the humble" (1 Pet. 5.5-6). Compare Philippians 2.3. We must remember that "pride goeth before destruction, and an haughty spirit before a fall" (Prov. 16.18).

- Pride was followed by *disobedience*. "And hearkened not to thy commandments, and refused to obey" (v.16-17). We began the Christian life by obeying God: "But God be thanked, that ye were the servants of sin, but ye have *obeyed from the heart* that form of doctrine which was delivered you" (Rom. 6.17). Luke tells us that "the word of God increased; and the number of the disciples multiplied in Jerusalem greatly; and a great company of the priests were *obedient to the faith*" (Acts 6.7). Paul tells us that the gospel has been "made known to all nations for the **obedience of faith**" (Rom. 16.26. Compare Romans 1.5. If we began the Christian life by obeying God, then we continue the Christian life on exactly the same basis. See, for example, 1 Peter 1.14. Compare 1 Samuel 15.22.

-    Disobedience was followed by **ingratitude.** "Neither were mindful of thy wonders that thou didst among them" (v.17). Compare Psalm 78.10-16. Unsaved men and women are marked by ingratitude: "When they knew God, they glorified him not as God, **neither were thankful**" (Rom. 1.21). The religious world will be "**unthankful**" in the "last days" (2 Tim. 3.1-5). It would be a shameful thing for believers to follow the pagan world and the religious world in this way. Hence we read, "In every thing give thanks: for this is the will of God in Christ Jesus concerning you" (1 Thess. 5.18).

-    Pride, disobedience and ingratitude were followed by **rebellion.** They "hardened their necks, and in their **rebellion** appointed a captain to return to their bondage" (v.17), referring to Numbers 14.4. It hardly seems credible that God's power and provision for them should be so quickly forgotten! We have the explanation in Hebrews 4.2, "For unto us was the gospel preached, as well as unto them: but the word preached did not profit them, **not being mixed with faith** in them that heard it". In Stephen's words: "To whom (Moses) our fathers would not obey, but thrust him from them, and in their hearts turned back again into Egypt" (Acts 7.39).

Their history served to warn them of the consequences of forgetfulness and disobedience, and was a forcible reminder "that those who do not learn the lessons of history are forever condemned to repeat them" (C.J. Barber). But in it all God was faithful to them: "**But** thou art a God ready to pardon, gracious and merciful, slow to anger, and of great kindness, and forsookest them not". Jeremiah makes the same point, even though Jerusalem was in ruins. See Lamentations 3.22-23. Even after the most fearful idolatry, God remained faithful: "Yea, when they had made them a molten calf, and said, This is thy God that brought thee up out of Egypt, and had wrought great provocations; **yet** thou in thy manifold mercies forsookest them not in the wilderness" (v.19). We should notice the key phrases here: "**forsookest them not**" (v.19); "**withheldest not**" (v.20). It should be remembered that while the wilderness **journey** was an essential part of God's discipline for Israel, the wilderness **wanderings** were the direct result of disobedience. See Deuteronomy 1.2 and 2.14: An eleven day journey took thirty-eight years! (It was no coincidence that the impotent man had lain by the pool of Bethesda for thirty-eight years, John 5.5).

But God did not withdraw His covenant blessings. *Direction remained*: "Yet thou in thy manifold mercies forsookest them not in the wilderness: the pillar of the cloud departed not from them by day, to lead them in the way; neither the pillar of fire by night, to shew them light, and the way wherein they should go" (v.19). *Instruction remained*: "Thou gavest also **thy good Spirit** to instruct them (v.20). See Isaiah 63.10-11: "But they rebelled, and vexed his holy spirit: therefore he was turned to be their enemy, and he fought against them. Then he remembered the days of old, Moses, and his people, saying, Where is he that brought them out of the sea with the shepherd of his flock? where is he that put his holy spirit within him (i.e. Moses)". See also Haggai 2.5. *Provision remained*: "Thou...withheldest not thy manna from their mouth, and gavest them water for their thirst. Yea, forty years didst thou sustain them in the wilderness, so that they lacked nothing; their clothes waxed not old, and their feet swelled not" (vv.20-21). See Deuteronomy 29.5. Clothing and footwear did not wear out. The believer is clothed with "the garments of salvation" (Isa. 61.10), and **they are permanent!** The nation was entirely upheld by God, and "lacked nothing". Their survival was a miracle, and it was all through God's "manifold mercies" (v.19).

iv) The covenant fulfilled in the conquest, vv.22-25
The words "possessed" and "possess" occur four times in these verses (vv.22,23,24,25). To summarise; "thou...broughtest them into the land, concerning which thou hadst promised to their fathers, that they should go in to possess it" (v.23). This fulfilled the promise recorded in v.15. The details follow:

- **They dwelt in the land, vv.22-24.** God's people occupied territory on the east of Jordan (v.22), and west of Jordan (vv.23-24). **He** gave them victory over those who attempted to impede their progress (v.22). For the defeat of Sihon king of Heshbon and Og king of Bashan, see Numbers 21. The people of God are victorious in the measure that they obey God. **He** multiplied Israel in the wilderness, so that they were sufficiently strong to possess "the land of Sihon, and the land of the king of Heshbon, and the land of Og king of Bashan", and to possess the land "promised to their fathers".

"So the children went in and possessed the land", that is, the generation that succeeded the Israelites who perished in the wilderness. God is able to keep His promises, even though His people are unworthy and disobedient. We too must 'possess our possessions'. God makes them available to us, but we must 'go in and possess the land'. God has done His part, now we must do ours. In the Lord's words to Joshua: "Every place that **the sole of your foot shall tread upon**, that have I given unto you, as I said unto Moses" (Joshua 1.3).

- **They defeated their enemies, v.24.** "Thou subduedst before them the inhabitants of the land, the Canaanites, and gavest them into their hands, with their kings, and the people of the land, that they might do with them as they would". God gave them victory. There was war in Canaan, just as there is warfare for us now. We must remember that while Canaan is not a picture of heaven (after all, we don't expect warfare in heaven!), it is certainly a picture of our present spiritual inheritance, and that does involve warfare. See Ephesians 6.10-20. Sadly, there is the possibility here of defeat as well.

- **They delighted in God's goodness, v.25.** There was nothing mean about God's provision for His people. "And they took strong cities, and a fat land, and possessed houses full of all goods, wells digged, vineyards, and oliveyards, and fruit trees in abundance: so they did eat, and were filled, and became fat, and delighted themselves in thy great goodness". It all reminds us that God's "divine power hath given unto us all things that pertain unto life and godliness" (2 Pet. 1.3). But there was danger: it is spelt out in Deuteronomy 6.10-12; 8.7-17. God posted a warning: "Beware!"

v) The covenant maintained to the restoration, vv.26-31
We must notice the particular reference to God's covenant mercy during this period. This is clearly emphasised: "according to thy **manifold mercies** (see v.19) thou gavest them saviours" (v.27); "many times didst thou deliver them according to thy **mercies**" (v.28); "Nevertheless for thy great **mercies'** sake thou didst not utterly consume them" (v.31). The period was marked by "great provocations" (v.26 with v.18)), but God was "gracious and merciful" (v.31). The section begins with the words, "Nevertheless **they**" (v.26) and ends, "Nevertheless...**thou**" (v.31). We must notice at least some of the details given:

- **They were disobedient to God, v.26.** "Nevertheless they were disobedient, and rebelled against thee, and cast thy law behind their backs, and slew thy prophets which testified against them to turn them to thee, and they wrought great provocations". The Lord Jesus referred to this in the parable of the wicked husbandmen (Matt. 21.33-46) and in His lament over Jerusalem (Luke 13.34). Stephen reminded the nation of their disobedience and rebellion: "Ye stiffnecked and uncircumcised in heart and ears, ye do always resist the Holy Ghost: as your fathers did, so do ye. Which of the prophets have not your fathers persecuted? and they have slain them which shewed before of the coming of the Just One; of whom ye have been now the betrayers and murderers" (Acts 7.51-53).

The sequence above is not without significance: they rejected God ("rebelled against *thee*"); they rejected the word of God ("cast *thy law* behind their backs"); they rejected the servants of God ("slew *thy prophets*"). Backsliding works in exactly the same way: *firstly*, no communion with God; *secondly*, no reading of God's word; *thirdly*, no fellowship with God's people. The first evidence we have of backsliding is often failure to attend assembly meetings, but it all starts long before that. Notice too that when people reject the *message* of God's word, they usually resent and reject the *messengers* as well. Sadly, it sometimes happens to a lesser or greater degree amongst Christians. Loyalty to God's word is not always popular.

- ***They were delivered to their enemies, vv.27-29.*** Disobedience brings bondage. Notice particular reference to the period of the Judges here. "According to thy manifold mercies thou gavest them saviours, who saved them out of the hand of their enemies". The Lord Jesus is of course the superlative and unique Saviour! He is infinitely greater than Othniel, Ehud, Barak, Gideon, Jephthah and Samson. Their strengths and weaknesses only serve to emphasise *His* greatness. This makes a very nice devotional study! The period of the Judges began with Israel's failure to expel remaining enemies, and continued to the era of Samuel. It ended with the cry, "Give us a king", which arose, amongst other things, from a desire for conformity to the world. See 1 Samuel 8.5.

The words, "withdrew the *shoulder*, and hardened their *neck*, and would not *hear*" (v.29) call for attention. The "*shoulder*" is the emblem of strength. It was the place where burdens were carried. See, for example Isaiah 9.6 and Luke 15.5. Preachers have happily emphasised that the scriptures assign *one* shoulder for the government of the universe (Isaiah 9.6), but *two* shoulders for the lost sheep (Luke 15.5)! To remove the shoulder therefore means the withdrawal of strength: "But they refused to hearken, and pulled away the shoulder" (Zech. 7.11). Israel refused to support and maintain the commandments of God. We frequently encounter hardened or stiff *necks* in Scripture. See, for example, Deuteronomy 9.6,13; Acts 7.51. It means to be unyielding and obstinate, like an animal that refuses to submit to the yoke (Jer. 27.12). Priscilla (ladies first here!) and Aquila were the exact reverse: "Greet Priscilla and Aquila my helpers in Christ Jesus: who have for my life laid down their own necks (it is actually in the singular: 'neck')" (Rom. 16.3-4).

- ***They were dominated by the nations, v.30.*** "Yet many years didst thou forbear them, and testified against them by *thy Spirit in thy prophets*; yet would they not give ear: therefore gavest thou them into the hand of the people of the lands". This carries solemn lessons for us. Refusal to heed to the voice of the Holy Spirit in the word of God will bring disastrous consequences. In this case,

Israel lost the blessings of God's presence and protection, and the joy of her God-given inheritance. As C.J.Barber observes, "every time history repeated itself, the price went up". Can **we** really expect anything less?

But they were not 'utterly consumed' or 'forsaken' (v.31): "**Nevertheless** for thy great mercies' sake thou didst not utterly consume them, nor forsake them; for thou art a gracious and merciful God". The Psalmist noted this too: "Nevertheless he regarded their affliction, when he heard their cry: and he remembered for them his covenant, and repented according to the multitude of his mercies. He made them also to be pitied of all those that carried them captives" (Psalm 106.44-46).

This brings us to the third section of the chapter, and to the object of this historical review.

3) THEIR APPEAL TO GOD, vv.32-38
In these verses we should notice **(a)** their appeal to God's mercy (v.32); **(b)** their acknowledgement of God's justice (vv.33-37).

a) Their appeal to God's mercy, v.32
"Now therefore, our God, the great, the mighty, and the terrible God, who keepest covenant and mercy, let not all the trouble seem little before thee, that hath come upon us, on our kings, on our princes, and on our priests, and on our prophets, and on our fathers, and on all thy people, since the time of the kings of Assyria unto this day". The "kings of Assyria" were the first of the successive world powers to menace and then subjugate Israel and Judah since their bondage in Egypt. We must notice the perfect blending of divine attributes. On the one hand, God is "the great, the mighty, and the terrible God": on the other, He is God that "keepest covenant and mercy". D.Kidner is worth quoting at length here: "**Great** is a reminder that God does not share our narrowness of vision or of being; **mighty** is a virile word, fit to describe the paladins who did exploits for David (2 Sam. 23.8-39), or "the King of glory...mighty in battle" (Psalm 24.8), or the divine prince of Isaiah 9.6. **Terrible** is misleading, for the word here means awe-inspiring, not ruthless". But He is, equally, a God of "covenant and mercy". In David's words, "a God full of compassion, and gracious, longsuffering, and plenteous in mercy and truth" (Psalm 86.15).

b) Their acknowledgement of God's justice, vv.33-37
"Howbeit thou art just in all that is brought upon us; for thou hast done right, but we have done wickedly". They had:

- **Rejected the law of God, v.34.** "Neither have our kings, our princes, our priests, nor our fathers, **kept thy law**, nor **hearkened unto thy commandments and thy testimonies**, wherewith thou didst testify against them".

- **Rejected the goodness of God, v.35.** "For they have not served thee in their kingdom, and in thy great goodness that thou gavest them, and in **the large and fat land which thou gavest before them**, neither turned they from their wicked works".

Failure to keep the **law of God** had brought servitude to the laws of others. Failure to appreciate the **goodness of God** had brought loss of that goodness to them, and benefit for others: "The land that thou gavest unto our fathers to eat the fruit thereof and the good thereof, behold, we are servants in it: and it yieldeth much increase unto the kings whom thou hast set over us because of our sins: also they have dominion over our bodies, and over our cattle, at their pleasure, and we are in great distress" (vv.36-37).

This painful confession is followed by action. "Those who prayed have asked for mercy (v.32), but do not mean to trade on it, as their 'binding declaration' (v.38) makes clear" (D.Kidner). "And because of all this we make a sure covenant, and write it; and our princes, Levites, and priests, seal unto it". The terms of their covenant with God are spelt out in Chapter 10.

But we must not leave it there. All of us have to admit failure. We have not been what we ought to be. These people were determined to renew their commitment to God. What about us?

READ CHAPTER 10

Their renewed commitment to God

The reading of the law in Chapter 8 produced two notable results: *(a)* a desire to put into practice something that had been allowed to lapse for a thousand years! (8.14-17); *(b)* a desire to renew the covenant with God. With this in view, the Levites led the people in prayer (9.6-38) in which *(i)* they recalled God's **covenant faithfulness** to His people, "Now therefore, our God, the great, the mighty, and the terrible God, who keepest **covenant and mercy**..." (v.32); *(ii)* they confessed their **national failure** to honour the covenant, "Thou art just in all that is brought upon us; for thou hast done right, but we have done wickedly" (v.33).

The faithfulness of God to the covenant with His people, and the unfaithfulness of the people to their obligations under the covenant, brought a resolve to renew the covenant. "And because of all this we make a **sure covenant**, and write it; and our princes, Levites, and priests, seal unto it" (9.38). This covenant is described and sealed in Chapter 10. The reading of Scripture in Chapter 8, brought **confession** of sin in Chapter 9, and **conformity** to God's will in Chapter 10. **Prayer** in Chapter 9 was followed by **practice** in Chapter 10.

We must now notice: *(1)* the people involved, vv.1-28; *(2)* the preparation involved (v.28); *(3)* the perception involved (v.28); *(4)* the promise involved vv.29-39).

1) THE PEOPLE INVOLVED, vv.1-28
In short, we have a record of the leaders of the people (vv.1-27) and "the rest of the people" (v.28).

a) The leaders of the people, vv.1-27
The leaders are represented by *(i)* the governor (v.1): "Now those that sealed were, Nehemiah, the **Tirshatha**, the son of Hachaliah"; *(ii)* the priests (vv.2-8); *(iii)* the Levites (vv.9-13); *(iv)* "The chief of the people" (vv.14-27). These classes formed the leadership (the four categories have no direct counterparts in the

New Testament), and their role here recalls 1 Peter 5.1-3, "The elders which are among you I exhort...feed the flock of God which is among you, taking the oversight thereof, not by constraint, but willingly; not for filthy lucre, but of a ready mind; neither as being lords over God's heritage ('not as lording it over your possessions', JND), but being **ensamples to the flock**". We should say, however, that although we are not all leaders, we are certainly all priests and servants (Levites), and therefore there is always room for deeper commitment in our priesthood and in our service!

b) The rest of the people, v.28
"And the rest of the people...clave to their brethren, their nobles", so there was a unity between the leaders and the people. The good example of the leaders was emulated by the people. They **all** wanted God's blessing! The lesson is clear. Devotion and fidelity to God **must never be the prerogative of the leadership**. **All** believers, whether leaders or otherwise, should be marked by these features. **All** believers need to be dedicated to God. Each assembly should comprise devoted brothers and sisters, and be led by godly men. But there is something else here: the fact that the "rest of the people...clave to their brethren, their nobles" was the result of the extensive reading and teaching given "before the street that was before the water gate" (8.3). Clear reading and explanation (8.8) had borne fruit!

2) THE PREPARATION INVOLVED, v.28
"And the rest of the people, the priests, the Levites, the porters, the singers, the Nethinims, and **all they that had separated themselves from the people of the lands unto the law of God**, their wives, their sons, and their daughters, every one having knowledge, and having understanding...clave to their brethren, their nobles..." Attention is drawn to:

a) Their separation negatively
"All they that had **separated** themselves **from** the people of the lands", clearly referring to the people who had earlier "**separated** themselves from all strangers, and stood and confessed their sins, and the iniquities of their fathers" (9.2). As we have seen before in our 'Nehemiah' studies, the New Testament reads similarly: "Be ye not unequally yoked together with unbelievers: for what fellowship hath righteousness with unrighteousness? and what communion hath light with darkness? and what concord hath Christ with Belial? or what part hath he that believeth with an infidel? and what agreement hath the temple of God with idols...wherefore come out from among them, and be ye **separate**, saith the Lord" (2 Cor. 6.14-17).

b) Their separation positively

"All they that had separated themselves...*unto* the law of God". We totally misrepresent our calling if we are known only for what we do *not* do, and where we do *not* go. In dealing with the subject, the New Testament puts the positive before the negative as follows: "I beseech you therefore, brethren, by the mercies of God, that (firstly) ye present your bodies a living sacrifice, holy, acceptable unto God, which is your reasonable service. And (secondly) be not conformed to this world..." (Rom. 12.1-2). The believers at Thessalonica "turned **to** God **from** idols" (1 Thess. 1.9).

3) THE PERCEPTION INVOLVED, v.28

These people acted with spiritual intelligence: "every one having knowledge, and having understanding". The need for perception in this way is emphasised by the apostle Paul: "present your bodies a living sacrifice, holy, acceptable unto God, which is your **reasonable** (or 'logical' from *logikos*) service" (Rom. 12.1); "Wherefore be ye not unwise, but **understanding** what the will of the Lord is" (Eph. 5.17). There seemed to be some **lack** of understanding at Corinth: "What? know ye not that your body is the temple of the Holy Ghost which is in you, which ye have of God, and ye are not your own? For ye are bought with a price: therefore glorify God in your body..." (1 Cor. 6.19-20). While we must submit to the teaching of God's word, whether we understand it at first or not, God does expect us to "grow in grace, and in the knowledge of our Lord and Saviour Jesus Christ" (2 Pet. 3.18). We should notice the order in Nehemiah's description of the people concerned: "every one having knowledge, and having understanding". We cannot possibly understand the meaning of God's word without getting to know what it actually says!

4) THE PROMISE INVOLVED, vv.29-39

The undertaking by leaders and people to obey the law, that is to keep the covenant, is expressed generally (v.29) and particularly (vv.30-39).

A) Generally, v.29

They "entered into a curse (referring to the expectation of judgment if they failed to comply with the law), and into an oath, to walk in God's law, which was given by Moses the servant of God, and to observe and do all the commandments of the Lord (*Jehovah*) our Lord (*Adonahy*: the Sovereign Lord: a plural word), and his judgments and his statutes". As we have regularly pointed out, Thomas Newberry describes the name *Jehovah* as "a combination in marvelous perfection of the three periods of existence in one word, the future, the present, and the past". He is the eternal God. *Adonahy* means 'Sovereign Lord, or Master'

(Thomas Newberry). God's people therefore undertook to obey the eternal God with absolute rights over them. They referred to Him as "the Lord **our** Lord". It expresses the immense privilege of God's people, and stresses His immense grace in choosing them. It also expresses their immense responsibility.

Their desire to "walk in God's law, which was given by Moses the servant of God" meant that they were willing to return to the beginning: back to "God's law, which was given by Moses". One thousand years made no difference at all: the law remained unchangeable. In the New Testament, Jude writes about "the faith which was **once delivered** unto the saints" (Jude v.3). We must never attempt to amend or update the word of God: it is complete in itself. Paul had this in mind when writing to Timothy: "And the things that thou hast heard of me among many witnesses, the **same** ('don't alter it, Timothy') commit thou to faithful men, who shall be able to teach others also" (2 Tim. 2.2).

B) Particularly, vv.30-39
The covenant involved three areas: **(a)** relationships with the "people of the land" (vv.30-31): they wanted the word of God to affect home and spiritual life; **(b)** recognition of the "seventh year" (v.31): they wanted the word of God to affect social life; **(c)** provision for "the house of...God" (vv.32-39): they wanted the word of God to affect their finances. All areas of life were to be governed by the will of God and the word of God.

a) Relationships with the people of the land, vv.30-31
This involved two areas in their lives: **(i)** no intermarriage (v.30); **(ii)** no violation of the sabbath (v.31).

i) No intermarriage, v.30. "That we would not give our daughters unto **the people of the land**, nor take their daughters for our sons". (Perhaps this is put first as it had been a major problem some years before: see Ezra chs. 9-10). God had made his mind and will clear on this issue: "neither shalt thou make marriages with them (the nations of Canaan); thy daughter thou shalt not give unto his son, nor his daughter shalt thou take unto thy son. For they will **turn away thy son from following me**, that they may serve other gods" (Deut. 7.3-4). But the book of Nehemiah ends sadly: "In those days also saw I Jews that had married wives of Ashdod, of Ammon, and of Moab: and their children spake half in the speech of Ashdod, and **could not speak in the Jews' language**, but according to the language of each people" (Neh. 13.23-29). Amongst other things, this reminds us that we must jealously safeguard our spiritual language. Many (but not all) modern hymns and choruses do little or nothing to help in this way.

This in an opportune moment to ask just how deeply **we** are moved by the word of God, whether through private reading or public teaching. Like Israel, our resolution can be so easily likened to the "early dew" (Hosea 6.4): it soon evaporates, and it is soon forgotten. Does Bible teaching really have an effect in our lives? God's people made a noble covenant here, but look what had happened by Chapter 13!

ii) No violation of the sabbath, v.31. "And if **the people of the land** bring ware or any victuals on the sabbath day to sell, that we would not buy it of them on the sabbath, or on the holy day". God's people were to live by different standards. Time set aside for the enjoyment of divine things was not to be eroded by the world. But by the end of the book, as above, the solemn undertaking here had been forgotten: "In those days saw I in Judah some treading wine presses on the sabbath, and bringing in sheaves, and lading asses...There dwelt men of Tyre also therein, which brought fish, and all manner of ware, and sold on the sabbath unto the children of Judah, and in Jerusalem" (Neh. 13.15-22).

The actual word "sabbath" occurs first in Exodus 16.23-30 with reference to the manna. This is rather beautiful. "See, for that the Lord hath given you the sabbath, therefore he giveth you on the sixth day the bread of two days; abide ye every man in his place, let no man go out of his place on the seventh day" (Exod. 16.29). While the sabbath and the Lord's day are quite distinct, the Lord's day does enable us to enjoy the sweetness of Christ in fellowship with His people, just as the sabbath enabled Israel to enjoy the sweetness of the manna without the distraction of daily toil.

b) Recognition of "the seventh year", v.31
The people undertook *(i)* to "leave the seventh year" and *(ii)* to forgo the "exaction of every debt". The release from debt took place "at the end of every seven years".

i) The land to rest during the seventh year. "Six years thou shalt sow thy field, and six years thou shalt prune thy vineyard, and gather in the fruit thereof; but in the seventh year shall be a sabbath of rest unto the land, a Sabbath for the Lord: thou shalt neither sow thy field, nor prune thy vineyard" (Lev. 25.3-4). God ensured that His people would not be hungry during "the sabbath of the land" (Lev. 25.20-21). They were reminded every seventh year that God was able to preserve and bless His people as tenants in His land. The divine Landlord made it clear that Canaan belonged to Him, that He cared for it, and that He would suitably care for those who worked in it for Him. *If we look after His interests, He will look after ours.*

ii) Debts to be forgiven at the end of each seventh year. "At the end of every seven years thou shalt make a release. And this is the manner of the release: Every creditor that lendeth aught unto his neighbour shall release it; he shall not exact it of his neighbour, or of his brother; because it is called the Lord's release" (Deut 15.1-2). Burdens were to be lifted, and "thou shalt open thine hand wide unto him (the poor brother)" (Deut. 15.8). *We need to practice the "release".* See 1 John 3.17-18.

c) Provision for "the house of God", vv.32-39

We cannot overlook the repeated expression, "*the house of our God*" or "*the house of the Lord*". The words occur nine times in vv.32-39. We should also notice the repeated word "*bring*". It occurs six times in vv.34-39. The "house of God" is a place that demands our presence. It is a place where we contribute ("bring"). Some people think only in terms of what they can *get out* of the assembly: we should think in terms of what we can *put into* the assembly! We must consider the following:

i) Making a contribution, vv.32-33. "Also we made ordinances for us, to charge ourselves yearly with the third part of a shekel for the service of the house of our God". This was not imposed by the Tirshatha: it was *voluntary.* The expression, "*charge ourselves* yearly", suggests standard figure. All could participate: there was no partiality. The New Testament has something similar to say on the subject: "Every man according as *he purposeth in his heart*, so let him give; not grudgingly, or of necessity: for God loveth a cheerful giver" (2 Cor. 9.7). Quite obviously, our stewardship involves rather more than transferring money from pocket to bag! We also need to be careful in our promises and pledges. See Ecclesiastes 5.2-7.

ii) Bringing the wood offering, v.34. This was not an offering actually detailed in the law. "And we cast the lots among the priests, the Levites, and the people, for the wood offering, to bring it into the house of our God, after the houses of our fathers, at times appointed year by year, to burn upon the altar of the Lord our God, as it is written in the law (see above)". In a different connection, Solomon said that "where no wood is, there the fire goeth out" (Prov. 26.20). The altar would grow cold without the wood offering. There would be no sweet savour offering. The wood offering had an important part to play. Perhaps this was one reason why the spies were to ascertain "whether there be wood therein (the land), or not" (Num. 13.20). The land was evidently well-wooded. God provided the fuel!

The word rendered "wood" is more often rendered "trees" in the Old Testament, and trees are often used as a picture of men. The godly man "shall be like a tree planted by the rivers of water" (Psalm 1.3). David said, "I have seen the wicked in great power, and spreading himself like a green bay tree" (Psalm 37.35). The wood offering can therefore be taken as a picture of our own lives. The wood did not in itself emit a "sweet savour", but it was upon that wood that the "sweet savour" of the offerings rose to God. This is so true of each one of us: we have no "sweet savour" in ourselves: but it is through us that the sweetness of Christ ascends to heaven.

It should be noticed that no particular wood was specified (v.34): evidently every kind was to be used. God looks for the sweetness of Christ through every one of us. All classes were involved: "the priests, the Levites, and the people" (v.34). This is interesting: normally the Nethinims and the sons of Solomon's servants were the burden-bearers, but only 392 of them had come back from Babylon (see Neh. 7.60). Dedicated men were in short supply, and therefore all were to be involved. *The wood was to be brought "into the house of our God".* It was to be presented to God: a picture of our lives lived for God. But this involved burden-bearing. It was carried by them. *The wood was to be divided before use.* See Genesis 22.3, where Abraham "clave the wood". No stately oak was laid upon that altar! The wood was reduced by cleaving it. This recalls the Saviour's teaching: "whosoever will save his life shall lose it" (Luke 9.24). *The wood was laid "in order" upon the fire* (Lev. 1.7): precisely the same expression is used of the burnt offering placed on the wood (Lev. 1.8). The same careful exercise in relation to the offerings themselves was required in connection with the wood. We need to be orderly in our spiritual exercise before God (Rom. 12.1). *The wood was completely consumed:* nothing was left, reminding us of Paul's words: "And I will very gladly spend and *be spent* for you" (2 Cor. 12.15). *The wood offering was continually required.* "And the fire upon the altar shall be burning in it; it shall not be put out: and the priest shall *burn wood* on it every morning, and lay the burnt offering in order upon it; and he shall burn thereon the fat of the peace offerings" (Lev. 6.12). A continual fire required continual fuel. There could be no burnt offering without the wood offering. It was to be brought "year by year" (Neh. 10.34), reminding us of the need for godly consistency.

iii) Bringing the firstfruits, v.35. God's people undertook "to bring the *firstfruits* of our ground, and the firstfruits of all fruit of all trees, year by year, unto the house of the Lord". This was a case of giving back to God what He had first given them (see Neh. 9.25). It was therefore a thankful acknowledgement that God was the Giver, and fulfilled the command of Moses: "The first of the firstfruits of thy land thou shalt bring into the house of the Lord thy God" (Exod. 23.19; 34.26). Detailed instructions followed: "And it shall be, when thou art come in unto the land which the Lord thy God giveth thee for an inheritance, and possessest it, and dwellest therein; that thou shalt take of the first of all the fruit of the earth, which thou shalt bring of thy land that the Lord thy God giveth thee, and shalt put it in a basket, and shalt go unto the place which the Lord thy God shall choose..." (Deut. 26.1-11). This is exactly what we should be doing during the week in preparation for the Lord's supper (1 Cor. 11.28).

In passing, do notice that it is the *"firstfruits"* of produce: the *"firstlings"* of animals, and the *"firstborn"* of children: for all three, see Numbers 18.8-19.

iv) Offering the firstborn, v.36. "Also the **firstborn** of our sons, and of our cattle, as it is written in the law, and the **firstlings** of our herds and of our flocks, to bring to the house of our God, unto the priests that minister in the house of our God". God claimed all the firstborn of the children of Israel, and the firstlings of their cattle: "And the Lord spake unto Moses, saying, Sanctify unto me all the firstborn, whatsoever openeth the womb among the children of Israel, both of man and of beast: it is mine" (Exod. 13.1-15). See also Leviticus 27.26-27. The Levites were to be taken "instead of all the firstborn among the children of Israel" (Num. 3.45). The procedure is explained in Numbers 3.40-51. There were 273 more firstborn than there were Levites, and these were redeemed at the rate of five shekels each. The proceeds were given to Aaron and his sons (Num. 3.46-48). The church is described as the "church of the firstborn" (Heb. 12.23). *God claims every believer for Himself.*

v) Offering the firstfruits of dough, v.37. "And that we should bring the **firstfruits** of our dough, and our offerings, and the fruit of all manner of trees, of wine and of oil, unto the priests, to the chambers of the house of our God; and the tithes of our ground unto the Levites, that the same Levites might have the tithes in all the cities of our tillage". Provision was made for the redemption of the "tithes" (Lev. 27.30-33). God's people were commanded to "Bring...all the tithes into the storehouse, that there may be meat in mine house, and prove me now herewith, saith the Lord of hosts, if I will not open you the windows of heaven, and pour you out a blessing, that there shall not be room enough to receive it" (Mal. 3.10). These passages refer to support for the servants of God, and for the service of God. Not only so, these offerings put the Levites in a position to offer their own tithe: "And the priest the son of Aaron shall be with the Levites, when the Levites take tithes: and the Levites shall bring up the **tithe of the tithes** unto the house of our God, to the chambers, into the treasure house" (v.38). In giving to the Lord for the use of His servants, we put them in a position to give to the Lord. Both the people and the Levites were to offer to God: "For the children of Israel **and the children of Levi** shall bring the offering of the corn, of the new wine, and the oil, unto the chambers, where are the vessels of the sanctuary, and the priests that minister, and the porters, and the singers: and we will not forsake the house of our God" (v.39). In the current context, to "forsake the house of our God" means failure to give practical support to those who ministered in it, and, alas that is just what happened. See Nehemiah 13.10-14; Malachi 3.7-12.

In summary, the words "firstfruits", "firstborn" and "firstlings" emphasise that God was to have **the best.** His interests were to be given **first place.** Not many years would elapse before God had to say, "And if ye offer the blind for sacrifice, is it not evil? and if ye offer the lame and the sick, is it not evil? offer it now unto thy governor; will he be pleased with thee, or accept thy person? saith the Lord of hosts?" (Mal. 1.8). But what about **our** contributions to the "house of God"? Work in connection with the local assembly, to which Paul refers in 1 Corinthians 3.9-17, demands materials of the highest quality. Are we only giving the second-best? In the words of Matthew Henry, "Though they paid great taxes to the king of Persia, and had much hardship put upon them, they would not make that an excuse for not paying the tithes, but would render to God the things that were His, as well as to Caesar the things that were his". Is that **our** attitude?

READ CHAPTER 11

Repopulating Jerusalem

We should read Chapter 11 in conjunction with Chapter 7, in which Nehemiah took a census of the people: "And my God put into mine heart to gather together the nobles, and the rulers, and the people, that they might be reckoned by genealogy" (7.5). We noticed that no further information is given in that passage, although there was a strong hint that the census was to be taken because "the city was large and great: but the people were few therein" (7.4). But now the purpose of that census becomes clear. It was taken in preparation for repopulating Jerusalem. The intervening chapters (ch.8-10) tell us how the people were **spiritually** prepared to dwell in the city. After all, "the place which the Lord shall choose to place his name there" (Deut. 16.2) required suitable people in residence. **It still does.** That is why Paul wrote to Timothy: "But if I tarry long, that thou mayest know how thou oughtest to behave thyself ('how men ought to behave themselves', RV) in the house of God, which is the church of the living God, the pillar and ground of the truth" (1 Tim. 3.15).

Nehemiah Chapter 11 may be divided into two major sections: *(1)* those that dwelt at Jerusalem (vv.1-19): "the rulers of the people dwelt at **Jerusalem**" (v.1)**;** *(2)* those that dwelt in Judah and Benjamin (vv.20-36): "the residue of Israel... were in **all the cities of Judah**".

1) THOSE THAT DWELT AT JERUSALEM, vv.1-19

"And the rulers of the people dwelt at Jerusalem: the rest of the people also cast lots, to bring one of ten to dwell in Jerusalem the holy city" (v.1). We should notice that *(a)* it was the place where God dwelt; *(b)* it was the place where God's people were to dwell.

a) It was the place where God dwelt

Jerusalem is called "**the holy city**" (vv.1,18). W.B.Pope (Ellicott's Commentary) observes that "Remembering the separation that had taken place (Chapter 9), and the recent covenant (Chapter 10), we see the solemnity of this epithet, now first used, and repeated in verse 18". This anticipates conditions at the end-time: "Then shall Jerusalem be holy, and there shall no strangers pass through her any more" (Joel 3.17).

As we have already said, Jerusalem was 'the place of the name' (Deut. 16.2,6). It was the place where He chose to dwell. We know, of course, that He actually dwelt in **the temple,** which Solomon called "the house which I have built for thy name" (2 Chron. 6.38). **Historical** Jerusalem was a city with a temple. "**New** Jerusalem" is also called "**the holy city**" (Rev. 21.2). Its advent is announced as follows: "Behold, the tabernacle of God is with men, and he will dwell with them". It is the "holy city" because it is the dwelling place of God. But unlike historical Jerusalem, it will have no temple: "And I saw no **temple** therein: for the Lord God Almighty and the Lamb are **the temple of it**" (Rev. 21.22).

The local assembly is called "the temple of God": "Know ye not that ye are **the temple of God**, and that the Spirit of God dwelleth in you? If any man defile **the temple of God**, him shall God destroy; for **the temple of God** is holy, which **temple** ye are" (1 Cor. 3.16-17). In this connection, we must be careful not to glory **in the assembly,** but **in the Lord** to whom it belongs. While we must teach and maintain "all the counsel of God" (Acts 20.27), we must never become proud of our orthodox practices: "He that glorieth, let him glory in **the Lord**" (1 Cor. 1.31). Like the temple in the Old Testament, the assembly will be an empty shell without His presence.

b) It was the place where God's people were to dwell

The words, "to dwell in Jerusalem" and their equivalent, occur in vv.1,2,3,4,6. Jerusalem was the centre of God's purposes. It was the place above all where He was worshipped and served. In the New Testament, that distinction belongs to the local assembly. In his connection we should notice the following: "when ye come **together in (the) church...**when ye **come together therefore into one place**" (1 Cor. 11.17-20).

While we regularly quote the words, "For where two or three are gathered together in my name ('unto my name', JND), there am I in the midst of them" (Matt. 18.20), the context makes it clear that the Lord Jesus is dealing here with church discipline. See vv.15-19. The passage should, in fact, be compared with 1 Corinthians 5.4-5, "In the name of our Lord Jesus Christ, when ye are gathered together, and my spirit, with the power of our Lord Jesus Christ, to deliver such an one unto Satan for the destruction of the flesh, that the spirit may be saved in the day of the Lord Jesus".

The local assembly is also the centre for evangelism: "from **you** sounded out the word of the Lord" (1 Thess. 1.8). It follows therefore that, like Jerusalem, the assembly is to be well supported: "not forsaking the assembling of ourselves together (not 'yourselves', but "ourselves": the writer speaks to himself as well!), as the manner of some is" (Heb. 10.25). (The words, "and so much the more, as ye see the day approaching" evidently refer, not to the Lord's coming, but to the fall of Jerusalem as predicted by the Lord Jesus some forty years previously. In view of pending national disaster, there was great need for fellowship and mutual encouragement).

We must now notice some significant references to the men who dwelt in Jerusalem, the 'place of the Name'. 1 Chronicles ch.9 expands the list in this chapter, and gives us glimpses of the temple servants at work. The passage illustrates 1 Corinthians 12.18-21: "But now hath God set the members every one of them in the body, as it hath pleased him. And if they were all one member, where were the body? But now are they many members, yet but one body". In Nehemiah ch.11 there were:

i) Leading men, v.1
"And the **rulers of** the people dwelt at Jerusalem". It would have been a poor example to "the **rest of** the people" if they had treated their responsibilities lightly, and taken up residence elsewhere. Peter writes, "The elders which are **among you** I exhort...Feed the flock of God which is **among you**" (1 Pet. 5.1-2). Shepherding the flock and itinerant preaching are not always mutually complementary. Quite often, the local assembly comes off worse!

ii) Willing men, v.2
"And the people blessed all the men, **that willingly offered themselves** to dwell at Jerusalem". (We cannot be certain whether this refers to the people in v.1, or to additional people). Deborah and Barak refer to people who "willingly offered themselves": "Praise ye the Lord for the avenging of Israel, when the people **willingly offered themselves**...My heart is toward the governors of Israel, **that offered themselves willingly** among the people" (Judges 5.2,9). Paul does the same: "For to their power (ability), I bear record, yea, and beyond their power they were **willing** of themselves; praying us with much entreaty that we would receive the gift, and take upon us the fellowship of the ministering to the saints" (2 Cor. 8.3-5).

Paul expresses his willingness to serve God as follows: "For God is my witness, whom I serve **with my spirit** in the gospel of his Son..." (Rom. 1.9). Elders are to serve willingly: "Feed ('shepherd', JND) the flock of God which is among you, taking the oversight thereof, not by constraint, but **willingly**; not for filthy lucre, but of a ready mind" (1 Pet. 5.2).

iii) Valiant men, v.6
"All the sons of Perez that dwelt at Jerusalem were four hundred threescore and eight **valiant men**". Others are mentioned later: "Amashai the son of Azareel, the son of Ahasai, the son of Meshillemoth, the son of Immer, and their brethren, **mighty men of valour**" (v.13-14). Paul was looking for "valiant men" in saying, "Finally, my brethren, be strong in the Lord, and in the power of his might...Wherefore take unto you the whole armour of God, that ye may be able to withstand in the evil day, and having done all, to stand. Stand therefore..." (Eph. 6.10-17). That is, "stand" **during**, and **after** "the evil day", which is any particular day. The apostle urged the believers at Corinth to "Watch ...stand fast in the faith, **quit you like men**, be strong" (1 Cor. 16.13). Jeremiah was obliged to charge Israel with bending "their tongues like their bow for lies: but they are **not valiant for the truth** upon the earth" (Jer. 9.3). We all need to 'stand up and be counted'.

iv) Overseeing men, v.9
"And Joel the son of Zichri was their **overseer**" (v.9). Others are mentioned later: "And their **overseer** was Zabdiel, the son of one of the **great men**" (v.14); "The **overseer** also of the Levites at Jerusalem was Uzzi the son of Bani..." (v.22). In this connection we should notice that "Shabbethai and Jozabad, of the chief of the Levites, had **the oversight of the outward business of the house of God**" (v.16). This is explained in the previous chapter where the people covenanted to make proper provision for "the house of our God". This included "the wood offering", "the firstfruits", "the firstborn" and "the firstlings". Shabbethai and Jozabad ensured that the house of God was provisioned and supplied.

It is the responsibility of New Testament overseers to ensure that the assembly, "the house of God" (1 Tim. 3.15), is spiritually provisioned and equipped. The fires of devotion to Christ must never go out, and the saints must be adequately fed.

v) Priestly men, vv.10-11
"Of the **priests:** Jedaiah the son of Joiarib, Jachin. Seraiah, the son of Hilkiah, the son of Meshullam, the son of Zadok, the son of Meraioth, the son of Ahitub, was the ruler of the house of God". The words, "Jedaiah **the son of** Joiarib", are doubtful: see JND footnote. According to W.B.Pope (Ellicott's Commentary), "This should read, Jedaiah, Joiarib, Jachin, three priestly families (1 Chronicles 9.10)".

We must never forget that every believer, young or old, brother or sister, knowledgeable or not so knowledgeable, is a priest. See 1 Peter 2.5,9. The 'place of the Name' today cannot function without priestly ministry. The word "priest" means, 'one who offers sacrifices'. It is through this ministry that God receives His portion in the worship of the assembly: "By him therefore let us offer the sacrifice of praise to God continually, that is, the fruit of our lips giving thanks to his name" (Heb. 13.15). Compare 1 Peter 2.5, and notice Acts 13.2, "As they ministered **to the Lord**", comparing this with Deut. 21.5, "And the priests the sons of Levi shall come near; for them the Lord thy God hath chosen **to minister unto him**".

vi) Working men, v12

"And their brethren that **did the work** of the house were eight hundred twenty and two". Such men are usually in short supply. When Ezra "viewed the people" (Ezra 8.15), he "found there none of the sons of Levi". We are to be "stedfast, unmoveable, always abounding in the work of the Lord, forasmuch as ye know that your labour is not in vain in the Lord" (1 Cor. 15.58). In the New Testament, this was not confined to brothers: Paul wrote, "Help those **women** which **laboured** with me in the gospel" (Phil. 4.3). Here the word "laboured" (*sunathleo*) means striving or contending along with a person. Other 'labouring' sisters are mentioned in the New Testament. For example, "Salute Tryphena and Tryphosa, who **labour** in the Lord. Salute the beloved Persis, which **laboured much** in the Lord" (Rom. 16.12). Here the word "labour" (*kopiao*) means 'laborious toil' (W.E. Vine).

vii) Praying men, v17

"And Mattaniah the son of Micha, the son of Zabdi, the son of Asaph, was **the principal to begin the thanksgiving in prayer**: and Bakbukiah **the second** among his brethren, and Abda the son of Shammua, the son of Galal, the son of Jeduthun". The chronicler records that David "appointed certain of the Levites to minister before the ark of the Lord, and to record, and to thank and praise the Lord God of Israel" (1 Chron. 16.4).

The house of God cannot function without prayer. This is why Paul puts prayer first in writing to Timothy: "I exhort therefore, that, first of all, supplications, prayers, intercessions, and giving of thanks, be made for all men" (1 Tim. 2.1). When Paul says, "I will therefore that (the) men pray everywhere, lifting up holy hands, without wrath and doubting (1 Tim 2.8), he means **two** things: *(a)* that **only the men** are to pray publicly in the assembly prayer meeting; *(b)* that the men are **not to keep silent!** We need to remember them both.

viii) Praising men, vv.22-23

"Of the sons of Asaph, **the singers were over the business of the house of God**". Not now, "the **outward** business of the house of God" (v.16). We should notice the provision for them: "For it was the **king's** commandment (presumably Artaxerxes) concerning them, that a certain portion should be for the singers, due for every day" (v.23). The singers were, of course, Levites (see 1 Chron. 15.16-22). "The business of the house of God" was in the charge of praising men! After all, someone who is always dour and doleful, who is always moaning and complaining, is not likely to make a good leader, or be a good example!

While the New Testament does not provide for trained singers or choir pieces, it does have something to say about singing. See 1 Corinthians 14.15, "I will sing with the spirit, and I will sing with the **understanding** also". While we enjoy good tunes, we must not forget the words of our hymns and choruses: hymn and chorus writers are not always good theologians! Paul deals with the subject in a later epistle: "speaking to yourselves in psalms and hymns and spiritual songs, singing and making melody in your heart to the Lord" (Eph. 5.19). The previous verse (v.18) refers to "the song of the drunkard" (Psalm 69.12): "And be not drunk with wine, wherein is excess". But here is singing of a totally different order! We are told that in the Greek text, the words "to yourselves" (Eph. 5.19) can signify 'one to another', but that it is more often "to yourselves". As A.Leckie *('What The Bible Teaches - Ephesians')* observes, "personal not public worship is the subject". Although the expression "making melody", means, literally, to 'sing with a stringed instrument accompaniment', here it is the heart that is the instrument!

The parallel passage in Colossians 3.16 can be better understood by punctuating as follows: "Let the word of Christ dwell in you richly in all wisdom; teaching and admonishing one another. In psalms and hymns and spiritual songs, singing with grace in your hearts to the Lord". The three expressions: "psalms and hymns and spiritual songs" are of interest. It has been suggested that the word "**psalms**" may have a wider connotation than the book of Psalms, and refers to expressions of praise, like the Psalms themselves, arising from experience with God. This may or may not be so. We **do** sing Psalm 23, to name but one! The word "**hymns**", meaning songs of praise, could well refer to New Testament compositions. "**Spiritual songs**" means a composition which expresses "some spiritual truth" (A. Leckie). Our hymn, 'Thou art the everlasting Word', certainly falls within that category.

ix) Vigilant men, v.19

"Moreover the porters, Akkub, Talmon, and their brethren **that kept the gates**, were an hundred seventy and two". The work of the porters is dealt with at length in 1 Chronicles 9.19-29; 26.1-19. The work required strength: "All these of the sons of Obed-edom: they and their sons and their brethren, able men for **strength for the service**, were threescore and two of Obed-edom. And Meshelemiah had sons and brethren, **strong men**, eighteen" (1 Chron. 26.8-9). After the death of Athaliah, Jehoiada "set the porters at the gates of the house of the Lord, that none which was **unclean in any thing should enter in**" (2 Chron. 23.19). In the days of Josiah, "the porters waited at every gate; **they might not depart from their service**; for their brethren the Levites prepared for them" (2 Chron. 35.15).

The need for spiritual "porters" remains: "For I know this, that after my departing shall grievous wolves enter in among you, not sparing the flock...Therefore watch, and remember, that by the space of three years I ceased not to warn every one night and day with tears" (Acts 20.29-31). The need is stressed by such passages as "false brethren unawares brought in" (Gal. 2.4); "there shall be false teachers among you, who privily shall bring in damnable heresies" (2 Pet. 2.1); "For there are certain men crept in unawares" (Jude v.4).

The Lord Jesus referred to the subject: "For the Son of man is as a man taking a far journey, who left his house, and gave authority to his servants, and to every man his work, and commanded the **porter** to watch" (Mark 13.34); "But he that entereth in by the door is the shepherd of the sheep. To him the **porter** openeth" (John 10.2-3).

2) THOSE THAT DWELL IN JUDAH AND BENJAMIN, vv.20-36

"And the residue of Israel, of the priests, and the Levites, were in all the cities of Judah, every one in his inheritance" (v.20). The "villages" (sometimes "towns", RV) of "**the children of Judah**" are listed in vv.25-30, and the "villages" of "**the children...of Benjamin**" in vv.31-35. Levites were found in the territory of both Judah and Benjamin (v.36).

We should notice that vv.21-24 are a parenthesis: vv.21-23 refer to the Nethinims and Levites **at Jerusalem,** and v.24 refers to the people's representative **at Shushan**: "And Pethahiah the son of Meshezabeel, of the children of Zerah the son of Judah, was at **the king's hand in all matters concerning the people**". The king had commissioners at court from his various dominions to advise on their affairs.

READ CHAPTER 12

"The dedication of the wall"

Nehemiah 12 describes "the dedication of the wall of Jerusalem" (v.27), accompanied by praise and thanksgiving to God. When the work was actually completed, even the enemies recognised "that this work was wrought of our God" (6.16). Now the time had come for God's people to "[give] thanks in the house of God" (v.40). It was certainly not a hastily-convened meeting! Whilst "the porters and the singers and the Levites" had been appointed on completion of the work (7.1), the dedication of the wall did not take place until some serious business had been transacted. The Scriptures were read in Chapter 8, and this led to the renewal of the covenant in Chapters 9 & 10, in preparation for full occupation of the city. After all, as we saw in our last study, "the place which the Lord shall choose to place his name there" (Deut. 16.2) required suitable people in residence. Jerusalem was not a museum piece: it was to be the centre of spiritual life. The *place* had been prepared, and the *people* had been prepared. A new era had dawned, and "the joy of Jerusalem was heard even afar off" (v.43).

The four major paragraphs in the chapter may be entitled: *(1)* preservation (vv.1-26); *(2)* purification (vv.27-30); *(3)* praise (vv.31-43); *(4)* provision (v.44-47).

1) PRESERVATION, vv.1-26

More names! To make matters worse, the list begins with "the priests and the Levites that went up with Zerubbabel the son of Shealtiel, and Jeshua" (v.1). So why do we need yet another note of people who returned from exile ninety years before? Surely Ezra 2 and Nehemiah 7 are quite sufficient! However, this is a rather specialised list. The whole section deals only with the priests and the Levites. C.J. Barber is certainly right in saying, "This register reminds us of the importance and power of godliness in the life of the nation". The priests and Levites represented the people before God. Failure here meant national disaster, and failure in *our* priestly worship and service through, for example, unconfessed sin, means disaster too. The list therefore reminded the people of former leaders and teachers, and said in effect: "*Remember* them which have the rule over you, who have spoken unto you the word of God: **whose faith follow**", (Heb. 13.7). The list emphasises three important things in connection with the priestly and Levitical families:

a) Their continuity

This is clear from the way in which the section is locked together. It commences with a list of the "chief of the priests and their brethren in the days of **Jeshua**" (v.7), and traces their descendants until the days of Nehemiah and Ezra: "These were in the days of Joiakim the **son of Jeshua**, the son of Jozadak, and in the days of **Nehemiah** the governor, and of **Ezra** the priest, the scribe" (v.26). The chapter ends with reference to the same period (v.47). Ezra and Nehemiah were both present at the dedication of the walls (vv.31,36).

God had preserved the priestly family through the 'last days' of Old Testament history. There had been a continuity of priestly ministry and Levitical service. In the case of the Levites, their ministry of praise (the singers) and purity (the porters) is emphasised (vv.8-9,24-25,45). How much we need to pray for the maintenance of this ministry in the 'last days' of the **present** dispensation! In this connection, we should notice the expression "begat" (vv.10-11). If priestly worship and Levitical service are to be preserved today, there must be spiritual **children.** We must pray therefore for the **salvation** of men and women! Those spiritual children then need to be taught, so that they too can worship and serve: "And the things that thou hast heard of me among many witnesses, the **same** commit thou to **faithful** men, who shall be **able** ('competent', JND) to teach others also" (2 Tim. 2.2).

b) Their authenticity

It is more than a list of names. We are given genealogies. The priests could declare their 'pedigree' (Num. 1.18). We must not forget what happened to the men who could not prove their priestly status in the days of Zerubbabel (7.63-65). They were "as polluted, put from the priesthood". Sadly, there are many people masquerading as religious leaders today (many of them are called 'priests') who fail the New Testament test, "Examine yourselves, whether ye be in the faith; prove your own selves" (2 Cor. 13.5). While there are unsaved priests in Christendom, there are no unsaved priests in the New Testament epistles!

c) Their unity

The two classes, "the priests" and the "Levites", are seen constantly together throughout the chapter, emphasising the relationship between priestly men and serving men (vv.1,22,30,44,47). This was a divinely-ordained relationship: "And the Lord said unto Aaron, Thou and thy sons and thy father's house with thee shall bear the iniquity of the sanctuary...and thy brethren also of the tribe of Levi, the tribe of thy father, bring thou with thee, **that they may be joined unto thee**, and minister unto thee" (Num. 18.1-2). We do not have people today who answer to priests and Levites respectively. We are **all** priests **and** Levites! All service for God should be undertaken in the spirit of priestly worship. See, for example, Romans 15.16, where the words, "ministering the gospel of God", refer to priestly service. The word "ministering" comes from a Greek word (*hierourgeo*) meaning a sacrificing priest.

As in all the Scriptures, the details given in these verses of the chapter will repay careful study. Just as a guide, it is important to notice that the 'spinal column' of the section lies in the succession of the high priestly family. This is summarised in vv.10-11: "And **Jeshua** begat Joiakim, **Joiakim** also begat Eliashib, and **Eliashib** begat Joiada, and **Joiada** begat Jonathan, and **Jonathan** begat **Jaddua**". These two verses co-ordinate the surrounding verses. In studying the passage, we should notice the way in which these verses are expanded: "**In the days of** Jeshua (v.7)...Joiakim (v.12)...Eliashib, Joiada, and Johanan, and Jaddua (v.22)". See the addendum.

Before we leave this section, we must reiterate that these detailed lists emphasise that God is interested in each one of His people. He does not bulk them all together. Our individual record is "on high" (Job 16.19). This should encourage us on one hand, and caution us on the other.

2) PURIFICATION, vv.27-30
Having seen how the priestly and Levitical families had been preserved through difficult days, this section of the chapter describes their preparation for the dedication of the wall: "And the priests and the Levites purified themselves, and purified the people, and the gates, and the wall" (v.30). Bearing in mind that this was an occasion of great rejoicing, the singers were required. Two things are emphasised:

a) Gathering for praise, vv.27-29
These verses emphasise the function of the singers: "they sought the Levites...to keep the dedication with gladness, both with thanksgivings, and with **singing**... and the sons of the **singers** gathered themselves together...the **singers** had builded them villages round about Jerusalem". Perhaps the Levitical singers were not in evidence as they should have been, and needed stirring up! After all, it does say that they "**sought** the Levites". We all need a prod now and then! Each of these three verses mentions Jerusalem, so praise and Jerusalem are closely connected! The place where the Lord put His Name should be a place of praise! It wasn't just a case of singing the right tune: they were going to "keep the dedication with **gladness**!" (v.27). We should notice:

i) The need for singers, v.27. "And at the dedication of the wall of Jerusalem they **sought** the Levites out of all their places, to bring them to Jerusalem, to keep the dedication with gladness, both with thanksgivings, and with singing, with cymbals, psalteries, and with harps". Do notice that it was the **Levites** who sang. The servants of God should be praising people! At the dedication of the temple, "the Levites which were the singers…stood at the east end of the altar, and with them an hundred and twenty priests sounding with trumpets… the trumpeters and singers were as one, to make one sound to be heard in praising and thanking the Lord" (2 Chron. 5.12-13). Whilst the New Testament does not envisage assembly choirs (and certainly not assembly trumpeters!), it is still true that "Whoso offereth praise glorifieth me" (Psalm 50.23). It has been nicely said that "'Today, there is only one choir, and we are all in it: and the Lord Jesus is the Leader of the praise" (A.Leckie). See Hebrews 2.12.

ii) The nearness of the singers, vv.28-29. "And the sons of the singers gathered themselves together, both out of the plain country round about Jerusalem, and from the villages of Netophathi; also from the house of Gilgal, and out of the fields of Geba and Azmaveth: for the singers had builded them **villages round about Jerusalem**". They lived near their spiritual centre! It isn't always possible to reside in the shadow of the assembly hall, but like David, our hearts should be there: "Lord, I have loved the habitation of thy house, and the place where thine honour dwelleth" (Psalm 26.8).

b) Purification before praise, v.30
"And the priests and the Levites purified themselves, and purified the people, and the gates, and the wall". The details are absorbing and significant.

i)   They purified themselves. This is so necessary: "let a man examine **himself** (not his brethren)" (1 Cor. 11.28). Provision is made for cleansing: "If we confess our sins, he is faithful and just to forgive us our sins, and to cleanse us from all unrighteousness" (1 John 1.9). We must notice that they purified **themselves** first. The Lord Jesus taught, "**first** cast out the beam out of thine own eye; and then shalt thou see clearly to cast out the mote out of thy brother's eye" (Matt. 7.3-5).

ii)   They purified the people. The priests and Levites were now in a position to help the people. We can only help fellow-believers when we are right with God ourselves: "Brethren, if a man be overtaken in a fault, ye which are **spiritual**, restore such an one in the spirit of meekness; considering thyself, lest thou also be tempted" (Gal. 6.1).

*iii) **They purified the gates and the wall.*** So the ***place*** was purified as well as the people. This just emphasises the epithet, "Jerusalem, the **holy city**" (11.1,18). It was a place set apart for God. The assembly (with all its members) should be exactly the same. Like the temple in the Old Testament, it should be a place where God is honoured and worshipped. After all, a biblical temple is a building in which 'every one speaks of his glory' (Psalm 29.9). The assembly is not a place where we ape the world with its entertainment and pursuits.

We are not told exactly how this purification was made. Perhaps help in this direction can be found in Exodus 19.10,14; Numbers 8.5-8. In all probability it was ceremonial cleansing, although it certainly reflected spiritual reality. Compare Ezra 6.21. However, the absence of detail suggests that this is not the main point. These people did not just sit down and let the world go by: they were active in their devotion to God. It is one thing just to come to assembly meetings: it is quite another to actively pursue God's interests. We must not be passive Christians.

3) PRAISE, vv.31-43
The big day dawned, and two processions marched in opposite directions along the rebuilt walls of Jerusalem (v.31). J.N. Darby calls them, "two great choirs and processions". Beneath their feet was material evidence of God's goodness and provision. After all, "this work was wrought of our God". It was praise all the way. The passage is punctuated by some delightful little expressions. For example "gave thanks" (vv.31,38,40); "stood still (v.39); "sang loud" (v.42); "offered great sacrifices" (v.43). It is all reminiscent of Psalm 48.12-14, "Walk about Zion, and go round about her: tell the towers thereof. Mark ye well her bulwarks, consider her palaces; that ye may tell it to the generation following. For this God is our God for ever and ever: he will be our guide even unto death". We are given details of the "two great companies":

a) The first company, vv.31-37
"Then I brought up the princes of Judah upon the wall, and appointed two great companies of them that gave thanks, whereof one went on the **right hand upon the wall** toward the dung gate" (v.31). Although we are not given the starting point, it is clear that this group marched anti-clockwise along the southern and then the eastern part of the wall: "on the right hand upon the wall toward the **dung gate**...and at the **fountain gate**, which was over against them, they went up by the stairs of the city of David, at the going up of the wall, above the house of David, even unto the **water gate** eastward". Consult the map!

These verses also describe the constitution of the party, which was evidently led

213

by none other than Ezra (v.36). Presumably, the "great companies of them that gave thanks" were the singers, the Levites. They were followed by "Hoshaiah, and half of the princes of Judah (see v.38 for the other half), and Azariah, Ezra, and Meshullam, Judah, and Benjamin, and Shemaiah, and Jeremiah" (vv.32-34). The princes were followed by "certain of the priests' sons with trumpets", accompanied by others with "the musical instruments of David the man of God" (vv.35-36). It is possible, just 'possible', that the trumpets were the **silver trumpets** of Numbers ch.10. These were to be blown on such occasions (Num. 10.10).

b) The second company, vv.38-39
"And the other company of them that gave thanks went over against them, and I (Nehemiah of course) after them, and the half of the people upon the wall, from beyond the tower of the furnaces even unto the broad wall; and from above the **gate of Ephraim**, and above the **old gate**, and above the **fish gate**, and the tower of Hananeel, and the tower of Meah, even unto the **sheep gate**: and they stood still in the **prison gate**". This party marched in a clockwise direction. Consult the map again! (See page 219).

c) Both companies, vv.40-43
"So stood the two companies of them that gave thanks in the house of God, and I, and the half of the rulers with me". So it was a case of going from "the prison gate" to "the house of God". A nice picture of sinners brought into God's presence! It is always important to "look unto the rock whence ye are hewn, and to the hole of the pit whence ye are digged" (Isa. 51.1). They "**stood still** in the prison gate". How glad we are that when we were in "the prison gate", we heard the Lord say, "Fear ye not, **stand still**, and see the salvation of the Lord" (Exodus 14.13). We should notice the following in connection with their thanksgiving in the house of God:

i) The enthusiasm of their praise.
"And the singers **sang loud**" (v.42). New Testament believers are not lacking in this respect: "And they worshipped him, and returned to Jerusalem with great joy: and were continually in the temple, **praising and blessing God**" (Luke 24.52-53); "And they, continuing daily with one accord in the temple, and breaking bread from house to house, did eat their meat with gladness and singleness of heart, **praising God**, and having favour with all the people" (Acts 2.46-47); "And at midnight Paul and Silas prayed, and **sang praises** unto God" (Acts 16.25).

There can be no doubt that the enthusiasm of the singers was shared by everybody. After all, they had just marched along the walls and, to quote D.Kidner, "every inch of these ramparts had its special memory for one group or another".

See Chapter 3. We must re-visit those gates, and recall their spiritual significance. **We** have good cause to 'sing loud' too!

ii) ***The orderliness of their praise.*** "And the singers sang loud, with Jezrahiah their overseer" (v.42). It was not discordant or disorderly. Everything was done under the 'beady eye' of Jezrahiah. We should compare this with Ezra 3.11, and we must not forget 1 Corinthians 14.40!

iii) ***The direction of their praise***. "Also that day they offered great sacrifices, and rejoiced: for God had made them to rejoice with great joy" (v.43). We should not overlook the fact that whole families were involved in this thanksgiving: "the wives also and the children rejoiced". This was not an exercise in self-congratulation. They said in effect, "The Lord hath done great things for us; whereof we are glad" (Psalm 126.3). Sacrifice and praise are nicely connected in the restoration of temple worship under Hezekiah: "And when the burnt offering began, the song of the Lord began also" (2 Chron. 29.27).

iv) ***The effect of their praise.*** "So that the joy of Jerusalem was heard even afar off" (v.43), recalling that "at midnight Paul and Silas prayed, and sang praises unto God: and the prisoners heard them ('and the prisoners listened to them', JND)" (Acts 16.25). God really does give "songs in the night"! (Job 35.10). As D.Kidner observes, "This time, in contrast to Ezra 3.13, it was no uncertain sound that was heard afar off". On the other hand 'tears and cheers' (C.E. Hocking) is not a bad combination!

4) PROVISION, vv.44-47
The final paragraph of the chapter emphasises the enthusiasm with which the priests and Levites were supported. Bearing in mind that they looked to the Lord for support, we should notice:

a) Their support was whole-hearted, v.44
"And at that time ('on that day', JND margin) were some appointed over the chambers..." So Nehemiah "struck while the iron was hot, gaining something practical from this moment of elation and goodwill" (D.Kidner). Nehemiah continues: "And at that time were some appointed over the chambers for the treasures, for the offerings, for the firstfruits, and for the tithes, to gather into them out of the fields of the cities the portions of the law for the priests and Levites: for Judah *rejoiced for the priests and for the Levites that waited*". (How much do we rejoice in the work of God's servants?). While the people were required to give under law, hence the words "the portions assigned by the law"

(JND), they did so with evident joy. This should be the spirit of our stewardship too: "Every man according as he purposeth in his heart, so let him give; not grudgingly, or of necessity: for God loveth a **cheerful** giver" (2 Cor. 9.7).

b) Their support was merited, vv.45-46
"And both the singers and the porters kept the ward of their God, and the ward of the purification, according to the commandment of David, and of Solomon his son" The idea of the word "ward" here is the "performance of an office or function" (Gesenius). These men 'waited on their ministry' (Rom. 12.7). They followed an excellent tradition: "For in the days of David and Asaph, of old there were chief of the singers, and songs of praise and thanksgiving unto God".

Men who follow the good traditions and practices of the word of God, are well worth supporting. Paul evidently alludes to the support of the priests ("they which wait at the altar") and Levites ("they which minister about holy things"), in saying "even so hath the Lord ordained that they which preach the gospel should live of the gospel" (1 Cor. 9.11-14). See also Galatians 6.6, "Let him that is taught in the word communicate unto him that teacheth in all good things".

c) Their support was consistent, v.47
"And all Israel in the days of **Zerubbabel**, and in the days of **Nehemiah**, gave the portions of the singers and the porters, every day his portion". Zerubbabel and Nehemiah stood at the beginning and end respectively of this particular period in Old Testament history. There had been consistent and regular ("every day") support throughout the period. The believers at Philippi were similar: "Now ye Philippians know also, that in the beginning of the gospel, when I departed from Macedonia, no church communicated with me as concerning giving and receiving, but ye only" (Phil. 4.15-16). Paul calls this, "your fellowship in the gospel from the first day until now" (Phil. 1.5).

d) Their support was shared, v.47
"And they sanctified holy things unto the Levites; and the Levites sanctified them **unto the children of Aaron**". This is called the "tithe of the tithes" (10.38), referring to Numbers 18.25-30 where the Levites were instructed to "give thereof the Lord's heave offering to Aaron the priest" (v.28). This "tithe of tithes" was "reckoned" to the Levites "as though it were the corn of the threshingfloor, and as the fulness of the winepress" (Num.18.27,30). In other words, although it was given to them by others in the first place, it was accepted as if they had harvested it themselves. We noticed the lesson in Chapter 10. In giving to the Lord for the use of His servants, we put **them** in a position to give to the Lord (10.38).

Addendum

The high priestly family
As noted above, the 'spinal column' of vv.1-26 lies in the succession of the high priestly family. This is summarised in vv.10-11: "And **Jeshua** begat Joiakim, **Joiakim** also begat Eliashib, and **Eliashib** begat Joiada, and **Joiada** begat Jonathan, and **Jonathan** begat **Jaddua**". These two verses co-ordinate the surrounding verses.

In studying the passage, we should observe the way in which these verses are expanded: *(a)* "in the days of **Jeshua**" (v.7): the first generation of high priests; *(b)* "in the days of **Joiakim**" (v.12); the second generation of high priests; *(c)* "in the days of **Eliashib**" (v.22): the third generation of high priests; *(d)* "in the days of Eliashib (as above), **Joiada**, and **Johanan**, and **Jaddua**" (v.22): the fourth, fifth and sixth generations of high priests. We must notice the details given in each case:

a) "In the days of Jeshua", vv.1-9
This refers to the first generation of high priests. These verses detail "the chief of the **priests**" (vv.1-7), and what we may call, borrowing the language of v.24, "the chief of the **Levites**" (vv.8-9). Our use of these words here finds some support from the expressions "***over*** the thanksgiving" (v.8) and "***over*** against them in the watches" (v.9). The Levites were divided into two classes:

- **The singers, v.8.** "Jeshua, Binnui, Kadmiel, Sherebiah, Judah, and Mattaniah, which was **over the thanksgiving**, he and his brethren".

- **The porters, v.9.** "Also Bakbukiah and Unni, their brethren, were **over against them in the watches**", or "over against them as watches" (JND). Gesenius gives the meaning of "watches" as "custody, guard".

To summarise, "in the days of Jeshua", that is, at the beginning of the period, there were priests and Levites, and amongst the Levites, there were men who led the praise, and men who acted as porters.

b) "In the days of Joiakim", vv.12-21
This refers to the second generation of high priests. These verses detail the children of the chief priests mentioned in vv.1-7, that is, the contemporaries of Joiakim himself. A further list of Joiakim's priestly contemporaries is given in vv.12-21. When the two lists (vv.1-7; vv.12-21) are compared it does seem that

some of the priests evidently served in the days of both Jeshua and Joiakim. The names of Levites who served in the days of Joiakim are given in vv.24-25. The list ends with the words, "These were in the days of Joiakim the son of Jeshua (also known as Joshua), the son of Jozadak, and in the days of Nehemiah the governor, and of Ezra the priest, the scribe" (v.26). This appears to be a general summary of the passage. Jozadak was the high priest at the time of the Babylonian captivity (1 Chron. 6.15).

c) "In the days of Eliashib", v.22
This refers to the third generation of high priests. "And Jeshua begat Joiakim, Joiakim also begat Eliashib" (v.10).

d) "In the days of Eliashib, Joiada, and Johanan, and Jaddua", v.22
Omitting reference to Eliashib (see above), **this refers to the fourth, fifth and sixth generations of high priests**: "and Eliashib (the third generation) begat Joiada, and Joiada begat Jonathan, and Jonathan begat Jaddua" (vv.10-11).

Reference is made here (v.22) to the "**Levites** in the days of Eliashib, Joiada, and Johanan (or Jonathan, v.11), and Jaddua". It is not clear why the names of the priests during the period were recorded, though not detailed, "to the reign of Darius the Persian". We should note the self-explanatory fact that "The sons of Levi, the chief of the fathers, were written in book of the chronicles" (referring to 1 Chronicles 9.14-18), even until the days of Johanan (the fifth generation: evidently the same as Jonathan, v.11) the son of Eliashib" (v.23). We should also note that the New Testament has something even better. Paul refers to his "**fellowlabourers** (the Levites were labourers), whose names are in the **book of life**" (Phil. 4.3). The "book of life" is even better than "the book of the chronicles!"

But it **is** clear that Levitical and priestly families had been preserved from the beginning of the period ("in the days of Jeshua") to the end of Old Testament history. The book of Nehemiah ends during the high priesthood of Eliashib (see 13.4-7), and therefore the high priesthoods of his son Joiada, his grandson Johanan, and his great grandson Jaddua, must take us beyond the events recorded in Nehemiah and at least to the days of Malachi.

The two classes of Levites detailed in vv.8-9, the singers and the porters, are now again specifically mentioned:

- **The singers, v.24.** "And the chief of the Levites: Hashabiah, Sherebiah, and Jeshua the son of Kadmiel, with their brethren over against them, **to praise and**

to give thanks, according to the commandment of David the man of God, ward over against ward". So they went back to the original command. There can be nothing better than following original instructions! The words, "David the **man of God**" (see also v.36) remind us that while at one stage in his life he was anything but "the man of God", he enjoyed the forgiveness and restoring grace of God!

- The porters, v.25. "Mattaniah, and Bakbukiah, Obadiah, Meshullam, Talmon, Akkub, were porters keeping the ward at the thresholds of the gates".

As already noted, a summary concludes the section. "These were in the days of Joiakim the son of Jeshua, the son of Jozadak, and in the days of Nehemiah the governor, and of Ezra the priest, the scribe" (v.26).

We conclude therefore, and this is the point of the section, that there were priests and Levites functioning to a greater or lesser degree, right the way through the period commencing with the return from Babylonian exile to the days actually beyond the book of Nehemiah, reaching, it seems, to the days of Malachi, when the priesthood evidently failed. See Malachi 2.1-10.

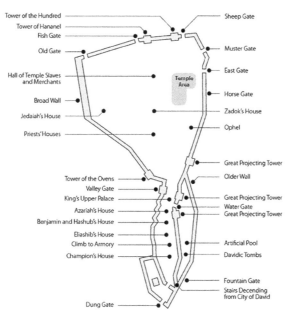

Jerusalem's Wall in Nehemiah's Day

READ CHAPTER 13

"I contended with them"

It would have been very nice indeed if the book of Nehemiah ended with Chapter 12! After all, just look at all the progress. The **place** had been prepared (Chapters 1-6), and the **people** had been prepared (Chapters 7-12). Everything was set fair for the future. A new era had dawned, and "the joy of Jerusalem was heard even afar off" (12.43).

But the book of Nehemiah does **not** end with Chapter 12! It ends with Chapter 13, and while this makes very discouraging reading, it is a salutary warning to us all: "Let him that thinketh he standeth take heed lest he fall" (1 Cor. 10.12). It is only fair to add that the chapter does end on a positive note: "Thus cleansed I them from all strangers, and appointed the wards of the priests and the Levites, every one in his business...Remember me, O my God, for good" (vv.30-31). In fact, each paragraph in the chapter ends in this way: see vv.9,12-14,21-22,30-31. Nehemiah never faltered or failed!

The roots of Nehemiah 13 lie in Chapter 10, where the people covenanted to obey God's word in various ways, including the following: *(i)* "that we would not give our daughters unto the people of the land, nor take their daughters for our sons" (10.30); *(ii)* "and if the people of the land bring ware or any other victuals on the sabbath day to sell, that we would not buy it of them on the sabbath, or on the holy day" (10.31); *(iii)* "that we should bring...the tithes of our ground unto the Levites, that the same Levites might have the tithes in all the cities of our tillage" (10.37).

The people made a good start (12.44-47), and all went well for about twelve years (compare 2.1 with 13.6), but in Nehemiah's absence, things deteriorated: *(i)* they failed to support the Levites (13.10-14); *(ii)* they failed to keep the sabbath (13.15-22); *(iii)* they failed to maintain separation from the nations (13.23-30). In each case, Nehemiah was obliged to '**contend**' with them (13.11,17,25). He was not afraid to "earnestly contend for the faith" (Jude v.3).

He was a man of deep conviction. The people made fine promises in Chapter 10, but failed to deliver. **We** are equally vulnerable. But failure does not excuse us from further commitment to God. Failure should lead us to seek His help with even greater determination!

We must notice again that all was well while Nehemiah was present in Jerusalem. His strong convictions held the people, but they failed to share them. When he was absent, spiritual standards slipped. It is not sufficient to have men of conviction at the helm of the assembly: we **all** need to be men and women of conviction. Nehemiah left Jerusalem with everything in good order, and returned to find disorder. It would be tragic if the **Lord Jesus** were to return and find **us** unfaithful to His word. Do remember that "we must all appear before the judgment seat of Christ; that every one may receive the things done in his body, according to that he hath done, whether it be good or bad" (2 Cor. 5.10). While Nehemiah recovered the situation, it wasn't long before decline set in again. Malachi, who evidently preached a little after Nehemiah, refers to lack of support for the Levites ("Will a man rob God? Yet ye have robbed me. But ye say, Wherein have we robbed thee? In tithes and offerings" (3.8-10), and intermarriage with pagan neighbours ("Judah hath profaned the holiness of the Lord which he loved, and hath married the daughter of a strange god", 2.11). Some people never learn! But do **we?**

In each of the three cases described above, the people deliberately flouted the word of God, and it all began when the priesthood failed. The compromise of Eliashib in preparing a chamber in the temple for Tobiah the Ammonite (v.4), led to decline elsewhere. This is always the case. Failure in devotion to God will bring failure everywhere.

Nehemiah Chapter 13 describes a fourfold failure: *(1)* failure to recognise the sanctity of God's house (vv.1-9); *(2)* failure to recognise the needs of God's servants (vv.10-14); *(3)* failure to recognise the blessings of God's rest (vv.15-22); *(4)* failure to recognise the separation of God's people (vv.23-29).

1) FAILURE TO RECOGNISE THE SANCTITY OF GOD'S HOUSE, vv.1-9
While, at first glance, it appears that vv.1-3 ("On that day") immediately follow 12.44-47, it is not quite so clear where vv.4-6 fit in with this, bearing in mind that they commence with the words, "And before this" We cannot be altogether certain of the chronology here, and this could be quite deliberate. Perhaps the Holy Spirit intends to teach us that the sad inward condition of God's people can produce outward decline at any time. Two things *are* clear however: *(i)* that

there was serious decline in Nehemiah's absence, and *(ii)* that vv.1-3 provide the background for vv.4-6. We should therefore notice:

a) The exclusion of the Ammonite and the Moabite, vv.1-3

The reading of the law revealed that "the Ammonite and the Moabite should not come into the congregation of God for ever" (v.1), referring to Deuteronomy 23.3-4. The relevance of this commandment to the passage is very clear: Tobiah was an Ammonite (2.10), and Sanballat (13.28) was evidently a Moabite. He is called "the Horonite" which suggests that he came from Horonaim in Moab (see 2.10, JND margin). He was related to Joiada, Eliashib's grandson. This makes Eliashib's provision for Tobiah, and Joiada's marriage to Sanballat's daughter, totally inexcusable. (Bearing in mind this prohibition, we should think carefully about the position of "Ruth, the Moabitess". How was it possible for her to be so richly blessed? There is, of course, a very positive answer!).

The word of God was heeded and obeyed: "Now it came to pass, when they had heard the law, that they separated from Israel all the mixed multitude". The "mixed multitude" (Exodus 12.38) had certainly caused problems in the past: they evidently led the protest in Numbers 11.4-6. We too must beware of the "mixed multitude". The response of the people was most encouraging at the time (v.3), but if we understand the chronology correctly, one aspect of the problem still needed to be addressed. This brings us to:

b) The provision for Tobiah the Ammonite, vv.4-5

"And before this, Eliashib **the priest**, having the oversight of the chamber of the house of our God, was allied unto Tobiah: and he had prepared for him a great chamber, where aforetime they laid the meat offerings, the frankincense..." (v.4-5). On hearing the Scriptures read, the **people** separated themselves from the "mixed multitude", but not **Eliashib** who, of all people, should have known better: "For **the priest's** lips should keep knowledge, and they should seek the law at his mouth: for he is the messenger of the Lord of hosts" (Mal. 2.7). When the wall was being rebuilt, it was Eliashib who set the pace (3.1). But now he engages in some very unsanctified conduct. In Chapter 3, he was employed in building a wall to keep Tobiah out. Now we find him preparing a chamber for Tobiah in the temple! Perhaps this is why "there is a suspicious absence of Eliashib's name throughout the high religious festivities of the preceding chapters" (Elicott's Commentary). Eliashib is certainly not alone in making changes to preserve a friendship. Believers can sometimes be valiant for assembly truth, until family interests and connections arise. Then things change. After all, Tobiah was not in fellowship with God's people, but he was a friend! We must beware of similar inconsistency.

We must notice what followed: "And he had prepared for him a great chamber, where **aforetime** they laid the meat offerings, the **frankincense**..." What a change of use! But, sadly, this frequently happens today. In the Old Testament, "the house of our God" (v.4) was the temple in Jerusalem. In the New Testament, it is the church, which is described, in its universal sense, as "an habitation of God through the Spirit" (Eph. 2.22), and in its local sense, as "the temple of God" where the "Spirit of God" dwells (1 Cor. 3.16). But so often worship gives place to whist, the Scriptures to socials, and the Gospel for games. A veritable chamber for Tobiah! God's interests are pushed out. The frankincense was all for God (see Lev. 2.2). In this, let alone in other ways, God was robbed. Compare Malachi 3.8-9. The assembly should be a place where God receives our worship and adoration as we remember His Son. It follows that if there is no frankincense in the chamber of our heart, there will be no frankincense in the assembly either.

c) The expulsion of Tobiah the Ammonite, vv.6-9

Attention is drawn here to at least three things. In the first place, Nehemiah calls this "evil": "And I came to Jerusalem, and understood of the **evil** that Eliashib did for Tobiah, in preparing him a chamber in the courts of the house of God" (v7). In the second place, Nehemiah was grieved by the situation: "and it **grieved me sore**" (v.8). He did not shrug his shoulders and put it down to 'the day in which we live'. In the third place, he threw out what was wrong, "Therefore I **cast forth** all the household stuff of Tobiah out of the chamber", and brought in what was right, "Then I commanded, and they cleansed the chambers: and thither **brought I again** the vessels of the house of God, with the meat offering and the frankincense" (vv.8-9). He certainly made a thorough job of it! All this reminds us, again, that the local assembly is "the temple of God" (1 Cor. 3.16) and that 'wicked persons' are to be "put away" (1 Cor. 5.13).

The results of Eliashib's compromise follow. When God's interests are invaded, and "the things concerning himself" (Luke 24.27) are rejected in favour of foreign interests, things decline **everywhere.** In this case, it robbed God's servants of support (vv.10-14), it deprived them of the blessings of God's rest (vv.15-22), and it affected their relationship with the world (vv.23-29). This brings us to:

2) FAILURE TO RECOGNISE THE NEEDS OF GOD'S SERVANTS, vv.10-14

The Levites served on behalf of the entire nation: See Numbers 8.9-11, "And thou shalt bring the Levites before the tabernacle of the congregation: and thou shalt gather the whole assembly of the children of Israel together: and thou shalt bring the Levites before the Lord: and the children of Israel shall **put their hands upon the Levites**: and Aaron shall offer the Levites before the Lord for an offering of the children of Israel, that they may execute the service of the Lord" (Num. 8.9-11). Since they served on behalf of the entire people, it follows that they should be supported by the entire people. But it was more than just giving to the Levites: "But the tithes of the children of Israel, which they offer as an heave offering **unto the Lord**, I have given to the Levites to inherit" (Num. 18.24).

Through lack of fellowship and support, the Levites were obliged to provide for themselves: "And I perceived that the portions of the Levites had not been given them: for the Levites and the singers, that did the work, were fled every man to his field" (v.10). They were unable to perform their proper functions through lack of support. To some extent, we can understand how this situation arose. The people could well have said, 'The priests obviously don't value divine things, so why should we? They simply followed the bad example of their religious leaders.

We have already noted (12.44-45), that 1 Corinthians 9 evidently alludes to the support of the priests and Levites: "If we have sown unto you spiritual things, is it a great thing if we shall reap your carnal things?...Do ye not know that they which minister about holy things (referring to the Levites) live of the things of the temple? and they which wait at the altar (the priests) are partakers with the altar? Even so hath the Lord ordained that they which preach the gospel should live of the gospel" (1 Cor. 9.11-14). If we all really recognised our responsibilities in connection with the Lord's work, there would be no shortage of finance.

Nehemiah's ministry was effective: "Then brought all Judah the tithe of the corn and the new wine and the oil into the treasuries" (v.12). Compare Malachi 3.10. Notice too, that there was proper accounting: "And I made treasurers over the treasuries, Shelemiah the priest, and Zadok the scribe, and of the Levites, Pedaiah: and next to them was Hanan the son of Zaccur, the son of Mattaniah: for they were counted faithful, and their office was to distribute unto their brethren" (v.13). Paul deals with this subject in 2 Corinthians 8.16-24, saying "avoiding this, that no man should blame us in this abundance which is administered by us: providing for honest things, not only in the sight of the Lord, but also in the sight of men" (vv.20-21). This brings us to:

3) FAILURE TO RECOGNISE THE BLESSINGS OF GOD'S REST, vv.15-22
The sabbath is first mentioned by that name in connection with the manna: "Tomorrow is the rest of the holy sabbath unto the Lord" (Exodus 16.23). On the sabbath day, God's people were able to enjoy the sweetness of the manna without effort and distraction. It was a reminder of deliverance from Egypt: "And remember that thou wast a servant in the land of Egypt, and that the Lord thy God brought thee out thence...therefore the Lord thy God commanded thee to keep the sabbath day" (Deut. 5.15). It was instituted for man's benefit: "The sabbath was made for man, and not man for the sabbath" (Mark 2.27), that is, the sabbath was made for man to enjoy, not to dominate and oppress him. It was an institution which expressed God's merciful consideration for man. It became the sign of God's covenant with Israel. See Exodus 31.12-18. "The Sabbath was never given to the nations in the same way as to Israel, and amid all the sins enumerated against the Gentiles, we do not find Sabbath-breaking ever mentioned. Nevertheless, it appears to be a principle of God's government of the earth that man and beast should have one day in seven as a respite from labour, all needing it physically" (*Morrish's New and Concise Bible Dictionary*).

The Sabbath is not "the Lord's day". This is "the first day of the week". The very words point to something entirely new and quite distinct from everything connected with the legal Sabbath. While "the Lord's day" does not carry the legal sanction assigned to the Sabbath, it is none the less an opportunity for God's people to express their love for Him in worship and service, which is itself a testimony to unbelievers. The flouting of "the Lord's day" generally, with the irresistible arrival of the 'Continental Sunday', is symptomatic of total disregard for God and His word. Believers should not willingly be party to it. In profaning the Sabbath, these Jews lost their distinctiveness: they were doing exactly the same as everyone else.

This raises wider issues. It highlights the dangers of commercialism. Business had invaded God's interests. For the second time, Nehemiah uses the word "evil": "What **evil** thing is this that ye do, and profane the sabbath day?" (v.17). Trade and commerce were in 'pole position' in their priorities, rather than the things of God. This is a warning for believers today. What do **we** put first in life? The Lord Jesus was addressing His **disciples** in saying, "For whosoever will save his life shall lose it; but whosoever shall lose his life for my sake and the gospel's, the same shall save it. For what shall it profit a man, if he shall gain the whole world, and lose his own soul?" (Mark 8.35-37).

We should notice the effect of these commercial practices. Business was brisk.

The 'commodity markets' (to coin a modern term) flourished. God's people were quite willing to deal in "wine, grapes, and figs" (v.15), but there was nothing for the Levites. God's interests were conveniently forgotten, and His servants faced a bleak future. It can be sadly true of believers that there is;

> Room for pleasure, room for business,
> But for Christ the crucified,
> Not a place where He can enter
> In the heart for which He died.

We should also notice that Israel had not learnt by experience: "Then I contended with the nobles of Judah, and said unto them, What evil thing is this that ye do, and profane the sabbath day? Did not your fathers thus, and did not our God bring all this evil upon us, and upon this city?" (vv.17-18). Jeremiah had sounded out God's warning in this connection: "But if ye will not hearken unto me to hallow the sabbath day, and not to bear a burden, even entering in at the gates of Jerusalem on the sabbath day; then will I kindle a fire in the gates thereof, and it shall devour the palaces of Jerusalem, and it shall not be quenched" (Jer. 17.19-27).

Old habits die hard. The guilty traders did not give in without a struggle. "So the merchants and sellers of all kind of ware lodged without Jerusalem once or twice" (v.20). But Nehemiah was quite determined in dealing with them: "Then I testified against them, and said unto them, Why lodge ye about the wall? if ye do so again, I will lay hands on you". The threat of physical violence concluded the matter: "From that time forth came they no more on the sabbath" (v.21). We too need to deal ruthlessly with everything and anything that militates against the Lord's interests in our lives. This brings us to:

4) FAILURE TO RECOGNISE THE SEPARATION OF GOD'S PEOPLE, vv.23-29

The situation described in the last two chapters of Ezra now reappears in the last chapter of Nehemiah. In the days of Ezra, "The people of Israel, and the priests, and the Levites, have not separated themselves from the people of the lands...for they have taken of their daughters for themselves, and for their sons: so that the holy seed have mingled themselves with the people of those lands" (Ezra 9.1-2). Ezra describes his reaction: "I rent my garment and my mantle, and plucked off the hair of *my* head and of *my* beard, and sat down astonied" (Ezra 9.3). Nehemiah went further: "I contended with them, and cursed them, and smote certain of them, and plucked off *their* hair..." (13.25). He would have ended up today in the Old Bailey, accused of grievous bodily harm!

This section highlights the dangers of marriage to an unbeliever, and reinforces the warning of the New Testament, "Be ye not unequally yoked together with unbelievers" (2 Cor. 6.14-18). The dangers are highlighted as follows:

i) **It is disastrous for the children.** They could not speak the language of God's people. That should be quite sufficient to show who was the dominant party in the marriage! "And their children spake half in the language of Ashdod, and could not speak in the Jews' language, but according to the language of each people" (v.24). This recalls the warning given by God in Deuteronomy 7.3-4, "Neither shalt thou make marriages with them; thy daughter thou shalt not give unto his son, nor his daughter shalt thou take unto thy son. For they will **turn away thy son from following me**". Believers with families should take note. What kind of language do the children speak? The language of the Scriptures or the language of the world? Whilst parents cannot guarantee the ultimate spirituality of their children, they should at least hear the right language in their formative years at home. We could rob our children of the benefits of Deuteronomy 31.9-13 and Nehemiah 8.1-18.

ii) **It ignores lessons from the past.** "Did not Solomon king of Israel sin by these things? yet among many nations was there no king like him, who was beloved of his God, and God made him king over all Israel: nevertheless **even him** did outlandish women cause to sin" (v.26). Advancing years can be as dangerous as youth. "It came to pass, when Solomon was old, that his wives (he had 700 wives and 300 concubines) turned away his heart after other gods" (1 Kings 11.1-4). What followed is quite unbelievable. See 1 Kings 11.5-8.

iii) **It is a sin against God himself.** "Shall we then hearken unto you to do all this great evil, to transgress against our God in marrying strange wives?" (v.27).

iv) **It endangers priesthood.** "And one of the sons of Joiada, the son of Eliashib the high priest, was son in law to Sanballat the Horonite: therefore I chased him from me. Remember them, O my God, because they have defiled the priesthood, and the covenant of the priesthood, and of the Levites" (vv.28-29). Bearing in mind that Eliashib was "allied unto Tobiah" (v.4), it is not altogether surprising that one of his grandsons was "son in law to Sanballat the Horonite". After all, Joiada wasn't set a very good example and, presumably, he was quite accustomed to the presence of foreigners in the family circle.

We must notice, in conclusion, the repetition of the words "**Remember me**" (v.31) Nehemiah had said this twice before: "**Remember me**, O my God, concerning this, and wipe not out my good deeds that I have done for the house of my God, and for the offices thereof" (v.14); "**Remember me**, O my God, concerning this also, and spare me according to the greatness of thy mercy" (v.22). See also 5.19. As we have said before, this must not be construed as boasting: the fact remains that Nehemiah acted alone, because there was no one else to whom he could turn. He had little fellowship. He was sustained by his personal relationship with God: hence the expression "**my** God", and, "O **my** God".

But as we have already observed, the book does end on a positive note: "Thus cleansed I them from all strangers, and appointed the wards of the priests and the Levites, every one in his business; and for the wood offering, at times appointed, and for the firstfruits" (vv.30-31). Everything had been properly restored - by **one man** who had the courage to put things right! We must be men and women of similar conviction: people whom God can use in the face of discouragement and difficulty. It is not without significance that Ezra and Nehemiah are placed together, as books and as men. If we fail in our priestly ministry before God, we will fail in our public life before men. The note on which the book concludes, "Remember me, O my God, for good", are the words of a man who, in the face of great odds externally, and in the face of great discouragement internally, had been unswervingly faithful. Centuries later, another man wrote, "I have fought a good fight, I have finished my course, I have kept the faith: henceforth there is laid up for me a crown of righteousness (a rightly adjusted crown of reward), which the Lord, the righteous judge, shall give me at that day" (2 Tim. 4.7-8).

What will WE be able to say at the end of life's journey?

Ezra, Nehemiah, Esther

ESTHER

by
John M Riddle

ESTHER

Introduction

For the purposes of this introduction, we will consider the following: *(1)* the position of the book; *(2)* the providence of God; *(3)* the purpose of the story; *(4)* the part of the characters.

1) THE POSITION OF THE BOOK
There are two ways to put the book in context, and we will deal with them in order of importance: *(a)* the spiritual context; *(b)* the historical context.

a) The spiritual context
Five Old Testament books cover the period of Israel's history after their return from exile in Babylon. They are, of course, the books of Ezra, Nehemiah, Haggai, Zechariah, and Malachi. Ezra, Haggai and Zechariah cover the rebuilding of the temple at Jerusalem. Nehemiah and Malachi deal with the rebuilding of the wall of Jerusalem, and the following decline.

The book of Esther belongs to the same period, and describes a crisis at the heart of the Persian empire. Unlike the books of Ezra and Nehemiah, books which describe the concerns of godly men in relation to Jerusalem and Judah, the Jewish characters in the story here evidently chose not to return to Jerusalem, and the unusual character of the book is largely due to this fact. It does not seem unjust to suggest that they belonged to the majority of exiles who once said, "How shall we sing the Lord's song in a strange land?" but settled down quite comfortably after all. The language of Psalm 137 had died on their lips: "If I forget thee, O Jerusalem, let my right hand forget her cunning. If I do not remember thee, let my tongue cleave to the roof of my mouth; if I prefer not Jerusalem above my chief joy" (vv.5-6). Others had turned their backs on Babylon, and returned to, "the place which the Lord shall choose to place his name there" (Deut. 16.2). **We must do the same.** The Ecumenical Movement will reach its goal in "MYSTERY, BABYLON THE GREAT, THE MOTHER OF HARLOTS AND ABOMINATIONS OF THE EARTH" (Rev. 17.5).

b) The historical context

The book can be dated by reference to "Ahasuerus...which reigned, from India even unto Ethiopia..." (1.1). The name "Ahasuerus" was apparently an official name for Persian kings, rather like the name Pharaoh in Egypt. There are two other Persian kings bearing the same title. See Daniel 9.1 and Ezra 4.6. The Persian king here is better known in history as Xerxes. His reign commenced in BC485, and therefore the events recorded in the book of Esther took place between, approximately, BC483 (see 1.3, "In the third year of his reign") and BC474 (see 3.7, "In the twelfth year of king Ahasuerus"). This means that we can place the book of Esther between the expeditions to Jerusalem led by Zerubbabel and Ezra respectively: in other words, in the sixty years between Ezra Chapter 6 and Ezra Chapter 7.

There is another interesting reference to the reign of Ahasuerus. Esther 2.16 tells us that Esther "was taken unto king Ahasuerus...in the seventh year of his reign". So it took something like four or five years to replace Vashti as queen. But why the delay? The answer appears to be that Ahasuerus was engaged in war. A feast of one hundred and eighty days' duration (1.4) almost seems an exaggeration until we discover that it was at this time that the king held a meeting at Susa to make arrangements for the invasion of Greece. Purely as a matter of interest, Xerxes (his Greek name) left Susa for the West in BC481, was eventually defeated at Salamis, and returned to Persia from Sardis in BC478. You won't find all this in the Bible - it will mean a trip to the library! (You will also discover that he was murdered in BC464 by two of his officers, Mithridates and Artabanus). So it was shortly after his return from the disastrous campaign against Greece, that he made Esther queen. Voila!

2) THE PROVIDENCE OF GOD

God is not mentioned in the book of Esther, just as He is not mentioned in the Song of Solomon. "This is the more remarkable, since in this short book of 167 verses, the Median King is mentioned 192 times, his kingdom is referred to 26 times, and his name, 'Ahasuerus' is given 29 times" (*The Companion Bible*, Appendix 60). The absence of God's name is quite unbelievable, until we remember that the Jews should never have been in Persia at all. The book therefore displays God's love and care for those who have little love and care for His commandments. Esther, queen of Persia, was in a totally wrong position for a Jewess, and Mordecai's position in the king's gate (a place of honour) was no better. He was quite unpatriotic. We find him sitting, by his own choice, at the gate of a heathen sovereign. Let's face it, neither Esther nor Mordecai are particularly saintly in their behaviour.

We have a parallel in the history of Abraham. Read Genesis 12.10-20, and you will discover that although God communicated with Abraham both before and after his stay in Egypt, He did not communicate with him whilst in Egypt. What is more, there is no record of Abraham communicating with God whilst he was in Egypt. He certainly did so before and after (Gen. 12.8 and 13.4), but not whilst in Egypt. But God was certainly at work behind the scenes: "the Lord plagued Pharaoh and his house with great plagues because of Sarai Abram's wife" (Gen. 12.17). So don't expect to hear God's voice, and don't think that you will go on speaking to Him, when you are outside His will. Disobedience silences the voice of God, and silences your voice as well.

God may not be named in the book of Esther, but His hand is constantly seen. Matthew Henry puts it like this: "though the name of God be not in it, His finger is". Vashti was deposed in most unjust circumstances, and the elevation of Esther raises some rather delicate questions. But her cousin was right in saying, "who knoweth whether thou art come to the kingdom for such a time as this?" (5.14). It was no accident that Mordecai uncovered the plot to assassinate Ahasuerus. It was no accident that the king had a sleepless night before the second banquet. (What a mercy that they didn't have sleeping pills in those days!). On the other hand, just suppose that Vashti had come when ordered by the king. Or suppose that Esther's parents had lived... But we mustn't 'suppose!' The book of Esther emphasises the providence and sovereignty of God - down to the smallest detail.

But don't trade on this. We must never think that to be used by God means divine approval. Just think about Balaam. He said some most sublime things, but he was nothing more than a wizard from Mesopotamia! God in His sovereignty may see fit to use us even when we are in a wrong position. But that doesn't mean that He endorses our position. See Romans 6.1-2, "What shall we say then? Shall we continue in sin, that grace may abound? God forbid..." Esther's queenhood was a violation of God's law – though overruled. **Our responsibility is to obey.** Our stance must be, 'this is the right thing to do – or the wrong thing to do – whatever may come of it'.

Let's say one further thing in connection with the absence of God's name in the book of Esther. It has often been stated that the Name of God **is** in the book, but in acrostic form. According to *The Companion Bible*, it is said to occur five times in this way. The compiler of *The Companion Bible* (mostly the work of E.W. Bullinger) tells us that in the book of Esther God's "working was secret and hidden: hence, the Name of 'Jehovah' is hidden secretly four times in this book, and the Name "Ehyeh" (I am that I am) once". If you wish to pursue this, get hold of a copy of "The Companion Bible" and Appendix 60, to which we have already referred. You have every good wish for success - but, seriously, E.W. Bullinger argues a good case. This doesn't mean that he 'argues a good case' everywhere!

3) THE PURPOSE OF THE STORY
Isaiah 54.17 states one of the outstanding lessons of the book of Esther: "No weapon that is formed against thee shall prosper". The book also recalls the words of Psalm 121.4, "Behold, he that keepeth Israel shall neither slumber nor sleep". This reminds us that we must not forget the prophetic significance of the book. But there is a greater issue at stake than even the preservation of the Jews. Israel's coming Messiah would be "of the seed of David according to the flesh" (Rom. 1.3). We have here therefore one of several attempts to destroy the royal line, with Haman a remarkable picture of Satan himself.

Undoubtedly, the book of Esther emphasises a general lesson, and this was very clearly stated by James Anderson many years ago in the *Believer's Magazine*: "The story is an epitome of the whole human story. It displays the wrong person getting promotion to power, but although that may appear to be unjust, it doesn't hinder the end of God's ways. The man destined to the gallows will yet have power and honour. It forms another chapter of the story of wrong being so often on the throne, but right will assuredly triumph at the last". This brings us, finally, to:

4) THE PART OF THE CHARACTERS
In our studies, we shall pay particular attention to Haman, Esther and Mordecai. But there are significant lessons for us from **Ahasuerus** and **Vashti.** For the time being, we will quote Ellicott's Bible Commentary in which Esther is dealt with by R. Sinker: "Ahasuerus is an ordinary specimen of an Eastern despot, who knows no law save the gratification of his own passions, and of the passing caprice of the moment. He sends for his queen in defiance of decency and courtesy, to grace a revel, and deposes her for a refusal simply indicative of self-respect; he is willing to order the destruction of a whole people throughout his empire, at the request of a favourite of the time; when the tide of favour turns, the favourite is not only disgraced, but he and all his family are ruthlessly destroyed, and Mordecai rises from a humble position to be the new vizier". So much for Ahasuerus! Mr. Sinker has got it pretty well summed up.

Now for a few preliminary suggestions in connection with Haman, Mordecai and Esther:

i) **HAMAN.** We have already said that Haman is a striking picture of Satan himself. There are many resemblances, and they culminate in Esther's statement: "The adversary and enemy is this wicked Haman" (7.6). Doesn't this remind you of 1 Peter 5.8 ("your **adversary** the devil, as a roaring lion, walketh about, seeking whom he may devour"); Matthew 13.39 ("the **enemy** that sowed them is the devil") and 1 John 3.12 ("Not as Cain, who was of that **wicked** one")? The murderous intentions of Haman recall the words of the Lord Jesus concerning Satan: "he was a murderer from the beginning" (John 8.44). Haman means, 'magnificent', and this recalls Ezekiel 28.12-19. Haman's ambition that every knee should bow to him, takes us to Matthew 4.9. However, the very means by which he endeavoured to dispose of Mordecai became the instrument of his own defeat. You can supply chapter and verse for that! We shall look at this more closely in due course.

ii) **MORDECAI.** Here is the man who refused to bow - the only man to do so - and we are immediately reminded that a Greater than Mordecai said, "the prince of this world cometh, and hath nothing in me" (John 14.30). Mordecai refused to exalt himself: even after he had been paraded through the streets in high honour, he "came again to the king's gate" (6.12). But he was "the man whom the king delighteth to honour" (6.9), and the book ends with Mordecai "great in the king's house" (9.4) and "great among the Jews" (10.3). Doesn't this remind us of Luke 1.32, "He shall be great..."? The man who had been condemned to death was elevated to the highest possible position. See Philippians 2.9-11.

iii) **ESTHER.** She was reminded that her privileges brought responsibility, and undertook the risks arising from intervention on behalf of others. (4.14-16). That's where we come in! We too have a ministry of intercession, and a mission of intervention. Like Priscilla and Aquila, there are times when we have to 'lay down our necks (singular, neck)' (Rom. 16.4). Are we willing to expose ourselves to risk in the service of God? Work for God is never easy. But look at the end of the story. Esther is with the man honoured above all. (9.29-31).

READ CHAPTER 1

Exit Vashti

The best comments on any part of the Bible are generally found in the Bible itself. You couldn't possibly do better than the following when it comes to the book of Esther – "Verily thou art a God that hidest thyself, O God of Israel, the Saviour" (Isa. 45.15). As we said in our introduction, God may not be named in the book of Esther, but His hand is constantly seen. How about this for another appropriate comment: "Behold, he that keepeth Israel shall neither slumber nor sleep"? (Psalm 121.4).

The way in which the book of Esther displays the providence of God, makes it quite unique in the Bible, and we don't have to wait long before it all starts to happen. The opening two Chapters alone describe three principle events: *(1)* the removal of Vashti; *(2)* the selection of Esther; *(3)* The loyalty of Mordecai. The first of these is dealt with in Chapter 1.

1) THE REMOVAL OF VASHTI, 1.1-22
The passage can be divided as follows *(a)* the feast of Ahasuerus (vv.1-9); *(b)* the refusal of Vashti (vv.10-12); *(c)* the advice of Memucan (vv.13-22)

a) The feast of Ahasuerus, vv.1-9
This incident is set against the background of a remarkable feast made by Ahasuerus for "all his princes and his servants; the power of Persia and Media, the nobles and princes of the provinces" (v.3). The feast lasted for approximately six months, and was followed by a further feast, lasting seven days, for "all the people that were present in Shushan the palace, both unto great and small" (v.5). Shushan (Hebrew), or Susa (Greek), was the winter capital of the Persian Empire, and was situated some two hundred miles east of Babylon. Daniel saw the place in a vision (see Daniel 8 - it's worth reading the whole chapter since it describes the rise of the Medo-Persian Empire and its defeat by Greece), and Nehemiah served Artaxerxes there (see Neh.1.1).

The outstanding feature of the narrative in vv.1-9 is its detail. In describing the extent of the kingdom: "This is Ahasuerus which reigned, from India even unto Ethiopia, over an hundred and seven and twenty provinces" (v.1); in describing the excellence of the kingdom: "He shewed the riches of his glorious kingdom and the honour of his excellent majesty" (v.4). Just look at the detail in the description of the feast in the "court of the garden of the king's palace" (vv.5-7). Even the drinking vessels are said to be "diverse one from another" (v.7).

Since "all Scripture is given by inspiration of God", we can be excused for asking the question, 'Why so much detail?' In view of the fact that we are reliably informed by competent historians that the feast was called to settle details for the invasion of Greece, we could also ask the question, 'Why the absence of detail?' After all, the book does not mention this most important event.

i) Why the surfeit of detail? We must remember that Esther describes people who, unlike the exiles who had returned to Jerusalem, possessed little - if any - interest in the glory of God. His glory was of no apparent concern to either Esther or Mordecai. They act without reference to Him. When God's glory is neither sought nor considered, human glory gains the ascendancy, and the graphic detail here emphasises this fact. We cannot doubt the magnificence of the Persian court, but it was godless glory. This is what God says about it all: "Let not the wise man glory in his wisdom, neither let the mighty man glory in his might, let not the rich man glory in his riches: but let him that glorieth glory in this, that he understandeth and knoweth me" (Jer. 9.23-24). Paul cites this passage in 1 Corinthians 1.31. The assembly is a place where, "No flesh should glory in his presence", and where, "He that glorieth, let him glory in the Lord". See also 1 Peter 1.24-25, "For all flesh is as grass, and all the glory of man as the flower of grass. The grass withereth, and the flower thereof falleth away: but the word of the Lord endureth for ever".

The Lord Jesus described the glory of Solomon as follows: "Consider the lilies of the field...And yet I say unto you, That even Solomon in all his glory was not arrayed like one of these" (Matt. 6.28-29). Solomon's court must have been breathtaking - the queen of Sheba certainly found it like that: "there was no more spirit in her" (1 Kings 10.5). But the glory of Solomon was very different from the glory of Ahaseurus. Read 1 Kings 3.5-15.

ii) Why the absence of detail? The proposed invasion of Greece by Persia was of undoubted importance in the purposes of God. See, again, Daniel Chapter 8 and, additionally, Daniel Chapter 11. The fourth Persian king in Daniel 11.2 is most probably Ahasuerus or, to give him his other name, Xerxes. But that is of minor importance in Esther. The welfare of God's people is much more important than the rise and fall of nations. That is why emphasis is placed here on what seems to be a comparatively unimportant internal problem. It is also the reason for the assignment of just two verses, Luke 3.1-2, to seven Very Important People by human standards (Tiberias Caesar, Pontius Pilate, Herod, Philip, Lysanias, Annas, Caiaphas), and three whole Chapters, Luke 1-3, to seven even more Very Important People by divine standards (Joseph, Mary, Zacharias, Elisabeth, John, Simeon, Anna). Although utterly obscure by human standards, God's seven are infinitely more valuable to Him than 'the world's seven'. The Lord Jesus stands, of course, incomparably alone.

2) The refusal of Vashti, vv.10-12
This paragraph raises some most interesting questions, although we must not lose sight of the fact that the entire story emphasises the providence of God.

i) Was Ahasuerus drunk? "On the seventh day, when the heart of the king was **merry** with wine…" (v.10). Let's take stock of the facts in endeavouring to assess the situation. We are told that there was "royal wine in abundance, according to the state of the king". We are also told that "the drinking was according to the law; none did compel: for so the king had appointed to all the officers of his house, that they should do according to every man's pleasure". John C. Whitcomb (*Esther - Triumph of God's Sovereignty*, Moody Press) writes as follows: "Usually the king pledged his guests to drink a certain amount, but now they could drink as much or as little as they desired". Whitcomb continues by quoting Herodotus: the Persians "are very fond of wine, and drink it in large quantities… It is also their general practice to deliberate upon affairs of weight when they are drunk…sometimes, however, they are sober at their first deliberation, but in this case they always reconsider the matter under the influence of wine". In all fairness, we are not told that this was a drunken revel, and we can only note that there was "wine in abundance" with no prohibition on over-indulgence nor upon abstemiousness. It would perhaps be perverse to add, 'but knowing human nature…'!

As to the king himself, the word "merry" in itself does not necessarily signify drunkenness. But it might be helpful to consider other occasions where the phrase is used: "And Abigail came to Nabal; and, behold, he held a feast in his house, like the feast of a king; and Nabal's heart was merry within him, for he was very drunken" (1 Sam. 25.36); "Now Absalom had commanded his servants, saying, Mark ye now when Amnon's heart is merry with wine" (2 Sam. 13.28). If the verse had said, 'the heart of the king was merry', then it could be construed to mean elation and joy. But, "merry with wine" does imply, at the very least, that he was not entirely sober!

ii) Was Vashti justified in refusing to appear? It could be argued that she should have come at the king's request, irrespective of his insobriety or otherwise. It could be argued that the king only wished to display the beauty of his wife. On the other hand, it could be argued that the request was unreasonable, particularly since after six days' drinking, the company would hardly clap politely, and murmur admiring approval! Perhaps it is hardly appropriate to superimpose Christian virtues on a Persian court, but it's worth remembering New Testament teaching: "Likewise, ye husbands, dwell with them according to knowledge, giving honour unto the wife, as unto the weaker vessel, and as being heirs together of the grace of life; that your prayers be not hindered" (1 Pet. 3.7). Ahasuerus doesn't seem to fit in there very well, does he?!

3) The advice of Memucan, vv.13-22

Vashti lost her crown, and 'Women's Lib.' was banished. It would be rather interesting to see what would happen today, wouldn't it?! (Only a man could write that!). Listen to the advice of Memucan, spokesman for the "seven princes of Persia and Media": "Vashti the queen hath not done wrong to the king only, but also to all the princes, and to all the people that are in all the provinces of the king Ahasuerus. For this deed of the queen shall come abroad unto all women, so that they shall despise their husbands in their eyes" (vv. 16-17). Notice that it is "all women" (v17), and "the ladies of Persia and Media" (v.18). The former means women in general, whilst the latter means 'the ladies of the aristocracy' (Whitcomb), i.e. the wives of the seven princes. The resulting decree required that "all the wives shall give to their husbands honour, both to great and small" (v.20), and "that every man should bear rule in his own house, and that it should be published according to the language of every people" (v.22). The last phrase has been rendered: "and should speak according to the language of his people" with the footnote, i.e. "should speak his own tongue" (JND). The meaning is a little obscure, but presumably indicates that "the rule of the husband in the house was to be shown by the fact that only the native tongue of the head of the house was to be used in the family" (C.F. Keil).

At first glance, all this seems quite remarkable in view of Biblical teaching. God had said, "It is not good that the man should be alone; I will make him an help meet for him" (Gen. 2.18). It is very important to distinguish between the two words, "help" and "meet". Eve was a "help" to Adam: not to lead or guide him, or to exercise authority over him: but to "help" him. On the other hand, Eve was not in any way inferior to Adam. She was his counterpart and answered to him in every way - she was "meet for him". Rightly understood, this does not produce male despotism and female subservience. The New Testament says, "Wives, submit yourselves unto your own husbands, as unto the Lord", that is, with the devotion in which they submit themselves to the Lord. It also says, "Husbands, love your wives...so ought men to love their wives as their own bodies" (Eph. 5.22,25-28). See also Colossians 3.18-19 and 1 Peter 3.1-7.

The royal decree now seems a little less impressive. It is very one-sided, and stresses the obligations of Persian wives with no reference to the obligations of Persian husbands. In summary, it falls far short of Bible teaching on the subject.

READ CHAPTER 2

Enter Esther

Before studying this Chapter, it might be helpful to notice that the book of Esther is not alone in displaying the providence of God. See, for example, Acts 18.1-3, "After these things Paul departed from Athens, and came to Corinth; and found a certain Jew named Aquila, born in Pontus, lately come from Italy, with his wife Priscilla *(because that Claudius had commanded all Jews to depart from Rome:)* and came unto them. And because he was of the same craft, he abode with them, and wrought: for by their occupation they were tentmakers". This is quite amazing. First of all, God moved Claudius Caesar to expel the Jews from Rome. There was no one higher in the world than the Roman Emperor - but that was no obstacle to God. Secondly, God overruled in the education and training of two obscure Jews. Claudius and Aquila and Priscilla were poles apart, and only God could put his hand upon people so diverse to further his purposes! As a result of it all, Paul found shelter and employment at Corinth. Just think about it: God did all this in order to plant an assembly in that wicked city.

But you don't have to go further than the birth of the Lord Jesus himself to see the providence of God displayed. Once again, God moved the Roman Emperor: "And it came to pass in those days, that there went out a decree from Caesar Augustus, that all the world should be taxed...and all went to be taxed, every one into his own city. And Joseph also went up from Galilee, out of the city of Nazareth..." (Luke 2.1-7). The decree of Cyrus (Ezra 1.1) is another clear example.

Makes you think, doesn't it? Well, if it doesn't make you think, it should! God works silently behind the scenes - *in all our lives.*

Esther Chapters 1 and 2 describe God's prior provision for His people. Haman has not yet come to power, and his infamous plan to eradicate the Jews has not yet been conceived. But God fully anticipated the attempted genocide of the Jews, and was already working for their deliverance. The significance of the opening two chapters becomes very clear indeed as the story unfolds. They describe three principle events: *(1)* the removal of Vashti (1.9-22); *(2)* the selection of Esther (2.1-20); *(3)* the loyalty of Mordecai (2.21-23).

1) THE REMOVAL OF VASHTI, 1.9-22
We have already considered the record of her removal in Chapter 1, and whatever the rights and wrongs of the unpleasant event, God - in His providence - was preparing the way for a new queen – Esther. So:

2) THE SELECTION OF ESTHER, 2.1-20
The chapter commences with a remorseful king. The statement, "he remembered Vashti" (v.1), apparently carries the thought of affectionate remembrance but, in view of the decree, there was little Ahasuerus could do about the situation. After all, the decree was irreversible: see 1.19. However, his courtiers had a good idea, but it was not such a good idea for the Persian girls. "Little imagination is needed to appreciate the horror caused by the round-up of these girls, whose fate it was to be carried away from their homes to be secluded for life as the king's concubines. What a liability to be beautiful!" (J.G. Baldwin, *The New Bible Commentary, Revised*). This statement is well supported by v.14, and the expression "round-up" is not exaggerated. The whole business was at "the king's commandment and his decree" (v.8).

There are perhaps three strands to this part of the story: *(a)* Esther and Mordecai (vv.5-11); *(b)* Esther and Hegai (vv.12-15); *(c)* Esther and Ahasuerus (vv.16-20).

a) Esther and Mordecai, vv.5-11
Esther plays a passive role. We know that she was "fair and beautiful" (v.7). We also know that she was assigned "seven maidens" and given "the best place of the house of the women" (v.9). Mordecai plays a more active role. We should notice the following:

i) **His ancestry, vv.5-6.** Think about these verses: they are more than bald statements of fact. In the first place, we have, again, the **providence of God.** "Now in Shushan the palace there was a certain Jew, whose name was Mordecai" (v.5). He could have been in Babylon, or Persepolis, or Ecbatana. But he was in Shushan! Was it purely coincidence - a quirk of fate? We know better than that. We're back to our introduction! God is in control of our movements.

Secondly, we have the **government of God**. He was a Benjamite, the great-grandson of Kish, "who had been carried away from Jerusalem with the captivity which had been carried away with Jeconiah king of Judah, whom

Nebuchadnezzar the king of Babylon had carried away" (v.6). The Babylonian captivity was the direct result of Judah's disobedience. Disobedience always brings captivity. See 2 Timothy 2.25-26: "In meekness instructing those that oppose themselves; if God peradventure will give them repentance to the acknowledging of the truth; and that they may recover themselves out of the snare of the devil, who are taken captive by him at his will" or 'to the will of God'.

ii) ***His adoption of Esther, v.7.*** "And he brought up Hadassah (meaning, in Hebrew, 'myrtle'), that is, Esther (meaning, it is generally assumed, in Persian, 'star'), his uncle's daughter…whom Mordecai, when her father and mother were dead, took for his own daughter". Notice, yet again, the providence of God: had someone else adopted Esther, she might have been anywhere but in Shushan.

Esther had nothing outside Mordecai: her old life had come to an end in her parent's grave. It's like that with us too. We have nothing outside of Christ. We too have been placed in a different family. Paul quotes Hosea in Romans 9.23-26: "And that he might make known the riches of his glory on the vessels of mercy, which he had afore prepared unto glory, even us, whom he hath called, not of the Jews only, but also of the Gentiles? As he saith also in Osee, I will call them my people, which were not my people; and her beloved, which was not beloved. And it shall come to pass, that in the place where it was said unto them, Ye are not my people; there shall they be called the children of the living God". See also Romans 8.15 ("ye have received the Spirit of adoption, whereby we cry, Abba, Father") and Ephesians 1.5 ("having predestinated us unto the adoption of children by Jesus Christ to himself").

iii) ***His instruction to Esther, v.10.*** "Esther had not shewed her people nor her kindred: for Mordecai had charged her that she should not shew it". See also v.20. Haman soon discovered Mordecai's ancestry (3.6), but Esther's nationality was not known to either Haman or Ahasuerus until Chapter 7.4. Whilst, again, the withholding of this information was providential, and Mordecai presumably had Esther's best interests before him, we must not take this as a spiritual precedent. Paul was very happy to reveal his connections: "There stood by me this night the angel of God, whose I am, and whom I serve…" (Acts 27.23). He is most positive in Romans 1.16, "For I am not ashamed of the gospel of Christ…" See also 2 Timothy 1.8, "Be not thou therefore ashamed of the testimony of our Lord, nor of me his prisoner: but be thou partaker of the afflictions of the gospel according to the power of God". So far as we are concerned, it is a case of 'nailing our colours to the mast'.

Ashamed to be a Christian!
Afraid the world should know
I'm on my way to Zion
Where joys eternal flow!
Afraid to wear Thy colours,
Or blush to follow Thee!
Forbid it, O my Saviour,
That I should ever be.

Now, let's suppose that Esther **had** declared her nationality. Yes, it is pure speculation, and perhaps we shouldn't do it! Possibly, Haman would not then have attempted to eradicate the Jews. Her confession might have saved an awful lot of trouble. Well, we just don't know, of course. But we do know that a clear confession of Christ at the earliest possible opportunity can save us from a lot of awkward situations later on. When people know that we belong to Christ, they often seem to know that there are certain things that we avoid, and so we don't have to end up making weak excuses when the 'crunch' comes.

iv) His concern for Esther, v.11. "And Mordecai walked every day before the court of the women's house, to know how Esther did, and what should become of her". She was no longer in his custody - that had passed to "Hegai, keeper of the women" (v.8). We just need to remember that this isn't the Western World of 2008. This is Persia BC 478 or thereabouts. In commanding Esther not to disclose her nationality, Mordecai was evidently endeavouring 'to make the best of a bad job'. She was certainly not free to pursue life outside, so he was anxious that she should progress to the best possible position inside. That would, at the very least, make life more tolerable for her. Hence his daily concern for her welfare. There certainly does not seem to be anything particularly selfish in his motives.

All of which reminds us of the concern which, as believers, we should show to each other. "And whether one member suffer, all the members suffer with it; or one member be honoured, all the members rejoice with it" (1 Cor. 12.26). See also 1 John 3.16-18, "Hereby perceive we the love (of God), because he laid down his life for us: and we ought to lay down our lives for the brethren..."

b Esther and Hegai, vv.12-15

We have already noticed that Hegai, "keeper of the women" (v.8), was most impressed with Esther, and that he had "preferred her and her (seven) maids unto the best place of the house of the women" (v.9). There is little need

245

to comment on the procedure described in vv.13-14. R. Sinker (Ellicott's Commentary), writing on v.3, says it all: "Called Hegai in verse 8; a eunuch whose special charge seems to have been the virgins, while another, named Shaashgaz (verse 14: according to Scofield the name means 'beautiful servant'), had the custody of the concubines. *The whole verse shows, as conclusively as anything could do, in how degrading an aspect Eastern women were, as a whole, viewed.* It was reserved for Christianity to indicate the true position of woman, not man's plaything, but the help meet for him, able to aid him in his spiritual and intellectual progress, yielding him intelligent obedience, not slavery". J.G. Baldwin says: "Though these girls had every luxury, and could choose any adornment to enhance their beauty, they returned from the king's presence to the house of the concubines, mere chattels, awaiting the king's pleasure, if indeed he ever remembered them again".

The statement that Esther was "fair and beautiful", is confirmed by the fact that "she required nothing but what Hegai the king's chamberlain, the keeper of the women, appointed. And Esther obtained favour in the sight of all them that looked upon her" (v.15). She needed no adornment (see v.13): the "oil of myrrh" and "sweet odours" (v.12) were sufficient. Whilst there can be no comparison between the situation at Shushan and the Christian wife, we are at least reminded of 1 Peter 3.3-5: "Whose adorning let it not be that outward adorning of plaiting the hair, and of wearing of gold, or of putting on of apparel; but let it be the hidden man of the heart, in that which is not corruptible..."

We are also reminded that if Esther entered the presence of Ahasuerus in the sweetness of the cosmetics provided by Hegai, then we "are unto God a sweet savour (*euodia*) of Christ" (2 Cor. 2.15). When Paul received the gifts from the assembly at Philippi, he described them as "an odour of a sweet smell, a sacrifice acceptable, wellpleasing to God" (Phil. 4.18). The two words rendered "*odour* (*osme*) of a *sweet smell* (*euodia*)" occur in Ephesians 5.2 which describes the fragrance of Christ himself: "And walk in love, as Christ also hath loved us, and hath given himself for us an offering and a sacrifice to God for a *sweetsmelling* (*euodia*) *savour* (*osme*)".

c) Esther and Ahasurus, vv.16-20

"And the king loved Esther above all the women...so that he set the royal crown upon her head, and made her queen instead of Vashti" (v.17). This was followed by "Esther's feast" (v.18). It all looks very romantic. Until, that is, we read v.19: "And when the virgins were gathered together the second time..." Whilst the passage does not give the purpose of this gathering, there can be little doubt that it was for the same reason as the first, vv.2-4. We must remember that Ahasuerus was a polygamist, and was constantly adding to his harem.

It all contrasts starkly with Ephesians 5.25: "Christ also loved the church, and **gave himself** for it". Ahasuerus gave Esther a crown and made her a feast: Christ "gave Himself".

But there's something else. Esther "obtained grace and favour" in the sight of Ahasuerus because of her beauty. But we enjoy divine grace in its truest sense. See 2 Timothy 1.9, "Who hath saved us, and called us with an holy calling, not according to our works, but according to His own purpose and grace, which was given us in Christ Jesus before the world began". In the words of the hymn:

> "Chosen, not for good in me,
> Wakened up from wrath to flee..."

We were "chosen...in him before the foundation of the world, that we should be holy and without blame before him: in love having predestinated us unto the adoption of children by Jesus Christ to himself, according to the good pleasure of his will" (Eph. 1.4-5, with a little re-punctuation).

Let's face it, the whole affair is shallow and empty. It was all outward show. Ahasuerus was only interested in beautiful women and sensuality. It all turned on "fair young virgins" (vv.2-3), and pleasing and delighting the king (vv.4,14). The whole court was obsessed with this - in exactly the same way as society today. Youth, beauty, physical attraction... There is "nothing new under the sun". Society has yet to learn that, "As a jewel of gold in a swine's snout, so is a fair woman which is without discretion" (Prov. 11.22). Natural beauty is temporary, **but our spiritual beauty in Christ is eternal.**

3) THE LOYALTY OF MORDECAI, 2.21-23
We have already noticed that Esther Chapters 1 and 2 describe God's prior provision for His people. A crisis loomed, and God knew all about it. The removal of Vashti, the selection of Esther, and now, the loyalty of Mordecai, were all part of God's providential care for the Jews.

Mordecai uncovered a plot to assassinate Ahasuerus, and the culprits were duly "hanged on a tree" (v.23). Two statements are particularly significant.

i) "Esther certified the king thereof in Mordecai's name", v.22. Mordecai could have remained silent about the plot. After all, Ahasuerus was a heathen king. He was Emperor of Persia, and the land of Mordecai's fathers was now just a province in the mighty Persian Empire. But he took steps to save the life of the king. On the other hand, perhaps Mordecai was acting in his own interests, and in Esther's interests. Had Ahasuerus died, Esther would no longer be queen, and Mordecai would have no representation at court. Whilst we cannot know what was in Mordecai's mind, we do know that God was again at work behind the scenes. We also know that Romans 13.7 teaches that we are to "render... to all their dues: tribute to whom tribute is due; custom to whom custom; fear to whom fear; honour to whom honour". This is because "the powers that be are ordained of God" (Rom. 13.1). 1 Peter 2.16-17 reinforces this: "As free, and not using your liberty for a cloak of maliciousness (wickedness); but as the servants of God. Honour all men. Love the brotherhood. Fear God. **Honour the king**".

ii) "It was written in the book of the chronicles before the king", v.23. Mordecai could have sought recognition for his loyalty to the king. Had he done so, events could have taken a totally different course. But because he did not seek such recognition at the time of the event, recognition came at the right moment in God's time! In God's providence, an entry was made in the official records, with immense results! The happy consequences of his humility are spelt out very clearly in Chapter 6. The man who sought no honour for himself, became "the man whom the king delighteth to honour" (6.7,9,11). This recalls 1 Peter 5.5-6, "Yea, all of you be subject one to another, and be clothed with humility: for God resisteth the proud, and giveth grace to the humble. **Humble yourselves therefore under the mighty hand of God, that he may exalt you in due time**".

But it also recalls another "Man whom the King delighteth to honour". He sought no recognition on earth. "Tell the vision (on the Mount of Transfiguration) to no man, until the Son of man be risen again from the dead" (Matt. 17.9). The Lord Jesus waited the Father's time, and "God also hath highly exalted him, and given him a name which is above every name..." (Phil.2.9).

READ CHAPTER 3

Enter Haman

Chapter 3 commences with significant words: "After these things..." (It was, in fact, some four to five years after Esther's enthronement: compare 2.16 with 3.7). It was only after God had providentially arranged matters of state for the good of His people (see Chapters 1-2), that Ahasuerus promoted "Haman the son of Hammedatha the Agagite, and advanced him, and set his seat above all the princes that were with him" (v.1). In introducing the book of Esther, we noticed that Haman is a striking picture of Satan himself, and the details here confirm this.

We must now consider *(1)* the rise of Haman (3.1-15); *(2)* the reaction of Mordecai (4.1-4); *(3)* the role of Hatach (4.5-10); *(4)* the responsibility of Esther (4.11-17).

1) THE RISE OF HAMAN, 3.1-15
In this connection we must notice *(a)* his identity; *(b)* his glory; *(c)* his authority; *(d)* his animosity; *(e)* his strategy; *(f)* his insensibility

a) The identity of Haman, v.1
He is "Haman...the Agagite". The name Agag, appears to be a title of the kings of Amalek. See Numbers 24.7, "His (Israel's) king shall be higher than Agag, and his kingdom shall be exalted". Compare 1 Samuel 15.8. After the battle between Israel and Amalek in Exodus 17.8-13, God had this to say; "I will utterly put out the remembrance of Amalek from under heaven". Moses subsequently built an altar "and called the name of it Jehovah-nissi (the Lord my banner): for he said, Because the Lord hath sworn that the Lord will have war with Amalek from generation to generation" (Ex. 17.14-16). Notice the margin reading of v.16: 'Because the hand of Amalek is against the throne of the Lord, the Lord will have...' The New Translation (JND) has "And he said, For the hand is on the throne of Jah; Jehovah will have war with Amalek from generation to generation!" While 1 Samuel 15 describes the slaughter of the Amalekites, it is evident from I Samuel 30 that some survived and continued their implacable hatred against Israel. Haman therefore represents a nation with deep hatred of God's people.

He attempted to reverse the judgment pronounced on Amalek on Deuteronomy 25.17-19, "thou shalt blot out the remembrance of Amalek from under heaven…"

It is only right to add that there was evidently a place in Media, later incorporated into the Persian Empire, called Agag, and some commentators feel that the name "Agagite" refers to this location.

b) The glory of Haman, v.1

We should notice his exalted position: "Set his seat above all the princes that were with him". This reminds us of Satan's exaltation. Let's say, first of all, that Satan was created by Christ. See Colossians 1: "For by him were all things created, that are in heaven, and that are in earth, visible and *invisible*, whether they be thrones, or dominions, or principalities, or powers: all things were created by him, and for him" (v.16). The statement, "visible and invisible, whether they be thrones, or dominions, or principalities, or powers", must include Satan himself. There are two passages which are often cited when describing Satan's former glory.

i) **Isaiah 14.1-17**, which takes up "this proverb against the king of Babylon" (v.4), and continues, "How art thou fallen from heaven, O Lucifer, son of the morning! how art thou cut down to the ground, which didst weaken the nations! For thou hast said in thine heart, I will ascend into heaven, I will exalt my throne above the stars of God: I will sit also upon the mount of the congregation, in the sides of the north: I will ascend above the heights of the clouds; I will be like the most High. Yet thou shalt be brought down to hell, to the sides of the pit" (vv.12-15).

ii) **Ezekiel 28.1-19,** which first addresses the "*prince* of Tyrus" (vv.l-10), and continues by addressing the "*king* of Tyrus" (vv.11-19). While there is some reason for saying that "Lucifer, son of the morning" is the king of Babylon, there seems little doubt that the king of Tyre is the spiritual master of the prince of Tyre. For example, "Thou sealest up the sum, full of wisdom, and perfect in beauty. Thou hast been in Eden the garden of God…Thou art the anointed cherub that covereth; and I have set thee so: thou wast upon the holy mountain of God; thou hast walked up and down in the midst of the stones of fire. Thou wast perfect in thy ways from the day that thou wast created, till iniquity was found in thee" (vv.12-15). It should be noted that the words, "Thou hast been in Eden the garden of God", do not necessarily refer to the garden of Eden in Genesis Chapters 2 & 3 The language seems rather to suggest a heavenly paradise, from which Satan was expelled.

Both Peter and Jude make it clear that although he is fallen, Satan must not be contemptuously dismissed. False teachers are "not afraid to speak evil of dignities. Whereas angels, which are greater in power and might, bring not railing accusation against them before the Lord" (2 Pet. 2.10-11). See also the parallel passage in Jude vv.9-10. For further comment, see the addendum.

c) The authority of Haman, v.2

"And all the king's servants, that were in the king's gate, bowed, and reverenced Haman". There was total recognition of his authority - but not quite, as we shall see later. Some centuries later, John wrote: "And we know that we are of God, and **the whole world lieth in wickedness** (better *'the wicked one'*)" (1 John 5.19).

d) The animosity of Haman, vv.2-5

"But Mordecai bowed not, nor did him reverence...and when Haman saw that Mordecai bowed not, nor did him reverence, then was Haman full of wrath". Mordecai's refusal to bow was a matter of conscience and principle - not spite. He was the one man who refused to bow to Haman, just as there were "seven thousand in Israel, all the knees which have not bowed unto Baal, and every mouth which hath not kissed him" (1 Kings 19.18), and just as some will refuse to bow to the Beast: "I saw the souls of them that were beheaded for the witness of Jesus, and for the word of God, and which had not worshipped the beast, neither his image, neither had received his mark upon their foreheads, or in their hands; and they lived and reigned with Christ a thousand years" (Rev. 20.4). The animosity of Satan towards Israel will continue until the point when "he knoweth that he hath but a short time" (Rev. 12.12) The same chapter (Revelation 12) tells us that "he persecuted the woman which brought forth the man child...and the dragon was wroth with the woman, and went to make war with the remnant of her seed..." (vv.13,17).

But there was another Man who refused to bow: Satan said, "All these things will I give thee, if thou wilt fall down and worship me" (Matt. 4.9). The Saviour answered: "Get thee hence, Satan: for it is written, Thou shalt worship the Lord thy God, and him only shalt thou serve" (Matt. 4.10-11). Hence Satan's animosity towards Him. See John 8.37-44, "Ye seek to kill me, because my word hath no place in you...Ye seek to kill me, a man that hath told you the truth...Ye are of your father the devil, and the lusts of your father ye will do. He was a murderer from the beginning..."

Notice that the king's servants "daily" urged Mordecai to bow (v.4). Potiphar's wife "spake to Joseph day by day" (Gen. 39.10). The Lord Jesus was "forty days tempted of the devil" (Luke 4.2). Can **we** expect anything less?

But supposing Mordecai **had** bowed to Haman. It would have saved an awful lot of trouble, wouldn't it? After all, does it really matter...? Just remember that *today's compromise is tomorrow's surrender.*

e) The strategy of Haman, vv.6-15

"Haman sought to destroy **all** the Jews that were throughout the whole kingdom of Ahasuerus, even the people of Mordecai" (v.6). "And the letters were sent by post into all the king's provinces, to destroy, to kill, and to cause to perish, **all** Jews, both young and old, little children and women, in one day..." (v.13). It was a case of genocide. Psalm 83 describes a confederacy of nations bent on exactly the same goal: "Come, and let us cut them off from being a nation; that the name of Israel may be no more in remembrance" (v.4). Revelation 16.13-14 makes clear that this confederacy will be initiated by Satan himself. Like Haman, Satan is certainly "the Jews' enemy" (v.10). "It is perfectly clear, then, that the titanic death-struggle of the book of Esther simply cannot be understood apart from the satanic purposes toward Israel which the general context of Scripture reveals" (John C. Whitcomb).

"That Haman's attempted genocide of the Jews is not an inconceivable fantasy has been learned from the Nazi Holocaust", and R. Gordis (*Megillat Esther*) poignantly recalls that "Anti-Semites have always hated the book and the Nazis forbade its reading in the crematoria and the concentration camps. In the dark days before their deaths, Jewish inmates of Auschwitz, Dachau, Treblinka and Bergen-Belsen wrote the book of Esther from memory and read it secretly on Purim" ((Extracted from an article by Edwin M. Yamauchi, *Bibliotheca Sacra*, April-June 1980).

In order to achieve his end, Haman totally misrepresented the Jews to Ahasuerus: "There is a certain people scattered abroad and dispersed among the people in all the provinces of thy kingdom; and their laws are diverse from all people; neither keep they the king's laws..." (v.8). This was totally unsupported, and recalls the words of the Lord Jesus: "When he (Satan) speaketh a lie, he speaketh of his own: for he is a liar, and the father of it" (John 8.44). We must be careful that we do not become "false accusers" (Titus 2.3). We must be careful to ensure that our apparent concern for the well-being of others does not mask personal ambition.

We should also notice that the king made sure that the attempt on his life was thoroughly investigated - "And when inquisition was made of the matter, it was found out" (2.23). But since his personal safety was not apparently endangered here, Ahasuerus accepted the word of Haman without the slightest demur.

There is no investigation now; he made no attempt to verify Haman's charge against the Jews ("neither keep they the king's laws"). We should remember the plain lesson of Deuteronomy 17.4-5, "And it be told thee (that idolatry was taking place), and thou hast heard of it, and inquired diligently, and, behold, it be true, and the thing certain, that such abomination is wrought in Israel: then (and not until then)" action was to be taken. We do tend to accept juicy bits of scandal about the Lord's people without verifying the facts, don't we?

Before broaching the matter with the king, Haman and the Persian astrologers determined "the exact day of the year which would be most propitious for the destruction of Israel" (J.C. Whitcomb). Reference to the occult, however, was subject to a higher authority, for "The lot is cast into the lap; but the whole disposing thereof is of the Lord" (Prov. 16.33).

f) The insensibility of Haman, v.15
"And the king and Haman sat down to drink; but the city Shushan was perplexed" (v.15). Haman had no care or concern about his victims, and we can be sure that Satan has no love for the souls of men either.

Addendum

The fall of Satan (see 'The glory of Haman' above, produced some very helpful discussion, although this was not entirely conclusive. As Wm. Hoste (*Bible Problems and Answers*) observes: "Perhaps there is scarcely any subject which lends itself more readily to speculation, and concerning which speculation ought to be more carefully avoided, than the mysterious fall of Satan". It does seem clear, however, that Satan entered the garden of Eden as a fallen creature. He was already the enemy of God and man. The Lord Jesus said "I beheld Satan as lightning fall from heaven" (Luke 10.18), and while some feel that this statement refers to the future (Revelation 12.9), it does seem more likely to refer to the past. The matter is dealt with most helpfully by N. Crawford (*What the Bible Teaches – Luke*). Here is part of his answer: "Why did the Lord mention it to the seventy? Two answers have been given to this question. First, to tell them that what they had experienced in casting out demons was to be expected, for the demons' leader was already fallen. Secondly, He detected a sense of vain glory in them because of their success, and tells them this fact to warn them of the danger of pride. The latter is the more likely answer and can be seen in 1 Timothy 3.6; the novice, if he is given responsibility too quickly, is in danger of being lifted up with pride, and of falling 'into the condemnation of the devil'".

READ CHAPTER 4

"For such a time as this"

In previous studies, we have used the expression, 'the providence of God'. The book of Esther displays God's "providential overruling", as opposed to His "supernatural intervening" (J. Sidlow Baxter: *Explore the Book*). Perhaps the time has come for a definition. The word 'providence' comes from two Latin words: *pro*, meaning '*before*', and *video,* meaning '*I see*'. It therefore means, 'activity arising from foresight'. "God arranged non-miraculous events to achieve a predetermined outcome - which makes it all the more miraculous! God may seem strangely silent, but He remains actively sovereign". (J. Sidlow Baxter).

The providential care of God for His people now becomes strikingly apparent, as Mordecai apparently realises for the first time: "who knoweth whether thou art come to the kingdom **for such a time as this?**" (v.14).

Three characters take an active part in the proceedings. We have already met Mordecai and Esther, but we now meet Hatach, "one of the king's chamberlains" (v.5). He plays a most important part in the story. We may not aspire to Mordecai or Esther, but we can all fulfil the role of Hatach! The chapter may therefore be divided as follows: *(1)* the reaction of Mordecai (vv.1-4); *(2)* the role of Hatach (vv.5-10); *(3)* the response of Esther (vv.11-17).

1) THE REACTION OF MORDECAI, vv.1-4

"When Mordecai perceived all that was done, Mordecai rent his clothes, and put on sackcloth with ashes, and went out into the midst of the city, and cried with a loud and bitter cry; and came even before the king's gate: for none might enter into the king's gate clothed with sackcloth" (vv.l-2). (Eastern potentates expected their subjects to be deliriously happy at all times: compare Nehemiah 2.1-2). Although Esther was "exceedingly grieved" when informed by her maids and chamberlains, it is evident that she was not aware of the reason for Mordecai's grief. See v.5. Ahasuerus had not confided in his queen and, by our standards, she seemed strangely insulated from the outside world. Bearing in mind that God's people were in peril, let's ask some questions:

i) **Are we concerned about the threat to our existence?** Yes, we have eternal life. The Lord Jesus said, "I give unto them eternal life; and they shall never perish..." (John 10.28). But we have a great enemy, and he is bent on destroying our testimony. We have already said that Haman is a striking picture of Satan himself. There are many resemblances, and they culminate in Esther's statement: "The adversary and enemy is this wicked Haman" (7.6). Doesn't this remind you of 1 Peter 5.8 ("your **adversary** the devil, as a roaring lion, walketh about, seeking whom he may devour"); Matthew 13.39 ("the **enemy** that sowed them is the devil") and 1 John 3.12 ("Not as Cain, who was of that **wicked** one")? Haman exhibited the character of his dark master, but "we are not ignorant of his devices" (2 Cor. 2.11), one of which is to transform himself "into an angel of light" (2 Cor. 11.14). Persecution is not nearly so successful as corruption.

But do we really care about the sad decline in spiritual power and faithfulness to the word of God? When Nehemiah learned that "the place which the Lord shall choose to place his name there" was in ruins, he could have shrugged his shoulders and carried on serving wine to the king, but he "sat down and wept, and mourned certain days, and fasted, and prayed before the God of heaven" (Neh. 1.4). Daniel was not a party to the sins which resulted in the Babylonian captivity, but he set his "face unto the Lord God, to seek by prayer and supplications, with fasting, and sackcloth, and ashes" (Dan. 9.3). Paul "ceased not to warn every one night and day with tears" as he anticipated "grievous wolves" from without, and "men ...speaking perverse things" from within (Acts 20.29-31).

ii) **Are we out of touch with the feelings of Christ?** In this case Esther was out of touch with the feelings of Mordecai. However, it would be rather unfair to criticise Esther. She was evidently cocooned from national life, and was blissfully unaware of the crisis. But what about us? The Lord Jesus wept over Jerusalem (Luke 19.41). Human misery touched Him deeply. See also Mark 7.34, 'And looking up to heaven he **groaned**' (JND). In that sense, how much do we know of the "fellowship of his sufferings?" We tend to become impervious and insensitive to human need. Generally speaking, we have surrounded ourselves with every creature comfort, and become quite unaware of a grieving Christ.

iii) **Are we out of touch with one another?** Ahasuerus certainly didn't communicate with his wife. Had he done so, a little queenly advice and good common sense might have nudged him in a completely different direction! Assembly elders need to be in constant touch with each other, and in constant touch with the flock. They also need, when necessary, to 'take on board' the views of sisters in fellowship. The Lord's people need to be in constant touch with each other. Paul might have acted entirely on his own authority in Acts 15, but "**they** (that is, the local 'brethren', v.1) determined that Paul and Barnabas... should go up to Jerusalem unto the apostles and elders about this question. And being brought on their way **by the church...**" (vv.l-3). Fellowship is vital.

2) THE ROLE OF HATACH, vv.5-10

The frequent reference to Hatach leaves you with the impression that he is mentioned quite deliberately. He must certainly not be overlooked. "Then called Esther for Hatach... and gave him a commandment to Mordecai...so Hatach went forth to Mordecai...and Mordecai told him of all that had happened unto him... also he gave him a copy of the writing of the decree...and Hatach came and told Esther the words of Mordecai. Again Esther spake unto Hatach, and gave him commandment unto Mordecai". Now let's see what we can learn from all this:

i) **No service for God escapes His notice.** Hatach isn't one of the big 'stars' in the story (forgive the play on Esther's name!), but he does valuable work. The Bible is just full of such examples. What about Paul's nephew in Acts 23? Or the little captive maid in 2 Kings 5? Just think what would have happened if the sons of Merari had found it rather *infra dig* to carry tent pegs and tent cords, and jettisoned them *en route* through the wilderness! None of us are in a position to compare different aspects of Christian service in terms of their importance. Everything is important, and everything is known to God. We know nothing about "Jesus, which is called Justus" (Col. 4.11), but God knows everything about him!

ii) **No service for God should be beneath our dignity.** Hatach was one of the "king's chamberlains" (v.5), but he was quite willing to act as a messenger boy! Just think about the Lord Jesus: "The Son of man came not to be ministered unto (that is, to be served), but to minister (that is, to serve), and to give his life a ransom for many" (Mark 10.45). Those of us who preach should never get 'too big for our spiritual boots', and we shouldn't encourage others to do so either. One assembly decided that since a brother in fellowship was a competent Bible teacher, he should be deleted from the cleaning rota! (Yes, it really did happen!).

iii) **No service for God should be undertaken without strict reference to His word.** Hatach was devoid of any ideas of his own! He had nothing to contribute to the dialogue between Esther and Mordecai. He simply repeated what he was told to say - without any embroidery. The Lord Jesus made this clear about His own ministry: "For I have not spoken of (from) myself; but the Father which sent me, he gave me a commandment, what I should say, and what I should speak" (John 12.49). Our business is to communicate the word of God: nothing more, and nothing less. Hatach did exactly what he was told, and repeated exactly what he was told.

iv) No service for God should be undertaken without strict personal integrity.
Esther obviously trusted Hatach implicitly: just think about "the delicate task she entrusted to him. And Mordecai must have trusted him too, for he divulged to him Esther's true nationality and thus her dangerous position" (J.C. Whitcomb). There was no tittle-tattle by Hatach. No betrayal of confidences. He was totally trustworthy, and could be safely relied upon to carry detailed information (v.7) and important instructions (v.8).

At the same time he was at considerable risk. Just suppose Haman had found out about his visits to Mordecai. There is always "risk" attached to service for God. Barnabas and Paul are described as "men that have hazarded their lives for the name of our Lord Jesus Christ" (Acts 15.26), and Paul tells us that Priscilla and Aquila had "for my life laid down their own necks ('neck', singular)", unlike the Tekoite nobles who "put not their necks to the work of their Lord" (Rom 16.3-4; Neh. 3.5).

3) THE RESPONSIBILITY OF ESTHER, vv.11-17
Mordecai had already urged Esther to intercede for the Jews before Ahasuerus (v.8). This section of the narrative emphasises at least three important matters:

a) The task seemed impossible, vv.11-12
Esther outlines court procedure: "Whosoever, whether man or woman, shall come unto the king into the inner court, who is not called, there is one law of his to put him to death, except such to whom the king shall hold out the golden sceptre, that he may live". That in itself hardly seems a problem - after all, Ahasuerus wasn't away fighting the Greeks, and we might have expected king and queen to spend some time together every day. But the king's affection (see 2.17) seemed to be cooling off a little, and Esther has to say, "I have not been called to come in unto the king these thirty days". To put it in plain words, Esther is saying, 'Sorry, but there's nothing much I can do about it'.

It's all too familiar, isn't it? 'We're living in the last days, you know...people are gospel-hardened aren't they (are they?)...it's a day of small things (quoting, out of context Zechariah 4.10)...people are so materialistic...more people in this country go to the mosque on Fridays than go to the Church of England on Sundays... anyway, the Lord is coming back'. The last remark seems to be an excuse for doing nothing! Nothing about preaching "the word; be instant in season, out of season..." (2 Tim. 4.2), that is, get on with gospel preaching whether the climate is favourable or not! We have become accustomed to fighting a rearguard action, and any thought of expansion seems quite out of the question. In our judgment (alas) it has become a battle for survival, rather than for territorial acquisition. Well, Mordecai is having none of it:

b) The task demands intervention, vv.13-14

During the Great War of 1914-1918, Lord Kitchener appealed for volunteers to fight the Germans. His portrait appeared on posters throughout the country with his stabbing finger and the words, "Your Country Needs **You**". Mordecai was on the same wavelength: "Who knoweth whether thou art come to the kingdom for such a time as this?" Only **she** had the opportunity to represent God's people. No one else could do it - but see **(ii)** below. We are all 'key people'. While we certainly wouldn't put ourselves in the same category of Jeremiah and Paul, we ought nevertheless to be people with divine convictions about our role in God's service. Jeremiah was told, "Before I formed thee in the belly I knew thee; and before thou camest forth out of the womb I sanctified thee, and I ordained thee a prophet unto the nations" (Jer. 1.5) and Paul evidently had this is mind in saying, "God, who separated me from my mother's womb, and called me by his grace, to reveal his Son in me, that I might preach him among the heathen" (Gal. 1.15-16).

There are three challenging strands in Mordecai's statement:

i) Failure on Esther's part would mean her own death.

"For if thou altogether holdest thy peace at this time, then shall there enlargement and deliverance arise to the Jews from another place; **but thou and thy father's house shall be destroyed**". Mordecai does not specify how this would happen - perhaps he was thinking of divine judgment. The lesson for us is very clear: failure to speak for Christ will mean the demise of our own testimony, and loss of reward at the judgment seat of Christ. The poor condition of many assemblies today - and the closure of many assemblies - is largely due to past failure in evangelism. It almost seems that sometimes assemblies reach a 'point of no return'. The assembly that holds its "peace at this time", and sits comfortably in its Gospel Hall - like Esther in the Persian palace - will ultimately lose its existence.

ii) Failure on Esther's part would not mean the annihilation of the Jews.
The threat of genocide was very real, but Mordecai obviously believed in the inerrancy of God's promises: "For if thou altogether holdest thy peace at this time, **then shall there enlargement and deliverance arise...from another place**..." These are telling words. Our failure does not mean the failure of God's purposes. God will continue His work, but we will cease to be "vessels unto honour..." This is precisely Mordecai's point -

iii) Failure on Esther's part would mean loss of the honour she would otherwise receive. Whilst Mordecai still does not mention God's Name, it seems clear that he had at least begun to recognise the providence of God. It now remained for Esther to fulfil the purpose which God intended for her. Mordecai doesn't speak with absolute certainty ("who knoweth...?") but **we** can: Esther **had**, indeed, "come to the kingdom for such a time as this".

Let's update this. If we believe that God controls and directs our movements, and has a plan for our lives, can we not then say, 'I have come to Cheshunt (or wherever you live) for such a time as this?' God has placed us where we are for a purpose. If we fulfil that purpose then we will hear the words, "Well done, thou good and faithful servant..." (Matt. 25.21). The alternative is loss of the reward which would have been otherwise given. Paul was very conscious of the fact that he had 'come to prison for such a time as this'. "But I would ye should understand, brethren, that the things which happened unto me have fallen out rather unto the furtherance of the gospel" (Phil. 1.12).

c) The task requires intercession, vv.15-17
Esther accepts the responsibility resting upon her, but it wasn't just a case of sweeping into the king's presence, and hoping for the best! She was well aware of the risks involved. Her mission of intervention demanded a ministry of intercession. "Go, gather together all the Jews that are present in Shushan, and fast ye for me, and neither eat nor drink three days, night or day: I also and my maidens will fast likewise; **and so will I go in unto the king**, which is not according to the law: and if I perish, I perish".

Once again, the task entrusted to Esther meant exposure to risk. The Lord Jesus was exposed to death itself in seeking the good of His sheep: "the good shepherd giveth his life for the sheep" (John 10.11)

But here is a problem: we have used the word 'intercession', but there is no mention of prayer to God. It is very clear that prayer was always associated with fasting. See, for example Nehemiah 1.4; Daniel 9.3. But evidently not here! As J. Sidlow Baxter observes, "Can we really believe that in a crisis which threatened death to every Jew in the Persian Empire, that there was no agonised calling upon the God of their fathers? Can we believe, too, that after the amazing deliverance which came to them, there was absolutely no voice of thanksgiving to God? There is only one possible inference - the silence was intentional!". No mention is made of prayer evidently to emphasise that in the book of Esther, God was 'working behind the scene, moving every scene which He is behind'.

One thing is very clear, we must never forget that the Lord's work demands self-denial and disciplined prayer.

READ CHAPTER 5

Favour with the king

The three days of fasting are over, and Esther fulfils her promise: "So will I go in unto the king...." (4.16). We should remember, from past chapters, God has got key people in position. **Esther** is in the palace. She is Queen of Persia. As a result of disclosing the assassination plot, **Mordecai** is also in position, although this is not yet apparent. The significance of his disclosure of the attempt on the king's life has not yet been revealed. Once Esther and Mordecai are in position (Chapters 1 & 2), we have (in Chapters 3 & 4), the rise of Haman (3.1-15), the reaction of Mordecai (4.1-4), the role of Hatach (4.5-10), and the responsibility of Esther (4.11-17).

There are three main paragraphs in this chapter: *(1)* Esther approaches the throne (vv.1-2); *(2)* Ahasuerus accepts her invitations (vv.3-8); *(3)* Haman anticipates victory (vv.9-14).

1) ESTHER APPROACHES THE THRONE, vv.1-2

These verses remind us of our approach to another throne. "Let us therefore come boldly unto the throne of grace, that we may obtain mercy, and find grace to help in time of need" (Heb. 4.16). Ahasuerus "sat upon his royal throne in the royal house". However splendid the scene, it cannot compare with "the throne of the Majesty in the heavens" (Heb. 8.1). Esther was not at all sure that the throne of Persia would prove to be a "throne of grace", but *we* know that the "throne of the Majesty in the heavens" *is also* a "throne of grace". We should notice *(a)* her alarm before the king; *(b)* her approach to the king; *(c)* her acceptance by the king.

a) Her alarm before the king

i) Esther was uncertain. What kind of reception would she receive? Would the golden sceptre be extended to her? She had explained the position to Mordecai in 4.11. There was a tremendous risk involved: "So will I go into the king, which is not according to the law: and if I perish, I perish". It is all far removed from Hebrews 4.16 and 10.19, "Let us *therefore* come *boldly* unto the throne of grace...Having therefore, brethren, **boldness** to enter into the holiest..." This does not mean that we approach God irreverently or carelessly: we must never abandon "the fear of the Lord". But we are able to "come boldly". The expression suggests freedom of speech. We can take everything 'to the Lord in prayer'. We can come "in full assurance of faith". Esther certainly didn't come that way!

Perhaps this is an opportunity to say, again, that service for God often carries risk. As we have already noted, the church at Jerusalem described Barnabas and Paul as "men that have hazarded ('given up', JND) their lives for the name of our Lord Jesus Christ" (Acts 15.26), and Priscilla and Aquilla certainly exposed themselves to risk: "who have for my life laid down their own necks ('neck)" (Rom. 16.4), or "who for my life staked ('risked, hazarded', margin) their own neck" (JND).

ii)   Esther was uninvited. "Whosoever...shall come unto the king in the inner court, **who is not called**, there is one law of his to put him to death...**I have not been called** to come in unto the king these thirty days" (4.11). There is no such restriction so far as we are concerned: "In every thing by prayer and supplication with thanksgiving let your requests be made known unto God" (Phil. 4.6). The Lord Jesus taught, "Ask, and it shall be given you; seek, and ye shall find; knock, and it shall be opened unto you" (Matt. 7.7). We have an unqualified divine invitation in Hebrews 10.22, "Let us draw near..." James says, "If any of you lack wisdom, let him ask of God..." (James 1.5).

iii)   Esther was unenthusiastic. She was willing to approach the king (see 4.16), but you could hardly expect her to relish the task! How about us? Has prayer become a chore - a duty that must be performed? David didn't think so: "My voice shalt thou hear in the morning, O Lord; in the morning will I direct my prayer unto thee, and will look up" (Psalm 5.3).

b) Her approach to the king
i)   Where did she come? She came to the throne of Persia - to the highest possible authority in the kingdom. She could not have gone higher. We have already noticed that we approach "the throne of the Majesty in the heavens" (Heb. 8.1).

ii) When did she come? "Now it came to pass on **the third day**..." You'll have no difficulty with that! The Lord Jesus "rose again the **third day** according to the scriptures" 1 Cor. 15.4). We approach God on the basis of Christ's death and resurrection. We "by him do believe in God, that raised him up from the dead, and gave him glory; that your faith and hope might be in God" (1 Pet. 1.21).

iii) How did she come? "Esther put on her royal apparel". We too have "royal apparel". Garments suitable for the presence of God. Once, like Joshua the high priest (Zech. 3.1-10), we were "clothed with filthy garments". But listen to this: "Behold, I have caused thine iniquity to pass from thee, and I will clothe thee with change of raiment..." We have been "made the righteousness of God in him" (2 Cor. 5.21). God has "made us accepted in the beloved" (Eph.1.6).

We must make sure that appropriate garments are always worn. Peter describes God's people as a "holy priesthood" in offering "spiritual sacrifices" in the "spiritual house". He also uses the expression "royal priesthood" in connection with our testimony before others: "that ye should shew forth the praises of him who hath called you out of darkness into his marvellous light" (1 Pet. 2.1-10). It is in connection with the latter that we are told: "Put ye on the Lord Jesus Christ, and make not provision for the flesh, to fulfil the lusts thereof" (Rom.13.14). But what about the future? The hymnwriter puts it like this:

> When I stand before the throne,
> Dressed in beauty not my own;
> When I see Thee as Thou art,
> Love Thee with unsinning heart:
> Then, Lord, shall I fully know,
> Not till then, how much I owe.

c) Her acceptance by the king

"She obtained favour in his sight: and the king held out to Esther the golden sceptre that was in his hand". We have already noticed that Esther had no right to enter the king's presence, and therefore she was only accepted on the basis of grace. As John C. Whitcomb says: 'The spiritual application to the gospel message is remarkable. Because of our sin, we cannot enter the presence of an infinitely holy God. But this same God, in His incomparable love and grace, has provided a plan whereby even the worst of sinners may enter His presence and touch, as it were, His golden scepter (American spelling)'. As Whitcomb points out, the picture is imperfect in view of the character of the ruler himself.

The sceptre displayed the right to rule: hence Esther's acceptance was invested with the highest possible authority. Notice Hebrews 1.8, "But unto the Son he saith...a sceptre of righteousness is the sceptre of thy kingdom".

Our acceptance is in Christ Himself: "But of him are ye in Christ Jesus, who of God is made unto us wisdom, and righteousness, and sanctification, and redemption (1 Cor. 1.30). In the words of Harry Bell, "Paul was on a tour of Corinth and was taken to the university (but Paul said, 'Christ is made unto us **wisdom**'); then to the law courts (but Paul said, 'Christ is made unto us **righteousness**'); then to the temple (but Paul said, 'Christ is made unto us **sanctification**'); then to the slave-market (but Paul said, 'Christ is made unto us **redemption**')".

2) AHASUERUS ACCEPTS HER INVITATIONS, vv.3-8

Instead of making her request at the king's invitation to do so (v.3), that is as soon as she entered his presence (vv1-2), Esther invited him to a banquet where he evidently expected the request to be made. Hence his second invitation: "What is thy petition? and it shall be granted thee: and what is thy request? even to the half of the kingdom it shall be performed" (v.6). But the request was delayed for the second time: "Let the king and Haman come to the banquet (a second banquet) that I shall prepare for them, and I will do tomorrow as the king hath said" (v.8). On the human level, this double delay hardly seemed sound policy: "Her second refusal was tempting fate. Postponing her real request another time was a most questionable gamble; any number of things could go wrong in the interval between the two dinners: the king's benevolent mood could change, for example, or Haman could learn of Esther's true feelings toward him, or of her relationship with Mordecai" (Carey A. Moore).

Why the delay? Haman was the king's favourite, and possibly Esther felt that her influence with the king was not sufficiently strong. Another banquet might get him in a really good mood! Or perhaps her courage failed at the last moment.

On the other hand, there was nothing underhand about Esther. Haman was present throughout. It must also be said that Esther's actions certainly saved the king's face. He might have been hard put to explain a sudden change of mind had Esther approached him without Haman present. But the circumstances described in Chapter 7 gave Ahasuerus all the justification he needed.

One thing, however, is very clear: it was not God's time. God had already determined that Ahasuerus needed a little insomnia plus some nice light reading to while away the hours! Having done that, He would then give Esther the opportunity and courage she needed to intercede for her people. We're back to God's providence: remember – *pro* and *video*. (God's 'video' is infinitely far better than the other sort!). Now, what lessons can we learn from all this?

i) **We needn't delay in making OUR requests.** We don't have to catch God in the right mood. "The eyes of the Lord are over the righteous, and his ears are open unto their prayers" (1 Pet. 3.12). Remember, "Let us therefore come boldly unto the throne of grace...". However, we mustn't forget that we should always approach the throne of God in a worshipful spirit, rather than blurting out our requests immediately.

ii) **We mustn't camouflage our real purpose.** If we arrange meetings for Gospel preaching, then let's make it quite clear that this is what we are about. People are hardly likely to be impressed if you advertise a talk on flower arranging, and then tell the audience that they're hell-deserving sinners! (Not quite so exaggerated as you might think). Paul asked his brethren at Ephesus to pray "that utterance may be given unto me, that I may open my mouth boldly, to make known the mystery of the gospel, for which I am an ambassador in bonds: that therein I may speak boldly, as I ought to speak" (Eph. 6.19-20). Jeremiah was told, "Speak unto them all that I command thee: be not dismayed at their faces, lest I confound thee before them" (Jer. 1.17).

iii) **We must be careful about rash promises.** Supposing Esther had asked for "half of the kingdom!" (vv.3,6). (Under current U.K. divorce legislation, she would, presumably, have got it! Perhaps she should have asked for "half the kingdom", and then ensured that her half contained all the Jews. That would have solved the problem!). Herod said exactly the same thing in Mark 6.23, only to be asked for the head of John the Baptist. Jephthah vowed "whatsoever cometh forth of the doors of my house to meet me, when I return in peace from the children of Ammon, shall surely be the Lord's, and I will offer it up for a burnt offering" (Judges 11.31). We all know what happened: you can argue till you're blue in the face, the passage is clear: he "did with her according to his vow which he had vowed" (v.39). So be careful what you say - or sing.

3) HAMAN ANTICIPATES VICTORY, vv.9-14

Before we look at the passage itself, it might be helpful to glance at the prophetic message of this book. At the end-time, the Jews will again be under threat of annihilation, and Haman - a picture of Satan, as we have seen - is also a picture of the "man of sin". Consider the following:

i) **His name.** "This **wicked** Haman" (7.6). See 2 Thessalonians 2.8, "Then shall that **Wicked** be revealed...."

ii) **His power.** Haman's rise was meteoric, and he had the power of life and death throughout the Persian Empire. Revelation 13 makes it very clear that the power of the "man of sin" is universal. (You will have to decide whether the "man of sin" in 2 Thessalonians 2 is the first or second beast of Revelation 13! The question is not so easily answered as you might suppose! But both have universal power).

iii) His pride. Just listen to Haman boasting to his wife and friends. Now listen to another boast: "Who opposeth and exalteth himself above all that is called God, or that is worshipped; so that he as God sitteth in the temple of God, shewing himself that he is God" (2 Thess. 2.4).

iv) His hate. Haman worked through political power for the Jews' destruction. It will happen again. See Revelation 13.15: "And he had power to give life unto the image of the beast, that the image of the beast should both speak, and cause that as many as would not worship the image of the beast should be killed".

v) His death. Haman's death was sudden and complete. One day he vaunts himself: the next day he hangs, as we would say today, 'by his own rope', only 'hanging' in those days was more akin to crucifixion. He was terrible whilst in power, but it was only for a few years - at the most some four or five years; compare 2.16 with 3.7. The end of the "man of sin" will be similar: "whom the Lord shall consume with the spirit of his mouth, and shall destroy with the brightness of his coming" (2 Thess. 2.8).

Note in passing that Haman had ten sons, and they were slain too (9.10). You might now like to read Revelation 17.2-13: "And the ten horns which thou sawest are ten kings, which have received no kingdom as yet; but receive power as kings one hour with the beast" (v.12).

Now, back to Esther Chapter 5. The outstanding feature of Haman in this passage, is his pride: notice

a) *His selfish pride*
Pride can have some nice angles. We talk about 'taking pride in our work', and about a 'proud father' or a 'proud mother'. But here is boastful pride.

i) He was proud of his possessions. "And Haman told them of the glory of his riches..." (v.11). He was soon to learn that "a man's life consisteth not in the abundance of things which he possesseth" (Luke 12.15).

ii) **He was proud of his posterity.** "And the multitude of his children". Well, Psalm 127 tells us that "children are an heritage of the Lord: and the fruit of the womb is his reward" (v.3).

iii) **He was proud of his promotion.** "And all the things wherein the king had promoted him". But listen to this: "Lift not up your horn on high: speak not with a stiff neck. For promotion cometh neither from the east, not from the west, nor from the south. But God is the judge: he putteth down one, and setteth up another" (Psalm 75.5-7).

iv) **He was proud of his privileges.** Just listen to him on the subject: "Yea, Esther the queen did let no man come in with the king unto the banquet that she had prepared but myself; and tomorrow am I invited unto her also with the king" (v.12). Apart from the king, he was the sole guest.

It's all summed up in Jeremiah 9.23-24: "Let not the wise man glory in his wisdom, neither let the mighty man glory in his might, let not the rich man glory in his riches: but let him that glorieth glory in this, that he understandeth and knoweth me, that I am the Lord which exercise lovingkindness, judgment, and righteousness, in the earth: for in these things I delight, saith the Lord".

b) His injured pride

"Yet all this availeth me nothing, so long as I see Mordecai the Jew sitting at the king's gate" (v.13). Pride of position consumes people. Revenge is the fruit of pride.

c) His placated pride

His wife and friends have the answer. Revenge will be sweet: "Then go thou in merrily with the king unto the banquet" (v.14). Everything looked good for Haman. But Chapter 6 follows. Pride is self-destructive. We leave Chapter 5 with Mordecai condemned to death by 'a prince of this world'. The "Lord of glory" was treated similarly by "the princes of this world" (1 Cor. 2.8).

READ CHAPTER 6

"The man whom the king delighteth to honour"

The words that stand at the head of these notes occur five times in this chapter. See vv.6,7,9(twice),11. The passage signals the beginning of Mordecai's rise to honour, and the beginning of Haman's journey to the gallows. We are given a glimpse of Mordecai's coming glory as "the man whom the king delighteth to honour". It is a foretaste of the day when "Mordecai the Jew was next unto king Ahasuerus, and great among the Jews" (10.3). All of which reminds us that "we see Jesus...crowned with glory and honour" (Heb. 2.9), and that His glory is soon to be fully displayed. But the beginning of Haman's downfall reminds us not only that Satan is already a defeated foe, but that ultimately he will be "cast out into the earth...having great wrath, because he knoweth that he hath but a short time" (Rev. 12.7-12). Haman's wife and friends were certainly convinced that he had "but a short time!" (v.13).

We'll study the chapter under four paragraph headings as follows: *(1)* a man who had not been honoured (vv.1-3); *(2)* a man who wanted to be honoured (vv.4-9); *(3)* a man who was publicly honoured (vv.10-11); *(4)* a man who would never be honoured (vv.12-14)

1) A MAN WHO HAD NOT BEEN HONOURED, vv.1-3
"And the king said, What honour and dignity hath been done to Mordecai for this? Then said the king's servants that ministered unto him, ***There is nothing done for him***" (v.3).

Notice, first of all, the perfect timing in every detail of the story:

i) ***It was the right night.*** "On ***that*** night could not the king sleep..." That is, the night before Esther's second banquet. If Ahasuerus had suffered a bout of insomnia on any other night, the story might have ended rather differently.

ii) ***It was the right book.*** "He commanded to bring the book of records of the chronicles; and they were read before the king". He could have endeavoured to while away the time in some other way (how about the court musicians?), or asked for a completely different book. It appears from Ezra 6.1-2 that the royal palaces had extensive archives.

iii) **It was the right entry.** "And it was found written, that Mordecai had told of Bigthana and Teresh...who sought to lay hand on the king Ahasuerus". They could have read from other parts of "the book of records of the chronicles".

iv) **It was the right question.** "What honour and dignity hath been done to Mordecai for this?" The king could have grunted approval, and let them read on!

Notice, secondly, that what had **not** happened was also perfectly timed. Just suppose Mordecai **had been** honoured at the time of the incident in question. Or suppose that he had clamoured for some kind of recognition or reward. Events could have turned out very differently. Now let's notice some important lessons:

a) God's providence is perfect
We have already noticed this in our studies. Let's quote J. Sidlow Baxter again: "God arranged non-miraculous events to achieve a predetermined outcome - which makes it all the more miraculous".

Now listen to Peter preaching on the day of Pentecost: "Him, being delivered by the determinate counsel and foreknowledge of God, ye have taken, and by wicked hands have crucified and slain" (Acts 2.23). Now it is Paul writing. "But I would ye should understand, brethren, that the things which happened unto me have fallen out rather unto the furtherance of the gospel" (Phil. 1.12). Aren't these New Testament examples of divine providence? How about something from the Old Testament? See, for example, 1 Sam 9.14, "And they (Saul and his servant) went up into the city: and when they were come into the city, behold, Samuel came out against them, for to go up to the high place". Just think about your own life now - you should be able to supply a few examples of your own!

b) God's Son must be honoured
Ahasuerus had failed to honour the man who had delivered him from death. "There is nothing done for him". We know that this was prearranged by God, but we would be quite wrong to put ourselves in this picture. The Lord Jesus has delivered us from death at infinite cost, and it would be a lamentably poor response on our part if we are failing to honour Him in our lives. Could it be said of us, "There is nothing done for **him**?" Listen to the New Testament again: "For the love of Christ constraineth us; because we thus judge, that if one died for

all, then were all dead: and that he died for all, that they which live should not henceforth live unto themselves, but **unto him** which died for them, and rose again" (2 Cor. 5.14-15). See also 1 Corinthians 6.20; "For ye are bought with a price: therefore glorify God…" Read Ecclesiastes 9.14-15. It is generally true in the world that "no man remembered that same poor man". But do **we** leave Him out of our calculations?

c) God's people must be humble
We have already noticed that Mordecai never clamoured for recognition. Solomon observed that "The fear of the Lord is the instruction of wisdom; and before honour is humility" (Prov. 15.33). This was preeminently true of the Lord Jesus. He was "obedient unto death, even the death of the cross. Wherefore God also hath highly exalted him, and given him a name which is above every name…" (Phil. 2.8-9). Peter writes: "Yea, all of you be subject one to another, and be clothed with humility: for God resisteth the proud, and giveth grace to the humble. Humble yourselves therefore under the mighty hand of God, that he may exalt you in due time" (1 Pet. 5.5-6)

2) A MAN WHO WANTED TO BE HONOURED, vv.4-9
Haman was dazzled by his own success. Ahasuerus had "advanced him, and set his seat above all the princes that were with him" (3.1; 5.11). Everything seemed set fair for him. He had enjoyed a private drink with the king (3.15), and was now to accompany the king to the queen's banquet. So, "Haman thought in his heart, To whom would the king delight to do honour more than to myself?" (v.6). It was even better than getting permission to hang Mordecai! He didn't have time to make that request anyway! Now let's notice some lessons:

a) He was obsessed with his own importance
You'll notice that it was an attitude of heart: "Now Haman thought in his heart". The previous reference to his heart reveals the same thing: having been invited to the banquet, "Then went Haman forth that day joyful and with a glad heart" (5.9). So Haman entered the king's presence with a very proud heart. Notice that he observed court etiquette: he was in the "outward court" (v.4), as opposed to the "inner court" of 5.1. See 4.11. But outward ceremony masked inward pride, and inward hatred for Mordecai. It's very easy to 'go through the motions', especially in assembly life. We like to be as orthodox as possible, and do exactly the right thing. Every 'i' is dotted, and every 't' is crossed. But sometimes it masks "anger…malice" (Col. 3.8), and other evils just waiting to be let loose.

How do we enter the King's presence? John the Baptist said, "He must increase, but I must decrease" (John 3.30). There was no decreasing with Haman. We can just imagine how Haman would have responded if Elisha had said to him, "What is to be done for thee? wouldest thou be spoken for to the king, or to the captain of the host?" He would have jumped at the opportunity! But just listen to the lovely answer from the "great woman" of Shunem: "I dwell among mine own people". No wonder she was "a great woman!" (2 Kings 4.8-13). Paul had to remind the proud Christians at Corinth that any ability they possessed was entirely God-given: "What hast thou that thou didst not receive? now if thou didst receive it, why dost thou glory, as if thou hadst not received it?" (1 Cor. 4.7). Whether it's our position, or gift, or whatever - none of us have any reason to "glory in his presence".

b) He was ambitious for the highest place
Just like Diotrephes: "Who loveth to have the preeminence among them" (3 John 9). Or like the Pharisees, "Ye love the uppermost seats in the synagogues" (Luke 11.43). The Lord Jesus taught that "Whosoever will be great among you, let him be your minister (*diakonos,* meaning 'servant'); and whosoever will be chief among you, let him be your servant (*doulos*)" (Matt. 20.26-27).

Haman sought recognition on a scale that put him almost on the level of the king himself. Just contrast this with the way Paul describes the status of the apostles in 1 Corinthians 4.9, "For I think that God hath set forth us the apostles last, as it were appointed to death: for we are made a spectacle unto the world, and to angels, and to men". The word "last" here is a technical term describing prisoners bringing up the rear of a triumphal procession and destined for the arena. Haman's aspirations remind us that in the end-time, the "man of sin" will sit "in the temple of God, shewing himself that he is God" (2 Thess. 2.4). How different to the Lord Jesus Who came "not to be ministered unto (to be served), but to minister (to serve), and to give his life a ransom for many" (Matt. 20.28).

c) He was totally unworthy of promotion
Mordecai had actually done something to benefit the king. But Haman, the king's favourite, had done nothing meritorious. All he had achieved was confusion at Shushan (3.15) and immense distress to Jewish citizens in the Persian Empire (4.3). But then, it's often true that the greatest chaos is caused by people who seek position and prominence.

3) A MAN WHO WAS PUBLICLY HONOURED, vv.10-11
Imagine the chagrin of Haman. "Make haste, and take the apparel and the

271

horse, as thou hast said, and do even so to Mordecai *the Jew*, that sitteth at the king's gate: let nothing fail of all that thou hast spoken" (v.10). The very position he sought and expected, was given to the man he had attempted to destroy. Assuming Lucifer to be the dark master of the king of Babylon (although this may not be the case), and speaking through him, we read: "For thou hast said in thine heart, I will ascend into heaven, I will exalt my throne above the stars of God: I will sit also upon the mount of the congregation, in the sides of the north: I will ascend above the heights of the clouds; I will be like the most High" (Isaiah 14.13-14). But the position, and more, sought by "Lucifer, son of the morning" belongs to Christ.

Ahasuerus was evidently reminded of Mordecai's nationality from the official records. But why didn't he immediately identify Mordecai with the people whose destruction he had recently authorised? The best answer is, simply, that he didn't know who Haman was describing in 3.8-9. Haman carefully avoided mentioning the Jews by name, and Ahasuerus made no attempt to verify the charge brought against them. He just accepted Haman's word for it!

a) He is "the MAN whom the king delighteth to honour"
You can build on this yourself. Start with Hebrews 10.12, "But this man, after he had offered one sacrifice for sins for ever, sat down on the right hand of God". Go on from there. Oh, and don't forget that the Lord Jesus is "*the* man whom the king delighteth to honour". He is, "*the* man Christ Jesus" (1 Tim 2.5).

b) He is "the man whom the KING delighteth to honour"
There could be no greater degree of honour. Mordecai received honour from the highest authority on earth. The Lord Jesus received honour from the highest Authority in heaven: "For he received *from God the Father* honour and glory, when there came such a voice to him from the *excellent glory*..." (2 Pet. 1.17), or "uttered to him *by* the excellent glory" (JND). The honour and glory bestowed upon Christ is *unique.* It is shared by none. "Wherefore God also hath highly exalted him, and given him a name (the name) which is above every name" (Phil. 2.9).

c) He is "the man whom the king DELIGHTETH to honour"
It was no grudging recognition. The scene on the mount of transfiguration was a picture of "the power and coming of our Lord Jesus Christ" (2 Peter 1.16). That is, of course, His second coming. The world will hear God say, "This is my *beloved* Son, in whom I am well pleased; hear ye *him*" (Matt. 17.5). He is the "King of nations" (Jer. 10.7).

d) He is "the man whom the king delighteth to HONOUR"

He was honoured by wearing the "royal apparel...which the king useth to wear, and the horse that the king rideth upon, and the crown royal which is set upon his head" (v.8). (We are told that the Hebrew means, literally, that the crown was worn by the horse! Well, the crown certainly isn't mentioned in vv.9,11). Mordecai was invested with royal honours, but that is nothing when compared to the honour bestowed upon Christ. "Jesus said, Now is the Son of man glorified, and God is glorified in him. If God be glorified in him, **God shall also glorify him in himself, and shall straightway glorify him**" (John 13.31-32).

Mordecai was honoured publicly. He was honoured in the very place where a gallows had been erected for him. We must remember at least two things here. Firstly, that the very word "gallows" is literally, 'tree', and that, secondly, the punishment intended for Mordecai was undoubtedly crucifixion, since hanging, in the usual meaning of the word, does not seem to have been employed by the Persians. Need we say any more? Christ will be proclaimed as "the man whom the king delighteth to honour", in the very world which nailed Him to "the tree". Whilst Mordecai "came again to the king's gate" (it doesn't say that he "sat in the king's gate" which **might** suggest that he returned to his "sackcloth with ashes", 4.1-2), God has said, "Sit thou at my right hand, until I make thine enemies thy footstool" (Psalm 110.1). Mordecai was brought "on horseback through the street of the city". The Lord Jesus will emerge from heaven seated on a "white horse" (Rev. 19.11).

John C. Whitcomb has it nicely: "Fourteen centuries earlier, Joseph, another Israelite, was thus honoured when the Pharaoh had him ride in his second chariot; and they proclaimed before him, 'Bow the knee!' (Genesis 41.43). Some day the entire universe will bow down before God's unique Son, Jesus Christ our Lord. (c/f Psalm 2.4-12; Philippians 2.10-11)".

4) A MAN WHO WOULD NEVER BE HONOURED, vv.12-14

Just try to imagine the turmoil in Haman's mind. R. Sinker (Ellicott's Commentary) puts it like this: "It would be a grim and curious study to analyse Haman's feelings at this juncture. Various thoughts were mingled there. Self-reproach, perhaps, that he had so thoughtlessly been the cause of the present display, bitter hatred of his rival now multiplied a thousandfold, and the evident knowledge that the game was played out, and that he was ruined. The more subtle the brain, the more truly must he have known this". Of course, Haman had not been in any way disgraced by leading Mordecai through the city: **but it was a terrible blow to his pride**. A humble man can cope far more easily with the blows of life than a proud man!

Once again, we encounter the words, "And Haman told..." But what a difference now! It was boastful pride in 5.11: it is bitter disappointment in 6.13. His wife's words in v.14 could well have been the last he ever heard her say. We certainly mustn't underestimate this lady. She certainly influenced her husband in 5.14, and correctly assessed the situation in 6.13. But was Zeresh speaking 'off the cuff', or was she giving Haman the benefit of careful observation? Had she noticed that somehow or the other, the Jew comes out on top? For example, Joseph with Pharaoh, and Daniel with Nebuchadnezzar. Or had she learnt that, "he that toucheth you toucheth the apple of his eye?" (Zech. 2.8). One thing is clear: the omens had changed, and so had the attitude of Haman's family and friends.

The Lord Jesus taught that "Whosoever exalteth himself shall be abased..." (Luke 14.11). Remember too that "pride goeth before destruction, and an haughty spirit before a fall" (Prov. 16.18). There could hardly be a better example than Haman.

READ CHAPTER 7

Exit Haman

Haman's friends and family had predicted his downfall (6.13), and now their worst fears were fulfilled. The Agagite had "begun to fall" in Chapter 6, and his "fall" is completed in Chapter 7. We have already noticed the prophetical implications of the story. After his expulsion from heaven (Revelation 12.9), Satan will vent his anger particularly on the Jewish nation: "And when the dragon saw that he was cast unto the earth, he persecuted the woman which brought forth the man child" (Rev. 12.13) He has, however, "but a short time" (v.12), and will be consigned to the abyss (Revelation 20.1-3) for a thousand years, before his ultimate consignment to the lake of fire where he will be "tormented day and night for ever and ever".

Whilst there can be no question about the prophetic significance of events described in the book of Esther, we have emphasised its practical lessons during our studies. We will do so again in this chapter, which may be divided as follows: *(1)* the cordiality of Ahasuerus (vv.1-2); *(2)* the concern of Esther (vv.3-4); *(3)* the character of the enemy (vv.5-6); *(4)* the condemnation of Haman (vv.7-8); *(5)* the counsel of Harbonah (vv.9-10).

1) THE CORDIALITY OF AHASUERUS, vv.1-2

There certainly seems to be a strong feeling of goodwill in the king's request: "What is thy petition, queen Esther? and it shall be granted thee: and what is thy request? and it shall be performed, even to the half of the kingdom". We have already speculated about this. The smile on his face would have probably vanished if Esther *had* asked for half of his kingdom! Even so, there can be no doubt that Ahasuerus was prepared to be generous to his queen. Perhaps his conscience reminded him that he had neglected her for thirty days! (4.11). Bearing in mind his tendency to sudden change, it seems more likely that he was in a particularly good mood at the time! Perhaps it was something to do with the wine!

We too come to a generous King. In the words of John Newton:

> "Thou art coming to a King:
> Large petitions with thee bring:
> For His grace and power are such,
> None can ever ask too much".

He is "able to do exceeding abundantly above all that we ask or think" (Eph. 3.20). The Lord Jesus taught, "If ye abide in me, and my words abide in you, ye shall ask what ye will, and it shall be done unto you" (John 15.7); "And in that day ye shall ask me nothing. Verily, verily, I say unto you, Whatsoever ye shall ask the Father in my name, he will give it you. Hitherto have ye asked nothing in my name: ask, and ye shall receive, that your joy may be full" (John 16.23-24). John certainly seems to refer to this in writing "whatsoever we ask, we receive of him, because we keep his commandments, and do those things that are pleasing in his sight...and this is the confidence that we have in him, that, if we ask any thing according to his will, he heareth us: and if we know that he hear us, whatsoever we ask, we know that we have the petitions that we desired of him" (1 John 3.22; 5.14-15). You'll notice, of course, that these words do not constitute a blank cheque. There are some very important conditions. Firstly, we must "keep his commandments, and do those things that are pleasing in his sight". This means that we are not likely to make selfish requests - that would hardly be "pleasing in his sight". Secondly, everything is subject "to his will". We cannot expect Him to answer our requests if they are unscriptural, or if it would be harmful to us in some way. But this in no way detracts from His ability, generosity, and desire to bless us abundantly. We can "come boldly unto the throne of grace, that we may obtain mercy, and find grace to help in time of need" (Heb. 4.16).

Perhaps we ought to say that our prayers should reflect the measure of our faith. For example, our faith might not be strong enough to ask for vast numbers to be saved in the area, but surely we can pray with complete faith that God will save souls in the district and enlarge the assembly. Whilst God "giveth to all men liberally, and upbraideth not", we must "ask in faith, nothing wavering" (James 1.5-8).

2) THE CONCERN OF ESTHER, vv.3-4

Esther takes the place of an intercessor, not merely for herself, but for her people. "If I have found favour in thy sight, O king, and if it please the king, let my life be given me at my petition, and my people at my request: for we are sold, I and my people, to be destroyed, to be slain, and to perish".

It is worth noticing that Esther first brought pleasure to the king - he was invited to a "banquet of wine" - and it is "wine that maketh glad the heart of man" (Psalm 104.15). Her intercession was set against the joy that she brought to Ahasuerus. We have already noted the lesson.

Notice, too, that Esther was so different to Haman: he carefully observed court etiquette (6.4), but it only masked his pride and hatred for the Jews. Esther humbly petitioned the king, with no thought for her personal advancement. We must notice:

a) She petitioned the king with a sense of acceptance
Esther had not encountered hostility on the part of Ahasuerus. She was conscious of royal favour. The golden sceptre had been extended to her on the previous day, and the king repeated his desire to accede to her request. The fact that we pray in the name of the Lord Jesus Christ is not a meaningless formula. It is the ground of our acceptance in the presence of God.

b) She petitioned the king without personal ambition
Ahasuerus had made a magnificent offer – "to the half of the kingdom" - but Esther was not concerned with increase in her personal wealth, or personal enhancement in any way. She was not an opportunist. By human standards, she missed a golden opportunity - something that only comes once in a lifetime! But she identifies herself with her own people: "my people...*we* are sold, I and *my* people...But if *we* had been sold for bondmen and bondwomen..." (This was, presumably, the first time the king knew that he had married a Jewess! See 2.10 and 2.20. Now she really had to 'nail her colours to the mast'.)

Doesn't this remind you of Moses?: "By faith Moses, when he was come to years, refused to be called the son of Pharaoh's daughter; choosing rather to suffer affliction with the people of God, than to enjoy the pleasures of sin for a season; esteeming the reproach of Christ greater riches than the treasures in Egypt" (Heb. 11.24-26). Doesn't this remind you too, again, of the "great woman" of Shunem?: "What is to be done for thee? wouldest thou be spoken for to the king, or to the captain of the host?". Not at all - she had no desire for high society: listen to this magnificent reply – "I dwell among mine own people" (2 Kings 4.8-13).

What about our ambitions? The welfare of God's people was more important to Esther than personal prestige. If we are genuinely concerned for one another, and really love one another, then we will take every opportunity to promote one another's welfare in every way. It is a case of "the members" having "the same care one for another" (1 Cor. 12.25). Sadly, to quote the hymn, 'Room for pleasure' and 'Room for business' displaces room for the Lord's people, and more serious even than that, 'But for Christ, the crucified, Not a place where He can enter in the heart for which He died'.

Talking about ambition, how about Solomon? "And God said, Ask what I shall give thee". What an offer! What a reply! "Give therefore thy servant an understanding heart to judge thy people, that I may discern between good and bad: for who is able to judge this thy so great a people?" (1 Kings 3.1-13). "And God gave Solomon wisdom and understanding exceeding much, and largeness of heart, even as the sand that is on the sea shore" (1 Kings 4.29). How about Elisha? "Ask what I shall do for thee". What an offer! What a reply! "And Elisha said, I pray thee, let a double portion of thy spirit be upon me" (2 Kings 2.9).

Still talking about ambition, listen to this: "Wherefore we labour (R.V. 'we make it our aim' with the margin 'Greek: are **ambitious**'), that, whether present or absent, we may be accepted ('well-pleasing') of him" (2 Cor. 5.9).

c) She petitioned the king with a sense of alarm
You can hear the urgency in her voice: "For we are sold, I and my people, to be destroyed, to be slain, and to perish". Esther was actually quoting the king's letter. See 3.13. This was no casual request. The lives of God's people were at stake. Need we say more? You can hear the urgency in the prayers of Epaphras; "always labouring fervently (one Greek word - with *agon* in the middle: put a 'y' on the end, and you've got it, well, almost) for you in prayers" (Col. 4.12). Read through the Psalms, and notice how often the words "cry" and "cried" occur. So many of the Psalms were written in times of dire danger.

Now, just one or two technicalities.

i) "We are **sold**". This refers, of course, to 3.9, where Haman said, "I will pay ten thousand talents of silver to the hands of those that have the charge of the business, to bring it into the king's treasuries". The words "those that have the charge of the business" refer, not to the 'business' of annihilating the Jews, but to those in charge of Persian business affairs. Haman offered to pay this vast sum of money to the royal treasury.

ii) "If we had been sold for bondmen and bondwomen, I had held my tongue". So far so good, at least they would have been alive. But what about, "**although *the enemy could not countervail ('compensate', JND) the king's damage*". This is not easy! Perhaps Ellicott's Commentary has the answer: "Haman, though willing to pay a large sum into the royal treasury, cannot thereby make up for the loss that king must incur by wholesale massacre being carried on in his realm".

3) THE CHARACTER OF THE ENEMY, vv.5-6
Once again, we are confronted by the problem of the king's apparent lapse of memory: "Who is he, and where is he, that durst presume in his heart to do so?" (v.5). He seemed to have forgotten that it was Haman's suggestion! Ahasuerus was very inattentive at times. We have already noticed that he never bothered to find out who Haman had in mind when he said "There is a certain people scattered abroad and dispersed among the people in all the provinces of thy kingdom; and their laws are diverse from all people; neither keep they the king's laws: therefore it is not for the king's profit to suffer them" (3.8-9). But Ahasuerus just didn't know who Haman was describing, and Haman was at pains not to tell him! On the other hand, we might be forgiven for thinking that the truth ought to be dawning on him by now. Perhaps he was drunk (again?); after all, it was a "banquet of wine" (v.2).

The important thing is to notice the description of Haman. "The **adversary** and **enemy** is this **wicked** Haman". We must never forget the identity of our opponent. He cannot rob us of eternal life, but he will certainly endeavour to destroy our testimony and ruin our service.

a) "Adversary"
This recalls 1 Peter 5.8: "Be sober, be vigilant; because your **adversary** the devil, as a roaring lion, walketh about, seeking whom he may devour". The word rendered "adversary" here is interesting: it means an opponent in a lawsuit, and could refer to the fact that Peter's first readers were faced with two alternatives: either to bow in emperor worship, or to refuse to do so, with the inevitable consequences. The word may therefore have the sense of "the accuser of our brethren" (Rev. 12.10). One thing is very clear, whatever tactics he employs, Satan is our opponent.

b) "Enemy"
This recalls Matthew 13.39: "The **enemy** that sowed them is the devil". The word conveys the idea of hate and hostility. So don't expect an easy passage.

c) "Wicked"
This recalls 1 John 3.11-12: "For this is the message that ye heard from the beginning, that we should love one another. Not as Cain, who was of that **wicked** one". The word means 'bad in effect, malignant' (W.E. Vine). It is the **active** form of evil.

4) THE CONDEMNATION OF HAMAN, vv.7-8

The man who had "begun to fall" in Chapter 6 is now plunging downwards. The grim forebodings of Zeresh must have rung in his ears as he went to the banquet. These forebodings became terror in v.6: "Then Haman was **terrified** before the king and the queen" (JND). First the king's anger (v.7), then the king put the worst possible interpretation on Haman's posture at the queen's couch, and finally, he is deprived of light itself. His face is covered: never again did he see the face of the king (v.8). His doom was sealed.

The man who endeavoured to destroy the Jews had to lead "a Jew in triumphal procession through the streets of the city, and now he has to plead with a Jewess for his very life!" (John C. Whitcomb). This can only remind us of the ascendancy of the Jew under the reign of Messiah: "And kings shall be thy nursing fathers, and their queens thy nursing mothers: they shall bow down to thee with their face toward the earth, and lick up the dust of thy feet" (Isa. 49.23); "The sons also of them that afflicted thee shall come bending unto thee; and all they that despised thee shall bow themselves down at the soles of thy feet" (Isa. 60.14).

5) THE COUNSEL OF HARBONAH, vv.9-10

We have met Harbonah before (1.10). An additional charge is laid by him against Haman: "Behold also, the gallows fifty cubits high (seventy-five feet: higher than a house: for all to see), which Haman had made for Mordecai, **who had spoken good for the king**". As if the existing charges were not enough, Haman was also guilty of plotting the death of a benefactor of the king.

We cannot escape the biblical significance of the words, "So they hanged Haman on the gallows that he had prepared for Mordecai". Here is an appropriate commentary: "Oh let the wickedness of the wicked come to an end...He made a pit, and digged it, and is fallen into the ditch which he made. His mischief shall return upon his own head, and his violent dealing shall come down upon his own pate" (Psalm 7.9-16). Compare Esther 9.25: "that his wicked device, which he devised against the Jews, should return upon his own head". See also Psalm 9.15-16; Proverbs 11.5-6. Remember Galatians 6.7, "Be not deceived; God is not mocked: for whatsoever a man soweth, that shall he also reap".

If the "king's wrath" was "pacified" with the execution of Haman, then divine wrath against Satan will be finally satisfied when he is consigned to the lake of fire.

READ CHAPTER 8

The Jews have "a good day"

The contents of this chapter are summed up in Esther's plea before Ahasuerus "to **put away the mischief of Haman the Agagite**, and his device that he had devised against the Jews...let it be written to **reverse the letters** devised by Haman the son of Hammedatha the Agagite, which he wrote to destroy the Jews which are in all the king's provinces" (vv.3,5). Haman was dead, but his plans remained in place, and the Jews were still in dire peril. They still "sat in the region and shadow of death" (Matt. 4.16), and lived in "fear of death" (Heb. 2.15).

We have already noticed that Haman is an apt picture of the devil. Esther describes him as follows: "The **adversary** and **enemy** is this **wicked** Haman" (7.6). As we have seen, Esther's description is certainly applicable to both Haman and Satan. Haman reminds us of Satan as "the adversary": "Be sober, be vigilant; because your **adversary** the devil, as a roaring lion, walketh about, seeking whom he may devour" (1 Pet. 5.8); he reminds us of Satan as the "enemy": "The **enemy** that sowed them is the devil" (Matt. 13.39); he reminds us of Satan as the "wicked one": "For this is the message that ye heard from the beginning, that we should love one another. Not as Cain, who was of that **wicked** one" (1 John 3.11-12).

We have also noticed that the very gallows erected for Mordecai, became the instrument of Haman's own death. Those gallows proclaimed the triumph of Mordecai rather than his humiliation. The very instrument designed by Haman for Mordecai's death became the instrument of his own death, which reminds us that the Lord Jesus came "that through death he might destroy him that had the power of death, that is, the devil". But the passage continues: "and deliver them who through fear of death were all their lifetime subject to bondage" (Heb. 2.14-15).

Satan, like Haman, is a defeated enemy. The Lord Jesus triumphed over him at Calvary. It is now a question of delivering those over whom he had "the power of death". John tells us that "for this purpose the Son of God was manifested, that he might destroy ('loosen' or 'undo') the works of the devil" (1 John 3.8). The Lord Jesus has not only defeated the enemy: He is able to completely reverse the effects of the enemy's power. That is certainly good news: even better than the news which brought to the Jews "joy and gladness, a feast and a good day" (8.17).

This chapter illustrates the fact that whilst men and women are delivered from Satan's power by divine decree, God's people are actively involved in intercession before His throne, and in proclamation of the good news. Let's now work through the chapter, looking - as always - for its relevance to ourselves. After all, "whatsoever things were written aforetime were written for our learning, that we through patience and comfort of the scriptures might have hope" (Rom. 15.4).

The chapter may be divided as follows: **(1)** ascendancy over the enemy (vv.1-2); **(2)** appeal for help (vv.3-6); **(3)** authority for the work (vv.7-10); **(4)** attacking the opposition (vv.11-13); **(5)** accelerating the good news (v.14); **(6)** anticipation of victory (vv.15-17).

1) ASCENDANCY OVER THE ENEMY, vv.1-2
"On that day did the king Ahasuerus give the house of Haman the Jews' enemy unto Esther the queen. And Mordecai came before the king; for Esther had told what he was unto her. And the king took off his ring, which he had taken from Haman, and gave it to Mordecai. And Esther set Mordecai over the house of Haman".

In our studies, we have taken Esther as a picture of God's people, and Mordecai as a picture of the Lord Jesus Christ. It is important to stress that this is an application. If we pressed Mordecai as a "type" of Christ, we could find ourselves in some difficulty. What would we then make of the words, "And Esther set Mordecai over the house of Haman?" Bearing this in mind, notice:

a) Esther received authority over the house of Haman
She is given "the house of Haman". The enemy is in the position of defeat. The New Testament does not minimise for one moment the strength of our spiritual opposition: "We wrestle not against flesh and blood, but against principalities, against powers, against the rulers of the darkness of this world" (Eph. 6.12). On the other hand we are told, "Ye are of God, little children, and have overcome them (the spirits which are "not of God"): because greater is he that is in you, than he that is in the world" (I John 4.4). While we are acutely conscious of Satan's "devices" (2 Cor. 2.11), and sometimes fail in the battle, the fact remains that

we do have immense superiority. Esther had all the power and authority of the throne of Persia: we have infinitely greater resources than even that. We can be "strong in the Lord, and in the power of his might" (Eph. 6.10). That power is displayed in a totally different way to worldly power: "they overcame him (Satan) by the blood of the Lamb, and by the word of their testimony; and they loved not their lives unto (the) death" (Rev. 12.11).

b) *Esther revealed her relationship with Mordecai*
"And Mordecai came before the king; for Esther had told what he was unto her". These are quite delightful words. Do we tell the King what Christ is to us? When we enter the presence of the King, we speak about Christ rather than about ourselves. We are reminded of this in Joseph's words, "Tell my father of all my glory in Egypt, and of all that ye have seen" (Gen. 45.13). (It is nice to speak well of each other too!)

c) *Esther resigns her authority in favour of Mordecai*
"And Esther set Mordecai over the house of Haman". She did not act herself: she deferred to her cousin. After all, he was the man with the king's ring. The Lord Jesus said, "All power (authority) is given unto me". Esther gave first place to Mordecai, and we must give first place to Christ.

2) *APPEAL FOR HELP*, vv.3-6
While Esther had been given a position of superiority over the house of Haman, this did not mean that the results of his rise to power had been automatically cancelled. The Jews were still under sentence of death on "the thirteenth day of the twelfth month" (3.13). How could that awful disaster be averted? Well, one thing is quite certain: it could not be averted without intercession. We should therefore notice:

a) *The depth of Esther's concern*
"And Esther spake yet again before the king, and fell down at his feet, and besought him with tears to put away the mischief of Haman" (v.3). In past studies, we have referred to the tears of Nehemiah ("I sat down and wept, and mourned certain days, and fasted, and prayed before the God of heaven", Neh. 1.4) and the tears of Paul ("serving the Lord with all humility of mind, and with many tears", Acts 20.19). How much are we really concerned about the spiritual welfare of men and women? Whilst Esther delayed her previous request (see 5.7-8), on this occasion she comes straight to the point. Again, it was on Mordecai's insistence (4.13-14) that she made the first approach, but now, so far as we can judge, she now uses her own initiative.

The depth and reality of Esther's feelings become even clearer in v.6. It's not now, "his device that he had devised against **the Jews**" (v.3), but "How can I endure to see the evil that shall come unto **my** people? or how can I endure to see the destruction of **my kindred**?" She identifies herself with the very people under threat, and displays her love for them.

b) The assurance of Esther's acceptance
"Then the king held out the golden sceptre toward Esther" (v.4). We have seen the "golden sceptre" before. It signified "favour in his sight" (5.2). Our acceptance is in Christ Himself. The strength of Esther's acceptance lay in the strength of the sceptre. It was the emblem of absolute power. Our acceptance is vested in the "King of kings".

c) The ground of Esther's appeal
"If it please the king, and if I have found favour in his sight, and the thing seem right before the king, and I be pleasing in his eyes" (v.5). These four conditions fall into two categories. First of all, the **proposal** must be acceptable to him: secondly, the **proposer** must be acceptable to him. Read 1 John 5.14 in connection with the first ("And this is the confidence that we have in him, that, if we ask anything according to his will, he heareth us"), and 1 John 3.22 in connection with the second ("And whatsoever we ask, we receive of him, because we keep his commandments, and do those things that are pleasing in his sight"). We encountered both verses in our last study.

3) AUTHORITY FOR THE WORK, vv.7-10
It is "in the king's name", and "with the king's ring", and by "the king's scribes" (vv.8-9). Mordecai acted as the king's executive: "He wrote in the king Ahasuerus' name, and sealed it with the king's ring, and sent letters by post on horseback, and riders on mules, camels, and young dromedaries" (v.10). The messengers carried good news on the highest possible authority. Let's recall Matthew 28.18-19 again: "And Jesus came and spake unto them, saying, **All power (authority) is given unto me in heaven and in earth. Go ye therefore**". The Saviour prayed, "As thou hast sent me into the world, even so have I also sent them into the world" (John 17.18). The Lord Jesus has absolute authority assigned to Him, and the good news of deliverance bears that very authority.

4) ATTACKING THE OPPOSITION, vv.11-13
The letters were quite specific. It wasn't a case of an all-out attack on everybody, but "to destroy, to slay, and to cause to perish, all the power of the people and province **that would assault them**" (v.11). See also v.13: "and that the Jews

should be ready against that day to avenge themselves **on their enemies**". So the battle was to be taken to the enemy. It wasn't a case of defence, but of attack. The Lord Jesus did exactly that: "who went about doing good, and healing all that were oppressed of the devil" (Acts 10.38). He stormed the strongholds of the enemy. Every street tracted, every home visited, every conversation with unsaved people about the gospel, is an excursion into enemy territory. The enemies of the Jews had been given a date on which to strike: now the Jews themselves were to strike on the very same date. The enemy waits to strike us, but we are to take the strike initiative ourselves. Needless to say, "the weapons of our warfare are not carnal, but mighty through God to the pulling down of strongholds" (2 Cor. 10.4). The overthrow of Jericho illustrates his perfectly, and there can be little doubt that Paul had this in mind when writing the above.

You will have noticed that v.11 was not quoted in full above. So what about the balance of the quotation - "and to cause to perish, all the power of the people and province that would assault them, **both little ones and women, and to take the spoil of them for a prey**"? First of all, we need to remember that we are not talking about **Christian** conduct. Esther does not belong to our own era where we follow the Saviour's teaching: "Love your enemies, bless them that curse you, do good to them that hate you, and pray for them which despitefully use you, and persecute you" (Matt. 5.44). The Lord Jesus exemplified this perfectly: "Father, forgive them; for they know not what they do" (Luke 23.34). Secondly, it has been pointed out that the difficult words are really a quotation of Haman's original decree (3.13), and therefore mean that the Jews were to destroy those who would assault them and their families, and who would rob them of their possessions. This certainly seems to be confirmed by 9.10 ("the ten sons of Haman...the enemy of the Jews, slew they") and 9.16 ("But the other Jews that were in the king's provinces gathered themselves together, and stood for their lives, and had rest from their enemies, and slew of their foes seventy and five thousand").

But which ever way we take v.11, the spiritual application is clear: we must be quite ruthless in spiritual warfare. Since it is the powers of darkness that keep men in "the region and shadow of death" (Matt. 4.16), we must use our spiritual weapons to the full.

5) ACCELERATING THE GOOD NEWS, v.14
No hanging about here! "So the posts that rode upon mules and camels went out, **being hastened and pressed on** by the king's commandment". (It was just the same previously, see 3.15: but then it was bad news). It reminds us of

1 Samuel 21.8: "the king's business required haste". (Try that on the police if you get caught speeding!). There was an urgency about the matter. Paul puts it like this: "But this I say, brethren, **the** (notice this) time is short: it remaineth, that both they that have wives be as though they had none; and they that weep, as though they wept not; and they that rejoice, as though they rejoiced not; and they that buy, as though they possessed not; and they that use this world, as not abusing (over using) it" (1 Cor. 7.29-31). Paul is dealing here with earthly ties in view of the imminence of Christ's return; hence "**the** time is short" - not just 'time is short'. We are to pursue His interests.

J.C. Whitcomb puts it nicely: "It has often been observed that this provides a remarkably cogent illustration of missionary work today. God's death sentence hangs over a sinful humanity, but He has also commanded us to hasten the message of salvation to every land (cf. Proverbs 24.11). Only by a knowledge of, and a response to, the second decree of saving grace through the Lord Jesus Christ can the terrible effects of the first decree of universal condemnation for sin be averted".

Why were the Persian postmen to ride at such speed? After all, the king's scribes were called "in the third month, that is, the month Sivan (June)" (v.9), but the actual date on which the Jews were to avenge themselves was not until "the twelfth month, which is the month Adar (March)" (v.12). The answer is two-fold. First of all, we need to remember that the Persian Empire was immense, and secondly, that the Jews needed plenty of time in which to plan their attack.

6) ANTICIPATION OF VICTORY, vv.15-17
Let's just notice two things in the final paragraph of this chapter: *(a)* Mordecai was exalted (v.15); *(b)* victory was expected (vv.16-17)

a) Mordecai was exalted, v.15
"And Mordecai went out from the presence of the king in royal apparel of blue and white, and with a great crown of gold, and with a garment of fine linen and purple". The city of Shushan had been "perplexed" when Haman was in the ascendancy (3.15): now the city "rejoiced and was glad". The reason for the joy of the Jews is obvious: their man had been exalted! So we read, "The Jews had light, and gladness, and joy, and honour".

We have every reason to rejoice in the exaltation of our Saviour. In a coming day, the Jews will have every reason to rejoice as well! They will then have "light, and gladness, and joy, and honour".

b) Victory was expected, vv.16-17.

"And in every province, and in every city, whithersoever the king's commandment and his decree came, the Jews had joy and gladness, a feast and a good day. And many of the people of the land became Jews; for the fear of the Jews fell upon them". Quite clearly, they were now in the ascendancy.

But what do you make of the closing words: "And many of the people of the land became Jews; for the fear of the Jews fell upon them?" Conviction or convenience? Mere profession or reality? The same questions could be asked today, couldn't they?

READ CHAPTER 9

"Mordecai waxed greater and greater"

"The thirteenth day of the twelfth month" now dawns. Haman intended it to be the day on which all the Jews in the Persian Empire would be eliminated. But it was now to be the day on which the Jews would destroy all their enemies. It's all summed up in the opening verse: "The day that the enemies of the Jews hoped to have power over them, (though it was turned to the contrary, that the Jews had rule over them that hated them;)" (v.1). There are three main paragraphs in the chapter: *(1)* the destruction of the enemy (vv.1-16); *(2)* the rejoicing of the Jews (vv.17-19); *(3)* the commemoration of victory (vv.20-32).

1) THE DESTRUCTION OF THE ENEMY, vv.1-16
In this section we should notice *(a)* how the enemy is described; *(b)* how the enemy was defeated.

a) How the enemy is described
i) *"The enemies of the Jews hoped to have power over them", v.1.* As you can see, the enemies were numerous. Haman evidently had many supporters. Peter warned his first readers to "be sober, be vigilant; because your adversary the devil, as a roaring lion, walketh about, seeking whom he may devour" (1 Pet. 5.8). The enemy was intent on far more than physical harm, as the following verse makes clear: "whom resist stedfast in the faith". His intention was to make these early Christians deny the faith. Paul reminds us that, like Haman, Satan has many eager supporters: they are called "principalities... powers...the rulers of the darkness of this world". Their objective is to defeat God's people. Hence the necessity to wear "the whole armour of God" so that we "may be able to withstand in the evil day, and having done all, to stand" (Eph. 6.11-13).

ii) *"Them that hated them...those that hated them", vv.1,5.* The Lord Jesus taught that "If the world hate you, ye know that it hated me before it hated you. If ye were of the world, the world would love his own: but because ye are not of the world, but I have chosen you out of the world, therefore the world hateth you...they hated me without a cause" (John 15.18-25). See also John 17.14 ("I have given them thy word; and the world hath hated them"). It is certainly very significant that having said that Cain was "of that wicked one", John continues, "Marvel not, my brethren, if the world hate you" (1 John 3.12-13). Haman certainly knew how to inflame hatred for the Jews, and Satan certainly knows how to do the same towards God's people today. We mustn't be under any illusions about this: we are hated people, and this is becoming increasingly obvious in the U.K. No wonder the Jews "stood for their lives" (v.16). Christian life is not a playground: it is a battle ground.

iii) "Such as sought their hurt", v.2. It was a deliberate and calculated strategy. As we have already noted, our "adversary the devil...walketh about, **seeking** whom he may devour". He looks for every opportunity to inflict damage.

> "Principalities and powers,
> Mustering their unseen array,
> Wait for thine unguarded hours,
> Watch, and pray".

b) How the enemy was defeated
i) The decisiveness with which victory was achieved. There was no doubt about the outcome. "The Jews had rule over them" (v.1); "No man could withstand them; for the fear of them fell upon all people" (v.2); "The Jews... did what they would unto those that hated them" (v.5). We must remember, of course, that in applying the lesson from this, we are thinking in terms of victory over Satan's power, rather than conquering people! Paul tells us more in 2 Corinthians about his persecutions and difficulties, than he does in any of his other letters: "Pressed out of measure, above strength, insomuch that we despaired even of life" (2 Cor. 1.8). But he also writes: "Now thanks be unto God, which always causeth us to triumph in Christ ('leads us in triumph in Christ'), and maketh manifest the savour of his knowledge by us in every place" (2 Cor. 2.14-16). He was under tremendous pressure, and suffered fearful persecution, but triumphed completely over the spiritual forces which opposed him. Hence we read, "For whatsoever is born of God overcometh the world: and this is the victory that overcometh the world, even our faith" (1 John 5.4).

Altogether, there were 800 killed in Shushan (vv.6,15) and 75,000 in the provinces (v.l6). Plus the ten sons of Haman, all of whom are named in vv.7-9. Since the Jews were only concerned with their enemies - they did not kill all and sundry - Haman's sons were obviously enemies of the Jews in the same way as their father. They shared his hatred, and this recalls the words of the Lord Jesus: "Ye are of your father the devil, and the lusts of your father ye will do. He was a murderer from the beginning, and abode not in the truth, because there is no truth in him" (John 8.44). Haman was certainly a liar (3.8), and a potential murderer (3.9). In this he reflected the character of his own dark master. Haman's sons were slain (v.10), and their bodies were publicly displayed (vv.13-14). People should be able to see that we too are victorious over the enemy.

ii) *The means by which victory was achieved.* "Thus the Jews smote all their enemies with the stroke of the sword" (v.5). This speaks for itself: "the sword of the Spirit, which is the word of God" (Eph. 6.17).

iii) *The power by which victory was achieved.* "And all the rulers of the provinces, and the lieutenants, and the deputies, and officers of the king, helped the Jews; because the fear of Mordecai fell upon them. For Mordecai was great in the king's house, and his fame went out throughout all the provinces: for this man Mordecai waxed greater and greater" (or "for the man Mordecai became continually greater", JND (vv.3-4). In short, the Jews were triumphant over their enemies through the power of an exalted man! Without Mordecai, the Jews would have been powerless, and their enemies would have achieved their object. Mordecai had vast resources under his command, and this serves to remind us that our Saviour is "the Lord of hosts". This can be rendered 'the Lord of armies'. He said "All power is given unto me in heaven and in earth" (Matt 28.18). The description of Mordecai's prowess - 'continually greater' (JND) will certainly remind us of some New Testament references to the Lord Jesus:

- *Mordecai was "great in the king's house", v.4.* We shall see more of this later, but let's stop and enjoy the fact that God has addressed Christ with these words, "Sit thou at my right hand, until I make thine enemies thy footstool...rule thou in the midst of thine enemies" (Psalm 110.1-2). Stop a little longer, and remember that "He shall be great, and shall be called the Son of the Highest: and the Lord God shall give unto him the throne of his father David" (Luke 1.32-33).

- *Mordecai's "fame went out throughout all the provinces", v.4.* The queen of Sheba said of Solomon, "thou exceedest the fame that I heard" (2 Chron. 9.6). But "a greater than Solomon is here!" (Luke 11.31). The world is yet to learn about the glory of Christ: "I will send those that escape of them unto the nations...that have not heard my fame, neither have seen my glory" (Isa. 66.19).

- **Mordecai "waxed greater and greater".** Doesn't this remind you of Isaiah 9.7: "Of the **increase** of His government and peace there shall be no end"? The kingdom of Christ will expand continually. But can we say that He is "greater and greater" in our lives?

2) THE REJOICING OF THE JEWS, vv.17-19
There were three main elements in the rejoicing of the Jews following the destruction of their enemies:

i) They rested. "On the fourteenth day of the same (month) **rested** they...and on the fourteenth thereof; and on the fifteenth day of the same they **rested**" (vv17,18). Historically of course, they rested after warfare, so that we could apply this with reference to Revelation 14.13; "Blessed are the dead which die in the Lord from henceforth: Yea, saith the Spirit, that they may rest from their labours; and their works do follow them". On the other hand, we must remember that whilst we remain here on earth's battleground, we can enjoy rest of soul. The Lord Jesus said, "Come unto me, all ye that labour and are heavy laden, and I will give you **rest**. Take my yoke upon you, and learn of me; for I am meek and lowly in heart: and ye shall find **rest** unto your souls" (Matt. 11.28-29). (The word translated "rest" here (*anapauo*) is rendered "refreshed" in 1 Cor. 16.18; 2 Cor. 7.13; Philm. 7,20).

ii) They feasted. "They...made it a day of **feasting** and gladness" (vv.17,18); "a day of gladness and **feasting**, and a good day" (v.19). Previously, there had been "great mourning...and **fasting**, and weeping, and wailing" (4.3). Whilst Isaiah 25.6 looks forward to coming blessing for Israel, we certainly enjoy God's rich provision now: "a feast of fat things, a feast of wines on the lees, of fat things full of marrow, of wines on the lees well refined". You see, we are **always** at the Lord's table: that is, always enjoying the provision which He makes for us. Incidentally, in the Old Testament, the Lord's table was the altar. See Malachi 1.7,12. That ought to help you sort out 1 Corinthians 10, and enable you to differentiate between the Lord's table and the Lord's supper!

iii) They sent portions. The Jews had "a good day, and of **sending portions one to another**" (v.19). Compare Nehemiah 8.10. So there was fellowship too amongst the victorious Jews. It's always nice to 'send portions' to each other: something you have been enjoying from the Scriptures is likely to cheer a brother or sister in Christ too!

> Have you had a kindness shown?
> Pass it on!
> Twas not given for thee alone:
> Pass it on!

But do note v.22: "sending portions one to another, and **gifts to the poor**". Don't forget the need to take this quite literally. See Galatians 2.10 ("Only they would that we should remember the poor"). Don't forget the masses of people around us who are spiritually impoverished.

3) THE COMMEMORATION OF VICTORY, vv.20-32

"And Mordecai wrote these things, and sent letters unto all the Jews that were in all the provinces of the king Ahasuerus, both nigh and far, to stablish this among them, that they should keep the fourteenth day of the month Adar, and the fifteenth day of the same, yearly" (vv.20-21). So the feast of Purim was instituted, taking its name from the lot cast by Haman (vv.24-26). It covered two days, the 14th and 15th Adar, commemorating the rest of the provincial Jews after the destruction of their enemies on the 13th Adar (v.17), and the rest of the city Jews after the destruction of their enemies on the 13th and 14th Adar (v.18). Let's just emphasise some features:

i) *It was to be observed by all the Jews.* "Mordecai...sent letters unto **all** the Jews that were in all the provinces" (v.20).

ii) *It was to be observed perpetually.* "And Mordecai wrote...to stablish this among them, that they should keep the fourteenth day of the month Adar, and the fifteenth day of the same, **yearly**" (vv.20-21), and "that these days should be remembered and kept throughout **every** generation, every family, every province, and every city; and that these days of Purim should **not fail** from among the Jews, nor the memorial of them perish from their seed" (v.28).

iii) It was established on the highest authority. "And **Mordecai** wrote these things...to stablish this among them" (vv.20-21); "Then Esther the queen, the daughter of Abihail, and Mordecai the Jew, wrote with all authority, to confirm this second letter of Purim...to confirm these days of Purim in their times appointed, according as Mordecai the Jew and Esther the queen had enjoined them" (vv.29-32).

iv) It was linked with fellowship. They were to keep the "fourteenth day of the month Adar...that they should make them days of feasting and joy, and of sending portions one to another, and gifts to the poor" (vv.21-22). So the feast of Purim was the occasion of joyful unity amongst God's people. It was central to their fellowship.

v) *It commemorated a crushing victory.* This is recalled in vv.24-25, which recite the rise and fall of Haman. This victory "turned...sorrow to joy, and... mourning into a good day" (v.22).

vi) *It was kept with a sense of commitment.* "And the Jew undertook to do as they had begun, and as Mordecai had written unto them" (v.23); "the Jews ordained, and took upon them, and upon their seed, and upon all such as joined themselves unto them, so as it should not fail, that they would keep these two days according to their writing, and according to their appointed time every year; and that these days should be remembered and kept throughout every generation..." (vv.27-28). Do notice the words, "to do as they had begun" (v.23). Sadly, it is often so different with us.

vii) *It was a testimony to others.* "And the decree of Esther confirmed these matters of Purim; and it was written *in the book*" (v.32). That is, "in the book of the (Persian) chronicles" (2.23; 6.1).

Now, having noticed all this, *we can go further and profitably apply the principles and purpose of 'the feast of Purim' to the Lord's supper.* The Lord Jesus said, "Take eat: this is my body, which is (broken) for you: this do in remembrance of me...This cup is the new testament in my blood: this do ye, as oft as ye drink it, in remembrance of me" (1 Cor. 11.24-25). Re-read the seven observations above, and jot down your conclusions.

READ CHAPTER 10

"The greatness of Mordecai"

We come to the grand finale of the book, and Esther doesn't get a mention! Whilst reference is made to Ahasuerus, even this only serves to emphasise the "greatness of Mordecai" (v.2). But the very language used to describe Mordecai, obliges us to turn over the pages of our Bibles until we read this of another Deliverer: "He shall be great, and shall be called the Son of the Highest: and the Lord God shall give unto him the throne of his father David: and he shall reign over the house of Jacob for ever; and of his kingdom there shall be no end" (Luke 1.32-33). The Lord Jesus is "great" in every sphere. It has been often said that no one attribute of the Lord Jesus is greater than any other, because He is great in every way.

i) He is *"a great prophet"*. "And there came a fear on all: and they glorified God, saying, That *a great prophet* is risen up among us" (Luke 7.16).

ii) He is *"a great priest"*. "Having *a great priest* ('an high priest', AV) over the house of God" (Heb. 10.21 RV).

iii) He is *"a great high priest"*. "Seeing then that we have *a great high priest*, that is passed into ('through') the heavens, Jesus the Son of God..." (Heb. 4.14).

iv) He is *"the great king"*. "Jerusalem...is the city of *the great King*" (Matt. 5.35). The Lord Jesus is citing Psalm 48.2 here.

v) He is *"the great shepherd of the sheep"*. "Now the God of peace, that brought again from the dead our Lord Jesus, that *great shepherd of the sheep*" (Heb. 13.20).

vi) He is *"the great God and our Saviour Jesus Christ"*. "Looking for that blessed hope, and the glorious appearing of *the great God and our Saviour Jesus Christ*" (Titus 2.13).

Esther Chapter 10 therefore reminds us of the coming glory of Christ, and we have no difficulty in applying the closing verse to Him: "great among the Jews, and accepted of the multitude of his brethren, seeking the wealth of his people, and speaking peace to all his seed". With this in mind, we ought to take another look at events described in the book of Esther. Preachers have often told us that 'coming events cast their shadows before them'. Let's quote John C. Whitcomb again: "It is perfectly clear, then, that the titanic death-struggle of the book of Esther simply cannot be understood apart from the satanic purposes toward Israel which the general context of Scripture reveals". Those 'satanic purposes' will culminate in an all-out attempt to annihilate Israel at the end-time. In this connection, we have already identified Haman as a picture of both Satan, and the "man of sin". What is more, Haman appears to be completely successful until the end of Chapter 5, just as Satan appears to be completely successful by the end of Revelation 13. Now let's recall what happened with effect from Esther 6:

i) **We are introduced to an exalted man.** He is "the man whom the king delighteth to honour" (6.6,7,9,11).

ii) **That exalted man intervenes on behalf of his people.** The day of their destruction becomes the day of their deliverance (8.8-14). Compare Zechariah 14.2-3: "For I will gather all nations against Jerusalem to battle; and the city shall be taken, and the houses rifled... then shall the Lord go forth, and fight against those nations".

iii) The Jews defeated their enemies, including Haman's ten sons (9.1-16). We must listen to Zechariah again: "In that day will I make the governors of Judah like an hearth of fire among the wood, and like a torch of fire in a sheaf; and they shall devour all the people round about" (Zech. 12.6). The enemy attack will be launched by the ten-part kingdom of the beast, but the invader will suffer the same fate as Haman's ten sons.

iv) **Having defeated their enemies, the Jews enjoyed rest and peace.** See 9.17-19. This recalls Israel's millennial blessings, when God's people will experience "joy and gladness, and cheerful feasts" (Zech. 8.19). Micah tells us that "they shall sit every man under his vine and under his fig tree; and none shall make them afraid" (Micah 4.4).

v) **The Jews remembered their deliverance.** See 9.30-32. They will again. When the "feast of tabernacles" is celebrated in the millennium, "every one that is left of all the nations which came against Jerusalem shall even go up from year to year to worship the King, the Lord of hosts" (Zech. 14.16).

vi) *The deliverer of the Jews is given the highest place.* He was "next unto king Ahasuerus" (10.3). The Lord Jesus will "sit and rule upon his throne (Zech. 6.13).

vii) *The deliverer of the Jews undertakes their welfare:* "Mordecai...seeking the wealth of his people" (10.3). Isaiah describes the care which will be bestowed upon the nation: "He shall feed his flock like a shepherd: he shall gather the lambs with his arm, and carry them in his bosom" (Isaiah 40.11).

That will do as an introduction. You will be able to expand the outline.

The "greatness of Mordecai" was enhanced by the stature of Ahasuerus, and it can only be for this reason that the Persian king is mentioned in the chapter. Mordecai was not "next" to some tin-pot third world dictator: he was "next" to a world-wide emperor. (Rather like the association between Joseph and Pharaoh). "And the king Ahasuerus laid a tribute upon the land, and upon the isles of the sea. And all the acts of his power and of his might...are they not written in the book of the chronicles of the kings of Media and Persia?" Mordecai was honoured by the supreme authority of the day. Notice two things:

1) HE WAS GREAT IN RELATION TO THE KING
i) "The greatness of Mordecai, whereunto the king advanced him" (v.2). We have noticed more than once, that Mordecai never sought his own glory. When he had good cause to clamour for reward, he made no attempt to secure it himself. He waited the king's pleasure. It is always delightful to turn to Philippians 2 and read of the Lord Jesus that "being found in fashion as a man, he humbled himself, and became obedient unto death, even the death of the cross. Wherefore God also hath highly exalted him" (Phil. 2.8-9). The Lord Jesus perfectly illustrated 1 Peter 5.6: "Humble yourselves therefore under the mighty hand of God, that he may exalt you in due time".

ii) "For Mordecai the Jew was next unto king Ahasuerus" (v.3). The Old Testament supplies further examples of the way in which the Jew always seems to get to the top. Think, again, about Joseph with Pharaoh, and Daniel with Nebuchadnezzar and Darius. (What about Disraeli with Queen Victoria?!). You'll notice how this is emphasised here: "For Mordecai **the Jew**". The hated Jew, whom Haman would have hanged, is "far above all". There was another Jew, of whom Peter said, "The God of our fathers raised up Jesus, whom ye slew and hanged on a tree. Him hath God exalted with his right hand to be a Prince and a Saviour" (Acts 5.30-31). If Mordecai was "next unto king Ahasuerus", then "the Lord said unto my Lord, Sit thou at my right hand, until I make thine enemies thy footstool" (Psalm 110.1).

2) *HE WAS GREAT IN RELATION TO HIS PEOPLE*
Four statements are made in v.3:

i) "Great among the Jews". The man who had delivered them, was honoured amongst them. The Lord Jesus is greater than the best of men. This is the point made in the Epistle to the Hebrews. It's not that the Lord Jesus is better than second rate men: He is better than first rate men.

He is greater than the most illustrious Jews of the past. "Then said the Jews unto him...art thou *greater* than our father Abraham, which is dead?" (John 8.52-53). The question was heavy with irony. But the answer is, 'Yes, He is greater than Abraham'. The Samaritan woman asked, "Art thou *greater* than our father Jacob, which gave us the well?" (John 4.12). The answer is, 'Yes, He is greater than Jacob', and "*greater* than Jonas...*greater* than Solomon". He is greater than all!

He will be "great among the Jews" in His coming reign. We have already referred to Luke 1.32-33: "He shall be great...and he shall reign over the house of Jacob for ever". The words, "And the Lord God shall give unto him the throne of his father David", cite Isaiah 9.7: "Upon the throne of David, and upon his kingdom, to order it, and to establish it with judgment and with justice from henceforth even for ever". But not only "great among the Jews": He will be 'Head over the heathen' (Psalm 18.43).

ii) "Accepted of the multitude of his brethren". The man who had delivered them was accepted by them. The Lord Jesus "came unto his own (things), and his own (people) received him not" (John 1.11). In the first instance, "neither did his brethren (His own family) believe in him" (John 7.5). Isaiah recounts the attitude of the nation: "He is despised and rejected of men...he was despised, and we esteemed him not" (Isaiah 53.3).

When He returns, "They shall look upon me whom they have pierced, and they shall mourn for him, as one mourneth for his only son..." (Zech. 12.10). At the same time, they will say: "Lo, this is our God; we have waited for him, and he will save us..." (Isaiah 25.9).

The blessing or otherwise of the Gentile nations in the millennial reign of Christ will depend on their attitude to the Jews during the great tribulation (Matthew 25.31-46). In this connection we should notice particularly that the King will say: "Inasmuch as ye have done it unto one of the least of these **my brethren**, ye have done it unto me" (v.40).

iii) "Seeking the wealth ('welfare', JND) of his people". The man who had delivered them, cared for them. When the Lord Jesus first came, it was 'seeking the welfare of His people': "Who went about doing good, and healing all that were oppressed of the devil...whom they slew and hanged on a tree" (Acts 10.38-39). When the Lord Jesus returns, it will be 'seeking the welfare of His people'. "He shall judge thy people with righteousness, and thy poor with judgment...He shall judge the poor of the people, he shall save the children of the needy, and shall break in pieces the oppressor" (Psalm 72.1-4).

iv) "Speaking peace to all his seed". The man who had delivered them, was favourable toward them. The Lord Jesus shall "see **his seed**, he shall prolong his days, and the pleasure of the Lord shall prosper in his hand" (Isa. 53.10). When He reigns, "all thy (Israel's) children shall be taught of the Lord; and great shall be **the peace** of thy children" (Isa. 54.13); "For thus saith the Lord, Behold, I will extend **peace** to her like a river" (Isa. 66.12). See also Psalm 22.30: "**A seed** shall serve him: it shall be accounted to the Lord for a generation".

But what about **our** relationship with the Lord Jesus? Can **we** apply the words, "his brethren...his people...his seed", to ourselves?

i) "His brethren". See John 20.17: "Go to **my brethren**, and say unto them, I ascend unto my Father, and your Father; and to my God, and your God". See also Hebrews 2.11-12: "For both he that sanctifieth and they who are sanctified are all of one: for which cause he is not ashamed to call them **brethren**, saying, I will declare thy name unto **my brethren**, in the midst of the church will I sing praise unto thee."

ii) "His people". See Romans 9.23-25: God has made known "the riches of his glory on the vessels of mercy, which he had afore prepared unto glory, even us, whom he hath called, not of the Jews only, but also of the Gentiles...As he saith also in Osee, I will call them **my people**, which were not my people".

iii) "His seed". See Hebrews 2.13: "Behold I and **the children** which God hath given me".

Ezra, Nehemiah, Esther